D1302277

CHALLENGES
AND
OPPORTUNITIES

FROM NOW TO 2001

Edited by
Howard F. Didsbury, Jr.

3o3
C437

WORLD FUTURE SOCIETY
Bethesda, MD • U.S.A.

Editor: Howard F. Didsbury, Jr.

Editorial Review Board:
Dierdre H. Banks, James J. Crider, David G. Cox,
Howard F. Didsbury, Jr. (chairman), Charles H. Little,
Theodore J. Maziarski, and Andrew A. Spekke

Staff Editor: Edward Cornish

Editorial Consultants:
James J. Crider, Frances Segraves, Cynthia Wagner

Editorial Assistant: Patty McNally

Production Manager: Susan Echard

Production Consultant: Jefferson Cornish

Typesetting: Ulla Bogdan

Layout: Graves Fowler & Associates

Cover Photography: Jeffrey M. Harrington

Published by:
World Future Society
4916 St. Elmo Avenue
Bethesda, Maryland 20814-5089 ● U.S.A.

Library of Congress Catalog Card Number: 86-50617

International Standard Book Number: 0-930242-31-9

Printed in the United States of America

Contents

Roots of Potential Conflict

Economics: Differing Perspectives

Continous Education for a Changing World

Wider Boundaries for More Effective Management

Epilogue: A Vision for Tomorrow

NOTE

This volume was prepared in conjunction with the World Future Society's conference, "FutureFocus: The Next Fifteen Years," held in New York City, July 13-17, 1986. The general chairman of the conference was Kenneth W. Hunter. Robert Lee Chartrand served as deputy general chairman. The staff director of the conference was Scott Foote.

The papers presented here were selected from a very large number submitted to the Editorial Review Committee. A number of distinguished papers whose subject matter did not lie within the limits of the volume could not be included.

Footnotes and other academic paraphernalia have been minimized to avoid disrupting the flow of the authors' ideas and insights.

INTRODUCTION

The spirit which animates many who are engaged in futures studies carries the conviction that the future offers a fertile field for human planning and action. Nothing can be done to alter the past—the future, however, is pregnant with possibility. The myriad difficult problems confronting humanity as it approaches the new millennium are colossal and in many instances their complexity is enormous. But it appears that the challenges before humanity are very largely the result of human action or inaction. Considered in this light the future is not foreordained. It is subject to being shaped by human desire and human will to a great degree. H.G. Wells in his book, *The Open Conspiracy,* stated it succinctly: "It is opportunity and not destiny we face."

The ethos of futures studies is in many respects akin to that of the Enlightenment—a faith in reason, in the power of education, in the importance of science and the accumulation of knowledge, and in the general common sense of humanity. Motivated by this exhilarating conviction, human beings have transformed their world dramatically and continue to do so. Information increases, knowledge accumulates and scientific and technological wonders multiply. But the fact that wisdom remains in critically short supply becomes evident almost daily. "Wisdom," the late Lord Ritchie-Calder often said, "is knowledge combined with judgment."

Can we turn the challenges before humanity into opportunities for creative, humane achievements? Can we attempt to see what *will* happen if a present course of action or inaction is pursued unaltered? Do we possess the wisdom to take advantage of our knowledge and utilize it in a judicious manner? Or are human beings "crisis animals"—only willing to take appropriate action after disaster? In the past the crisis-animal mentality—though regrettable—was not universal in its catastrophic implications. As this is no longer the case, there is sound reason for special global apprehension.

In the fifteenth year before the dawn of the new millennium two events have occurred—disastrous and tragic—which may have a long range beneficial effect on humanity. These events are the space shuttle Challenger and Chernobyl nuclear disasters occurring on

January 28 and April 26, 1986, respectively. Taken together these tragic events may illustrate spectacularly the fragility of technological undertakings on the one hand and the horrendous threat of nuclear radiation dispersal globally. The effect of these two events may do more to arouse humanity to the need for appropriate and timely exertion than have all of the previous decades of dire warnings and moral exhortations. The need for concrete action to reduce such global perils becomes clear. Action transcending cultural, ideological and political differences should now be determined. Should this development not happen, it may take a third event to facilitate it: a nuclear exchange by accident or design most probably between one or two Third World Powers! Such an event will clearly demonstrate the absurdity of concepts of neutrality, non-combatants and theaters of war. Everywhere everyone will be a participant without choice in the nuclear madness. A grim scenario indeed!

In the face of such an appalling eventuality, futurists for the most part still tend to be optimists of sorts. They are convinced that with wisdom and determination humanity's prospects can be made brighter. Challenges can be transformed into opportunities for human cooperation and development. The papers in this volume, in the main, reflect this conviction.

An Outline of the Book

The contributions to this volume have been grouped into six main sections, with a preface and an epilogue.

Preface

Confronted as we are with a world of accelerating change, complexity and interrelatedness, we grope for solutions to problems but are all too frequently stymied in our efforts. The underlying problem which frustrates our endeavors according to Stafford Beer in "Powerless Power: Goodwill's Paradox" is what he terms "reductionism." Reductionism is, in fact, one of the greatest impediments to the solutions of problems of social complexity.

"Reductionism is defined," according to Beer, "as that approach to problems which breaks the total system into tiny pieces, works out an understanding of each piece, and creates a minimal conjecture as to how the tiny pieces are related. This is how our whole civilization operates—or (to put it another way) fails to work." What is needed is a multidisciplinary approach to complexity in which we "redefine the problem, redesign the system." Beer urges a comprehensive methodology in place of the current reductionist mode of thinking.

Crisis Management and Conflict Resolution

In "The Future of Crisis Control and Conflict Resolution," William Exton, Jr. offers "a rationale for the control of crises" which entails consideration of a number of factors ranging from crisis causation to psychological impact. In the course of outlining "the most promising program" for the management of crises, he shows a meticulous concern for precision in definition, conceptual clarity and a care in the classification of crises based on the major factor causing a particular crisis.

In his essay, "Information Technology for Emergency Management: The Many Potentials," Robert Lee Chartrand draws attention to the fact that there is a growing concern that on all levels of government—local, state and federal—there is inadequate preparation to cope with technological and natural emergencies. The sheer complexity and jurisdictional diversity of potential crises and emergencies "have caused lawmakers and program managers to reexamine the effectiveness of our crisis (or emergency) management capability." Chartrand suggests that "the development of advanced information systems" is a key factor in improving this capability.

In a discussion of topics relevant to crisis management, a sound understanding of "risk" is crucial. Frederick Forscher offers an incisive summary of the increasing importance of understanding risk assessment—"risks to the individual and risks to the society—and how to assess it and how to manage it." It is clear from his analysis that the pursuit of a "risk free society" is a delusion.

Before attempting to construct a model for crisis resolution, Scott J. Schroeder believes it is important to understand the meaning of the term "crisis" and the characteristics of a crisis situation. In "Futures Applications of Crisis Management Theory," he explores these prerequisites in the context of corporate crisis management. He notes that when it comes to a crisis situation, mismanagement is generally the rule rather than the exception because most organizations lack a crisis resolution plan. Schroeder outlines the proper steps in crisis management.

"Decision making relating to crises and conflicts calls for special abilities in anticipating these adverse conditions before they come to pass. Successful handling of such situations depends in great measure, T. K. Das asserts, "on the ability to see into the future for changes in attendant circumstances." However, not all persons charged with handling such challenges "have that special attribute of looking into the distant future." In "Future Orientations of Decision Makers and the Reality of Strategic Thinking," Das suggests that "strategic thinking in reality is often merely extrapolations of near-term insights rather than a genuinely longer-horizon exercise." In support of this observation, he draws upon his own recent research. Finally, he considers practical implications of different future orientations and their relation to strategic thinking.

The program outlined in Jeffrey H. Kravitz and Robert G. Peluso's paper, "Crisis Management Training: Preparing Managers for Mine Emergency Operations," has applicability to almost any organization. The program as described relies upon interview and feedback techniques, emergency simulations and role playing, assessment center methods, and informational presentations.

Richard K. Curtis' "Terrorism: Crisis Intervention and Fluctuation Theory" offers some stimulating insights into various short range methods for combatting it, for example, submission, retaliation and deterrence. Curtis suggests that "Fluctuation Theory," as proposed by Nobel Laureate Ilya Prigogine, serves as a useful paradigm in analyzing terrorism and the most effective means of coping with it.

Progress Toward Mutual Global Security

In Dietrich Fischer's "Dissuasion: Toward an Active Peace Policy" we have a judicious survey of a number of approaches aimed at preventing nuclear war. He firmly believes that it is possible to achieve both peace and security and presents a proposal which illustrates how this can be achieved.

"The key to an effective policy of dissuading aggression is the recognition that it is not sufficient to make war disastrous for a potential aggressor; it is equally important to make peace as attractive for him as possible." "The most effective independent strategy to prevent war is *dissuasion,*" Fischer declares, "a combination of a broad range of measures that not only seek to punish aggression, but also to reward peaceful cooperation."

Considering the challenges facing humanity as we approach the 21st century, Glenn A. Olds cites with approval Buckminster Fuller's perceptive observation, "Mankind is now taking its final exam." In the course of his presentation, Olds raises several crucial questions, two of which are "Do we have enough intelligence and moral will to save us from human self-destruct?" and "Do we have the capability and will to unite nations to rid the world of war, democratize international relations, promote economic and social development, insure basic human rights and the rule of law, and harmonize the actions of nations?"

Several things must be done. We need to renew an attitude of hope for the development and mission of the United Nations. We must seek ways of creating a new and moral rational economic order. There is a need to create a United Nations military power. In addition, reform is needed in the United Nations structure "in the interest of nonduplication, simplification, and efficiency."

Like Glenn A. Olds, Jan Tinbergen sees the United Nations as a vital force in humanity's future. In "Strengthening the United Nations" he offers a number of concrete proposals to enhance the efficacy of United Nations institutions based on the bold assumption that in the future the United Nations will develop into "a system of world government or world government." For instance, at present the way member-nations are represented in the General Assembly is subject to important criticism. Representation in the Assembly *"must reflect differences in population size"* and, in addition, " . . . at least for the time being . . . a nation's representation should also depend on its *income per capita.*" One important institution which is lacking in the present structure of the United Nations is a "World Treasury." Efforts should be made to do away with voluntary contributions and replace them with some form of world taxes. A sound financial foundation would permit the United Nations to engage in development projects.

"It is now possible to combine existing technologies to make sophisticated and more holistic explorations of various scenarios for solving global social problems." Parker Rossman and Takeshi Utsumi, the authors of "Waging Peace With Globally Inter-connected Computers" set out to explain how this can be done. "Many small computers in different countries can be inter-connected through globally distributed network processing and information processing, into modeling and simulation instruments as powerful as those used by the Pentagon for war gaming."

Alvin M. Saperstein's paper "Provocative Versus Non-provocative Use of the New Smart Weapons: Organization Makes the Difference" draws attention to a crucial issue: "In a world of hostile independent nations, the requirements for conflict resolution are linked to the need for non-provocative defense." Saperstein concludes "Together, new technology and new organization can provide effective non-provocative defense, thus initiating an era of 'common security'."

"Political conflict involves the conflict of norms, yet resolution of political conflict requires that the disputants share some norms about conflict resolution. This presents a problem at the global level, where no such shared normative framework exists." Donald W. Michael and Walter Truett Anderson's "Norms in Conflict and Confusion: Six Stories in Search of an Author" presents six major worldviews each of which is in conflict with the others. The authors find that "none is adequate to serve as the normative framework for a global society." Regardless of this fact, the authors believe "a society will inevitably come into being, but not without conflict and great stress for individuals and institutions of governance."

After explaining some basic concepts about the nature of the modern world system, W. Warren Wagar explores six ways of preventing future wars in his "Peace by Revolution: Civilian-based Offense." The first two methods rely on military initiatives (deterrence and strategic defense). The second pair, disarmament and federation, rely on the initiatives of nation-states. The third pair, civilian-based defense and civilian-based offense, rely as the name implies on initiatives of private citizens. The last avenue to peace is the one favored by Wagar as the title of his paper suggests.

Roots of Potential Conflict

In this section are grouped a number of authors whose papers may serve to alert the reader to emerging areas of discord and conflict.

The first one by Robert P. Weber entitled "First You Pet Your Reptile" raises the most serious fundamental question as he draws attention to the fact that our inner brain—which we humans have in common with reptiles—is more powerful than we thought. This inner brain not only has an agenda of its own, but may frustrate our desire for needed change by the way it filters input and output from the cortex. The reptilian "brain" with its emphasis upon survival may offer continuous resistance to change. This opposition to needed change in human survival values and patterns must be taken into account in our planning for appropriate change.

For his part, David Macarov thinks much of our thinking is far removed from the reality which is developing around us. We persist in thinking in terms of a world that is rapidly disappearing. In "Value Conflicts and Their Resolution in the World of Work" he notes that automation has created "a situation where almost all of the human work needed is performed by a small minority of people, work can no longer be regarded as the be-all and end-all of life, the measure of a person's worth, the only method of structuring time, and the preferred method of seeking self-actualization. Other activities and characteristics will take their place in the pantheon of values, dethroning work as the central activity. These may be cooperativeness, altruism, neighborliness, creativity, honesty, religiosity, or humor."

"The Implications of Future Scenarios for Conflict Resolution in the United States" by Wallace Warfield presents several scenarios—alarming and grim—and depicts what race and cultural relations may be like in each of these scenarios. The author suggests a process that should be employed if all disparate groups in our society are to move equitably into the future. "The mediation function is integral to this process of transformation for it is essentially a humanist-optimist view of society that plays an 'agent of reality' role to manage the accompanying conflicts."

"Whether we survive as a truly democratic society or head down the road towards repressive centralism, depends upon the success of mediating institutions in demonstrating that solutions can be negotiated where everyone wins something."

"We are witnessing a new form of public militancy in the United States," observes Randall L. Scheel. "It can be called private disobedience and is characterized by deliberate acts of protest, sometimes violent, directed against the private sector." In the next 15 years we can anticipate increased growth in this new and alarming phenomenon.

Economics: Differing Perspectives

Weston H. Agor's "Using Brain Skill Assessments to Increase Productivity in Development Administration" describes how brain skill and management styles (BMS) assessments can be employed to increase productivity by management executives in developing countries. BMS programs combined with the ongoing training programs can serve to increase productivity significantly. Agor documents BMS results based on the results of testing over 2,000 managers and the experience gained from implementing in-depth BMS programs in several countries.

"The Future Potential of Increased Intra-Developing Countries Trade" presents three scenarios in which the trade of developing countries is examined. Stanley J. Lawson and Douglas O. Walker's three scenarios are: "High World Growth," "Medium World Growth," and "Low World Growth." The authors point out "Underlying all scenarios are projections of gross domestic product . . . (made) for 124 individual countries."

The high world growth scenario is "based on the assumption that national and international policies will be directed toward the achievement of a substantial rise in growth in every developing country, an acceleration that reflects growth potentialities created by significant changes in domestic politics and in the international economic environment." "A medium world growth scenario is based on the general assumption that long-term historical factors determining growth and trends of international trade in the world economy will continue into the future largely unchanged." Lastly, " . . . The low growth scenario assumes that the extraordinary slow-down in the growth of the world economy in the first half of the 1980s will end, with some moderate improvement as the decade unfolds. During the 1990s, growth is assumed to continue at a rate substantially below that recorded in the 1970s."

"The comparison of the experiences of Japan and the West suggests that Japan's semi-permanent trade surplus vis à vis the West may be explained by differences in lifestyles between the Japanese and Westerners, differences that can be explained mainly by public policy orientations, which, in turn, reflect the different needs and aspirations of late- and early-industrializers." Shigeko N. Fukai's analysis in "An Alternative to the Free Trade System" suggests that "as noneconomic, qualitative goals become more important than maximization of material production and consumption, the twin concepts of material self-sufficiency and non-material interdependence may replace the free trade doctrine as a guiding principle of an alternative international socioeconomic order."

Our economic difficulties result from an "excessive competition and overcapacity in both industry and agriculture." "The basic problem is this: many industries now produce or could produce with existing capacity, much more than can be sold at prices that bring reasonable profits." asserts Frederick C. Thayer in his essay "Avoiding a Crash: Public Investment, Private Regulation." "This worldwide 'glut' of products and services threatens to exert deflationary pressure on the global economy, increasing today's already high unemployment and pressuring industries burdened by overcapacity to make desperate attempts to dump their surpluses overseas." What can we do? "Because overcapacity is both the inevitable outcome of unrestricted competition and a recurring cause of depressions, we can avoid future worldwide despressions only by inventing mechanisms to restrict excessive competition and ensure full employment." "Only permanent regulation—whether formal or informal—can prevent overcapacity and overproduction and thus ensure a smoothly functioning and growing world economy."

Continuous Education for a Changing World

Confronted with global cultural diversity and technological complexity "what is needed is an overhauling of the learning systems and their transformation so as to make them socio-culturally relevant and capable of facing the challenges which change has brought about."

In his paper, "Learning Needs in a Changing World: Human Resources in a Knowledge Civilization," Mahdi Elmandjra cites issues which must be considered in any "reassessment of learning needs and the optimalization of human resources in a changing world."

We need to know much more about "the untapped human resources which could greatly improve the quality of life and enhance creativity." " . . . We still know very little about how our learning process functions."

Mahdi Elmandjra is convinced that "There is not a country in the world today that does not have the local ways and means to eradicate illiteracy and to develop its human potential. What most countries lack is the political will and the courage to do so—in spite of or because of the great socio-political transformations which education brings about." In the course of his paper he enumerates 13 "learning needs" which will contribute to the utilization of human resources.

Harold G. Shane's "Globalized Media: Toward Community or Catastrophe on the Planet?" is a succinct summary of some of the most important problems raised by the electronic telecommunications media: political, social, economic, and educational. Though somewhat captivated by potential technological marvels, Shane speaks of the absolute need for both teachers and students to become "better informed with respect to commercialism, gilded or slanted news, and the political aspects of television and press." The danger of being swamped in a flood of information ("infoglut") is emphasized. " . . . Students must be helped to develop the insights needed to enable each of them to interpret and to respond intelligently "to a bewildering mass of information and the variety of distortions it is subject to by skilled manipulators. In sum, there is a paramount need to develop an informed healthy skepticism when confronted with the full range of media: press, radio and television."

Characteristics of the much-talked-about "information society" are enumerated and their implications for education in such a society are discussed in Harlan Cleveland's "Educating for the Information Society." In an information society a premium is placed upon integrative thinking and an interdisciplinary approach to problem-solving. As Cleveland considers "Education . . . the drivewheel of citizenship in the *informatized* society" (my emphasis added), he outlines a "core curriculum" for "future oriented students."

At a time when there is so much discussion as to the direction education should take: general or career-oriented, Cleveland counsels "The number and quality of 'jobs' will be a function not of physical constraints but of the human imagination."

Wider Boundaries for More Effective Management

The two papers included in this section are concerned with expanding "boundaries" to ensure more effective management: the first on a regional level; the second on a global scale.

"With the Federal government retrenching from fiscal assistance, State and Local governments must find new ways of increasing efficiency in service delivery to deal with the fiscal crisis that will result."

Existing regional councils are a ready tool for local governments," Thomas J. Christofel points out in "Regional Councils: Today's Governmental Tool for the 21st Century," since as future oriented organizations, they correlate with the regional economies and have the flexibility to deal with autonomous local governments." "Regional councils, as bottom-up organizations, are tools unique to the region they serve. They are ready tools for the crises of today and tomorrow."

Leigh S. Shaffer and Samuel F. Moore offer in their paper "'Good Fences Make Good Neighbors': The Limits of the Territorial Solution" a critique of "the territorial solution" to problems of social conflict. They show clearly that in today's world there is a distinct class of problems—environmental problems—for which the conventional territorial solution is not only inappropriate but useless. This class of problems involve whole ecosystems and usually transcend political boundaries.

A Vision for Tomorrow

We conclude this volume with Don Toppin's "Toward the Great Millennium" which serves as an epilogue. Toppin offers us a vision of the bright prospects for a great new age for all humanity if we only have the wisdom and determination to work together for the dawn of such an age. Like Jan Tinbergen and Glenn A. Olds, Toppin believes the United Nations has a vital role to play in ushering in a bright new age.

"It is now reasonable to prophesy that we are approaching the dawn of the greatest cultural epoch since the beginning of human life on earth provided that a fresh transcendent campaign for a positive future, already launched in the consciousness of billions, is as successful as it must be. The alternatives are too horrible to mention!"

—Howard F. Didsbury, Jr.

Preface

POWERLESS POWER: GOODWILL'S PARADOX

by

Stafford Beer

The Nature of the Problem

Reductionism is defined as that approach to problems which breaks the total system into tiny pieces, works out an understanding of each piece, and creates a minimal conjecture as to how the tiny pieces are related. This is how our whole civilization operates—or fails to work.

Aspects of our world work very well indeed. Radio sets work. Reductionism shows us how they work. Yet strangely enough, when we have all the elements spread out over the table, and a circuit diagram to go with them, we have no component called "Sinatra's voice." Take a railway engine apart: there is no "speed" in there. Chop up the human brain, and you will not find a component called "compassion." He that hath ears to hear will instantly realize from this why so much rot is talked about "artificial intelligence." You can have an artificial heart, because we can dig out a heart. But it's a waste of time to talk about artificial intelligence, because no one ever dug out intelligence in the first place.

So why are we lured into such things? It is because reductionism declares that if you go on chopping pieces into smaller pieces, you will eventually understand *everything*. We got to the atom, thence to the release of energy in terms of smaller particles, thence to the bomb. By pursuing knowledge of the basic cells of the nervous system and of gas molecules, and by poking down into the genetic codes of the living cell, we have equipped ourselves with nerve gases and biological weapons. We hear little of these; but they are just as dangerous, and every bit as insane, as nuclear warheads. So although reduction has proven an effective methodology, it does tend to have reductionist outcomes! Then who shall undertake re-synthesis? Who will put Humpty Dumpty together again?

Stafford Beer is currently Professor of Cybernetics (part-time) at the University of Manchester, UK; Adjunct Professor of Social Systems Sciences at the University of Pennsylvania, US; and President of the World Organization of General Systems and Cybernetics.

3

Consider some of the outcomes that we face, and we shall quickly spot the next layer of the reductionist problem.

Once I was Chairman of a Committee of the Royal Statistical Society. Richard Doll was a member. He and his colleague Bradford Hill had discovered an association between smoking and lung cancer. But no one could demonstrate a causal relationship. And still that simple causality eludes us. That was thirty years ago, however, and folk are just not arguing any more: that cause is won.

But it did take thirty years. And the mode of simple causality retains its grip on our reductionist society. Only the other week the President of the United States was looking for a "clearer causal link" to show that pollution causes environmental damage to Canada. Meanwhile the Prime Minister of Britain wants "evidence" that Britain's acid rain has decimated the Scandinavian forests. Everyone knows that ecological systems are extremely complicated. They also know that some lakes and streams have the acidic constitution of lemon juice. What could possibly have caused that? In a reductionist world we shall never find out. Experimental rats have been smoking cigarettes for years and years, and they just don't develop lung carcinoma . . .

What happens when we turn to the ecology of humankind? Here are nine abstract nouns—which is about as many as anyone can handle. As I list them . . .

I ask you to consider whether, in the experience of your own lifetime, they might be related. Here goes: unemployment; drug abuse; decaying neighborhoods; malnutrition; crime; family disintegration; juvenile prostitution; decline of religion; riots in the streets.

There are, as a mathematical fact, seventy-two relationships among nine things. Which is "the cause" of what? It is not so much a question that *nobody knows,* as that *the question is fatuous.* The reductionist methodology leads to a notion of causality that just will not stick. But the great professions adhere to reductionism, trying to consider the seventy-two relationships one at a time. They are not Systemic in their outlook whatsoever—and I have worked closely with most.

Mrs. Thatcher has not accepted any responsibility for acid rain; and she says that street rioting is merely criminal. She is both a chemist and a lawyer. Both disciplines operate on a notion of causality that died its philosophic death with the philosopher David Hume, who died in 1776.

What about medicine?

A few years back I was trying to help a young woman. She was diabetic, and attended a clinic. She was epileptic, and had routine consultancy for that. She had a psychiatrist attending to something called a multiple personality. Her parents had called in a homeopathic specialist. Her GP beamed and said that she had the best possible advice. The *person,* we rightly call her the *individual,* in the middle of this muddle, was altogether lost and disregarded. She had exerted her unity, in face of all this reductionism, in a love affair. Then, all

4

alone because she wrongly chose her man, she decided on abortion. She was nineteen. If you will enlarge on this picture in the societal domain, you may ask: Who *is* the ill/well person? Is she literate or illiterate? Numerate or innumerate? Can she speak a foreign language? Does she have degrees? Oh, well, ask Education. Employed or unemployed? Does she pay tax—how much? Ask that of someone else. And what's her credit worth, and has she been abroad, and is she in the police computer? If so, is that because of felony, or technical offense, or because a policeman did not like her manner?

We cut up *people* into tiny bits, and shuffle them around. Then who shall undertake re-synthesis?

I am sure you realize that I could go on with this for pages: probing into business and industry, into government, into politics, into that most victimized third world. Always we should find a reductionist methodology, and always a childlike notion of causality to back it up.

So let's move on instead. There is, after all, a great deal of apparent goodwill around. I have undertaken various studies in both the Health and Education sectors of Ontario. No one is hiding in these trying to wreck the Province. My work over the years in Ottawa has touched on a dozen ministries and agencies. Everyone has goodwill.

But to whom could you say this: There is an ecumenical trend of unemployment to reach about a *billion* soon after the Year 2000. Canada is privileged in the short run. But quite soon we have to alter the meaning of the word "job."

To whom could you say: "Government's benignity to small business, the backbone of the economy, is at the root of its failures?"

I believe both these things. Why cannot they be resolved? I give you a direct reply. People are daunted by complicated systems. They run away from the seventy-two-fold connectivity of my nine elements. Nine? How many elements does a businessman or a politician reckon he is dealing with? A thousand, perhaps? Then a *million* (minus one!) relationships have to be handled. Reductionism just won't work in societal systems, unless you reduce to a police state—and cancel out most of the complexity. Direct causality won't work either, unless you cancel out complexity and reduce to a police state. The devil of it is: you can see it actually happening, even in our "democratic" western world . . .

But people *are* daunted by complicated systems, and so they use the reductionist—causal models with which they can cope. At that point, although they have power, they render themselves powerless. They perceive that there is nothing they can do. And that is true, insofar as they have blocked-off potential solutions *by definition*.

Consider: We must reduce the deficit. We cannot abandon defense of our land, we cannot "lose control" of law and order, we cannot alienate our business interests that create our weaith, and we cannot put off tourists or frighten off foreign investors. Too bad . . . we have "no alternative" but to junk our welfare programs. That might increase unemployment, drug abuse, and seven more elements? Oh come now, no causal connections have been proven . . .

5

There is no alternative—not because that's true, but because the logic is set up to *admit* no alternative.

Here is an apocryphal story.

This little girl comes up to me, views my beard a little askance, and says: "were you in Noah's Ark?" "Oh, c'mon," I say: "Of course I wasn't." "Then why weren't you drowned?" This story well defines a *double-bind*.

Typically management faces two of them.

(i) *Problems* do not respect the management structure. The production problem has its roots in sales, but sales is not listening—and anyway only changes in production control can produce results. You want to teach transdisciplinary cybernetics? Whichever Faculty takes you on, you are not in another Faculty's Ark—and you *are* drowned. In government it is very much worse, especially because the structures that ought to be changed are enshrined in legislation.

Problems in the end become the cherished property of those who have them. If you find that incredible, think of the individual and chronic illness. The problems are often what defines identity.

(ii) *Planning* parallels the organization. It has to: otherwise who would commission the work or engage in the planning process? It turns out then that what we intend to do is what we do now—with knobs on.

Add 10% each year to the market research budget, and eventually we shall know *everything*. Add a little more tax to all the usual tax targets, and eventually the deficit will vanish. It does not work like that. We have to find a planning mode that is not homologous with the organizational structure if we are ever to find solutions.

If we could generate a novel plan that did not parallel the organization, *then* we could set up an interdepartmental task force to consider that. But you cannot expect such a task force to generate a novel plan. The dear people will sit in a ring like death-watch beetles holding hands, trying to prop up the existing structure. These kinds of double-bind are goodwill's paradox. "We will embrace change—so long as it involves no actual alteration."

But Why a Foundation?

The reason for this approach is *freedom:* freedom from classifications, freedom from paradigm, freedom from organizational structure.

That also means "freedom from grants!" You cannot obtain a grant without accepting a structure, adopting its paradigm, and talking its linguistic conventions. It follows that you cannot redefine a problem: great chunks of your redefinition will be in someone else's territory. Besides, you have had to agree in advance what will count as an answer—so no real solution can possibly emerge. Always we end up with reductionist refinements of solutions we already have. Of these one thing alone is known: *they don't work.*

So this is why I never applied for a grant in a lifetime's professional work. I have been paid to tackle problems, whether as a salaried manager or a hired consultant, and have therefore had the freedom to look at every dimension of the problem and to hunt it down distant paths.

The Foundation seeks to extend that freedom to another generation of problem-solvers. We have a multidisciplinary group here in Toronto, and they have taken this initiative. There are smaller, less cohesive groups in Montreal, Ottawa and Vancouver. There is a group in Britain (more than twenty strong) that has gathered itself around multiple uses of one part of my work. There are embryonic groups in Continental Europe, in Scandinavia, in India, in Mexico, in Venezuela, Argentina and Brazil. There are other such "gangs" in at least four major regions of the United States, and another in Australia.

Among all these good people there are those concerned closely with my science and philosophy; others are concerned with management and government, and my experiences there. I published collections of poetry and paintings because of a late realizatism that so many people have interest in aesthetics—which are not frills decorating their lives but intrinsic to their vision of what it is to be human. More and more people are ready to discuss spiritual insights, which is why I have a limited practice in teaching a brand of meditative yoga—exercised for forty years.

If the use of my name can provide a focus to help even a few people redefine themselves, *then* to redefine a few networks of "whole" people; and if those people under this Foundation's transdisciplinary logo are then enabled to redefine problems: what a work we have begun!

Be assured that I am not going to travel the world whipping up frenzies. I want to think about problems, solve, resolve or dissolve them, and to facilitate those who "turn up," in their various ways— but usually as refugees from some institutional containment. The prime resources of the Foundation are those people and their prepared minds. I want nothing, and like to "stay put."

Some of you will, I realize, be saying: So what's the bottom line?

I will mention just one project that is ringing in my head. The decentralization of management and the nature of resultant diversified autonomy has been a major aspect of my work, and is much more considered now than it was 20 or 30 years ago. Recently I have developed a completely new cybernetic theory for making all this operational. It draws heavily on the work of Buckminster Fuller, in unity with my own. I want to run experiments on this. Think of all the groups that I just mentioned. All have access to microcomputers and to international networks. Most of them (not I!) has his/her own machine.

What a wonderful piece of research—provided it has no limitations. It would mean one thing to communes and cooperatives, another to the native peoples of Canada, another to Queen's Park or Ottawa, another to the corporation, another to the multinational and to the UN.

7

The bottom line shows up all right, if people in power gather their internal power to refute the institutional powerlessness that is thrust on them. Someone, somewhere has to have the guts. Sometimes, it happens.

If it sounds like magic, it is not. The truth of the matter is shockingly simple: you do not have to rob Peter to pay Paul. In our society, everything we need extra is being lost in *waste*. You cannot stop waste by cancelling programs, decimating staff, and thereby creating more problems than you solve.

What you do is *redefine the problem, redesign the system*. When managers or ministers have the will to do that, the saving—as I have seen it—is between one and two thirds.

The claim is staggering.

Our needs are few.

Crisis Management
and
Conflict Resolution

THE FUTURE OF CRISIS CONTROL

AND

CONFLICT RESOLUTION

by

William Exton, Jr.

The term "crisis" is usually applied to situations which are perceived (usually quite subjectively) as involving an immediate threat of unacceptable adverse consequences. Such perceptions usually appear to require, quite urgently, decisions and actions aimed at preventing or forestalling such extremely undesirable developments; or—at least—delaying them, or minimizing their adverse effects.

The terms "crisis" and "conflict resolution" must be regarded as relative, since popular usage applies them to any kind of situation, from an argument over what to watch on the family's TV, to a military incursion across national borders. And, in fact, some families, and some neighbors—and even some nations—have been able to resolve conflicting interests without a sense of actual—or even impending—crisis; while some other families, neighbors and nations seem to be in states of permanent crisis—or to move habitually from one crisis to the next. And the two terms are also related, in the sense that failures or inadequacies or unforeseen consequences of "conflict resolution" may lead to "crisis."

Since crises impose memorably dramatic—even traumatic—experiences on those threatened or involved; and since important—sometimes even vital—values are at risk, the kind of "management" or "handling" applied to a crisis becomes a matter of the most serious concern. When the crisis is national—or even international—in scale, the related functioning of those affecting—or failing to affect—the outcome goes down as a milestone in history. But the same considerations hold—in principle, though on a lesser scale—for the behavior of individuals involved in the crises of organizations, families, ventures, marriages, friendships, etc.

While the highly general "definition" suggested in the first paragraph would apply to virtually any set of circumstances regarded—by those affected—as constituting "a crisis," it is nevertheless determinable that: 1) there are crises of many kinds; 2) crises can be usefully

William Exton, Jr., is a management consultant for the international consulting firm of William Exton, Jr. and Associates, New York, New York.

11

classified according to functionally significant characteristics; and, 3) the effectiveness of the "management" or "handling" of crises can be shown to depend on the degree to which the measures employed can be and are adapted to the functional nature of the crisis itself (independently of the competence with which they are implemented).

It is the purpose of this paper to present a rationale for the control of crises. This requires considerations of a number of factors: causation (including agency, motivation, objective, etc.); degrees and aspects of urgency; foreseeable consequences (direct, indirect, contingent, etc.); reactive potentials (resources, capabilities, etc.); and psychological aspects (fear, courage, weakness, determination, confidence, morale, etc.). And, of course, it also requires consideration of appropriate measures for the obtaining, interpretation, utilization, evaluation and rational exploitation of information; and of developing the optimum strategy and tactics for application of the dynamic inputs which may be available, obtainable, and disposable.

It can be useful to classify perceived crises according to the major factor of causation. Thus a primary classification would distinguish between those having their origins in nature (earthquakes; volcanic eruptions; floods; droughts; tidal waves; catastrophic weather phenomena such as hurricanes, typhoons, tornadoes, excessive rainfall, etc.; epidemics; and other phenomena usually ascribed to "natural causes") as well as those resulting from accidents of all kinds, when occasioned by impersonal factors, or unintentionally by some human agency; all of these in contrast to those originating in conscious, deliberate, purposeful human behavior.

The latter category, again, can be usefully subdivided according to the degree of purposiveness and deliberation in the causative behavior; which—usually—originates in conflicting interests. This would range from one extreme of *planned* crisis, such as the bombing of Pearl Harbor by the Japanese in 1941, to the other extreme of *unplanned* crisis causation, such as Lord North's imposition of the Stamp Tax on England's American colonies. There is also the kind of crisis resulting from human behavior that cannot be specifically ascribed to identified purposing initiators, such as "inflation," or those affecting general environmental conditions (i.e.: regional soil erosion, smog, acid rain damage, etc.).[1]

There are other classifiable distinctions among the very diverse varieties of crises to which we are all too frequently subjected, and these distinctions may be of considerable importance in their control. There is the aspect of predictability: to what extent can—and should—a crisis be foreseen? Related to this is the question of the degree of visibility of the causative factors, over time: can they and should they be detected and identified? And, in this connection, of course, there is also the matter of the availability of feasible means of preventing the foreseeable crisis or minimizing its deleterious effects; or of delaying it.

In the matter of warnings of the imminence of crises, scientific advances increasingly provide the basis for some degree of enhance-

12

ment of control of a growing number of kinds of crisis. Such advances range in application from the predictability of earthquakes, volcanic eruptions and catastrophic weather patterns, to the gathering of military intelligence by increasingly sophisticated electronic means, and by satellite surveillance; from the increasingly sophisticated sociological techniques which measure the moods of the popular psyche, to the maturing sociometric forecasts that provide the data necessary for the forestalling of crisis in economic spheres.

Undoubtedly, the future will see quantum progress in our capability to detect ever earlier stages of the causation of many kinds of possible crises; enabling us to exert, to the fullest, all our potentials for preventing or minimizing them.

But—to leap ahead—just as the initial significance of a perceived crisis lies in its *potential* effect, so its *actual* effect often depends on the reactions of those affected—or threatened. And all such reactions must depend upon three basic elements.

First, the resources which may be, or can be made, available to those who would react in a positive way—rather than with the negative reaction of passive submission. But any physical and technological resources which may be available are likely to be useless without two equally essential (and essentially interrelated) factors, in the form of intangible resources. These are: the adequacy of the *competence* available and in position to make the essential evaluations and carry out the necessary decisions; and—indispensably—the *will* to act with dedication to the threatened values; and to do so as courageously and determinedly as may be necessary.

In all probability, this latter element—the *will* to surmount the crisis—will assure that whatever competence may be available will be exerted to its maximum capabilities; and that it will thus increase the probability of achieving the planned result, despite any inadequacy of other resources that makes such an outcome appear hopeless to others.

From the stock market crisis of 1929 to the bombing of Pearl Harbor; from the successive aggressions of Hitler to the Soviet invasion of East Bloc satellites; from the wild fluctuations in petroleum prices (since the advent of OPEC) to the lethal pollution of communities and water resources; from the urgent emergencies affecting individuals, families and neighborhoods, to confrontations and hostilities that bring the United Nations to desperate deliberations—we have ample evidence of a major truth: crises can be and have been foreseen. But—too often—nothing—or too little—is done about them, usually, until they became unmistakably, unavoidably, extremely and urgently menacing.

In other words, tolerable, acceptable situations are allowed to deteriorate into dangerous—even desperate—crises; even though it *is* possible to foresee such developments. And avoidable crises have been allowed to develop unhindered even when such developments *were* foreseen—and warned against—by some who simply were not listened to.

In each such case, the three basic requisites for the management of crises, as specified above, could have been mobilized and brought to bear. And it can be argued persuasively that they could have made it possible to prevent development of many, if not all, such crises, or—at least—to keep them from attaining their ultimate forms, and to counter them more effectivley.

If only the *will* to overcome the crises could be activated when adverse developments are first detected, then (usually) fewer resources and lesser competencies are required. And if these are provided at earlier stages, many major calamities can be avoided—or, at least—confined to less damaging consequences.

It is all very well, of course, to echo—in essence—such proverbial wisdom as "an ounce of prevention is worth a pound of cure" and "when there is no wisdom, the people perish"—not to mention: "Those who ignore history are condemned to repeat it." But it is still an inescapable truism that many crises *can* be avoided, or (at least) minimized, in their adverse effects, if only there is the perceptiveness to anticipate them and the *will* to forestall their development.

How can we increase the probability that these two conditions will be met? And if there is a way to accomplish this, how do we go about it?

The most promising program surely includes these elements:

1) Identify the values that will not be readily surrendered or compromised.

2) Be aware of values that are, or appear to be, opposed to our own; alert to their manifestations; and judicious about the actual and potential coincidence and opposition of such values so that the underlying essentials and the possibly aggravating inessentials of a potential crisis may be clearly identified.

3) Develop the function of perceiving a potential threat or counter to such values, in any event, activity, process, development, utterance or behavior; focusing primarily on those potential sources of adverse effects which carefully evaluated experience will suggest, "Eternal vigilance is the price"—not only of liberty, but of the protection and maintenance of any vulnerable value.

4) Inform and educate, in advance—on a generic basis—all those who share the values that may be menaced, so that they understand what they risk if a crisis develops. Encourage them to enhance their consciousness of the importance—to them!—of the values that may be involved. But teach them, also, to discriminate among values, so that priorities are understood. (In an imperfect world, we cannot regard *all* the values we cherish as sacrosanct. Let us be fully aware of what we will risk, and what we will not; what is, and what is not, negotiable; in effect, what values justify a crisis reaction to conditions which menace them, and which are not so sacred.

5) Anticipate and prepare for those contingencies which can develop into crises. (This may involve being prepared to meet a crisis before one is anticipated.)

14

6) Coordinate the implementation of Elements 1-5, above, providing physical and technological resources adequate to satisfy the implied requirements of Element 5, and creating optimum resources for the earliest detection of potential crises and for the dedication that alone can assure the *will* to protect and defend fundamental values.

Notes

1. Situations arising from a wide range of causative conditions often result in crises of a personal, individual nature—within the larger crisis. These originate in the *"internal* conflicts of interest"* which trouble—and often render indecisive—those who find themselves unable to perceive—and/or accept—a preponderance of positively viewed values in connection with any suggested, available or feasible option. Such indecisiveness tends to affect, in various ways, the principled analytical, sensitive and highly perceptive— rather than the dogmatic, single-minded and callous.

INFORMATION TECHNOLOGY FOR

EMERGENCY MANAGEMENT:

THE MANY POTENTIALS

by

Robert Lee Chartrand

There is a growing concern in many sectors of government and society that we as a Nation—at the Federal level, as well as in the States and localities—are inadequately prepared to cope with the technological and natural emergencies which affect people and property. The very complexity of our societal structure, as reflected in jurisdictional conflicts over responsibility and the accelerated development and use of new energy sources, pesticides, and fertilizers with toxic side effects, have caused lawmakers and program managers to reexamine the effectiveness of our crisis (or emergency) management capability. One critical facet of improving this potentiality— through improved mitigation, preparedness, response, and recovery mechanisms and procedures—is the development of advanced information systems for acquiring, storing, processing, retrieving, and sharing essential data that may be used by emergency managers.

A Range of Crises

The range of emergencies or "disasters" which must be coped with, whether of natural or man-caused origin, is large: floods, earthquakes, fires, assassinations, riots, terrorist attacks, nuclear meltdowns, toxic spills, and so forth. The awesome nature of many of these, as reflected in Hearn's description of a Gulf hurricane, continues to be a source of deep concern and cause for responsive official action.

... there burst upon the ears of all a fearful and unfamiliar sound, as of a colossal cannonade—rolling up from the south, with volleying lightnings. Vastly and swiftly, nearer and nearer it came—a ponderous and unbroken thunder roll, terrible as the long muttering of an earthquake.

—(Lafacadio Hearn—Chita)

Robert Chartrand is a senior specialist, information policy and technology. This paper is reprinted, with permission, from CRS Review, *November-December 1984.* CRS Review *is published by Congressional Research Service, a department of Congress.*

Experience has shown that information is critical in anticipating or dealing with many types of disasters, and as improved technologies have become available they have been added to the inventory of equipment and related methodology which can be applied to EM tasks. A selective recital of disaster types and the havoc ensuing from their occurrence is instructive:

- Boating and aircraft emergencies—Several hundred persons died in 1982 in off-shore sinkings; and in FY 1982 6,414 fishing vessels required SAR(Search and Rescue) assistance, plus 49,834 such incidents involving recreational boats. In addition, the FAA reported (in FY 1982), that 3,394 air carrier and general aviation accidents took place.
- Floods—During 1983, according to NOAA, 204 persons died and property losses exceeded $4 billion as a result of floods caused by accumulated snowfall runoff, dam breakage, or intensive rainfall.
- Hazardous materials spills (in transit)—The National Transportation Safety Board (NTSB) estimates that 250,000 hazardous materials shipments are made daily. Transportation accidents—train, truck, barge—involving such cargoes have accounted for about 25 deaths per year over the past decade, in interstate accidents alone. In 1971 there were 2,225 hazardous releases, but by 1980 the statistic had increased to 16,115.
- Nuclear powerplant accidents—Although Three Mile Island is the only "major" accident in recent years, there were 3,804 LER(Licensee Event Reports) documented instances (in 1980) where performance exceeded technical design parameters. Filed with the Nuclear Regulatory Commission (NRC), these reports came from 69 commercial nuclear plants: 753 accidents were attributed to human errors and 2,174 to equipment malfunction.
- Tornadoes—These destructive weather aberrations account for millions of dollars in damage and numerous deaths each year. The "super outbreak" in a 10-State area in 1974 involved 148 reported tornadoes which caused 315 deaths and $600 million in property loss. In FY 1982, FEMA responded to 181 tornado warnings or touchdowns.

Other types of emergencies, while happening with less frequency, are still of high concern to Federal, State, and local officials alike. Earthquakes, volcanic eruptions, and hurricanes can be highly destructive and while infrequent when compared with some other forms of disasters, can wreak severe damage. Domestic terrorism, still modest in numbers, remains a menace of serious concern to authorities. In 1981, 31 terrorist incidents were reported in the United States, climbing to 52 in 1982.

In many instances, responsible governmental agencies and private groups have failed, in the words of Rep. Albert Gore, Jr. of Tennessee—during the 1981 hearings conducted by his Subcommittee on Investigations and Oversight of the House Committee on Science and Technology—"to bring to bear either the technology or the management capability needed to respond quickly and effectively to the demands of stress situations."

In the opinion of many governmental and private sector leaders the improvement of the quality of information—narrative, statistical, graphic—which must be accessible to emergency managers is a *sine qua non;* "profiles" of need and use must be established, and data categories of overlapping utilization have to be identified. Also underscored is the need for methods of keeping such files current, and dispatching updated "essential elements of information" to outlying users; these deserve review and refinement. In essence, a requirement has been articulated to create a coordinated hierarchical information and communications capability that can fulfill known emergency management needs.

Evolving Information Technology Support

The benefits and limitations of using information technology—computers, telecommunications, microform systems, audio and video devices—in emergency management situations are imperfectly understood. Among the questions to be asked: What can technology do to better manage vital information? Can technology enhance the determination of information validity, indicating misinformation or "disinformation?" Should small-scale experiments and practical case studies be undertaken to better understand the man-machine interfaces involved in advanced systems for emergency use? In some instances these considerations may be better understood by studying the experience of those in comparable (e.g., command-and-control) environments in the military/intelligence arenas.

As traditional technologies—photography, telephone, radio—are augmented by more sophisticated systems, the ability of the community threatened or already affected by a given disaster to act on its own behalf is enhanced. And while Federal or State funding and technical assistance may be solicited, most local communities attempt to achieve a fairly high degree of self-sufficiency for coping with all but the extraordinary emergency.

Illustrative of the major uses of advanced information technology in crisis-related functions are:

- 800 minicomputer warning systems in use throughout the country;
- a variety of airborne platforms such as the NASA U-2 and NOAA Flying Laboratories, along with sophisticated satellites featuring multi-sensor collection systems;
- the large masses of data stored in computerized or microfilm files (e.g., National Hurricane Center);
- the rapid retrieval of key data utilizing on-line access systems, by users located in emergency operations centers (EOC), mobile units, or other remote (local EM) sites; and
- the varied communications conduits—landlines, airwaves, including satellite systems (e.g., Inmarsat)—for transmitting key data.

The emergency management capability which serves our society cannot help but be changed over time by the incorporation of these and other innovations, and it is such an evolutionary process as this which motivated the late Marshall McLuhan to remind the world as long ago as 1967 that:

> Environments are not passive wrappings, but are, rather, active processes which are invisible. The groundrules, pervasive structure, and over-all patterns of environments elude easy perception . . . The interplay between the old and the new environments creates many problems and confusions.

Institutional Roles and Responsibilities

As might be imagined, the substitution of machine for human decisionmaking, long an expressed fear in many arenas of operation, has not been advocated but the growing panoply of sensors (aloft and aground), processors, and disseminators—the result of human inventiveness—has instigated the rethinking of old positions. During the past five years, with the establishment of the Federal Emergency Management Agency (FEMA), there has been increasingly collaborative action within the Federal governmental community. Included among the organizations with recognized roles and responsibilities in emergency management, who attend such concerns, are:

Federal agencies, such as FEMA, VA, USGS, NWS, NOAA, DOD, and many more
State and local governments (including task forces)
Regional commissions
Private sector consultants and information services
Information "clearinghouses"
Organizational "watch centers"
National coordinating groups
Private sector contractors—corporate, university, not-for-profit

Today, there is a sizable cadre responsible for anticipating and coping with an array of crises either of natural or man-caused origins. Earlier in our Nation's history, such duties tended to be performed largely by quasi-volunteer groups, usually in a reactive mode. But now there are more than 12,000 designated "emergency managers"—variously full- or part-time—who are involved in all four phases of emergency management (EM). These forces have learned that James Michener was correct when he pointed out that:

> . . . [our] balance in life consists of handling in real time those problems which cannot be delayed, then recalling more significant data during periods of reflection, when long-term decisions can be developed.

Since 1950, the President has declared over 700 major disasters, ranging from the Johnstown, Pennsylvania flood of 1977, and Hurricanes Camille (1969) and Agnes (1972) to the less sweeping but nonetheless damaging tornado "super outbreak" in the Central

States (1974) or the increasingly frequent in transit spills of hazardous waste materials (16,115 in 1980). And while this may well have to be viewed as only "one small pattern in a tapestry of struggle," more and more people and property are being affected as established patterns of communication, transportation, and other regular activities of urban and rural dwellers alike are upset.

Focal Action by the Congress

The boundaries of congressional cognizance of this area necessarily and not surprisingly encompass the full spectrum of emergency management activities, whether occurring before, during, or after a disaster. The commonality of these closely interrelated activity parameters and the ways in which sophisticated information technology can enhance the ability of governmental and private sector organizations to confront disasters continue to demand further attention by both executive and legislative overseers.

Several high priority issues have been identified which are of such high priority that their consideration is imperative:

- Is there a current, valid long-range plan addressing the role of communications networks in emergency situations?
- Has the optimum use of advanced information technologies in various disaster scenarios been studied, and plans for their operational utilization developed?
- Have priorities been determined for the creation, maintenance, and use of those essential information files which may be available to decisionmakers during emergencies?
- Are the advantages and disadvantages of various technologies employed in anticipating or responding to natural or man-caused disasters understood by those managers or operators responsible for their use?
- Will secure communications be available in contingency situations?
- Is there a need to review present emergency management concepts and plans, particularly those concerning the roles of "watch centers," networks, and key human resources?

Within the context of the recent establishment of the Federal Emergency Management Agency (FEMA) and congressional oversight activities focusing on civil defense and related activities, a need has been perceived for study and action which could include:

1. Taking advantage of the technology that is already on the shelf to upgrade our emergency management systems around the country.
2. Developing in our civilian managers the sensitivity to train for emergency situations and give priority to utilizing simulation in their regular work.
3. Drawing upon the expertise that has been developed in the national security arena in order to better deal with natural disasters.

20

During the 97th and 98th Congress, the Subcommittee on Investigations and Oversight, chaired by Representative Gore of the House Committee on Science and Technology, undertook a multi-faceted exploration of the role of information technology in emergency management. Early in the endeavor, it was noted that:

> The subject of disasters is not one that many of us care to dwell on. Earthquakes, fires, assassinations, terrorist attacks and nuclear melt-downs are the stuff of Hollywood and we like to keep it that way. As a result of this "out of sight, out of mind" ethic, our society is often ill-equipped to deal with emergencies when they do arise.

Present and potential uses of computers and telecommunications received primary attention as the Subcommittee considered their value in preventing or coping with both technological and natural disasters. In the 97th Congress, following a roundtable discussion led by Rep. Gore, two days of hearings were held on September 29 and 30, 1981, with expert testimony by acknowledged public and private sector leaders in the field. Subsequently, a technical forum was sponsored by the Subcommittee on November 23, 1981, and featured participation by 17 senior individuals who engaged in structured discussions and on-line demonstrations of technology-supported information systems.

The second phase of Subcommittee activity in this focal area occurred in the first session of the 98th Congress, with the convening of a combined two-day hearing and workshop, on November 16 and 17, 1983, and three special videotaped panels. The highlights of these various Subcommittee initiatives are featured in a committee print prepared by the Congressional Research Service.

Analogous Civilian and Military Challenge

As a result of these undertakings on Capitol Hill, it was discerned that part of the problem in emergency management may stem from the existing discrete systems in which military and civilian disaster experts operate. Some suggest that civilian managers must be afforded the opportunity for sustained orientation and training, including participation in simulated and actual emergency exercises. Proponents argue that the Nation could thus take advantage of the expertise that has been developed in the national security area and apply that to natural disaster situations.

Involving both military and civilian forces in certain types of emergencies implies a sharing of resources and responsibility, which in turn depend not only upon on-site cooperation but prior planning for manpower and materials' disposition. Similarly, the private sector groups which comprise NVOAD (National Voluntary Organizations Active in Disaster) often are involved in and can benefit from such action, including the receipt of automated forecasts and historical data. Such coordination and marshalling of available human and technological resources are required to meet the challenges and crises of the future.

Human and Machine Response Resources

With the immense impact of computers and telecommunications on society and government, and the understandable lag in appreciation of the multitudinous ways that they are altering our daily lives and thinking, the hesitation of emergency management forces to fully accept these innovations is comprehensible. The dilemma faced by persons at every level of authority and in every walk of life was stated trenchantly by George Will:

> . . . in the modern age people routinely rely on systems they do not understand . . . [they are] acting on faith, faith in strangers using skills that are as strange to laymen as Lilliput was to Gulliver.

With all of the advances achieved as a result of the ingenuity of man, the *human factor* remains paramount. Working to maintain the stability which underlies the general welfare, while striving to ensure sufficient emergency preparedness and plan perceptively for "continuity government" under unsought *in extremis* conditions, the leadership must often agree that "There is nothing more difficult of success, nor more dangerous to handle, than to initiate a new order of things." Yet, if the citizenry of this Nation is to survive the many convolutions introduced or facilitated by this electronic wizardry, the sweeping ramifications of the new systems—financial, commercial, social service, emergency preparedness—have to be understood, adapted, and trusted.

The Media Involvement Expands

In very recent times, a spate of destructive incidents—virtually all receiving maximum factual and interpretive coverage by reporters and television crews—has initiated a transition from somewhat detached enthrallment with such phenomena in the abstract to a fuller perception of the real cost and chaos of the actual happenings. There have been the eruptions of Mount St. Helens (1980), a precipitous climb in transit toxic spills, near-record numbers of tornadoes (reaching hitherto untouched areas), and in another realm, the persistent threat of a domestic terrorist incursion such as during the recent Olympic Games. Instances of so-called "multiple disasters" also are on the rise, as when the Air Florida crash in the Potomac River during a snowstorm (early in 1982) coincided with a Metro railcar crash in Washington or in the case when one debacle may cause yet another to occur. For example: an earthquake ruptures a dam which in turn triggers flooding.

One notable development on the media front, insofar as treatment of emergencies and their control operations was concerned, has been a series of widely viewed television "docudramas" including "The Day After" (ABC, November 20, 1983), "The Crisis Game" (ABC, November 22-25, 1983), "Special Bulletin" (NBC, March 20, 1983), and "If I Were President" (ABC, August 6, 1980), all attracting large audiences. These feature presentations concentrated on the decision-making process involved in attempting to cope with an impending nuclear war, a terrorist-caused catastrophe, or a crisis brought about by those protesting certain forms of military preparedness.

While the functioning of "crisis control centers" is featured, there is also telling commentary regarding the interplay between decision-makers in such a mechanism as well as their relationship with external forces. The portrayed participation of several very senior officials (Cabinet members, White House advisors, military leaders) lent an authenticity to the depiction of crisis management.

Several facets of emergency management, including the use of various technologies, appeared in these episodes. A meaningful perspective on this focal activity was offered by Dr. Jacques F. Vallee in his presentation (1981) before the congressionally-sponsored "Technical Forum:"

> The contribution that the emergency management community can expect from new information technology will not come from better or faster gadgets, but from greater understanding of the group dynamics of crisis situations, from a greater ability to prepare for such situations through sophisticated simulations and training, and from a finer analysis of their qualitative and quantitative characteristics.

Effective Crisis Management: An Unflagging Need

The *durability* and *flexibility* of emergency management systems are critical parameters for functional effectiveness. There is an upswing in simulations and actual exercising of certain crisis handling systems to test their execution of vital operations under stress. This constitutes one facet of "quality control" which can be a crucial underpinning for any such system.

To many, if not most emergency managers, the criteria is *the delivery of needed information* that is accurate, timely, comprehensive (where possible), and relevant to the challenge at hand. The "system" or "tool" may be incidental and if its performance is unreliable—whether in terms of linking networks or simply retrieving a piece of key data—then the responsible office may opt to return to a simpler, more trustworthy capability.

The acquisition, verification, and transmittal of information have always been critical in meeting a variety of crises ranging from small-scale localized disasters to larger emergency situations affecting a wide geographic area. *Information technology* as never before has come to offer a wide range of potentials for enhancing the effectiveness of crisis organizations—both governmental institutions and designated authorities within the private domain—responsible for emergency warning and notification, situation assessment, decision-making during crises, and dissemination of essential information for responsive action.

References

1. Kupperman, Robert H., and D. Trent. *Terrorism,* Stanford, CA, Hoover Institution Press, Stanford University, 1979. 450 p.

2. Littlejohn, Robert F. *Crisis Management: A Team Approach.* New York, American Management Association, 1983. 54 p.

3. National Academy of Sciences, National Research Council. *The Role of Science and Technology in Emergency Management.* Washington, 1982. 90 p.

4. Society for Computer Simulation. *Computer Simulation in Emergency Planning.* [Proceedings of a conference, Jan. 27-29, 1983, San Diego, CA] edited by John M. Carroll. La Jolla, CA, Jan. 1983. 115 p.

5. "The New Information Technology in Emergency Management." *Hazard Monthly,* December 1981: 7-11, 13.

6. U.S. Congress. House Committee on Science and Technology. Subcommittee on Investigations and Oversight. *Information Technology for Emergency Management.* Committee print. 98th Congress, 2nd session. Washington, U.S. Government Printing Office, 1984. 456 p.

7. U.S. General Accounting Office. Consolidation of Federal assistance resources will enhance the Federal-State emergency management effort. Washington, August 30, 1983. 88 p.

8. U.S. General Accounting Office. Federal involvement in the Mount St. Helens disaster: past expenditures and future needs. Washington, November 15, 1982. 133 p.

UNDERSTANDING RISKS

by

Frederick Forscher

Risk Assessment and Risk Management

Day and night, everywhere we turn, we are surrounded by a multitude of risks, some large and some so minimal that they can easily be overlooked, but all demanding, sooner or later, to be recognized (i.e. assessed) and dealt with (i.e. managed). Risks seem like the invisible radio signals that fill the air around us, some clear and some very faint, but all want to be heard.

With increased understanding of what is going on about us, we became aware of many risks previously unknown, and—as a consequence of the industrial revolution—became aware of the increased spectrum of risks (i.e. ranging from the old fashion toxic, mechanical and seismic—to electrical, chemical, radioactive, carcinogenic, and mutative). With better instruments, and a greater variety of instruments, we can now detect and assess the risks which previous generations could not. In fact, *Risk Assessment* has recently become a scientific/mathematical discipline of its own. On the other hand, *Risk Management* has not progressed very much since the days of the Voo-Doo doctor, the religious dogma, or the revealed truth (i.e. personal convictions). Risk assessment and risk management are like diagnostic and therapeutic activities in medicine. With our new instruments we are now able to diagnose conditions that years ago we didn't even know existed. We can also now understand how some treatments address the symptoms rather than the (diagnosed) cause of the disease. Compare that to an uninformed risk reduction in which we really don't address the root cause of the problem. And, just like treatment is no cure, risk avoidance is no solution.

Here, it is also important to point out that fear is not a measure of risk; whether it is fear of flying, or fear of radiation, or fear of AIDS. Fears are based on perceived risks and strongly held convictions that can—in some cases—lead to clinical anxieties and other mental health problems. While such problems are unfortunate, the

---

Frederick Forscher is president of Energy Management Consultants, Inc., Pittsburgh, Pennsylvania.

management of these *mental* health risks is not regulated by Federal agencies that otherwise are charged with the protection of the "health and safety of the public and the quality of the environment."

This paper deals with the subject of risk—risks to the individual and risks to the society—and how to assess it and how to manage it. The risks that we are discussing here—the non-economic risks—are all energy related, whether they are toxic, bio-chemical, electromagnetic, mechanical or radioactive; all are undesirable energy conversion processes that are controllable via a rational decision-making process called risk management. It is well to remind the reader that every decision, and every action, is energy related, and that energy should be the subject of public concern, the focus of our national policies, and the goal of our planning effort.

Risk management (i.e. the decision-making process) in today's industrial societies, which includes the Western world *and* the Communist bloc, follows essentially two different perceptions of what is true: the scientific truth or the revealed truth. The first type of risk management was not very successful in the past because risk assessment was not scientifically based; i.e., the diagnosis was not clear enough to make a confident prediction for risk reduction. The second kind of risk management, while occasionally successful in the past, lost much of its power today because of its inability to forecast events with confidence. "In God we trust" was a good motto about 200 years ago; today we often say "God helps those who help themselves." It seems that we are today in the precarious position where the number of voters with confidence in rational (scientific) risk management is about balanced by the number of voters that believe that the good old days should be our guide to decision making. As for the possible stalemate between the scientific and revealed truth, have no fear; the third kind of truth will take over as surely as time marches on. The third truth, the historical truth, is what comes about naturally, unpredicted by science or religion, but more and more the domain of the explanatory sciences like sociology, economics, or evolution.

Living Can Be Dangerous to Your Health

As technology spreads through the social organism, each individual is confronted with ever more difficult decisions; i.e. each decision maker must understand the risk and then decide what to do about it. What follows in this section is based on Dr. Bernard Cohen's pioneering effort to educate the public in understanding risk. (*Before It's Too Late,* B.L. Cohen, Plenum Press, NY, 1983.)

We view taking risks as foolhardy, irrational, and to be avoided. Training children to avoid risk is an all-important duty of parenthood. Risks imposed on us by others are generally considered to be entirely unacceptable. Unfortunately life is not like that. Everything we do involves risk. There are dangers in every type of travel, but there are dangers in staying home—40% of all fatal accidents occur there. There are dangers in eating—food is probably the most important cause of cancer and of several other diseases—but most people

26

eat more than necessary. There are dangers in breathing—air pollution probably kills at least 10,000 Americans each year, inhaling *natural* radioactivity is believed to kill a similar number and many diseases are contracted by inhaling germs. There are dangers in working— 12,000 Americans are killed each year in job-related accidents, and probably ten times that number die from job-related illness—but most alternatives to working are even more dangerous. There are dangers in exercising and dangers in not getting enough exercise. Risk is an unavoidable part of our everyday lives. Truly: Living Is Dangerous.

There are many ways of expressing quantified risk, but here we will use just one, the "loss of life expectancy" (LLE); i.e., the average amount by which one's life is shortened by the risk under consideration. The LLE is the product of the probability for a risk to cause death and the consequences in terms of lost life expectancy if it does cause death. As an example, statistics indicate that an average 40 year old American man will live another 34.8 years. If he takes a risk that has a 1% chance of being immediately fatal, it causes an LLE of 0.348 years (0.01 x 34.8). This does not mean that he will die 0.348 years sooner as a result of taking this risk, but if 1000 people his age took this risk, 10 might die immediately, having their lives shortened by 34.8 years, while the other 990 would not have their lives shortened at all. Hence, the average lost lifetime for the 1000 people would be 0.348 years. This is the LLE from that risk. Table 1 compares several LLEs that are due to various risks.

It seems to me that these comparisons are the all-important bottom line in the nuclear debate. Nuclear power is being rejected because it is viewed as being too risky, but the best way for a person to understand a risk is to compare it with other risks with which he is familiar. These comparisons are therefore the best way for members of the public to understand the risks of nuclear power. All of the endless technical facts thrown at people are unimportant and unnecessary if they only understand these few simple risk comparisons. But somehow they are never told these facts. The media rarely give them, and even nuclear advocates hardly ever quote them. Yet, these LLEs are not disputed by anybody, so that the question of whom to trust among the many "experts" does not really enter here.

There are other considerations that enter. Some people are more willing to accept natural risks than man-made risks, but nearly all of the risks we have considered are man-made and are the price we pay for the benefits of civilization. Recently, the acceptance of natural risks has been jolted by the radon problem. Radon is a radioactive gas that seeps silently from rock to soil into homes in certain areas in this country. EPA estimates that between 5,000 and 20,000 people die each year in the nation from lung cancer caused by radon. More than a million U.S. homes may have excessive radon levels, i.e. multiple levels over those defined by EPA as acceptably safe. Some homes were tested and showed 100 times and even nearly 1000 times the radon concentration that the EPA recommends as a maximum.

Table 1

Loss of Life Expectancy (LLE) Due to Various Risks

Activity or risk	Days LLE
Being male rather than female	2,800
Heart disease	2,100
Being unmarried	2,000
Being black rather than white (in US)	2,000
Cigarettes (1 pack/day)	1,600
Working as a coalminer	1,100
Cancer	980
30 lb overweight	900
Grade-school dropout	800
Being poor	700
Stroke	520
15 lb overweight	450
All accidents	435
Vietnam army duty	400
Living in southeastern US (South Carolina, Mississippi, Georgia, Louisiana, Alabama)	350
Mining or construction work (due to accidents only)	320
Motor vehicle accidents	200
Pneumonia, influenza	130
Alcohol	130
Suicide	95
Homicide	90
Occupational accidents (average)	74
Small cars (versus standard size)	50
Drowning	40
Speed limit 55-65 mph	40
Falls	39
Poison + suffocation + asphyxiation	37
Fire, burns	27
Radiation work, age 18-65	12
Firearms	11
Diet drinks (one per day throughout life)	2
All electric power in U.S., nuclear (UCS)	1.5
Hurricanes, tornadoes	1
Airline crashes	1
Dam failures	0.5
Spending lifetime near nuclear power plant	0.4
All electric power in US Nuclear (NRC)	0.03

In virtually all cases, the occupants of the homes are unaware of the hazard because radon has no taste, odor or color. Suddenly, the resale value of these radon-infested homes dropped sharply; yet, the mortgage payments must be kept up. Are these families now "voluntarily" or "involuntarily" accepting the risk of living in these homes?

Who is going to pay for relocating these families or for modifying their homes so as to assure acceptable radon levels for its occupants? In connection with the concern of voluntary versus involuntary risks, it should be pointed out that accidents to pedestrians (i.e. involuntary) account for 20% of deaths from predominantly voluntary motor vehicle accidents. Similarly, deaths from fires, burns, falls, poison, and suffocation, are not usually due to voluntary risk taking.

Since reactor meltdowns are accidents, they should be compared with other accidents. There are dam failure accidents which could kill 200,000 people within a few hours; they are estimated to be far more probable than a bad nuclear meltdown accident. The idea that a reactor meltdown accident is uniquely or even unusually catastrophic is grossly erroneous.

What Does It Cost To Manage Risks?

Let us now move from the assessment of risks to the management, and ask what it takes to reduce these risks to acceptable levels. If we should find, for example, that the cost per human life saved becomes excessively high so as to affect our national economy, we would then need to balance the benefits (i.e. saving a life) against the price we have to pay in terms of the welfare of all the people. Reducing our national wealth can have a disastrous impact on public health, amounting to hundreds of days of LLE. It is clearly counter-productive to eliminate one risk if by doing so one introduces other risks that are even greater. In all our efforts to minimize risk, we must therefore consider the risks of alternatives.

It may seem immoral and inhumane even to consider the monetary cost of saving lives, but the fact is that a great many of our risks can be reduced by spending money. A few years ago, air bags were offered as optional safety equipment on several types of automobiles, but they are no longer offered because not enough people were willing to buy them. They were proven to be effective and safe—an estimated 15,000 lives per year would be saved if they were installed in all cars. There is no discomfort or inconvenience connected with them. They have only one drawback—they cost too much.

If there were a smoke alarm in every home, it is estimated that 2,000 fewer people would die each year in fires. Even with a generous allowance for costs of installation and maintenance, this works out to a life saved for every $60,000 spent, but only 25% of American homes have smoke alarms.

And what about the government? We pay a large share of our income to national, state, and local governments to protect us. The government can hire scientists or solicit testimony from experts to determine risks and benefits, or even to develop new methods for protecting us. They could set the standards for: "How safe is safe enough," and in doing so would perhaps be responsible for any fatality as a result of the standard. So, instead, the Congress (and other legislatures) create Regulatory Agencies and Commissions to set

Table 2

Cost per fatality averted (1975 dollars) implied by various societal activities (left column) and cost per 20 years of added life expectancy (right column).

Item	$ per fatality averted	$ per 20-yr. life expectancy
Medical screening and care		
Cervical cancer	25,000	13,000
Breast cancer	80,000	60,000
Lung cancer	70,000	70,000
Colorectal cancer		
Fecal blood tests	10,000	10,000
Proctoscopy	30,000	30,000
Multiple screening	26,000	20,000
Hypertension control	75,000	75,000
Kidney dialysis	200,000	440,000
Mobile intensive care units	30,000	75,000
Traffic safety		
Auto safety equipment—1966-1970	130,000	65,000
Steering column improvement	100,000	50,000
Air bags, driver only	320,000	160,000
Tire inspection	400,000	200,000
Rescue helicopters	65,000	33,000
Passive three-point harness	250,000	125,000
Passive torso belt-knee bar	110,000	55,000
Driver education	90,000	45,000
Highway construction maintenance practice	20,000	10,000
Regulatory and warning signs	34,000	17,000
Guardrail improvements	34,000	17,000
Skid resistance	42,000	21,000
Bridge rails and parapets	46,000	23,000
Wrong-way entry avoidance	50,000	25,000
Impact absorbing roadside devices	108,000	54,000
Breakaway sign, lighting posts	116,000	58,000
Median barrier improvement	228,000	114,000
Clear roadside recovery area	284,000	142,000
Miscellaneous nonradiation		
Expanded immunization in Indonesia	100	50
Food for overseas relief	5,300	2,500
Sulfur scrubbers in power plants	500,000	1,000,000
Smoke alarms in homes	60,000	40,000
Higher pay for risky jobs	260,000	150,000
Coalmine safety	22,000,000	13,000,000
Other mine safety	34,000,000	20,000,000
Coke fume standards	4,500,000	2,500,000
Air force pilot safety	2,000,000	1,000,000
Civilian aircraft (France)	1,200,000	600,000
Radiation related activities		
Radium in drinking water	2,500,000	2,500,000
Medical X-ray equipment	3,600	3,600
OMB* guidelines	7,000,000	7,000,000
Radwaste practice—general	10,000,000	10,000,000
Radwaste practice—^{131}I	100,000,000	100,000,000
Defense high-level waste	200,000,000	200,000,000

*OMB is the Office of Management and Budget which monitors U.S. Government spending.
From B.L. Cohen, *Before It's Too Late,* Plenum Press, New York, 1983.

standards. We now have the FDA, FAA, NRC, EPA, OSHA, CPSC. In the aggregate these agencies constitute a fourth branch of government. Every day the Federal Register is filled with regulations (and standards) that affect you and me in practically every endeavor and—of equal importance—establishes inadvertently the cost to the taxpayer for each life saved and for each risk managed.

The regulatory process deals with future events and their associated uncertainties. In regulating risks, uncertainties are inevitable and can never be reduced to zero, no matter how much effort is applied to control the design or the operation, or other aspects of the practical systems. In regulating systems that are considered safe unless proven guilty (i.e., foods) it is the regulating agency that has to prove risk beyond a reasonable doubt. Regulation of systems considered guilty unless proven safe (i.e., pesticides) requires the producer to prove safety beyond a reasonable doubt. These two examples represent the extremes in uncertainty acceptance. Regardless of who has to provide the risk assessment, the prediction of risk involves a sequence of individual models whose reliability (i.e., public confidence) depends on their completeness, their embodied cause/effect relationships, and their data base. The combined uncertainties resulting from such risk assessments can be very large and usually overwhelm a quantitative risk prediction. It is for this reason that B.L. Cohen and others propose comparative risk analyses as the only practical alternative for public understanding.

Nuclear power is a typical victim of the media-instigated public perception of risk without the benefit of comparative risk analysis. The Atomic Energy Act of 1954 provides the statutory framework for the safety requirements now existing for today's commercial nuclear power plants. Plant licensing standards and the NRC regulatory decisions on safety improvements have as an underpinning the statutory requirement "to find that the operation of a commercial nuclear plant will present no undue risk to public health and safety." Questions arise from these statutory mandates as to what constitutes an undue risk—for example, where on the scale of potential risks should a member of the public have no special concern about residing in the proximity to an operating nuclear power plant? What constitutes an adequate level of protection to the public health and safety? How much of society's resources should be allocated or redirected toward plant safety improvements? How much backfitting of an existing plant need be accomplished to further the cause of the statutory mandate?

Presently, the law provides little guidance toward answering these questions. Fundamentally, this issue developed, because our founding fathers could not foresee the problems of safety, and so concentrated on justice. But, safety, like justice, is in the eyes of the beholder. Safety, like the idea of justice, can become a tool of the political demagogue. In many respects, this constitutional void has given rise to our litigative society, to adversarial relations where cooperation is called for, and to the interminable liability cases under the tort

31

laws. Clearly, a major legislative initiative in this important arena of science and society is called for; in fact it is long overdue.

Government officials are elected by a constituency and must be responsive to the public concern of their constituency. So, if the public is much more concerned about the dangers of radiation than about highways or medical hazards, the government will spend much more to protect them from the former than from the latter. In a democracy like ours, the public calls the shots. The problem is in the public's perception of where it needs protection, in its failure to understand and quantify risk and to put various risks in proper perspective.

FUTURES APPLICATIONS
OF CRISIS MANAGEMENT THEORY

by

Scott J. Schroeder

The transition from an industrial to an information age has thrust upon the global community a period of rapid change. Changes are occurring in many areas of both the external and internal environments of man. For example, in the external environment we see changes in the biosphere, in our economies, and in our technology base, to name a few. Internally, we are experiencing shifts in our value systems, in our personal identities, and in the confidence with which we face the future. The tension of transition and its accompanying responsibility has pushed man toward the propensity for creating or experiencing crisis, due both to the lack of decision time allotted by the changing environment and to its resulting frustration in the face of required action. Many of our more recent examples of this type of crisis have been in the form of terrorism: the Iranian hostage crisis, the TWA hijacking, and the airport attacks in Italy. The global community, though, is also faced with crises which some may prefer to call issues, such as world food shortages, East-West relations, and environmental degradation. Thus, crisis has become commonplace, and dealing with crisis has become an integral component of futures studies and the creation of the future. In general, however, we are poorly equipped for managing crisis on a personal or global level. Corporate America, on the other hand, has become familiar with crisis management and has developed sound methodologies for handling urgent problem situations. By examining these theories of crisis management in business, their application to futures planning and problem resolution can be understood. Initially, though, we must determine the meaning and characteristics of the term "crisis."

"Crisis" is a word which is often misused and overused in our society. People who are comfortable with a certain routine and are averse to change may designate any deviation from an established pattern a crisis. It is no wonder, then, with our rapidly changing

Scott J. Schroeder is Dean of Business Operations and Dean of General Education, DeVry Institute of Technology, Phoenix, Arizona.

environments, that many claim we are living in an era of crisis (we may be, but for a different reason, which will be explored later). This all-encompassing definition both distorts our perception and mis-represents the severity of the true crises we now face.

Generally, "a crisis is a critical situation, a turning point . . . characterized by a sense of urgency" (Horne). In a business sense, however, there are five specific characteristics which would lead a situation to be labeled a crisis. There must be the risk that the situation will 1) intensify, 2) lead to close scrutiny of the organization by the media or the government, 3) interfere with customary opera-tions, 4) damage the image of the organization or its C.E.O., and 5) harm the company's bottom line in any way. While the middle three apply specifically to business, the first and fifth requirements are applicable on a broad-based, futures planning level. That is, we must ask ourselves first if the problem will grow if it is left alone. For example, will our environmental situation worsen if current levels of pollution and misuse continue? In addition, we must determine whether the problem will detrimentally affect our global bottom line, meaning our quality of life rather than basic economic condition.

In light of these characteristics, it is important to develop a reliable methodology for determining their existence. Allan Cohen of Babson College has formulated several steps which aid in identifying actual crisis situations. First, one should use several sources of data. Gathering information from different sources provides both a check for overall veracity and the potential for gaining specialized knowl-edge from insiders on specific aspects of the potential crisis. Second, look at the track records of the people claiming that a crisis exists. As mentioned previously, every organization includes people who view any deviation from routine as a crisis. In addition, others are eternal pessimists who will foresee the organization's downfall in any event. The information provided by these individuals must there-fore be taken in the context with that of other sources. Third, one should monitor his own tendency to over- or underdramatize. Both of these tendencies can prove harmful and thus should be accounted for in making final judgments. Fourth, more time should initially be devoted to defining the problem than to devising its solutions. Especially in business, there is an action orientation which results in the desire to put out fires as soon as possible; smoke signals, however, can be misleading. Therefore, care is required to ensure problem, not just symptom, identification. Finally, Cohen warns that even the perception of a crisis, if widespread, can be a crisis itself. A wave of emotion can spread quickly, and "a group that is convinced that collapse is imminent tends to act in ways that increase the chance of collapse" (Cohen, p.37). By following these guidelines, one should be better able to identify and test the existence of crisis characteristics.

Even if it is determined that a current problem is not a crisis, it may still be an important issue, and often the issues of today, if unresolved will become the crises of tomorrow. As a result, crisis management and issues management are closely related. In fact, important issues may best be thought of as pre-crisis situations. In this light, business and society, spurred on by the potential for lower costs, both emotional and financial, could reduce procrastination and prevent, rather than resolve, many crises. For example, in his book *One Hundred Pages for the Future,* Aurelio Peccei describes ten major global crises of our time, most of which were just beginning to surface as issues twenty or thirty years ago. As a result of their neglect, these issues (such as the demographic explosion and the world debt structure) have grown into crises of tremendous proportion which now will require massive, if not divine, efforts in order to be resolved. Thus, important issues, if ignored or mismanaged, can evolve into more costly crisis situations.

The importance of handling issues as they arise is underscored by the fact that only fifty percent of corporations have a plan for managing a crisis. Furthermore, even among those companies with a plan, crises are frequently dealt with improperly or in a superficial manner. By identifying the pattern of typical crisis mismanagement, a basis can be formed for constructing an effective response method. As should be clear by the first step toward mismanagement involves failing to recognize and act upon warning signals until a crisis actually exists. For example, according to *The New York Times'* investigation of the chemical disaster in Bhopal which killed over two thousand people, Union Carbide managers knew about mechanical problems in the plant several months before the accident and about faulty safety devices for several weeks. The second step toward crisis mismanagement is to employ, due to mounting pressures, the most immediate solution. The problem's significance and its potential impact on the company or society, on the other hand, call for the most reasonably effective solution. The third step in mismanagement is the inability or unwillingness to communicate with the public. One of Dow Chemical's directors, Donald R. Stephanson, states that "if you aren't geared up and ready to inform the public, you will be judged guilty until proven innocent" (Symonds, p. 75). A company's communication need not be definitive, especially at the early stages of a crisis, but it must demonstrate the desire to provide appropriate information. Finally, poor managers never rise above the emotional aspect of the crisis. That is, faced with a shocking experience, the manager, primarily due to inadequate preparation, is unable to implement steps to resolve the crisis situation.

Thus, the steps toward mismanagement provide a foundation for the design of an effective crisis management method. Implied in this discussion is the requirement of planning for crisis. One approach, employed by President Reagan when he took office, is to establish a crisis management team, comprised of leaders within the organization. President Reagan's team, for example, included the Vice President, Secretary of State, Secretary of Defense, National Security Advisor, and Director of the C.I.A. Under normal operating conditions, the team identifies various potential crises, designs a detailed game plan (including the all-important communications network), and assigns response accountabilities. As a result, when a crisis occurs, the team is able to respond immediately and work through the shock factor toward problem resolution.

In addition, although this point is often debated, it is important that the top executive of the organization, either in business or in government, be involved. There should be no delegation of the primary role in a crisis because the top executive will be watched no matter who is doing the acting, and if he is not involved it will only bring him under greater suspicion and scrutiny, thereby only adding to the fire. If nothing else, the top executive should be the primary spokesperson, delivering prepared statements about the crisis.

The third guideline to proper crisis management is that the organization involved should take the initiative in handling the situation. That is, it should reach out first to those affected, the media, and the general public. For instance, in the Bhopal disaster, Union Carbide Chairman Warren Anderson flew to India to express concern for victims of the accident. In addition, announcements by the company that it was establishing a disaster aid fund and that it would not reopen the plant without Indian approval helped to diffuse the public's anger over the situation. Johnson & Johnson's response to the first Tylenol poisonings provides another example of initiative. Company officials immediately notified the public and the medical profession, started a massive recall, and reintroduced the product within six weeks in a triple-sealed safety package. Both of these examples emphasize that approaching crisis situations in what John Naisbitt would call a "high touch" manner can ease tensions and even improve the organization's image among the public. A "high touch" response to crisis is perhaps the most crucial element of crisis management aside from planning.

The next aspect of successful crisis management is communication. As mentioned, organizations should communicate with the media and the public as soon as possible during a crisis, if only to express awareness and concern. It is important to remember that the media will get its information somewhere, if not from the organization, then possibly from some less reliable source. As a result, saying nothing can hinder crisis efforts and make the organization appear as though it has something to hide. Equally essential, however, is that the organization avoid speculation about the crisis and that it defer definitive explanations until all the facts are known. Within the organization, employees must be informed of the crisis and given some reassurance if possible. If employees panic, due to rumors or lack of consultation, resolving the crisis will be only more difficult. Therefore, part of the planning process must include the establishment of a communications network listing all parties, both internal and external to the organization, which must be contacted in case of an emergency. Also, crisis communication should focus on the shared objectives between the organization and those affected by the situation. In this way, a bond can be formed which will elicit support for organizational efforts, as opposed to the divisive results of a confrontational approach. Because court action connotes an adversarial situation it should be avoided if at all possible. Although this may result in additional immediate costs, as it did with Union Carbide's provision of a disaster relief fund, focusing on shared objectives and attempting to avoid legal battles can provide a long-term boost to the company's image. Finally, the organization should keep communication lines open during non-crisis periods, informing the public of significant issues concerning its operations. This is especially important for organizations involved with futures planning. For example, at the beginning of 1985, the U.S.A. for Africa organization attempted to focus on and provide support for the famine situation in parts of Africa. The program received tremendous immediate response, which gave some temporary relief but by no means solved the problem. If the organization does not keep the public informed about issues related to its activities, then the problem will appear to have been resolved, and the issue will soon be forgotten.

The final guideline for crisis management is that action is required. This may seem self evident, but it is a principle violated by many companies. Some avoid action thinking that the problem will disappear if left alone, while others get caught in the paralysis of analysis, and still others believe that crisis management requires just a public relations effort. True crises, however, require resolution, not coverup or "massaging," and they must involve the line managers of the business. Although initiative and communication are needed, only action will provide successful results.

Given the framework for proper crisis management, an understanding of the basic characteristics of an effective crisis manager is important. To a large extent, these characteristics are required of all managers in our turbulent and uncertain times. First of all, the crisis manager must be forward thinking and have a broad view of the situation. That is, long-term results must receive primary consideration, and the manager must understand and have an open mind toward the different sides of the issue or problem at hand. Second, the crisis manager must be flexible and willing to depart from established rules if needed. A bureaucratic leader who desires regimentation and lives by the book may crumble when forced to deal with an unexpected crisis for which there are no rules or regulations. Consequently, another important characteristic is the ability to keep cool under pressure. Crises are most often emotional, pressure-filled situations which require a calm, soft-spoken leader to rise above them and provide a resolution. Lastly, the crisis manager must be able to foster "cooperative confrontation" (Horne, p.22). Cooperation here means the ability to get individuals representing different, often opposing, sides of the issue or crisis together in order to communicate. Confrontation should not be taken in a negative sense but rather as a willingness to discuss the real problem, not just side issues or symptoms of the crisis. Otherwise, agreement may be reached on a superficial level, and the crisis manager has still moved no closer to a solution of the actual problem. We see this frequently in international political negotiations.

Thus, through the definition of "crisis" it is clear that current literature on crisis management is applicable to non-business situations. In a larger sense, we are currently living in a time of crisis due to our avoidance of significant issues as they evolved. Our current crises extend from the external destruction of our environment to the internal demise of personal identities and value systems. In addition, our ever advancing technology, unaccompanied by comparable development of mankind, leaves us even more susceptible to crises in the future.

In order to resolve the larger crises of our time, it is necessary to develop specific plans which will result in concerted and effective effort rather than disjointed complaints never followed up by meaningful action. This, first of all, requires leadership. Despite Toffler's claim in *The Third Wave* that strong leadership will be replaced by local and individual action, this will never solve our largest global problems because efforts, even if they occur, will not be focused, and it is the responsibility of our leaders, in every sector, to provide that focus and support. This does not, however, mean that as individuals we are not responsible for taking the initiative in resolving problems whenever possible. Exactly the opposite is true, since ultimately our crises will be handled at a grass roots level.

As a result, the importance of communications in international futures planning becomes clear. There must be, as in corporate crisis management, open communication lines at all levels both within and across nations. Just as a corporate crisis cannot be solved through the actions of the chief executive alone, neither can those of even greater size on a national or international level. Both of these require a team effort, which extends to all members of the organization, state, nation, and planet. In the final analysis, we must in both corporate and global crises take action, for all the communication in the world will not solve any problems itself. Thus, given the tools for constructive crisis management, it is important that we begin to do our individual best in working to create a desirable future. As Aurelio Peccei states in *One Hundred Pages for the Future,* "The main thing is to begin, and to begin well."

References

1. Cohen, Allan R. "Crisis Management: How to Turn Disasters Into Advantages." *Management Review,* August 1982: 27-28 and 37-40.

2. Fink, Steven. "Coping With Crisis." *Nation's Business,* August 1984: 52R-53R.

3. Horne, Grant N. "Mediating Conflict in a Crisis." *Public Relations Journal,* January 1983: 22-23.

4. Kuechle, David. "Crisis Management an Executive Quagmire." *Business Quarterly,* Spring 1985: 53-70.

5. Levy, Robert. "Crisis Public Relations." *Dun's Business Month,* August 1983: 50-53.

6. Littlejohn, Robert F. *Crisis Management—A Team Approach*. New York: AMA Membership Publications, 1983.

7. Peccei, Aurelio. *One Hundred Pages for the Future*. New York: Pergamon Press, Inc., 1981: p. 165.

8. Robinson, Alice M. "Expect the Unexpected." *Security Management*, June 1985: 49-51.

9. Smart, Lucien E. "ABC's of Crisis Communications Planning." *Public Utilities Fortnightly*, August 22, 1985: 4 and 8.

10. Symonds, William C. "How Companies are Learning to Prepare for the Worst." *Business Week*, December 23, 1985: 74-76.

11. Vickery, Hugh B. "It's the Press. There's a Crisis. What Now?" *Association Management*, March 1983: 46-51.

FUTURE ORIENTATIONS OF DECISION MAKERS
AND
THE REALITY OF STRATEGIC THINKING

by

T.K. Das

It is widely acknowledged that there will be an increasing need in the future for decision making under adverse conditions of crises and conflicts. At a minimum, this calls for special skills in anticipating the nature of these situations before they come to pass. Strategic thinking enables us to get a head start in that regard. However, not all individuals may have that special attribute of looking into the distant future.

For instance, we need to question whether there are sufficient grounds to presume that all experienced decision makers are equally superior in strategic thinking by virtue of their professional seniority. Could it be that some of them, irrespective of their seniority, can "see" more into the future than others? Are there limitations on strategic thinking on account of an individual's future orientation? What are the implications of individual future orientations for the practice of decision making in organizations?

Insights into such questions are critical for understanding and improving the decision-making processes for managing crises and resolving conflicts. However, knowledge about these issues would be forthcoming only when we recognize the central role of decision makers acting as individuals. Such an individual-centered conception of decision processes would serve to partially offset the current pre-occupation with the rational-analytic mode, and help in better appreciating the real-world situation. The subjective attributes of the decision makers, while difficult to capture in quantitative terms, are nevertheless critical in determining the nature and content of any decision-making process.

This fundamental assumption of the center-stage role of individual decision makers makes it possible for us to investigate the subjective "grasp" that individuals have about the future time dimension. Future orientation is critical because it is related to the ability to engage in strategic thinking.

T.K. Das is assistant professor of Strategic Management, College of Business Administration at Texas Tech University, Lubbock, Texas.

One critical implication relates to the expectation about focusing on the future (the next fifteen years). The assumption is that all decision makers have in some sense an adequate "grasp" of the temporal dimension. Clearly, however, if an individual is intrinsically oriented toward the near-term future, it may not be prudent to expect any realism in decisions covering long time horizons. It is suggested here that strategic thinking in reality is often merely extrapolations of near-term insights rather than a genuinely longer-horizon exercise. This is supported by the author's research (briefly reported) with a large sample of upper-level U.S. business executives.

Successful management of crises and resolution of conflicts depend in great measure on the ability to "see" into the future in terms of what changes may occur both before and after policy interventions. The "distant future" orientations of certain individuals may well provide that extra edge in grappling with the increasingly intractable problems of a changeful world. A knowledge of the future, however tenuous, gives additional preparedness in confronting and tackling crises and conflicts. Such "tacit knowledge" of the future, to borrow Michael Polanyi's term, may not be assumed automatically for all who lay claim to expertise in strategic thinking based primarily on length of experience, elevated hierarchical positions or high responsibilities. Indeed, most individuals who are routinely involved in decisions requiring strategic thinking may well lack the requisite future orientation.

The consequences of all decisions are necessarily envisioned and evaluated against the backdrop of the flow of time. Crisis management, as any other area of management, draws upon the ability to visualize the effects of actions and interventions as the decision situation continues over time. The playing-out of myriad interacting forces impinging on a decision situation is inevitably formed by the temporal dimension. It thus seems pertinent to inquire about the nature of a decision maker's appreciation of the flow of time. Specifically, it is important to separate various decision makers by their ability to envision the unfolding of the future as it pertains to the problematical situation. Research has established that individuals differ in their visualizations of the future and their relative awareness of the near-term and distant future.

However, despite such findings, the subjective contemporary orientation of an individual has received hardly any recognition in the literature on decision-making and futures studies. It is all the more curious that the subject of futures research has relied almost exclusively on objective factors and quantitative models. In cases where human judgmental inputs have been included in such exercises, both futures research and forecasting have failed to recognize the fact that these judgments should be balanced by a particular individual's ability to "see" into the future. Indeed, when it comes to distant decision situations, a "near future" type of decision maker would not be contributing anything substantive in the form of judgmental assessments. This person, by the nature of his or her near-term orientation (without being conscious of the fact, of course), would be "contributing" merely mundane extrapolations based on restricted-horizon expertise. Unfortunately, these estimates are usually, albeit unwittingly, clothed as expert judgmental inputs on plainly distant future issues. The dangers of taking such "contributions" at their face value, mistaking the essentially pedestrian for the strategically substantive, are only too obvious. It is not too difficult to imagine the extent of the errors made by misplaced faith in the presumed "expertise" in cases involving such decisions.

The temporal dimension is the primary one in the four-dimensional space-time continuum that is almost universally recognized. The notion of the primacy of the time dimension has been widely supported. Apparently, however, time continues to retain its status as the "hidden dimension" of all decision making. In particular, there is hardly any recognition of the role of the psychological future orientation of individuals in the decision-making process. This is especially unfortunate when the decisions are essentially long-term in nature and involve significant issues. It is clear that future orientations of decision makers have intimate relevance to strategic thinking. The reality of strategic thinking seems to be different from the prevailing notion that its long-term character is unaffected by the individual decision maker's subjective orientation.

The findings of recent research indicate that there are significant differences between decision makers in their orientation toward the future. These differences have also been found to be associated with other dimensions relevant to decision-making, such as preferences for planning horizons and perceptions of planning backgrounds.

In a study involving 269 upper-level business executives in the United States, the author has found that those with a "distant" future time orientation tended to prefer longer planning horizons. On the other hand, executives with a "near" future orientation preferred shorter planning horizons. These findings were valid across all corporate titles of the executives, from Executive Vice Presidents to Assistant Vice Presidents. (For further details, see the author's *The Subjective Side of Strategy Making: Future Orientations and Perceptions of Executives,* Praeger, New York, 1986.) Since corporate planning objectives are constrained by the planning horizons chosen, it is very likely that executives negotiate over these objectives partly on the basis of their individual preferences for planning horizons. Hence their future orientations have a decided impact on the determination of strategic planning objectives and horizons.

Another study examined the temporal concerns of chief executive officers of 37 small and medium-size high technology companies. The researcher investigated the relationships between the temporal perspectives of the CEOs and what he termed as strategic attention. The study found several linkages between the temporal perspective of the CEOs and their strategic attention.

It is clear that one needs to recognize the differences that exist in the future orientations of individual decision makers. Furthermore, and more to the point, it is important to remember that these individual differences in future orientations are associated with other decision-related factors. This becomes particularly critical in the case of decisions which require good strategic thinking as a fundamental requisite. The current reality of strategic thinking is that this crucial subjective factor of future orientation is not taken into account. As a result, much of what passes for strategic decision making may well be no more than pedestrian extrapolations of near-term insights. That reality of strategic thinking could be changed, and obviously needs to be changed, by recognizing the future orientations of decision makers. This is no more of a tall order than one where the risk propensities, technical skills, leadership styles, interpersonal competence, general intelligence, street smarts, personal values, and other such factors are considered while assigning decision makers to appropriate responsibilities. We need, first, to recognize that not all high-level decision makers have the necessary ability for strategic thinking. Second, we need to consider ways of selecting individuals with "distant future" orientation for decision situations with long-term implications. Other decision makers, with "near future" orientations would, by the same logic, be more suitable for short-term decision situations. Indeed, the decision makers with a special knack for strategic thinking may well be unsuitable, in practical terms, for decision situations with short temporal horizons, in view of their distinct predilection for considering all matters in the longer perspective.

CRISIS MANAGEMENT TRAINING: PREPARING MANAGERS FOR MINE EMERGENCY OPERATIONS

by

Jeffery H. Kravitz and Robert G. Peluso

It is inevitable that each of our lives will be affected by crises at one time or another. On a micro scale, our individual reactions to crisis situations has direct influence upon ourselves, families, friends, and the organizations in which we participate. From a macro perspective, the decisions of world leaders during crisis affects millions of people. These decisions can have direct bearing upon individual health, freedom, and in the extreme case—survival.

Virtually no organization—irrespective of its size, nature of business, or location—is immune from a crisis situation. Emergencies can arise at any time and from many causes, but the effect is always the same—damage to people and property. Planning for emergencies must be accomplished in much the same way as an effective organization plans for its business strategies—as far in advance as possible, with the objective to minimize losses. Profit comes from restoring business back to "normal" within the shortest time-frame practicable. How quickly this occurs is directly related to the effectiveness and abilities of an organization's managers under emergency conditions.

Contemporary management theory supports the contention that managerial style should be contingent upon the interaction between people and situations. Management styles that work in relatively stable environments may be ineffective or dysfunctional in dynamic, high-stress emergency situations.

Effective crisis management requires managers to become highly competent in group dynamics and group problem-solving abilities. Emergency procedures must be reinforced and appropriate knowledge must be learned and shared among key individuals. The most effective and efficient utilization of all resources must be accomplished.

A program has been developed for the improvement of crisis management skills in the U.S. Mine Safety and Health Administration. MSHA's Managerial Emergency Responsiveness Development Pro-

Jeffery H. Kravitz is chief of Mine Emergency Operations, Mine Safety and Health Administration. Robert G. Peluso is chief of the Pittsburgh Health Technology Center, Mine Safety and Health Administration.

gram (MERD) has been beneficial for the improvement and development of emergency management capabilities utilizing interview and survey feedback techniques, emergency simulations and role playing, assessment center methods with feedback, tutorials, and knowledge tests. Although this program was designed specifically for MSHA managers, the same concept can be applied within any organization.

Crisis and Crisis Management Defined

Crisis is mainly characterized by three major elements: Threat, Time, and Surprise (Hermann, 1972). Threat is a potential hindrance to some state or goal desired by an organization or individual. It occurs if the decision makers recognize it and believe that it will hinder attaining goals. Decision time is short when the situation will be altered in the near future, after which no decision can be made, or the decision can be made only under less favorable circumstances. Surprise refers to lack of awareness by the decision makers that the crisis situation is likely to occur, but is not equated with the lack of a planned response to the situation. Even if plans exist, an individual can be surprised. For a crisis to exist, all three elements must be present.

Several authors (Weiner and Kahn, 1962; Miller and Iscoe, 1963) have identified a variety of characteristics associated with a crisis situation:

- A crisis is often a turning point in an unfolding sequence of events or actions;
- A crisis is a situation in which the requirement for action is high in the minds and planning of participants;
- A crisis is followed by an important outcome whose consequences and effects will shape the future of the parties to the crisis;
- A crisis is a convergence of events whose combination produces a new set of circumstances;
- A crisis is a period in which uncertainties about the assessment of the situation and alternatives for dealing with it increases;
- A crisis is a situation in which control over events and their effects decreases;
- A crisis is characterized by a sense of urgency, which often produces stress and anxiety among people;
- A crisis is a circumstance or set of circumstances in which information available to participants is usually inadequate;
- A crisis is characterized by increased time pressures for those involved;
- A crisis is marked by changes in the relations among participants; and
- Crisis increases tension among people.

Crisis management is not mismanagement. Some organizations appear to operate in a continual state of crisis treating each new situation as a surprising, potentially threatening event, calling for quick reactive measures and decisions. These types of organizations are mismanaged, and, as a result, are not capable of managing a true crisis when such a situation arises.

Effective crisis management, on the other hand, is a systematic, orderly response to crisis situations in such a manner that, by pre-arrangement, a specific segment of an organization is designated to deal with the crisis utilizing any available organizational resources, while the major part of the organization can continue functioning normally. It is a technique, and set of skills, for both avoiding emergencies, and planning for the unavoidable ones, in order to mitigate their unfortunate consequences. Effective crisis management, therefore, mandates development of a set of special skills for managing an organization under conditions of intense stress.

Stress and Crisis Management

Chief among the reported effects of stress on managers are tiredness and sheer fatigue (Horvath, 1959; Lazarus, 1963). If continued for long periods, fatigue leads to increased irritability, to paranoid reactions, to heightened suspiciousness, hostility, and increased defensiveness.

The effect of psychological stress on performance depends, to a large extent, upon the stress reaction based upon individual conditioning, and the complexity of the task to be performed. Mild stress often facilitates performance, especially if responses are uncomplicated or well learned. As stress increases, performance generally worsens; and with very intense stress, complete disintegration of performance can occur. The more complex the task, the more likely that stress will disrupt performance.

If stress is intense and if it persists, there is a tendency for more recent, and usually more complex, behavior to disappear, and simpler and more basic forms of behavior to reappear. Usually such regression involves simplification of basic perceptual and motivational processes within individuals. In the case of motivation, stress has usually been found to activate the more basic survival needs and to minimize those motives located higher up on the hierarchy of human needs.

Shifts in personality traits have also been discovered to occur during crisis conditions. Energetic, active people tend to behave even more energetically and actively under stress. Anxious people become more anxious, repressors repress more—especially if they consider it important to operate that way (Schroder, et al., 1967).

Stress has been found to also affect the way individuals relate to others. Researchers have found that people operating in leader roles who are more task-oriented than human relations-oriented will tend to become much more task-oriented under pressure, until they finally neglect human relations altogether. Also, people who are primarily human relations-oriented will, under sufficient stress, pay less attention to the task and attend more to the human relations involved (Fiedler, 1967).

Along similar lines, a fairly recent study of executive perceptions of corporate crises (Smart, 1980) has examined executive preferences for various managerial styles during normal and crisis situations. The results of this study indicate that executives favor a process management style of task performance during non-crisis periods; however, their preferences shifted toward a specific task direction during crisis periods.

The study went on to report that there was a consensus among executives that a democratic style of management was most suitable during normal conditions; however, during crises, there was a significant shift in preferences toward a more autocratic style.

There was agreement among executives that during normal times it is important to achieve a balanced management style stressing both the human needs and the production goals of the organization. However, there was a significant shift towards preferences for a more problem-solving orientation during crises.

During normal times, most executives agreed that the achievement of job satisfaction for subordinates is an important goal. During crisis, however, there is a highly significant shift away from this norm.

The study indicated that executives were willing to trade-off high employee morale for increased production during crisis: In normal times, high morale is an important organizational goal; however, during crisis, there is a significant shift towards greater emphasis on productivity.

Finally, one other stress-interaction effect can be mentioned at this point concerning delegation of decisions within organizations. When a crisis strikes an organization, there is a tendency for the highest executives and their immediate staffs to become immersed in all the details of the crisis due to the importance of the valuable resources being threatened. Since crisis decision making is typically made by face-to-face groups, middle management groups within the organization tend to become shunted out of the primary crisis decision making process, except for a role in implementing decisions at higher levels. As a crisis lasts longer, or becomes more intense, those at the top of the organizational hierarchy draw more and more decision-making responsibilities to themselves—decisions that would normally be delegated to others. Typically, this tends to shorten lines of communication to operational personnel even further and can possibly lead to alienation (Milburn, 1972).

Crisis Management During Mine Emergencies

Both the Coal Mine Safety and Health and Metal and Nonmetal suborganizations within MSHA operate district and subdistrict offices throughout the United States which report to the headquarters in Arlington, Virginia. During mine emergency operations, these managers operate within their respective jurisdictions and become MSHA's key on-site representatives. Federal law requires mine

47

operators to notify these persons whenever a significant mine accident occurs. A significant accident is considered to be:

- A fatal injury;
- A mine fire, not extinguished within 30 minutes;
- A mine explosion or ignition;
- A mine inundation;
- An entrapment of any person;
- Any accident requiring mine rescue and recovery; and
- Any physical event at a mine which causes death to persons other than persons on the mine property.

Once a district or subdistrict manager has been notified of a significant accident, he communicates this information to headquarters officials then takes whatever actions he determines necessary to help protect lives of persons involved in the accident and those who are engaged in rescue and recovery activities. Although these managers do have the legal right to supervise and direct the rescue and recovery operations, this extreme authority is seldom exercised. Normally, our managers will act as part of an ad hoc team composed of representatives from the involved mining company, state and local agencies, and the mine workers.

As part of this team, our managers act as advisors and coordinators while providing federal resources to facilitate emergency operations. Such resources may include: on-site gas analyses, ventilation consultation, mine stability analyses, site communications, seismic location of trapped miners, borehole and rescue drilling, television and borehole probes, and logistics support and personnel. To the fullest extent possible, however, the major responsibility for conducting effective rescue and recovery operations is left with the mining company.

Crisis Management Training Program

Since it is mandatory for MSHA managers to play a major role in the effective crisis management of mine emergencies, in 1980, a comprehensive program was initiated to internally assess our organization's emergency response capabilities and the adequacy of managerial training for crisis situations. This objective was accomplished utilizing a combination of in-depth interviews and survey feedback methodologies.

All MSHA district managers and many key members of the headquarters staff were individually interviewed to obtain information regarding past organizational and managerial performance during emergencies. Specifically, issues such as overall emergency performance, adequacy of existing emergency procedures, relationships with internal and external parties, adequacy of emergency training, and organizational policies were addressed.

Several significant issues precipitated from the interview data. This information was consolidated in a questionnaire format and these questionnaires were administered to three groups: district managers, subdistrict managers, and headquarters staff. An extraordinarily high response rate of 91% was obtained indicating a high degree of enthusiasm for the program under consideration.

Information from an analysis of the questionnaire results was presented to MSHA headquarters personnel. This information indicated a strong need to develop a crisis management training mechanism which would emphasize emergency problem solving, procedures and role clarification, and provide an exchange of knowledge which would be useful to managers participating in rescue and recovery activities.

Therefore, it was necessary to create a training program which would facilitate the development of crisis management skills and abilities for our managers. Specifically, this required considering training exercises that would incorporate use of group dynamics and group-problem solving techniques. It was also desired to reinforce knowledge and use of MSHA emergency procedures and to share appropriate technical knowledge and experiences among our managers.

The resulting seminar was designed so that it could be implemented within a two-day time period. The format included the following: psychometric, self-evaluation exercises assessing individual learning style, leadership style, and conflict resolution style; group problem solving exercises emphasizing emergency simulations and role playing exercises; emergency procedures exercises and reviews; a knowledge test requiring composite group responses; videotaped individual interview sessions; and several interactive informational presentations.

For this first seminar, three groups, each consisting of two district managers and ten subdistrict managers were formed for group problem-solving and interactive exercises. A competitive atmosphere was created between these groups as they were told how they would be scored on a group performance basis during four exercises: a group problem-solving emergency simulation, an emergency procedure prioritization exercise, role playing during an emergency simulation, and an extensive mine emergency knowledge and information review tests.

Our strategy in developing this program was to combine all previous exercises and presentations designed to provide skills and knowledge that would be utilized by the managers during the role-playing emergency simulations. These simulations are actually the heart of the training program, allowing a dynamic combination of techniques to be utilized consecutively. The exercise is modeled after actual past, or potential emergency situations with the objective of making the situation as authentic as possible. The development of such an exercise requires a team of experts who can provide up-to-date knowledge including: mine ventilation, gas analysis, mine rescue and recovery, drilling, and particular mining conditions and layouts. At several stages throughout the exercise development process, critiques of the technical content of the simulation exercise is encouraged. The ultimate critique of the exercise, however, occurs during a full dress rehearsal and prototype testing of the simulation utilizing members from the same organization from which participants will come. During this stage all final corrections and changes in content or procedures is incorporated into the exercise.

The role-playing training technique gives participants the opportunity to experience problems, explore solutions, and interact with other personalities which may actually exist during actual mine emergency operations. Needless to say, the success of this method is heavily dependent upon the participant's willingness to actually adopt the various roles and behave as persons simulated in the real world.

The success of the exercise is also extremely dependent upon the quality of feedback which can be given to participants when the exercise is finished. This is accomplished in several ways. The primary feedback mechanism is through the use of trained observers. The group of observers is composed of members of the simulation development committee, and those persons who have helped pre-test the simulations. Observers utilize checklists which are developed simultaneously with the simulation exercise.

Behaviors and actions are noted as the simulation progresses and are consolidated in a meeting of observers after the simulation has been completed. A critique is given to each group in intragroup feedback sessions, at which time the suggested solution to the exercise is revealed to each group. Detailed feedback is given during these sessions and difficult issues are resolved through a group discussion process. Later in that same day, groups are brought together in an intergroup feedback session where individual groups discuss their solutions with the consolidated group of participants. An additional form of feedback is accomplished at the end of the seminar through the group viewing of the edited videotape consisting of segments from each group's role playing exercise.

Program Evaluation

An evaluation of the program was accomplished utilizing a specially designed questionnaire. Managers were queried regarding the degree to which they found the program to be interesting, how helpful they thought the program was, how much they learned about managerial behavior in emergency situations, and the design and coordination of the program. Figure 1 shows the results of the questionnaire survey.

As can be seen, there was an overwhelming positive response to the program. Responses to more detailed questions revealed that the managers obviously liked the emergency simulations best out of all the seminar activities. Improvement recommendations included need for more detailed simulations and more specific feedback from experienced individuals.

As you may now realize, the managers were not the only ones to receive feedback. Feedback must flow both ways if a program is to be improved and valued.

Evaluation Questionnaire

Purpose: The purpose of this questionnaire is to obtain your honest opinion of the Mine Emergency Readiness Development Program you recently completed. In addition to five (5) prepared questions in Section 1, there are five (5) questions in Section 2, which provide an opportunity for you to express yourself more fully.

Section 1. (5 questions) (Mark only one (1) answer for each question, place an X on the bar in front of your answer.)

1. Did you find the Program interesting?	30	Almost Always	88%
	4	Somewhat	
	0	Seldom	
2. In a general way, how helpful do you think the Program was to you?	28	Very Helpful	93%
	6	Helped Some	
	0	A Waste of Time	
3. How much did you learn about management behavior in emergency situations?	20	A Great Deal	59%
	13	Some	
	1	Very Little	
4. Did the coordinators offer clear explanations of the activities?	31	Almost Always	91%
	3	Somewhat	
	0	Seldom	
5. Was there enough group discussion of the activities?	1	Too Much	91%
	31	About Right	
	2	Not Enough	

Program Improvement Modifications

It has now been four years since our initial MERD program was implemented. Four iterations of the MERD program have now successfully been completed for Coal, and three iterations for Metal and Nonmetal. The brief discussion which follows covers modifications made to improve the program and key things learned along the way to aid the development of future programs.

MSHA remains committed to the philosophy that simulation exercises should be built upon knowledge supplied during preceding presentations, thus, the first day of our seminar is devoted entirely to informational presentations.

In past seminars, the simulation exercises were the most popular activity essentially giving the managers what they wanted. The simulations in our first seminar were conducted during a two-hour period. Now, our simulations are held during a five-hour period through the morning and lunch, with feedback sessions and additional presentations conducted in the afternoon. While our first exercises only simulated surface conditions, our exercises now simulate both surface and underground conditions. Also, the total seminar length has now been expanded from two to three days, allowing us to run two complete simulations. A mine fire problem is conducted during the second day of the seminar, and a mine explosion exercise is performed during the third day. A listing of roles played during each exercise is shown in Figure 2.

Feedback sessions have also been expanded to one hour each for intragroup and intergroup discussions, and the quality of feedback has also improved since our initial seminar through the use of more detailed checklists and better observational techniques. It seems that our managers literally thrive on feedback, and no matter how much feedback time is planned into our agenda, there are always requests for more.

In conclusion, here are some key factors to be considered if you are thinking about developing a program similar to ours for your organization. First, it is extremely important to spend adequate preparation time and to utilize all available organizational resources to assure a quality product. Lack of organizational commitment, time, and resources will invariably lead to a crisis in the program you attempt to create—confusion and uncoordination efforts will result. As in all worthwhile similar endeavors, what people get out of a program is directly proportional to the quality and amount of effort that goes into the development process.

Our second bit of advice is to get everybody involved. Utilize the unique sources of expertise that exists within your organization. Experts should be used as key members of the development committee. Include the invaluable experience of such experts for informational presentations—build them into your agenda.

Thirdly, when you develop a crisis management program, it is wise to build in a flexibility that allows most or part of the program to be transmitted or utilized in other parts and levels of the organization. For example, although our program focuses upon the development of District and Subdistrict managers, simulations from these seminars have been reused and conducted for supervisors, inspectors, and members of our mine rescue teams.

Finally, it is of utmost importance to keep in touch with your managers to be aware of their continually changing training needs. Ideally, a needs analysis should be performed on a regular basis utilizing interview and survey feedback techniques. As a person grows within an organization, they need change. While a program was successful two years ago, it may be found to be repetitious or boring today. Ideally, crisis management programs should be conducted on an annual or bi-annual basis. Our program is continually challenged to supply interesting and useful information for our managers to help improve their skills and abilities—to make them better crisis managers.

References

1. Fiedler, F.E. *A Theory of Leadership Effectiveness*. (New York: McGraw-Hill Book Co., 1967), p. 147.

Figure 2:

Listing of Mine Fire Roles

Role

Surface Personnel	**Group I**	**Group II**	**Group III**

Mine Superintendent
  and Spokesman

State Representative

Representative of
  the Miners

Safety Director Telephone

Recorder

Underground Personnel
(Fresh Air Base)

Mine Foreman 1

Mine Foreman 2

Briefing Officer 1
  (Section Foreman)

Briefing Officer 2
  (Section Foreman)

State Representative

MSHA Representative

Representative of
  the Miners

Recorder

Mine Rescue Team

Captain — Team 1 & 3

Captain — Team 2 & 4

Rescue Team Controllers
Fresh Air Base Controllers
Fresh Air Base Evaluators
Surface Controllers

53

2. Hermann, C.F. "Threat, Time, and Surprise: A Simulation of International Crisis." In Charles F. Hermann (ed.) *International Crises: Insights from Behavioral Research*. (New York: Free Press, 1972) pp. 187-211.

3. Horvath, F.E. "Psychological Stress: A Review of Definitions and Experimental Research." In L.V. Bertalanffy and A. Rapoport, eds., *General Systems: Yearbook of the Society for General Systems Research,* Vol. 4, 1959.

4. Lazarus, R. "A Laboratory Approach to the Dynamics of Psychological Stress." (*Administrative Science Quarterly,* 8, September, 1963), pp. 192-213.

5. Milburn, T.W. "The Management of Crisis." In Charles F. Hermann, (ed.) *International Crises Insights from Behavioral Research*. (New York: Free Press, 1972) pp. 259-277.

6. Miller, K., and I. Iscoe "The Concept of Crisis." (*Human Organization,* Vol. 22, Fall 1963) pp. 195-201.

7. Schroder, H.M., M.J. Driver, and S. Streufert *Human Information Processing*. (New York: Holt, Rinehart and Wilson, 1967).

8. Smart, C. *A Study of Executive Perceptions of Corporate Crises*. Doctoral Dissertation, University of British Columbia, 1980.

9. Wiener, A.J., and H. Kahn *Crisis and Arms Control*. (Harmon-on-Hudson Institute, 1962).

TERRORISM:
CRISIS INTERVENTION AND
FLUCTUATION THEORY

by

Richard K. Curtis

Terrorism, defined as the use of violence primarily against civilian targets for political ends, is rapidly reaching epidemic proportions. According to a recent Rand Corporation analysis, international terrorism is increasing 12-15% a year.[1] It is more difficult to assess intranational terrorism, especially in closed societies. But whether intranational or international, terrorism is becoming a way of life the world over. In addition there is developing a loose but global infrastructure that helps sustain terrorism. This institutionalization of terrorism depends on certain governments providing logistical backing as well as sanctuary and training. This semipermanent subculture of terrorism is emerging, with overlapping personnel and common sources of financing and weapons supply.[2]

Terrorism is increasing in both frequency and intensity. Ironically the relationship between them seems to be inverse, so that the more frequent the acts the less the impact on the media, requiring greater escalation of intensity to command the world's headlines. Targets are becoming more indiscriminate and perpetrators harder to identify and punish. Recently a bomb tore through a Naples-Milan express train, killing 15 passengers and injuring 150. Various groups, including the neo-fascist Black Order, the left-wing Red Brigades, and an Islamic guerrilla faction all claimed credit for the act.[3]

Is there any effective way of coping with terrorism? We should distinguish short-range from long-range solutions. In the short term, various solutions have been tried, some more effective than others. The first solution is *submission*. When TWA Flight 847 was hijacked recently the lives of 39 American tourists were weighed against the release of some 766 Lebanese, mostly Shiites, held in Israel for previous acts of terrorism. What did the hijackers want? In addition to the release of their fellow terrorists they wanted publicity for their cause, humiliation for the United States, and a wedge to be driven

---

Richard K. Curtis is Professor of Speech Communication at Indiana University, Indianapolis.

55

between Israel and our country. To a remarkable degree they succeeded in securing all four goals.

The second short range solution is *retaliation*. When 4 Soviet officials were recently kidnapped by Lebanese extremists and one of them was killed, the KGB went into action. They kidnapped 12 Lebanese extremists and killed one of them. They then returned the body to the Shiite leader with the message: "Release our three hostages or we will shoot yours one by one." The 3 remaining Soviets were released immediately. More importantly, no further terrorist acts have been directed against the Soviets. The world had been put on notice that terrorism against the Soviet Union would not be tolerated. Retaliation would be swift and sure.[4]

The third short range solution is *deterrence*. A multi-billion dollar program is now under way to bolster the security of our country's embassies. Airport security has been tightened measurably following the recent airport bombings at Rome and Vienna. British police guarding Heathrow Airport in London now walk with machine guns at the ready. Yet the world remains remarkably vulnerable. Every public form of transportation, every public meeting place, are potential targets. A second form of deterrence has been suggested in developing an alliance of democratic nations against terrorism. Modeled after Alcoholics Anonymous, this would be a kind of Waverers Anonymous, with nations bolstering other nations in resisting demands and, if necessary, in retaliating. And what is proposed if a nation "falls off the wagon?" What do we do with Greece when it returns a hijacker to TWA Flight 847, or with Switzerland when it releases a member of the Islamic Jihad caught preparing to bomb the American embassy in Rome, or with Israel when it releases hundreds of confined terrorists to perpetrate further acts? Some would suggest that we pillory them in the press, for all the world to see.[5] Just how difficult the last solution is can readily be seen in the refusal of other nations to join us in imposing economic sanctions against Libya, despite evidence that the airport terrorists were trained there. At the time of this writing Qadaffy has served notice that his country will gladly serve as a training ground for any terrorists willing to take on his nemesis, the Israel-American alliance.

Of the various short-range solutions to terrorism, it seems that the only one that has been effective has been retaliation. Anatol Rapoport has distinguished among three value systems currently embraced in our world. The ethics of *resignation,* largely confined to Oriental countries, would appear to suggest submission as the proper course in combatting terrorism. The ethics of *activism,* heralded by the slogan "the end justifies the means," is exemplified by the Russian Revolution and the subsequent course of Communism. The ethics of activism appears to be rooted largely in the future. Communism, for example, tends to excuse its extremes in view of the ideal state toward which it is presumably struggling. The ethics of *retribution,* by contrast, appears to be rooted largely in the past, with the basic idea of setting things right, of restoring the status quo. The retaliation response of the Soviets toward terrorism appears to combine both the ethics of activism and retribution.[6] But in their retribution ethics the Soviets part company dramatically with the West. The Soviets simply kidnapped 12 suspected terrorists and started to kill them. In the West, by contrast, retribution is practiced by singling out those who are, in fact, guilty. And here, of course, is the rub. For, unless they are killed, wounded, or captured during the act, it appears to be extremely difficult to pinpoint the guilty.

Occasionally it happens that we can bring the actual perpetrators to justice, as is happening with the attempted assassination of the Pope. But it seems that the major means of combatting terrorism for the West will have to be deterrence. It is important to distinguish between active and passive deterrence and between long-range and short-range deterrence. Passive deterrence consists of tightening airport security, fortifying our embassies, and the like. Active deterrence consists of developing an alliance of nations dedicated to swift retribution through a united intelligence network as well as to identifying and isolating those nations that sponsor terrorism, and imposing group sanctions against them. All of these tend to be short-range solutions. There is a further form of deterrence, both active and long-range, that occupies the thrust of this paper.

Here we are primarily concerned with determining the underlying causes of terrorism and seeking to redress grievances, apparent or real.

Let us note at the outset the great risk under which terrorists typically work. This is clearly seen in the recent airport attacks at Rome and Vienna, in which three of the four terrorists were killed on the spot, and the fourth wounded. These were desperate men, perhaps laboring under the delusion that, like the Kamikaze pilots of World War II, their eternal reward was sufficient as martyrs in a holy cause. Why do people, presumably rational people, put themselves at such risk? It appears that their hope of redressing their grievances short of terrorism is thwarted. It is no surprise that the most fertile breeding ground for terrorists is the typical refugee camp. Displaced people with no home, no work, and no hope eventually become desperate.

Fluctuation theory is based on the work done by Ilya Prigogine, for which he was awarded the Nobel Prize in 1977. Very simply, what he did was to take fluctuation theory as derived from physics and chemistry and apply it to living systems, particularly to the origin of living systems on earth.

Perhaps the simplest illustration of fluctuation theory occurs with the so-called Benard instability. Heat a pan of liquid from below and, initially, the heat will pass through the liquid by means of *conduction,* with molecules in wild disarray. Increasing disorder continues to occur until, at a certain well defined gradient, a new method of heat transfer occurs in *convection.* Instantaneously and spontaneously eddies or whirlpools occur in a whole new pattern or new order that is more efficient in energy transfer. Because such structures appear to occur spontaneously out of dissipative disorder, Prigogine has referred to them as dissipative structures.

Without involving ourselves in the sophisticated mathematics of the non-linear equations involved, we can summarize Prigogine's findings. All living systems, including social systems, communicate with the external world through a separating surface, a "skin," corresponding to the integumentary organ of the individual. Typically, conditions prevailing outside the skin differ from those inside, including population numbers and energy per unit of volume and area. These differences comprise systemic constraints, inducing a flow of material and kinetic energy within the system. As long as the system remains open, subject to information flows within and without, fluctuations will occur. These fluctuations serve to keep the system in a basic instability from which new dissipative structures will arise.[7]

Fluctuation theory appears to provide an increasingly useful paradigm for explaining the development of human societies. It has been applied to population dynamics by R. May,[8] to spatial ordering by L. Segel and J.L. Jackson,[9] to vehicular traffic flows by Prigogine and R. Herman,[10] to the progressive urbanization of a geographical area by P. Allen, J.L. Deneubourg, and S. Pahaut,[11] and to the social system levels of the Katchin tribes of highland Burma by Deneubourg and Pahaut. In the last application the researchers were able to inject fluctuations in the "average" behavior of a particular organizational structure, thus triggering the change between two clearly identifiable forms of social organization.[12]

In addition, Ervin Laszlo borrowed the refined mathematical techniques of Prigogine and applied them to social systems in an attempt to define self-organization.[13] Others have applied fluctuation theory not only to the analyzing of social issues but to particular technologies, such as the designing of cars and buildings.[14]

In the field of sociology, fluctuation theory appears to fit the central thesis of C. Wright Mills that human society is characterized not as much by stasis as by change, and radical change at that. Since Mills, other sociologists, including Horowitz, have come to see society as characterized not by stability but by change.[15] Alfred North Whitehead recognized the place of radical change in society when he wrote, "The major advances in civilization are processes that all but wreck the societies in which they occur."[16] One has only to think of the major changes in our own country, including its birth, the abolition of slavery, the Great Depression and development of the welfare state, the Civil Rights movement, and the ending of the Vietnam war to recount major instances of the cost of radical change.

It is the contention of this paper that major advances do not have to require devastated societies, if only we heed the warning signs, in this case the terrorist acts of extremism. Let us take the example of a terrorist who did as much as anybody to foment rebellion and bring about the Civil War in our country. John Brown, an ardent abolitionist who vowed revenge when five "free-soilers" in Kansas were killed, took matters in his own hands as a divine mission. One night in May of 1856, he led four of his sons and three other men to the cabins of suspected proslavery settlers, dragged five men out and hacked them to death. Three years later, with the support of several prominent Bostonians, he gathered an armed and disciplined band of 16 white men and 5 black men and set up a paramilitary headquarters near Harpers Ferry in West Virginia. There he planned to seize a nearby armory as the first step in a program of insurrection. Launching his attack, he quickly took the armory and then rounded up some 60 leading men of the area to hold as hostages. In a day or two, however, he was forced to surrender to a small band of U.S. Marines led by Col. Robert E. Lee. Brown was tried and hanged. Though the Harpers Ferry raid failed to do what Brown had in mind in starting a general movement toward escape and freedom on the part of the slaves, he immeasurably heightened the sectional feelings that eventuated in the Civil War. Once war came, Union soldiers took the cue from Emerson and Thoreau that Brown was a hero and a saint, and immortalized him in the song, "John Brown's Body," and his soul went "marching on." Thus the terrorist became the legendary martyr in the cause of freedom.

Let us draw several lessons from this account. In the first place, one man's terrorist is another man's freedom fighter. Our present administration, for example, labels the rebels in Nicaragua "freedom fighters" regardless of their acts of terrorism that have been well documented, and the Sandinistas "terrorists" for their alleged acts of terrorism. In El Salvador, by contrast, the government's soldiers are "freedom fighters" despite well-documented acts of terrorism, while the rebels are "terrorists."

A more important lesson to be drawn from the John Brown account is the place of the terrorist as a catalyst of revolution. Before the overthrow of the Shah of Iran there were increasing acts of terrorism by extremists among a dissident populace. In turn these were suppressed by sterner measures by the Shah's security forces until, at last, revolution overthrew the Shah and a new order was imposed. Here was a dissipative structure in the form of a social mutation. We are currently witnessing a similar situation in South Africa.

The most effective means of countering terrorism, in South Africa as elsewhere, is to identify and ameliorate the source of contention that is creating the social asymmetry. Compounding the place of terrorism as a catalyst is the virtually instantaneous communication that is rapidly making ours one world. The occupation and devastation of remote Tibet by the Chinese, for example, now appears in our living rooms via "Sixty Minutes." One of the major purposes of terrorists, to call attention to some injustice, real or imagined, is increasingly realized in this electronic age.

In fluctuation theory it is significant that as a system is pushed beyond its center of equilibrium—not so much a point as a range—the fluctuations or asymmetries are both quantized and exponential. Quantized means that perturbations proceed by steps rather than by degrees. Exponential means that increasing perturbations require not simply additive amounts of energy but rather multiplicative amounts. Exponential increases in heat are required to drive conduction currents in the Benard instability past the "saddle point," as Prigogine labels it, where dissipative structures arise. Exponential increases in energy are likewise required in the marginal instabilities of society to drive perturbations to the point where corresponding new patterns emerge. It appears that two sources of energy are able to provide that threshold in the latter case. The first is the terrorist, with his acts perpetrated primarily to call attention to his cause. The second is the newsman capable of providing an instantaneous mass audience for the terrorist. These twin catalysts are capable of inducing synergistic amounts of energy sufficient to produce cataclysmic upheavals and entirely new orders.

It is noteworthy that relatively closed societies such as the Soviet Union are relatively immune to acts of terrorism. When they do occur, few learn of them, and they lose their catalytic power. Prime Minister Botha's recent declaration of certain hot spots in South Africa as being off limits to newsmen recognizes the power of the press to exacerbate the effect of terrorism.

It appears that the more open a society is the more vulnerable it is to terrorism, at least in the short run. Long accustomed to individual freedom as the centerpost of our democracy, we Americans blanch at the thought of secret dossiers and hit lists being prepared by our security forces. We treasure a society with maximum openness, convinced that the Founding Fathers' system of checks and balances as the principal means of controlling the use of power is meaningless without open lines of communication. It is only in an open society that we can heed the perturbations as they develop and make corrections before these perturbations develop into rebellion and revolution. Our social system is much more sensitive to feedback, especially negative feedback, than is a closed system. On the other hand, our system is, at least in the short run, more vulnerable to the terrorist.

Summary

There have developed three distinctive ways of coping with the terrorism that is increasingly becoming a way of life in our world: submission, retaliation, and deterrence. Submission, an extension of the resignation system of ethics, is perhaps the least effective method, in that it provides reinforcement for further terrorism. Retaliation, when indiscriminate, contradicts the basic sanctity of individual life that serves as a cornerstone of democratic society. Only when retaliation in the form of retribution for the guilty is practiced do we have an effective short range method for coping. Deterrence, whether active or passive, appears to be the most promising method. Fluctuation theory contributes to our understanding of terrorism by noting that all systems, including social systems, may be driven in their perturbations to the point where new patterns or orders— dissipative structures—appear. To drive a system to that threshold requires increased energy that is both quantized and exponential. The terrorism of extremists is ideally suited in an open society of mass media to serve as the synergetic catalyst to drive social systems out of their equilibrium range to that threshold where a new order can appear. Comparatively closed societies, though subject to acts of terrorism, tend to mute those acts whereas more open societies further exacerbate them through communication networks. Yet it remains that in open societies deterrence is more effective than in authoritarian societies because in the very act of publicizing terrorism we are moved to take corrective action before revolution occurs.

Notes

1. *The Indianapolis Star,* December 4, 1985, p. 1, quoting *The Future Course of International Terrorism,* a report by Brian M. Jenkins for the Rand Corporation.

2. *Newsweek,* January 6, 1986, p. 60, quoting the same report.

3. Ibid.

4. Herbert London, "The Effectiveness of Force to Thwart Terrorism," *The Indianapolis Star,* January 6, 1986.

5. "Unfinished Business," editorial, *The New Republic,* July 29, 1985, pp. 7-8.

6. Anatol Rapoport, *Operational Philosophy,* New York: Harper and Brothers, 1953, Chapter 9.

7. G. Nicolis and I. Prigogine, *Self-Organization in Nonequilibrium Systems. From Dissipative Structures to Order Through Fluctuations,* New York: John Wiley and Sons, 1977.

8. R. May, *Model Ecosystems,* Princeton, NJ: Princeton University Press, 1973.

9. L. Segel and J.L. Jackson, quoted in *Journal of Theoretical Biology,* Volume 37, 1972.

10. Ilya Prigogine and R. Herman, *Kinetic Theory of Vehicular Traffic,* New York: Elsevier, 1971.

11. P. Allen, et al., unpublished manuscript, to be published.

12. J.L. Deneubourg and S. Pahaut, unpublished manuscript, 1977.

13. Ervin Laszlo, *A Strategy for the Future,* New York: Braziller, 1974.

14. Will Lepkowski, "The Social Thermodynamics of Ilya Prigogine," *Chemical and Engineering News,* April 16, 1979.

15. "The New Sociology," *Time,* January 5, 1970.

16. Alfred North Whitehead, *Adventures in Ideas,* New York: Mentor Books, 1933.

Progress Toward
Mutual Global Security

DISSUASION: TOWARD AN ACTIVE
PEACE POLICY

by

Dietrich Fischer

With the goal of maintaining national security, the United States and the Soviet Union have, over the last four decades, gradually built the capacity for human extinction, without anyone deliberately wanting it and, until recently, without our being quite aware of it.

The discovery of the phenomenon of nuclear winter was more or less a coincidence (Sagan, 1983). When the U.S. spacecraft Mariner 9 circled Mars in 1971, it observed a cooling of the Martian surface caused by a dust storm in the atmosphere. This observation led scientists to calculate the temperature changes on the earth's surface that would result from the dust and smoke clouds covering the earth after a nuclear war. The cooling was found to be so severe, on all continents, that any human survivors might starve to death. (The only way to know for certain would be to try it out.)

Without this accidental discovery, a nation might have brought about human extinction, without anticipating it, in a futile attempt to save itself by destroying the nuclear forces of its opponent in a preemptive strike. Yet Colin Gray and Keith Payne (1980;25) have advocated such an "intelligent U.S. offensive strategy, wedded to homeland defenses, (which) should reduce U.S. casualties to approximately 20 million." They criticize the thought that "because the United States could lose as many as 20 million people, it should not save the 80 million or more who would otherwise be a risk" (p.27). They declare that "nuclear war is unlikely to be an essentially meaningless, terminal event. Instead it is likely to be waged to coerce the Soviet Union to give up some recent gain" (p.26).

It has now become apparent that even if a surprise counterforce strike aimed at destroying the nuclear forces of an opponent were 100 percent "successful," even if the other side were rendered in-

Dietrich Fischer, economist and faculty member at New York University, New York, New York. His most recent book is Preventing War in the Nuclear Age. This paper is reprinted with permission: Dietrich Fischer, "Dissuasion: Toward an Active Peace Policy," from Avner Cohen and Steven Lee, eds., *Nuclear Weapons and the Future of Humanity* (Totowa, NJ: Rowman & Allanheld, 1986), pp. 375-390.

capable of retaliation, the ensuing changes in the global climate would probably destroy the attacking nation as well, and all the other nations of the earth. In that sense, nuclear weapons have now been recognized as being similar in their effect to biological weapons. Biologically active killers could multiply and spread around the earth, sparing no country from their effects if they were used on a large scale. This insight made it relatively easy to conclude the 1972 treaty banning biological weapons (SIPRI 1982; 227). No nation would choose to use weapons that obviously would also kill its own population.

At least we have now become better aware of the far-reaching consequences of the use of nuclear weapons. Of course, this knowledge alone by no means guarantees that we will not use nuclear weapons to bring about human extinction. But at least we can no longer claim ignorance.

Almost everyone (except, perhaps, Gray and Payne) agrees that a nuclear war must be avoided. Opinions diverge as to how this is best to be done. Some emphasize national security as the overriding goal and advocate higher arms expenditures. Others stress the need for peace and advocate arms reductions, even if unilateral. One almost gets the impression that a choice must be made between security or peace. But there is no security without peace in the nuclear age. Both goals must be, and can be, pursued simultaneously. We will see that the crucial issue is not simply one of quantity, whether to spend *more* or *less* for defense, but of the *type* of defense that is most effective in achieving a secure peace.

A number of approaches aimed at preventing nuclear war will be examined in the following. To be effective, a clear understanding is needed of each method's promises and risks, the support it enjoys, and the opposition it faces. Some approaches can be taken independently by either side, while other approaches require mutual cooperation. Independent measures are, in a certain sense, easier to implement, because they do not depend on the uncertain outcome of complicated negotiations with an adversary. They can also buy time to give us a better chance to work out the more fundamental changes required in the international system to prevent nuclear war, and war in general. But independent strategies are usually less far-reaching, and cannot give as lasting security as measures based on mutual agreement.

Among steps requiring mutual agreement are, in the short term, various bilateral arms control and disarmament proposals. In the longer term, they must include the development of mechanisms to resolve international conflicts in other ways than through war. Even total mutual nuclear disarmament will be insufficient to guarantee against a nuclear holocaust. If nations continue to settle their differences through war, the temptation will always remain that one side or the other might build nuclear weapons again to avert defeat. The knowledge of how to make these weapons cannot be eradicated as long as civilization exists.

The dispute whether short-term or long-term measures are more important is futile. As Jonathan Schell (1984) has aptly put it, such a dispute is comparable to an argument over whether the victim of an accident bleeding slowly to death needs an ambulance or major surgery. Obviously, he needs both.

This paper will be limited to a discussion of some *independent* strategies that have been proposed for nuclear powers to protect their national security: defense, deterrence, preemption, and dissuasion. We will examine which strategies may help reduce the likelihood of nuclear war, and which of them may actually increase it.

Defense

The concept of defensive arms has attractive aspects. Such arms are useful to prevent aggression, but by themselves cannot be used to carry out aggression. If a country builds conventional antitank and antiaircraft weapons, but no tanks and bombers, a neighboring country will not feel threatened by such purely defensive weapons. As long as the neighbor has no plans to invade the country so equipped, it has nothing to fear. If a country builds bomb shelters for its civilian population, its people are somewhat protected against conventional bombing raids, but such shelters do not threaten anyone else.

There are, indeed, very good reasons to concentrate on purely defensive equipment in the area of conventional arms, and to avoid deliberately the construction of offensive arms that must be perceived as a potential threat by adversaries, regardless of any declared intentions as to their use. The best way to prove purely defensive intentions is not to acquire the objective capability for offense. A concentration on defense alone does not generate mutual fear, and therefore has much less tendency to stimulate an arms race than a buildup of offensive arms. If we possess the capacity to carry out offensive military operations, no matter what our intentions may be, potential opponents will see us as a threat to their security and will seek ways and means to eliminate that threat. This, in turn, will reduce our own security.

Can concentrating on pure defense also serve to protect a nation against a potential nuclear attack? Ronald Reagan, in his so-called "star-wars" speech of 23 March 1983, proposed that the United States develop space-based beam weapons that could destroy nuclear missiles in flight. He even offered to share such a defensive technology with the Soviet Union at some future time. He added, "I have become more and more deeply convinced that the human spirit must be capable of rising above dealing with other nations and human beings by threatening their existence. . . Would it not be better to save lives than to avenge them?"

The underlying idea is praiseworthy, but the proposal has some serious flaws. First, let us try to imagine the U.S. reaction if the Soviet Union announced it was going to develop a space-based defense against nuclear missiles (while keeping its own missiles). The U.S. would be frightened, and would have reason to be: such a technology could theoretically enable the U.S.S.R. to subject the U.S. to nuclear blackmail with no threat of retaliation. Even if the U.S.S.R. promised to make that technology available to the U.S., the U.S. would (and should) hesitate to base its security on such a promise. The U.S. would probably want to increase its nuclear arsenal so it could penetrate any Soviet defense and maintain its potential to deter a Soviet attack. And it must be assumed that the Soviet reaction to the proposed U.S. development would be exactly the same.

Second, laser or particle beams in space can be effective only against ballistic missiles that leave the atmosphere. The United States has already developed the counterweapon to such a defense: the cruise missile, which follows the ground at low altitude. It must be expected that the Soviet Union will soon possess an equally advanced cruise missile program. This renders space-based beam weapons ineffective against the latest generation of missiles.

Third, the space stations that would be used to emit laser or particle beams to destroy missiles could themselves be destroyed by hostile beams. They would be extremely vulnerable. During a crisis, each side would first want to destroy the other's space stations before their own were destroyed. Therefore, such a technology would add a new element of instability. This problem would be particularly serious, since one such space station could emit many beams and could potentially destroy several of the opponent's stations, thus giving an "advantage" to the side that would strike first.

Therefore, such plans to develop a "nonthreatening" defense against a nuclear attack, as attractive as they may sound, will not work. Indeed, no effective military defense against nuclear weapons is known today. Blast and fallout shelters can give only limited protection and that only at a great distance from a nuclear explosion; they offer no protection against a direct hit. Most importantly, they offer no protection against the nuclear winter. Antiballistic missile systems of any degree of reliability would be extremely difficult to construct, and it would be much cheaper to circumvent them with more ballistic missiles.

The main concern, however, is not that defense against a nuclear attack is not sufficiently effective. That alone would be no reason to pursue research in that area, in the hope of being able to develop an effective defensive scheme sometime in the future. More serious is the fact that any defense, even a partial one, if combined with offensive arms, makes the combination of the two more threatening than the offensive arms alone. Nuclear missiles combined with a defense against missiles are more threatening than nuclear missiles alone. No sane leader would ever want to initiate a nuclear war so long as he knows that his country is vulnerble to retaliation. But if there is some protection against retaliation,the first use of nuclear weapons might become conceivable to certain people under certain circumstances. Even if the "defense" were not effective in reality, if some people believed it effective, this might lead them to take irrational steps.

Nuclear weapons not combined with any defense will serve only the function of deterring others from using them—through the threat of retaliation. But if a nation that possesses nuclear arms begins to build up a massive civil defense program, whether in the form of shelters, evacuation plans, or beam weapons in space, an adversary has reason to wonder whether that nation is preparing itself to launch a first strike. This is the reason why many oppose civil defense against nuclear weapons. Not only do such plans deceive the public by giving it the false impression that protection against nuclear war is possible, but they may make nuclear war more likely by giving the impression that the nation is preparing itself to launch a nuclear attack. (The situation is different, of course, if a country that does not possess nuclear weapons and has no plans to acquire any builds civil defense shelters. Such measures may turn out to be useless in case of major nuclear war; but at least they are harmless, since they cannot possibly be misperceived as preparations to initiate a nuclear war.)

Since defense is not feasible as protection against a nuclear attack, alternative methods have been devised. Three of them can be briefly characterized as follows:

- Deterrence: the threat to retaliate in kind against a nation launching a nuclear attack.
- Preemption: destruction of an opponent's nuclear weapons before he can use them against us.
- Dissuasion: convincing a potential opponent, without evoking fear, that peaceful relations are more attractive to both sides than war.

These three methods will be examined in the next three sections.

Deterrence

The basic idea behind deterrence is that even though we cannot physically prevent an opponent from attacking us with nuclear weapons, we may be able to keep his finger from the button by the realization that we could retaliate if he were to attack us first.

Bernard Brodie is considered the founder of this concept, although he did not use the word "deterrence." He recognized that the invention of nuclear arms had fundamentally altered the nature of war. In 1946 he wrote, "Thus far the chief purpose of our military establishment has been to win wars. From now on its chief purpose must be to avert them" (quoted in Schell:52). Robert Oppenheimer failed to anticipate that. "Rightly observing that nuclear weapons could not be defended against (he) called them inherently 'aggressive' weapons and predicted that they would inevitably be used in lightening-swift aggressive war" (Schell:64). Brodie replied that when a potential aggressor realized his opponent possessed the same weapons and was ready to retaliate, this would stop the aggressor. This insight

69

has become the foundation of much of current nuclear strategy. Brodie stressed that this was not an end in itself, but only a temporary measure to gain more time to work out a radical restructuring of the present world system toward world government. Albert Einstein believed that world government was the only method to save the world from nuclear destruction.

An idea that may appear closely related to the concept of deterrence is that we must intimidate an opponent and instill fear in him so that he will not dare to attack us. Richard Pipes (1982) correctly observed that Soviet leaders are far more frightened by U.S. discussions of a counterforce strategy (aimed at destroying Soviet nuclear missiles) than they are by a countervalue strategy (aimed at destroying Soviet cities in retaliation against a nuclear attack on the United States). He seemed to imply from this observation that therefore a counterforce strategy was a more effective deterrent than a countervalue strategy because the Soviet leadership was more afraid of it. A similar argument maintains that we should deliberately leave a potential opponent in the dark about our intentions, to make him constantly worry what we might or might not do. During his 1980 presidential campaign, Ronald Reagan refused to rule out the possibility of a preemptive nuclear strike by the United States, arguing that the U.S. should never guarantee to an enemy what it won't do. He said, "Don't you open up the possibility of being hit by a surprise nuclear attack far more if you assure the rest of the world that under no circumstances would you ever be the first to fire those bombs?" (Scheer 1982:240-41). We will come back to these concepts, but first we will examine the essence of deterrence somewhat more closely.

Basically, deterrence means to avert a hostile threat by posing a counterthreat *in response*. There are logically four possible ways of responding to threats, not all of which meet the criterion of deterrence:

1. We can threaten an opponent if he threatens us, and not threaten him if he does not. This is the only posture that should properly be called "deterrence."
2. We can threaten an opponent regardless of whether or not he threatens us. This is a sort of extreme "hardline" posture.
3. We can refuse to threaten an opponent under any circumstances. This is a sort of "pacifist" posture.
4. We can threaten an opponent when he does not threaten us (when he appears weak) and not threaten him when he threatens us (being cautious and retreating when he appears dangerous). This posture is the logical opposite of deterrence and may be called "appeasement." Instead of deterring aggression, it invites aggression.

Equating deterrence with threatening an opponent is too ambiguous; it is necessary to specify when an opponent ought to be threatened. If we threaten him under the wrong circumstances, we

70

may inadvertently provoke aggression. The popular idea that if an opponent feels threatened he will not dare to attack is too simplistic. How important it is, for our own security, not to threaten an opponent as long as he does not threaten us, does not yet appear to be widely understood.

In a computer tournament of repeated plays of a prisoner's dilemma game, as reported by Douglas Hofstadter (1983), Robert Axelrod (1984) found that the winning strategy, which was most successful in soliciting cooperation from an opponent, was "Tit for Tat": cooperate if the other side does, and retaliate with a one-time move of noncooperation if the other side refuses to cooperate on the preceding move. In general, he observed that the strategies that did well had the following four characteristics in common: a) they never initiated noncooperation; b) they did not passively accept noncooperation, but retaliated immediately; c) they did not retaliate excessively (and thus escalate "hostility"), but immediately cooperated again after retaliating once; and d) they were simple and transparent, making it easy for the opponent to discover how he would respond. The same four principles also seem to make sense for an effective strategy of deterrence (although we cannot afford to learn from repeated mistakes, as in a computer simulation).

In the real world, we do not normally face simple dichotomies like "cooperation" or "noncooperation" on the part of an opponent. Should a nation, for example, retaliate with nuclear weapons against conventional aggression, or only against a nuclear attack? NATO's current policy is one of "extended" deterrence, implying the threat of using nuclear weapons first in case of a Soviet conventional attack on Western Europe. Bundy, Kennan, McNamara, and Smith (1982) have advocated a transition to a policy of no-first-use of nuclear weapons, after strengthening NATO's conventional defense. They emphasize that in an age of rough nuclear parity between the United States and the Soviet Union, an escalation to nuclear war would clearly be suicidal and might therefore no longer be credible.

There are some benefits and risks associated with each course of action, and which one is favored depends on how those in power assess the various costs and risks. The threat of relying on the first use of nuclear weapons, if the opponent believes it, no doubt contributes to reducing the likelihood of conventional aggression; but it increases the likelihood of a nuclear war. A policy of no-first-use without a strengthening of conventional defense would increase the likelihood of conventional war, but reduce the likelihood of a nuclear war. A policy of no-first-use, combined with a stronger conventional defense, would reduce the likelihood both of nuclear war and also of conventional war (because there is less reason to doubt that conventional defense would be used—it is more credible). On the other hand, such a posture might involve somewhat higher defense expenditures.

Those who think that a conventional war is almost as serious as a nuclear war and is quite likely unless deterred by the threat of first use of nuclear weapons will favor a policy of first use. Those who consider a nuclear war far more serious, and who expect that an opponent would retaliate with nuclear weapons against a nuclear first strike, rather than capitulating, will favor a policy of no-first-use. Those who consider war in general to be probable will favor higher conventional defense spending. (As mentioned in the previous section, it is important that these expenditures are for defensive, not offensive conventional arms.) Those who consider aggression to be very unlikely will prefer reduced defense expenditures.

It should be clear that a policy of no-first-use is a strong deterrent against an opponent's use of nuclear weapons, because he knows that as long as he does not use nuclear weapons, he will not suffer a nuclear attack, but that if he uses them, he faces the prospect of nuclear retaliation. If we threaten to use nuclear weapons first, deterrence against a nuclear attack is undermined.

Of course, more is needed than a mere pledge not to use nuclear weapons first. Nuclear forces must be restructured so their first use would never make any military sense, for either side. It has been said that even though the Soviet Union made a no-first-use pledge, it could not be trusted, and therefore the United States should not commit itself to a no-first-use policy. But there is no need to trust the other side in order to adopt no-first-use policy. It is in a country's own interest to pursue such a policy, and make it as convincing to an opponent as possible. A mere pledge adds little to one's own security. A commitment to no-first-use that is believed by the other side, because we follow it up with a removal of first-strike weapons, adds much more to effective nuclear deterrence and thus to a country's own security.

To spare the efforts required for a credible conventional defense, some pursue a policy that risks a nuclear holocaust, which might lead to human extinction. I personally find their arguments unconvincing.

The threat of the first use of nuclear weapons in case of a conventional war does not necessarily deter a conventional war. Wars can sometimes escalate rapidly from a small incident, and there is usually no agreement between the two sides concerning who made the first move. Each side tends to claim, and probably often believes, that the other side started the war. There is always *something* the other side did first. Unless we put a clear firebreak between conventional and nuclear war, a small misunderstanding could escalate to a nuclear holocaust.

If deterrence intended to prevent the other side's use of nuclear weapons is to be effective, it must be credible. An exaggerated threat may suffer in terms of credibility. The threat to launch a full-scale counterattack in response to the firing of a single missile would widen the catastrophe, instead of containing it, and might not even be believed, since it would obviously be suicidal by destroying the earth's environment. Bundy (1982) has emphasized that to deter a nuclear attack, it is not necessary to threaten retaliation on the same scale, or even an increased scale. He writes, "the losses that would be sustained in receiving an attack of 100 megatons far outweigh any 'gains' in delivering ten times as much to an enemy."* A nuclear power may not want to encourage nuclear blackmail by totally acquiescing to it; but it will certainly not want to escalate the conflict further through excessive retaliation if ever the nuclear threshold should be crossed, and instead will seek to convince the aggressor to terminate the war as rapidly as possible. A lesser retaliation is probably a more effective way to prevent an opponent from using nuclear weapons, because there will be less doubt in his mind about the resolve to carry it out, if necessary. An exaggerated threat is less believable.

In order to offer credible deterrence against a nuclear attack, it is not necessary to possess the same number of nuclear weapons as an opponent. All that is necessary is to be able to convince him that he would not be able to totally destroy our retaliatory force in a surprise attack. Solly Zuckerman (1982) has pointed out that even though the British and French nuclear forces are much smaller than those of the Soviet Union, they are sufficient to deter a nuclear attack on those countries, because even a lesser retaliation would still be a formidable punishment. This concept is called "minimum deterrence."

The recent discovery of the phenomenon of nuclear winter has shown a large-scale retaliation to be potentially suicidal, because it could destroy the life-sustaining environment. The likely result of this insight will be a gradual shift by the superpowers away from the very powerful hydrogen bombs they now possess to weapons with much lower yield, which are less likely to trigger a nuclear winter and cause self-destruction.

It is even conceivable that a new deterrence strategy based on highly accurate missiles with conventional warheads may emerge. Such retaliation against a nuclear attack would probably be aimed at such critical assets as communication centers and the bunkers hiding top government officials. This strategy of "decapitation" could be defended on the ground that it would make clear to top leaders that launching an attack would endanger themselves, not only others. But it may not be wise to carry out such a threat, because there might be no leaders left with whom to negotiate a rapid end to a war. The result, again, could be human extinction.

A saner approach to the prevention of war than such horrendous schemes of mutual threats is dissuasion, which will be discussed below. But first we have to consider an even more dangerous strategy, which has seriously been proposed.

---

*We now know that even attacks of 100 megatons, about 1 percent of the superpowers' nuclear arsenals, could result in a nuclear winter. But the principle that the threat of lesser retaliation is a more than adequate deterrent remains valid.

Preemption

A preemptive first strike seeks to destroy an opponent's nuclear forces before they can be launched.

The Harvard Nuclear Study Group (1983) discusses what it calls the "usability paradox;" to serve the role of a credible deterrent, nuclear weapons must be "usable," but they must not be so usable that they might be launched by accident or miscalculation. The group writes:

> Threats to destroy each other's populations are so suicidal in a world of mutual vulnerability that they are simply not credible for all types of deterrence (presumably including "extended" deterrence) against a conventional attack. Threats against military targets have a greater credibility that has the virtue of enhancing deterrence (p. 108).

Obviously, a U.S. nuclear attack on Soviet cities in case of Soviet aggression against NATO would lack credibility, because the Soviet Union could then retaliate against U.S. cities. Such a threat would be credible only as a desperate response to a Soviet nuclear attack on U.S. cities. This lack of credibility is indeed a problem with "extended" (or overextended) deterrence.

Would a threat to attack Soviet nuclear missile silos help the situation because it is more credible, as Richard Pipes (1982) has claimed? In fact, a threat of a preemptive counterforce strike will not deter an attack, but rather provoke one. A counterforce strike against missile silos requires a credible first-strike capacity, the ability to disarm the opponent in a surprise attack by destroying all (or almost all) his nuclear forces. It would be suicidal to launch a partial attack, which would cause certain retaliation. Since not every nuclear warhead can destroy its target with certainty, more nuclear warheads are needed for a preemptive counterforce strike than there are targets to destroy. This has led to an intense arms competition, with each side trying to possess enough warheads to pose a credible threat against the nuclear forces of the opponent. The invention of MIRVs (Multiple Independently-targetable Reentry Vehicles) has greatly increased the chance of a successful first strike, and has brought increased instability.

A common notion holds that strategic stability is enhanced by parity. If both sides have about equal nuclear strength, neither could "win" a war, and the situation is stable, because both sides are deterred from starting a war. If one side has superior forces, it could "win" a nuclear war and is therefore not deterred, which leads to instability. We will see that this notion is incorrect. (A related notion holds that what guarantees peace is military superiority—of one's own side, of course. One's own side is seen in the role of the police force, the other side as the criminal. The stronger the police, the more peaceful the world is. But when both sides believe this, a rapid arms race results.)

I will show that parity (or a "balance of forces") is neither necessary nor sufficient for stability. Let us consider a hypothetical situation in which two opponents possess only land-based nuclear missiles whose accuracy is so high that a nuclear warhead can destroy its target (a missile in its silo) with a 90 percent probability. We will look at two cases, one without parity but stability, and another case in which there is perfect parity and yet great instability.

Assume first that one side has 2000 missiles, each with a single warhead, and the other side has only 1000 missiles with a single warhead each. Although there is a great imbalance, neither side could destroy the other side's nuclear missiles in a surprise attack. The side with fewer missiles could not destroy more than half of the other side's missiles. The side that can aim 2000 warheads at 1000 missiles can target two warheads at each missile, increasing the probability of destroying a particular target to 99 percent. But the probability of destroying all 1000 missiles is very low $(.99)^{1000}$ or less than 10^{-4}. Thus neither side could preempt the other, and there is a certain measure of stability, despite the absence of parity.

With MIRVs, we can have a situation where each side can destroy the other's nuclear forces totally, provided it strikes first. Assume that each side possesses 1000 nuclear warheads on 100 missiles with ten warheads each. Each side can now aim ten warheads at each missile of the opponent. This increases the probability of destroying a given target to almost a certainty (99.999 999 99 percent). The probability of destroying all 100 of the opponent's missiles is also extremely high, 99.999 999 percent. Whoever strikes first can disarm the opponent; whoever waits takes a grave risk. Such a situation is obviously highly unstable, despite the perfect balance of forces. (Of course, these situations assume the use of very "low-yield" nuclear warheads, or the nuclear winter could destroy the aggressor, even without any retaliation.) This shows that parity does not guarantee, nor is it necessary for, stability. Far more important than to strive for "parity" is to maintain stability.

The traditional obsession with "parity," "balance of forces," "superiority," and "inferiority" has become obsolete with nuclear weapons. It is still true that numerical superiority can cause "psychological" instability—the other side's desire to "catch up"—and should be avoided for that reason. But such superiority cannot usually be translated into any military advantage, as long as the other side possesses a survivable capacity to retaliate. On the other hand, if the nuclear forces of both sides are highly destructive and at the same time vulnerable (such as MIRVs), then *neither side* may possess a survivable deterrent, despite a perfect balance. In that case, there can be instability even *with* parity.

One strategy that has been proposed to save stability even in the presence of MIRVs is "launch-on-warning." But such a strategy could bring even greater instability, given that there have been numerous false warnings of a nuclear attack in the past. Such a strategy could lead to an accidental nuclear war. During the debate following the television film "The Day After" in November 1983, Henry Kissinger and Robert McNamara agreed that a strategy of launch-on-warning was too dangerous. But while McNamara proposed that the U.S. government categorically say so, Kissinger thought it would be more prudent to leave the Soviet Union with the impression that the United States might consider a launch-on-warning, to deter the Soviets from attempting a preemptive strike. If a policy is too risky, how can it be credible? Even worse, if the Soviet leaders believed that the U.S. had adopted a launch-on-warning policy (as Kissinger would like them to believe), the Soviets might feel under pressure to adopt the same strategy, so as not to "fall behind" the U.S. This could have disastrous consequences for civilization.

Fortunately, we are not yet in such a dangerous situation, despite the introduction of MIRVs. Both the United States and the Soviet Union also possess nuclear submarines, which cannot yet be reliably detected, and so provide an invulnerable deterrent force. But strenuous efforts on both sides to develop antisubmarine warfare capability, are moving us toward a strategically highly unstable situation. It is useless to destroy a submarine after it has launched its missiles, so the only sensible application of antisubmarine warfare is preemptive.

The development of a counterforce capability has been defended with the argument that "of course, we would never strike first, but if they hit us with some nuclear missiles, we would certainly want to make sure that they cannot follow up." This kind of reasoning credits the opponents with only a low level of intelligence by assuming they would launch only a few missiles and open themselves up to a massive counterforce strike against their remaining missiles. (This is as if someone encountered a sleeping lion and instead of escaping quietly or seeking to kill him instantly were to sting him with a needle.)

A strategy of "nuclear war fighting," of seeking to "prevail" in a nuclear exchange through counterforce targeting aimed at "damage limitation" to one's own side, is a departure from mutual deterrence in an extremely dangerous direction. A strategy of nuclear deterrence is not necessarily the same as "mutual assured destruction" (MAD). Such a strategy would deter only an all-out attack, and would have no credible response against a limited nuclear attack. It has therefore been rightly criticized. There is a need to possess a credible deterrent against attacks on any scale. Retaliation on a lower scale may be aimed at military bases or military industries—but it must *not* be aimed at nuclear missiles, since that would invite a nuclear attack rather than deterring it.

How can an adversary determine whether his opponent's missiles are aimed at his military industries (e.g., oil refineries, munitions factories, etc.) or at hardened missile silos? If a country has the *capacity* to destroy missiles in their silos, the other side must assume the worst, and may thus be tempted to launch a preemptive counterforce strike during a grave crisis. To prove that it has no intention to launch a preemptive strike against nuclear missiles, it is in a country's own interest not to acquire that capability, e.g., by possessing a relatively small number of warheads that could not destroy all the opponent's nuclear forces, or by possessing weapons with relatively low accuracy. To destroy an oil refinery does not require extreme precision, as does the destruction of a hardened missile silo.

There are in fact two different types of counterforce strategies. One is purely retaliatory, but is aimed at the opponent's military assets, with the exception of his nuclear missiles. The other strategy (which requires very precise nuclear warheads in large numbers) is aimed at the opponent's nuclear forces. This strategy is not available for retaliation (after the opponent has launched his nuclear missiles) and therefore makes sense only for a disarming surprise attack. Yet this second extremely dangerous and destabilizing strategy rather than the first is what is normally understood by a "counterforce" strategy.

It should now be clear why Soviet generals are more frightened by a counterforce strategy (against missiles) than by a countervalue strategy (against cities) on the part of the United States, as Pipes (1982) has emphasized. The reason is not that they put greater value on their missiles than on their citizens, but that they know the United States would never launch a surprise attack on their cities, which would inevitably provoke retaliation. But if missiles are aimed at missiles, a surprise attack is more credible. This does not imply that a counterforce strategy is a more credible deterrent. On the contrary, it could frighten the Soviet Union into attempting a preemptive strike.

Even if the Soviet Union has adopted a counterforce strategy, as Pipes claims, the U.S. should not imitate such folly. A strategy of preemption is the logical opposite of a prudent strategy of deterrence. Instead of deterring an attack, it invites one. It signals to an opponent, "if you destroy us, you are safe, but if you leave us alone, you are at risk of being destroyed." A country that pursues a strategy of preemption with nuclear weapons endangers all of us, and possibly all future generations. If the person in command of the United States nuclear arsenal believes in the effectiveness of a preemptive counterforce threat (even without the intention of actually carrying it out), there is reason for profound concern.

Dissuasion

The key to an effective policy of dissuading aggression is the recognition that it is not sufficient to make war disastrous for a potential aggressor; it is equally important to make peace as attractive for him as possible. If the status quo appears unbearable to an adversary, his incentive to maintain peace is weakened.

War can be made less attractive in two ways, by increasing an opponent's losses in case he attacks, and by reducing any gains he might expect from his aggression. Similarly, peace can be made more attractive in two ways, by increasing an adversary's gains if he keeps peace, and by reducing any losses he may perceive to suffer. Gains and losses should be understood in a much broader sense than involving only economic and military assets, or even the loss of lives. Such intangibles as prestige or humiliation, or the adherence to religious or ideological principles, are often high on the list of values of national leaders. (Underestimation of the importance of such values can lead to unfortunate misunderstandings.) There are thus four basic approaches to dissuading aggression. Military defense and deterrence have concentrated only on the first of these four possibilities. Johan Galtung (1968, 1984) has called the last three options "nonmilitary defense."

Increasing an opponent's losses in case of aggressive actions is usually considered a purely military task. But even here diplomatic and economic sanctions can be applied. For example, when Iran took some 50 U.S. diplomats hostage after the United States had admitted the former Shah of Iran for medical treatment, the United States froze Iranian bank accounts in retaliation. But the expectation that a combination of military threats and the promise of financial rewards would change Khomeini's mind turned out to be a miscalculation. Money held little attraction for the ascetic Khomeini, who had been deeply offended by the U.S. hospitality extended to the Shah, under whose regime he had been imprisoned. Yet this should not be too surprising. Even the U.S. government is more attached to certain high principles than it is inclined to bend to threats and material rewards. It would have been inconceivable for the U.S. government to extradite the Shah under Iranian pressure. Why should the U.S. have expected Khomeini to react any differently?

A more successful use of nonmilitary sanctions, with some admirable features, was practiced by the Sandinista rebels in Nicaragua, based on their realistic assessment of the U.S. political process and public psychology. When in 1979 Somoza's troops, in cold blood, killed a U.S. journalist who had been reporting on their atrocities, this was shown on U.S. television, and weakened U.S. support for Somoza.

Reducing the gains an aggressor may hope to win can involve sabotage in occupied territory. Such measures are hardly applicable to the superpowers, who are more concerned about a potential nuclear attack than about an invasion of their territory. But such methods may be effective in dissuading aggression in other parts of the world that could spread to a superpower confrontation. For example, even if Saudi Arabia may not possess the military forces to keep out an invasion, it could threaten to blow up its oil wells and pipelines to keep them from foreign occupation. Similar tactics were used successfully by Sweden during World War II, which deterred a German invasion by threatening, among other things, to blow up its iron ore mines. Switzerland had no useful natural resources for that purpose, but it threatened to blow up its Alpine tunnels. If U.S. allies can deter aggression by such strategies, their dependence on U.S. intervention will be reduced, thereby increasing the security of the United States as well. On the other hand, threatening the first use of nuclear weapons in case of a Soviet move into the Persian Gulf region (the so-called "Carter doctrine") lacks credibility, because this would, according to Richard Barnet (1981:77), "vaporize the oil along with the civilization that depended on it."

Not only possession of physical assets, but also control of the population (perhaps as a workforce for war industries) may be an aggressor's objective. To frustrate such aims, the population can offer passive resistance. No government can function without a minimal amount of voluntary cooperation from its subjects. This applies also to an occupation regime. Such tactics were used successfully by Norway's teachers, who went on strike in 1942 to protest a planned nazification of the schools. Quisling, the Norwegian prime minister, threatened to execute some teachers, but in the end had to give up the plan, as it would only have further alienated the Norwegian population from his pro-Nazi regime (Sharp 1973:88-89).

To make peace more attractive, one can avoid subjecting an adversary to economic pressures, humiliation, or threats as long as he keeps peace. It is counterproductive to exert a "steady" economic pressure on an opponent. For example, if the United States were to "declare economic and technical war on the Soviet Union . . . as a peacetime complement to military strategy" (from "Pentagon Draws Up First Strategy for Fighting a Long Nuclear War," *New York Times,* 30 May 1982), as advocated in the 1984-88 U.S. defense guidance plan signed by Reagan's Defense Secretary Caspar Weinberger, this would reduce the Soviet Union's incentive to keep such a peace, instead of increasing it.

The imposition of heavy war reparations payments on Germany in the 1919 Versailles Peace Treaty made it easy for Hitler to campaign on the promise of abrogating that peace treaty. Lord Keynes, a member of the British delegation to Versailles, warned that such a heavy economic burden would cause social instability, but was ignored. The United States pursued a more successful peace policy after World War II, by granting economic assistance to its former enemies, Germany and Japan, as well as to other countries, in the form of the Marshall Plan.

If a country wants to keep peace, it should abstain from actions it would consider to be acts of war by the other side. For example, the "rescue mission" in Grenada was hailed as a U.S. success, freeing the island from Cubans who were allegedly building a Soviet/Cuban military base in the Western Hemisphere. But imagine the U.S. reaction if the Soviet Union had "rescued" the island of Diego Garcia in the Indian Ocean from U.S. forces who were building an American military base in the "Eastern Hemisphere." (If a superpower allows its military forces to be drawn into conflict by unpredictable political events in any small country, such as Grenada, Lebanon, or Afghanistan, this is analogous to connecting a powderkeg to dozens of fuses, any one of which could be ignited at any moment.)

To increase an adversary's gains from keeping peace, mutually beneficial trade and scientific and cultural exchanges may be set up, as well as assistance offered in case of natural disasters. There is always room for substantial mutual benefits from closer U.S.-

Soviet cooperation in such fields as medicine, energy research, exchange of new manufacturing techniques, and joint space exploration. Unlike physical resources, knowledge is not lost when given away. The drastic improvement in U.S.-Chinese relations came about through mutually beneficial contacts. China gained U.S. technology, and U.S. corporations gained access to the huge Chinese market. Numerous Americans have visited China since the resumption of relations, and thousands of Chinese have come to study in the United States. China has begun to experiment with a more market-oriented approach to economic management, and some Americans have begun to study the Chinese public health system. If the United States had sent marines and bombers into China, and scholars and symphony orchestras into Vietnam, instead of the other way round, U.S. relations with these two countries would probably be the reverse of what they are today: friendly relations with Vietnam, and rather tense relations with China.

The use or threat of force is not only immoral but counter-productive to a country's true interests. Relying mainly on threats to pursue foreign policy goals and to maintain national security invites counter-threats, creates fear and anger, and is likely to lead to mutual escalation. With nonmilitary forms of defense, there is no fear of escalation; on the contrary, we would wish for mutual escalation. If others tried to be more secure by making peace more attractive for us, we would welcome such steps. We need not wait for reciprocity, but can initiate such measures independently, in our own interest.

Cooperation with an opponent may seem to be a dangerous form of appeasement, but in fact it is the exact opposite. Appeasement means to yield to an opponent when he behaves aggressively, and in this way to encourage more aggression. If we cooperate with a potential opponent as long as he keeps peace, and make it clear that such cooperation would cease in case of war, aggression is discouraged.

In today's highly militarized world, an exclusive reliance on nonmilitary defense is not sufficient. But nonmilitary defense measures can certainly add to a country's security, without posing any threat to other countries. Any nation that neglects to supplement its military defense with such nonmilitary strategies takes an unnecessary risk to its security. A broad range of redundant measures, all aimed at making peace more attractive and war less attractive for a potential aggressor, provides a higher degree of security than concentration on "the" most effective method alone.

Conclusion

It is necessary with all efforts to pursue negotiations toward disarmament and toward the establishment of an effective legal system at the global level. But it would be risky to rely solely on negotiations to achieve greater security, given the poor record of negotiations in the past. It is also necessary to take steps that any nation can take independently, without risk, without having to wait for agreement on reciprocity from other nations. As Kenneth Boulding once said, agreement is a scarce resource, and whenever we can do without it, this is preferable.

What measures can a nation take on its own to reduce the risk of nuclear war? We have seen that *defense* against nuclear weapons is currently infeasible; even worse, it could be destabilizing and actually increase the danger of war. *Deterrence* has worked up to now, but is too risky an approach in the long run. If it were to break down, the consequences could be apocalyptic. "Extended" deterrence has lost credibility, since the first use of nuclear weapons would most likely be suicidal. A policy of no-first-use ought to be combined with a stronger conventional defense to protect against conventional aggression. A strategy of "nuclear war fighting" and "damage limitation" through *preemption* invites a preemptive nuclear attack from the other side, rather than deterring it. It should be abandoned out of self-interest.

Those advocating a preemptive strategy may be victims of a linguistic confusion. The word "strength" has two different meanings, which are not always clearly distinguished. "Strength" can mean the ability to inflict harm on others, or the ability to prevent others from harming oneself. While the second form of strength is helpful, the first form is counterproductive. What is needed is a second-strike capability, and the *absence* of any first-strike capability. A second-strike capability is offered by a *survivable* retaliatory force, widely dispersed, possibly mobile, which cannot be wiped out in a surprise attack, but which is itself insufficient for a disarming first strike. A typical first-strike arsenal consists of nuclear weapons that are extremely destructive but vulnerable (e.g., with multiple warheads), so that they would either have to be used first or be lost.

Greater security depends not on higher or lower military spending, but on a *different* security strategy. The most effective independent strategy to prevent war is *dissuasion,* a combination of a broad range of measures that not only seek to punish aggression, but also to reward peaceful cooperation. Until mutual nuclear disarmament can be achieved, such a policy will include minimum nuclear deterrence against any nuclear attack, in the form of *lesser* retaliation against military targets (not against civilians, and not against nuclear forces—since this could be misperceived as a preemptive strategy by an opponent). But such a policy will deliberately avoid any effort to achieve nuclear "superiority." Talk of "winning" a nuclear war is self-defeating. It only puts pressure on the opponent to lay to rest such dangerous illusions with a massive nuclear buildup.

The more an opponent is faced with threats, humiliating verbal attacks, and unacceptable economic pressures, the less attractive the status quo will appear to him, and the weaker will be his incentive to maintain peace. Only a formidable threat in case of war can then make war seem even less attractive. On the other hand, the greater the efforts to make peace more attractive, through economic and diplomatic approaches, the less reliance need be put on deterrence to maintain peace. (England and France, for example, maintain such close economic, political, and cultural relations that nuclear deterrence plays no role in their mutual relations, even though both could destroy each other totally.)

A comprehensive policy of dissuasion is *robust* in the sense that it will work under a wide range of different assumptions. Other national security doctrines may be based on specific assumptions, and will fail if those assumptions do not hold. For example, a search for military superiority provides security only if the other side accepts inferiority. Unilateral steps toward disarmament bring the desired result—reciprocity—only if the other side is motivated by fear alone; it fails if the other side has aggressive intentions. Dissuasion works regardless of whether the opponent is motivated by aggressive intentions, by fear, or by a desire to cooperate, and regardless of whether the opponent's offensive capabilities are strong or weak. (Hong Kong is extremely weak militarily compared to China, but by providing China with a large portion of its foreign exchange earnings, Hong Kong has made it more attractive for China not to seize it by military force.)

Dissuasion is an active, positive peace policy, not merely a reaction to threats, as deterrence is.

Conflicts will probably always be with us, but this does not mean that international conflicts need to be resolved through war. Better mechanisms exist. Some have suggested that we should learn from sports, a ritualized form of conflict, in which certain rules ensure that neither side is fatally hurt. But we can do even better. In sports, the idea still prevails that in order to win, one has to defeat the opponent. Businessmen have a different approach. Unless a business deal is beneficial to both sides, it will not be realized. In approaching international conflicts, we could learn much from business mentality.

To dissuade aggression, it is necessary to make it clear that aggression cannot succeed. But it is equally important to recognize the legitimate desire of other nations also to be secure. If we pose a threat to the security of others—or even if we only allow them to perceive us mistakenly as a threat—they will naturally seek ways and means to eliminate that threat. Threatening others can be suicidal in the nuclear age.

References

1. Axelrod, Robert. 1984. *The Evolution of Cooperation.* New York: Basic Books.

2. Barnet, Richard. 1981. *Real Security.* New York:Simon & Schuster.

3. Bundy, McGeorge. 1982. "'No First Use' Needs Careful Study." *Bulletin of the Atomic Scientists.*

4. Bundy, McGeorge, George F. Kennan, Robert S. McNamara, and Gerard Smith. 1982. "Nuclear Weapons and the Atlantic Alliance." *Foreign Affairs* 60, no.4:753-68.

5. Fischer, Dietrich. 1984. *Preventing War in the Nuclear Age.* Totowa, NJ: Rowman & Allanheld.

6. Galtung, Johan. 1968. "On the Strategy of Nonmilitary Defense: Some

Proposals and Problems." *In Peace and Justice: Unity or Dilemma?*, ed. Bartels. Catholic University of Nijmegen, Institute of Peace Research. Reprinted 1976 in Galtung, *Essays in Peace Research,* Vol. 2. Copenhagen: Christian Ejlers, 378-426. ———1984. *There Are Alternatives! Four Roads to Peace and Security.* Chester Springs, PA:Dufour.

7. Gray, Colin S., and Keith Payne. 1980. "Victory Is Possible." *Foreign Policy.* 39, pp. 14-27.

8. Harvard Nuclear Study Group. 1983. *Living With Nuclear Weapons.* New York: Bantam Books.

9. Hofstadter, Douglas R. 1983. "Computer Tournaments of the Prisoner's Dilemma Suggest How Cooperation Evolves." *Scientific American.* 248, no. 5 (May).

10. Pipes, Richard. 1982. "Why the Soviet Union Thinks It Could Fight and Win a Nuclear War." In *The Defense Policies of Nations,* ed. Douglas J. Murray and Paul R. Viotti. Baltimore: Johns Hopkins University Press.

11. Sagan, Carl. 1983. "Nuclear War and Climatic Catastrophe." *Foreign Affairs.* 62, no. 2:257-92.

12. Scheer, Robert. 1982. *With Enough Shovels: Reagan, Bush and Nuclear War.* New York: Random House.

13. Schell, Jonathan. 1984. "The Abolition." *The New Yorker,* 2 and 9 January.

14. Sharp, Gene. 1973. *The Politics of Nonviolent Action.* Boston: Porter Sargent.

15. SIPRI. 1982. *The Arms Race and Arms Control.* Stockholm International Peace Research Institute.

16. Zuckerman, Solly. 1982. *Nuclear Illusion and Reality.* New York:Viking Press.

HUMANITY'S FINAL EXAM

by

Glenn A. Olds

Exams are exacting. They measure mastery. They expose incompetence and charlatans. They invite an objectivity beyond personal preference or protection. They help to unveil the truth. They let the world know, and ourselves as well, how we really are doing.

That is why Bucky Fuller's trenchant phrase, "Mankind is now taking its final exam," is appropriate as we contemplate the future of humanity.

The questions before us are clear.

1. Do we have enough intelligence and moral will to save us from human self-destruction?
2. Can we orchestrate our deep and divisive differences to avert mounting violence and potential destruction?
3. Can we order the resources of the earth and the productivity of persons sufficiently to support our enlarging human family in growing equity and betterment?
4. Do we have the knowledge and will to cut down the gap between the haves and have-nots, the rich and poor, to dampen the fires of revolution and violence that stalks the earth?
5. Does might make right, really? Or is there some more reasonable ground for resolving conflict in the world, adjudicating justice, and ensuring human rights everywhere?
6. Has the force of law been replaced by the law of force? What is to become of the sanctity and sanction of international contract and binding agreement?
7. Do we have the capability and will to unite nations to rid the world of war, democratize international relations, promote economic and social development, ensure basic human rights and the rule of law, and harmonize the actions of nations?

These are hard questions. How are we doing on our answers? A prophetic picture comes to mind as a mood backdrop for our reply.

One of my old and good friends for many years, Ben Schmucher, served the International YMCA by meeting, at the airport and docks

---

Glenn A. Olds is president of the Alaska Pacific University and former U.S. Ambassador to the United Nations Economic and Social Council.

of New York, students coming to this country to study from abroad. A few years ago, he told me of visiting their son teaching at Miami University in Oxford, Ohio, at Christmas time. He and his wife had worked hard to find an appropriate gift for their five-year-old grandson. They finally settled on a globe, neatly fit in a cradled arm and base, to sit on the boy's desk. The boy was so delighted with the gift, Ben said, he never let the world out of his hands for the full week they were there.

Their final night, Ben was telling me, he and his son were sitting in the living room discussing the trip to Africa he was about to take, when he discovered, with the swiftly shifting geography of Africa, his son, a physics professor, didn't know where his dad was going.

Seeing the grandson's bedroom door ajar and his world cradled in his arms even in his sleep, Ben said to his son, "Get the globe, and I'll show you where we will be."

He said his son crossed the room, pushed the door full ajar, tiptoed to the bed, slipped the boy's sleeping fingers from around the globe, and got back to the doorway into the living room, when his grandson leaped bolt upright in bed, and shouted, "Hey, Dad, where you goin' with my world?"

That is the real question, isn't it? And children, with the innocence of perception of the "Emperor's New Clothes," are troubled. It used to be thought they were troubled because they thought we were confused and didn't know. But now, the anxiety deepens. What they fear is we really do know, but we are wrong!

They know this tiny earth of ours is one. They've seen it through moonshot eyes as this solitary home within a million wandering stars, our spaceship earth. They know we make it here, or a dark night swallows their hard star adventure. Yet, they see us quarreling over turf, boundaries, barriers, languages, political divisions, superpowers with fire power to destroy forever this place, our home. Why do we seem bent on going down that road?

They know might does not make right, or clubs would make men out of children and bullies would be followed freely. They understand the power of right when it stands all alone, and freely. Why then is there such confidence in might? Why so little trust in right to triumph over wrong?

They know we are our brothers' keeper. That so long as any baby cries of hunger when I have more bread than I can eat, I should give him some. Yet, they wonder why so many starve, in the midst of the world's and our plenty.

They dimly sense the president is right when he says no one can win a nuclear war; that we build military strength so we will not have to use it. Yet, they wonder, if there is enough nuclear fire power to destroy any enemy in the world, and/or, alas, even the world, why we are any safer when we multiply that power by ten or more.

They understand that the material has always been servant of the spiritual; that we do not live by bread alone; that there are some things more precious even than life, and we should be prepared to die for them. Yet, they are puzzled, we seem less committed to *live* for those values more important than bread, and willing even to sacrifice them simply and swiftly for the material.

Their little minds have already grasped some simple demographics of our world. They know there are about 100 babies born every 60 seconds in our world. Of those 100, they know 20 will not survive to the age of one; 60 will never see the inside of a formal schoolroom; 50 will never experience primary medical care; 45 will die before they are 45; and 40 will struggle to survive on less than $250 a year.

They know that our definition of poverty is much higher than the highest economic achievement of two-thirds of the world, and that the percentage of what we have been willing to share with that impoverished world is the lowest in our history, less than 1% of our gross national product, when it was 11% after World War II, during the founding of the United Nations and the Marshall Plan. They know our life expectancy is double theirs, our literacy almost complete, and health care assured to almost everyone. Small wonder they are asking, "Hey, Dad, where *are* you going with my world?"

They are beginning to understand that the health of the United Nations is a measure of the world's health. It is a thermometer of the world's fever, a measure of its blood pressure, a clue to its vital signs and general health.

To test how we are doing, then, is to ask about our blood pressure, our handling of our highs and lows, control of fever, the condition of our heart, our mental health, our flexibility and strength, our immune system—in short, our global fitness.

I shall borrow this medical metaphor, for evaluation of how we are doing with our exam. It will help us if we see how the body, the United Nations, is designed, to better understand its functioning.

It was Reinhold Niebuhr who said, "Man's hunger for liberty and justice makes government possible; his appetite for power and its perversity makes it necessary." This double dimension of the human spirit is the central theme of the United Nations. The *liberating,* nurturing *function* underpins the Economic and Social Council, the Trustee Council, most of the Commissions and Specialized Agencies, and roughly 85% of the work of the U.N. The *restraining* function, cribbing individuals and nations' appetite for power, constitutes the primary function of the Security Council. And, the task of orchestrating all this, in that noisy schoolroom we call democracy, which Churchill described as our "last best hope on earth," is the General Assembly, and its staff and that of the entire system, the Secretariat.

A little over forty years is a short time, as history goes, to measure the health of this global effort at management, conciliation, and peaceful coexistence. The pace of change, and mounting complexity, makes it even more difficult. Remember, the number of independent nations brought into its system has tripled. Seven hundred million people have emerged from colonial rule under its care. The population of earth has more than doubled in this time. Science and technology have put a man on the moon, penetrated outer and inner space, in unparalleled dimensions. Communications by satellite have linked us simultaneously in a global village.

Diagnosis

What does the final exam show?

In conditions of the heart, our compassion for the world's need, we have rarely been so well. Think of it. Over 52% of the women of the world have been liberated from the status of slaves, chattel, or just plain property. The United Nations Commission on the Status of Women, its two international conferences in Mexico, and most recently in Kenya, has led in giving a whole new lease on life for half the population of the globe. UNICEF, created a year after the United Nations' founding, has brought a new dignity to childhood, a new caring for the young that is global and compelling. Creation of UNRWA, relief for the Palestine refugees created in 1949, in the wake of the Middle East struggle of 1947-49, endures through the incredible strife of that war-torn country, and the creation of the U.N. Office for Refugees in 1951 now tends over 10 million displaced and dispossessed of the earth. Adoption of the Universal Declaration of Human Rights, championed by our own Eleanor Roosevelt and adopted without dissent in 1948, gave us a high-water mark for assessing human behavior for all time to come. The Trustee Council has virtually worked its way out of a job with only one trusteeship left, out of all the colonial areas of the world. And most, if not all, of these new nations are modeled and inspired by democratic constitutional and representative government.

Formation of the Fund for U.N. Population Activities in 1969, the U.N. Disaster Relief Organization in 1972, the World Food Council in 1974, and the current response to African famine and relief and recently in Cambodia and around the world attest to the strengthening of the arteries of compassion of the heart.

In terms of the circulatory system, essential to the internal flow of energies, the United Nations global functions of orchestration are unsurpassed. Think of the functions of the International Telecommunications Union (predating but now incorporated in the U.N.). We take for granted this daily link together with the United Postal Union that makes it possible to write and speak to anyone in the world. The International Civil Aviation Organization keeps traffic in the sky rational and moving, and even now addresses the scourge of terrorism and highjacking.

Think of the patent and copyright protection of the World Intellectual Property Organization, the orchestration of Tariff and Trade in GATT, the International Maritime Organization, the World Health Organization that has driven the major scourges of the earth from our planet, the World Bank and International Monetary Fund for harmonizing our currency, the Food and Agriculture Organization, International Development Association, and the Regional Economic Commissions for Europe, Asia and the Pacific, Latin America, Africa, and most recently Western Asia. Each links, in a special way, like spokes of a wheel, connections that make the world go round.

And what of our mental health, capacity for stress tolerance, and general fitness. "A measure of maturity," I tell my students, "is the dimension of dissonance you can contain peaceably." The dialogue of the General Assembly still goes on, with its occasional shoe pounding, walkouts, and screaming accusations. But, on balance, the world is still talking, and on occasion rises to eloquence befitting a parliament of nations. In spite of our critique and withdrawal from UNESCO, over its politization, its role in rolling back illiteracy, sharing the educational, scientific traditions of the world has been immense. Establishment of UNITAR (the United Nations Institute for Training and Research) under U.S. initiative, and more recently, has been the founding of the U.N. University, headquartered in Tokyo, yet mobilizing in dispersion the intelligence of the world to address our most intractable and enduring problems. Work of the Atomic Energy Commission furthers the peaceful exploration of this marvelous and intricate domain. The U.N. Environmental program launched in Stockholm in 1972 as the world's first effort to monitor the care and tending of our small planet, conventions and conferences on transfer of science and technology, narcotics and drugs, laws relating to the frontiers of space and the seas, and anticipation of the future and the world's program for development are all vitally and remarkably at work to humanize and organize our world.

On the *restraining function,* where we have had more visibility and less success, in the function of the Security Council, we would do well to remember the successful efforts at curbing and restraining power the U.N. has successfully forged. We have almost forgotten the resolution of 1959 on disarmament; the 1959 Antarctic treaty concept on a nuclear Free Zone; the McCloy-Zorin-U.S./USSR initiated agreement of 1961 as a basis for negotiating toward disarmament; the 1964 treaty banning nuclear weapon tests in the atmosphere; the 1966 treaty governing the use and exploration of outer space; the 1967 treaty prohibiting nuclear weapons in Latin America; the 1968 treaty on non-proliferation of nuclear weapons; the 1971 treaty banning nuclear and other weapons on the seabed and ocean floor; the 1972 convention on bacterial warfare; the 1977 convention against environmental modification techniques; and the 1980 convention on prohibition of certain conventional weapons for despoiling the environment.

The rehearsal of the constructive action of the U.N. Security Council, and the good Offices of the Secretary General to avert the prospect of escalating war, are too legion to mention. We remember the loss of one of our most sensitive statesmen and Secretary Generals, Dag Hammarskjold, on one such mission in the Congo. And there are many more, less celebrated. It should be sufficient to remind ourselves we have been spared anything resembling a World War since the U.N.'s founding. And to paraphrase Ann Landers's remarks on education, "If you think education is costly, try ignorance." I would say,

"If you think the U.N.'s peace efforts have been costly or minimal, try war."

We find it hard to remember the total annual U.N. budget is roughly about $3.00 per person in the U.S. or less than the price of a good movie as our global insurance policy. Actually, our U.S. contribution runs about 75 cents per person. When I was at the U.N. as your Ambassador in 1969-71, the cost of the whole U.N. was about one-third the budget of the New York City Fire Department, and we were putting out fires all over the world.

Prognosis

What are our prospects for passing the test? I tell my students, "If you leap from a cliff, you don't defy the law of gravity, you illustrate it." This is the *reality test* we are coming to understand. It is increasingly clear that angry rhetoric, fear, and manipulative diversions cannot hide the *reality* of our interdependent world. That is the primordial fact. What happens anywhere, happens everywhere. And, that is not merely good Einsteinian General Theory; that is how our world works. And, work it does. You can't harvest grapes from thistles. You can't plant seeds of distrust, injustice, and bellicose power, and reap trust, justice, and peace. You get what you sow!

Ignoring this causal interconnection as we do, it would be an irrational world if we weren't in trouble. How could we believe in a faithful God or a dependable Universe if we could flaunt the nature of things and get away with it. It is because we are beginning to understand that our ideas, attitudes, and actions have consequences, and that since "wars begin in the minds of men, peace must begin there also," that we are beginning to adjust to the *reality test*. We are lowering our rhetoric and recovering some candor, integrity, and plain common sense in more and more of our dealings with one another and our world.

The moral test is slowly emerging as well. We found the conscience of the world awakened and with us on Afghanistan, the Iranian hostages, the African famine effort, and will increasingly as the ethical insights of every culture unmask the raw injustice of arbitrary power. I am unable to understand much less explain our recent action on the World Court, but believe we are not ready as a people, nor is the world, to abandon the force of law for the law of force. We have paid too dear a price to crawl out of that cave, to go back without a qualm of conscience. We've thrown too much tea overboard for that.

The *rational* test is emerging in the midst of our tired defense of narrow nationalisms and parochial patriots. U Thant was right. Every citizen has a double loyalty: to his nation, his roots, his people, and to the world, its survival, and all the people. We know Franklin was right. "We hang together, or we all hang separately." It was true of the colonies, and it is now true of the nations in our shrinking world. *Justice* demands universality. "So long as any man is in chains, I am not free." We are no stronger than our weakest link. The ideologues and totalitarians of the earth are finding that when minds opened, ever so small, the reach for liberating truth, more universal principles, breaks out. This is the lifeblood of science, the natural juices of the mind, and why the world now strains against the narrower bounds that have claimed and defined our past.

The *maturity test* turns on growing recognition that even on the playground and marketplace, "You can't win 'em all." It has seemed strange to me that as Americans we should have such difficulty understanding this. In the World Series it is really *big league* when you hit one in three. Yet, in matters of international consequence we want to hold out the demand to bat a thousand. Ambassador Kirkpatrick did a study during her tenure at the U.N. to score the U.N. members on their record, especially when they voted with or for us. She was troubled to report we enjoyed support of most of the U.N. members only 1 out of 3 votes. Were we a party in power in a nation, of course, we would be unseated with that record. But in the international arena, with 159 other nations, that's not bad, and if you look at the record on the big issues, we've batted better than .333, with a few home runs, and that's big league!

Prescription

Finally, what prescription can we provide? First, we need a renewal of attitude, hope, and resolve that steeled the founding and early years of the U.N. To those of you who feel in the world's arena your small voice won't count, let me remind you, "you are the government." I learned this my second week as Ambassador. I was getting an inch-thick pile of cables and instruction daily from Washington on all the issues we were facing, and I came home one evening lamenting to Eva, "Honey, those people in Washington don't know any more than I do." To which she replied, "Why should they, in a government of the people, by the people, and for the people? Glenn, the government *is* you!"

You are important. Blossom where you are planted. Build bridges of understanding where you stand. There is no time to tell you the triumphs of personal diplomacy inside and outside of government known to me. Though we failed to get the Summit in Alaska where I thought it should be, the two solitary men meeting in Geneva soon may do more to open new dimensions and dialogue in the world than we can imagine. Have we forgotten, in the midst of all our sad memories, it was a solitary man, Richard Nixon, who opened the new China to the West, and with it, one-fifth of the population of the world?

Little things can become big in the international theater. Remember Gary Powers, a handful of Americans in Tehran, a daring intercept in the sky. Do not discount a solitary voice. It was Wayne Morse, a solitary voice in the name of international law, who raised the first protest over Vietnam in the U.S. Senate. History may yet record he may have seen more wisely than the rest.

Second, we can raise the knowledge of our economic interdependence into a demand for a new and more rational international economic and monetary system. When I raised this prospect in my first speech in Geneva in 1969 as your Ambassador, I nearly lost my job. I observed that the international monetary system was bankrupt; that it was clear that gold, sterling, and then oil were inadequate bases for a currency. Money, I observed, is a medium of exchange. It is nothing in itself. I observed further that all we had to exchange were goods and services. I proposed we convert the World Bank into an international trade exchange, and showed by computer printout through the year 2040, that a free trade, rational exchange of goods and services, on the basis of global supply and demand, with 7% profit per year permitted, would turn the world into a prosperous, exciting, and just marketplace. There is no space to tell you what that "innocence abroad" nearly cost me. But, it is still true, and about time to try.

Third, we can remind the nations of the world, and especially those with veto power, of the wisdom in exercise of Articles 47-52, which have to do with nations providing military power to the Secretary General to implement Security Council Resolutions re: threats to the Peace. Whenever it has been truly tried, it has worked. I urged our Department of Defense when I went to Kent State after the shooting and burning of the ROTC building, to establish a track in the ROTC programs on our universities across the country for training in International Peacekeeping, a role that Lebanon reveals we are ill-prepared to play but increasingly must play. The legislation for an Academy of Peace, for which my old classmate and now senior U.S. Senator Hatfield of Oregon worked, had this in mind as well. It remains to be seen what may come of this noble intent when they are finished with it, but the prescription is sound.

Fourth, we can work for a radical revision of the U.N. system, in the interest of nonduplication, simplification, and efficiency. Every bureaucracy suffers from metentelosis, the Greek word which describes the tendency to turn a *means* into an *end*. The U.N. needs a staff training college for its Secretariat, a recommendation I worked for a decade ago. The art of international management cannot be practiced by novices without instruction, and seniority often perpetuates mediocrity. Sir Robert Jackson performed such a study for the UNDP in 1970 with incisive and inclusive insight. It was called the U.N. Capacity Study. We could dust it off and press its discussion and implementation or even do better. The way to improve a game is not to take one's marbles and go home, but insist on improving the performance. The U.N. University was originally proposed as a nonpolitical instrument of self-correction and self-renewal for this purpose. Unhappily, through U.S. neglect, it has never realized its promise.

Finally, if man's extremities are often God's opportunities as I believe, what can the urgency and ultimacy of the exam before us inspire us to do:

1. We can press to have a piece of the multi-billion dollar "Star Wars research" modified to be "Star Peace research," and work on the laser beam technology to find a way to transmit energy

by laser from any source to its target, economically, accurately, and peaceably. I have argued for years that by the year 2000 we would be able to do this. This defensive interest now has been appropriated. Think of what it would mean if we could eliminate consideration and cost of energy transmission from the site of its origin to its user anywhere on earth. Tap the geothermal power of eastern, central and southern Oregon, or leapfrog the pipeline from Prudhoe Bay. Get energy from where it is to where it is needed, cheaply and safely, and it will transform the world.

2. In the face of the world's famine and hunger, find new and inventive ways to farm the sea. Oregon's Sea Grant competency at Oregon State, its seasoned experience in Alaska and canneries, suggests leadership for innovation. Why not find a way to impregnate wheat from eastern Oregon and the interior with fish meal from the residue of the canneries from the Pacific, multiplying its protein content and nutritional value and marketed like rice to the entire Pacific.

3. And last, why not convert the nervous nagging of a restless Mount St. Helens fruitlessly perking away her internal heat with periodic eruption, into a steady stream of released heat, to convert Oregon and Washington's magnificent water supply of the Columbia basin into steam, to drive non-polluting turbines to create new, cheap, and efficient energy for the region, and a prototype technology, that will tap the locked heat generated by the rubbing of the Pacific and North American plates that meet at our coastline and the Cascades into power to drive our world. We have the technology to do it now.

If this seems too far out, let me remind you that it has often been wars, in the past, that have spurred economy, technology, and innovation. That day is passed, as nuclear weapons have made war obsolete. It is now time to find global, peacetime alternatives.

Bucky was no doubt right, "We are taking our final exam."

STRENGTHENING THE UNITED NATIONS

by

Jan Tinbergen

The fortieth anniversary of the United Nations was an appropriate occasion to *look back* and attempt to *evaluate* its achievements as well as its failures. It is desirable also to *look forward*. The world is facing a great number of very serious problems for which solutions have to be found. It is inconceivable that such solutions can be found without the United Nations. It has rightly been said that if there was no such organization, it would have to be invented.

A set of proposals to enhance the efficacy of the family of United Nations institutions should be derived from a bold concept, namely that in the future this family shall develop into a system of *world government* or *world management*. In order to arrive at useful proposals we should be inspired by what at present can be observed at one level lower, that is in *well-governed nations,* if we think of government activities, or in *well-organized transnational enterprises* if we think of how to manage the planet Earth. The idea of learning from one level lower in a hierarchy has been launched by Scharpf in a study on European integration and the hierarchical structure of the Federal Republic of Germany and an analysis of what this author calls *Politikverflechtung* (policy interwovenness is perhaps an English translation). We are not going to pursue this latter phenomenon; instead our problem area includes, apart from governing or managing the planet, also whether some of the justified criticisms of member nations of the United Nations can be met.

One important criticism of this category is *the way member-nations are represented in the General Assembly:* one vote for each member, whether it be the United States or an island in the Caribbean, or Luxembourg. In well-run nations the system of representation is one vote per adult citizen, implying that, in the House of Representatives of the United States of America, California is represented by many more members than, say Rhode Island. In other words, the representation in the General Assembly must *reflect differences in population*

Jan Tinbergen is professor emeritus at the University of Leiden, The Hague, Netherlands. He shared the Nobel Prize in economics in 1969.

size. If we go back some time in the history of democratic countries, we shall also find that in an earlier phase voting rights of citizens depended on their *income* or on the taxes paid. Since the world as a whole can be considered to be in an earlier stage of development than the most developed countries, it makes sense to, at least for the time being, let a member nation's representation also depend on its *income per capita*. This happens to be the case in the two Bretton Woods institutions, the World Bank Group (World Bank, International Development Association and International Finance Corporation) and the International Monetary Fund (IMF). The low income countries' members of these institutions want to have more votes than they now have and this is in accordance with the historical development of well-organized nation states. But at the same time some influence, for a well-defined period, of income per capita of member states of the United Nations, is also in accordance with that historical development.

A second problem of efficiency in decision making is that they *be made at the optimal level*. Within a well-run nation state we observe that—often as the outcome of trial and error, or of historical development—decisions on different problems are made at *different levels within the national hierarchy* of authorities, from municipalities, to states and to the federal government, possibly with additional intermediate levels. Problems regarding local citizens only will be solved as a rule by local decisions. Problems affecting the state and no other state's citizens are decided upon by state authorities. But state activities affecting other states' population as well will be made at the federal level. In principle the optimal level of decision making should be such that *all whose welfare is affected by a decision are represented* at that level. Among the levels qualifying for this principle—if there are more—the *lowest* level should be chosen since this implies a maximum of participation (or democracy). This may not apply in cases where a particular expertise to decide is involved and such expertise is not available at the lowest level. For some of the highly technical problems that must be solved today this expertise may indeed be scarce.

Applying these principles to the United Nations means that most decisions must be left in the hands of national or lower authorities which *remain sovereign in these matters*. However, there are groups of problems which involve several nations. In such cases the decisions have to be made at *supra-national levels,* whether continental or world level. It is for those problems that the United Nations family of institutions has been created. The Bretton Woods financial institutions have been mentioned already; international loans evidently affect the welfare of at least two, often more, nations. This also applies to international trade; but the International Trade Organization negotiated in Havana was not ratified by the US. Instead the General Agreement on Tariffs and Trade (GATT) was concluded, followed later by the United Nations Conference on Trade and Development (UNCTAD). We don't intend to give a complete list, but an important new institution is the United Nations Environment Program dealing with *environmental pollution* of which it is quite clear that pollution activities in one country affect the environment in other countries. Acid rain is a relatively new but serious threat to human welfare.

By far the most important institution in this supranational area is the UN *Security Council,* established to settle international conflicts and avoiding armed conflicts.

This brings us to the third problem where a lesson may be drawn from the experience of well-organized nations. *Within such nations armed conflicts should no longer exist.*

The essence of the structure of a well-organized nation is that the various institutions which together constitute such a nation have the *competence* to decide their area of authority and the *power* to enforce their decisions. These are the two elements that United Nations institutions, and in particular the Security Council, do not have. For the UN to become effective the institutions must have competence and power. For the Security Council this means that no veto can paralyze its decisions and that a Peace Force is available—if necessary—for the enforcement of Security Council decisions.

Here we are faced with the *fundamental problem:* how can the two superpowers cooperate in maintaining world security? It is their mutual suspicion which brought into the Security Council the paralyzing veto power. Although not only the two superpowers are involved, their cooperation nevertheless is the core of the necessary structure; if a solution is found here, the solution of the other existing conflicts will be *relatively* simple.

A well-known truth is that cooperation in more difficult situations can be attained only if a *common danger* threatens the two (or more) partners. In today's world that common danger first of all is a nuclear war, or even a war. A conventional war in all probability would not remain conventional, and, moreover, has grown in destructive power more than is usually believed.

A beginning of an understanding of the mortal danger of a nuclear war has developed. The fact that a nuclear attack, in the presence of today's armament levels, (i) cannot be won and (ii) constitutes suicide is beginning to spread among American and Russian politicians. Formulated differently, there is a beginning of an understanding that security can only be *common security.* Attempts to find, by research, a "defense shield" against a rocket attack, can only avoid the danger of first-strike capability by one of the two if that research be *undertaken jointly.*

Alva Myrdal (1976) experienced one common tendency in the superpowers' attitude: they were not interested in other countries' contributions to the Geneva negotiations in the Disarmament Commission. This attitude makes the superpowers responsible—vis-a-vis the rest of the world—for security. It is doubtful, obviously, whether the ideas listed have already penetrated sufficiently into the minds of the superpowers' leadership, to make them cooperate in the way required for world security. Some additional incentives are needed. Could these be found in trade policies of the European Community and Japan? This would seem to be an interesting field for political research.

In our comparative study of the United Nations and the United States one more subject seems interesting. Does a well-organized country as the United States—or any other well-organized country— have institutions which are lacking in the United Nations, even after all existing institutions get the competence and the power they need for an optimal management of the earth? After, that is, FAO has been given the competence and power of a Ministry of Agriculture, IMF the competence and power of a World Central Bank, GATT and UNCTAD those of a Ministry of Trade, and so on, will one important institution be lacking?

I am thinking of a *World Treasury*. In every well-organized country the Treasury (or Ministry of Finance) is probably the most important Ministry. I submit that the world community cannot be managed well without a Treasury. Among the tasks of a Treasury that are important for the world community I want to discuss two.

First, a Treasury takes care of financing, mainly with the aid of taxes, the tasks the government is responsible for. Taxes are levied on the basis of principles laid down in tax legislation which warrants equal treatment of all taxable subjects. It would replace the voluntary character of today's contributions to the United Nations.

Secondly, a Treasury is able to finance a number of development projects out of current revenue (i.e. the current budget and not a capital budget). Current financing has the advantage that it does not create a debt, and that no discussion of interest on and repayment of a loan is necessary. It simplifies considerably some well-defined parts of development expenditures, presumably expenditures for infrastructure, but not necessarily only these.

After having analyzed the lessons that can be drawn from a comparison of the United Nations family of institutions with a well-run nation we may add some lessons possibly to be drawn from a comparison with a well-run (transnational) enterprise. The reader may wonder whether such a comparison makes sense. Presumably it is less natural than the comparison with a nation, but since on various occasions nations have been compared with enterprises, some sense must be given to the second comparative analysis proposed.

One feature of a well-run enterprise that may imply a check of the operation of the United Nations is the concept of *span of control*. As is well known, in a business hierarchy each level of authority plays a role in the supervision and coordination of the next-lower level; and each member of some level supervises and coordinates a limited number of members of that next-lower level. The number is called the *span of control* and is considered to be related to how efficiently it can be supervised and controlled by one person. The choice of this number also indirectly determines the number of levels between the top executive and the work floor. In that respect we distinguish between flat and steep hierarchies. Clearly this piece of philosophy deals with the executive tasks of the hierarchy and not with the information from the base to the top. It does not apply to the supervising activities of a parliament, where the number of supervisors (the members of parliament) are far more numerous than the number of ministers.

The way in which the concept of span of control may be of some use in analyzing the operation of "managing the planet" is in whether the real management of a number of world affairs can be done efficiently in such a large meeting as the General Assembly of 12 to 15 members, consisting of some of the very large countries whereas the smaller ones are united into federations of, on the average, a similar number of members. Small countries would not be deprived of influencing the management, but would participate in a two-level discussion. Inversely, the execution of an agreed upon policy would be supervised in a two-step procedure.

The concept of span of control might be illustrated with an example from environmental policy. Some environmental anti-pollution policy (of rivers and canals, for instance, or of acid rain) may be dealt with at the level of the very large countries or of the federations of the smaller countries, for instance the European Community. Other environmental problems must be dealt with at the world level, such as the pollution of the oceans or of the atmosphere.

A second example of a lesson to be learned from large enterprises may be the division of labor between the members of top management. The Chief Executive Board of the World, Ltd. (or the World, Inc. or the World Central Committee) has a limited number of members, and the responsibilities are distributed between them, mindful of their special abilities and interests. Just as a corporation executive deals with product groups and purchasing countries groups, by giving each member one product group and one country group and so supervising the matrix of this two-dimensional set of responsibilities, the World Chief Executive Board distributes over its members each of the subjects it is responsible for. Here too there will be "product groups" corresponding with the ministries mentioned, "country groups" whose interests *and* whose obligations constitute responsibilities and, in fact, more dimensions, such as personnel policy, which exist as well with the enterprises. Mathematically the word matrix only covers a two-dimensional set of responsibilities; more than two dimensions are covered by the term tensor, and we should speak of a tensor structure of the Board's set of responsibilities. This second example seems to show that the comparison with an enterprise, understandably, may be more relevant for the internal problems of the UN institutions.

WAGING PEACE
WITH GLOBALLY INTER-CONNECTED
COMPUTERS

by

Parker Rossman and Takeshi Utsumi

Powerful New Tools for Collective Intelligence

Society needs much more sophisticated tools to deal with complex global problems which so overwhelm the world's leaders that they are tempted to simplistic solutions. Benedict Nightingale (1985) writes, for example, about playwright Michael Frayn's concern for "the awesome complexity of the world, and . . . desperate attempts to reduce it to nice, neat shape." In the same issue, James Gleick (1985) reported how the mathematician, Benoit Mandelbrot, has expanded the work of scholars who "missed a whole range of things" because they "simply didn't have the tools" they needed to deal with "complexity (which) has been developing slowly in many disciplines for nearly a generation." Mandelbrot's work, he said, is a part of the revolution in understanding chaos, the study of turbulence and disorder in a whole range of phenomena.

Now, however, powerful new computer-communication and simulation tools can make it possible, as never before in history, for any intelligent citizen to have a hand in developing new alternatives to war and other complex international problems.

Even the political geniuses, and perhaps there are a few, have not been able to keep in mind all they need to know and understand to deal with the whole complexity of global interrelations. But computers, combined with other electronic technology, can now make possible mind-tools for a powerful new "collective intelligence."

Computers Plus What?

Rossman begins each chapter of his book (1985) with descriptions of tools that might be interconnected for powerful explorations through collective intelligence:

Parker Rossman is the former dean of the Ecumenical Continuing Education Center, Yale University. Takeshi Utsumi is the president of Global Information Services (GIS), Inc., Flushing, New York.

98

1) The meshing of phone and computer systems into a single mode, combined with expert systems and data banks via satellites creates a new tool with breathtaking possibilities. Computer expert systems, as intelligent assistants, can fuse the knowledge of many specialists into tools to deal with complex problems.
2) The work of one huge computer can be done by a distributed network of many interconnecting microcomputers which make up a reasoning system, stocked with all necessary knowledge. Access to information stored on optical videodisks, with a high-powered laser diode, can be obtained within seconds, e.g., over one dozen volumes of an encyclopedia can be packed into a single shiny 5¼ inch disk—even including color illustrations and moving pictures and very possibly with voice and music annotations in the future.
3) A global computer network can be a major new tool for coordinating complex information, planning and goal-setting, and for mobilizing resources. Computer modeling and simulations to explore risks and possibilities then become a powerful tool for calculating the consequences of experimental change by the people of different views and disciplines in various countries who created those cooperative simulation models.
4) Fifth generation computer tools, instead of solving problems step-by-step, can break complex projects up into thousands of units, each to be worked on simultaneously by different computers all over the world. This so-called distributed, asynchronous parallel processing resembles numerous neurons in the human brain. The fusing of expertise through networks of minds can result as thousands of interconnected computers help people work simultaneously on different aspects of the same problem or project, particularly on the utmost crisis facing humankind, i.e., preventing nuclear war and holocaust.

Peace Games

The technology now exists, for example, to interconnect hundreds or thousands of personal computers, in different countries, through distributed network and information processing, into modeling and simulation instruments for playing "peace games" on the scale of Pentagon war games.

When legislation was proposed for a U.S. Peace Academy, like West Point and Annapolis, many asked what peacemaking skills it would teach? Utsumi's proposal suggests an exciting answer beyond the training of conventional state department personnel, or even of negotiation skills like Terry Waite who sought release of American hostages in Lebanon for the Archbishop of Canterbury. All kinds of possibilities for waging peace could be explored through computer simulations to see what might work, to discover results before risks are actually taken. Developing expertise in modeling and gaming can be combined in global systems, with a cascading effect, to empower explorations of new international institutions, to remodel existing ones. New precision can come into the diagnosis of problems and the definition of issues and alternatives. It is now possible to combine existing technologies to make possible sophisticated and more holistic explorations of various scenarios in solving global social problems by the people and for the people of the entire world.

Tools?

Is it appropriate to use such words as "tool" or "instrument" for combinations of so many different kinds of technology into a more powerful "system?" As the bulldozer becomes one component in a system for empowering human hands to do physical work—to move mountains—so now existing components can be combined to empower human minds to deal with overwhelmingly complex "mental mountains?" When we speak of "peace games" (the term coined by Utsumi, 1977) some people persist in visualizing some little computer games to play on a screen, where we are talking about research and planning to manage complexity and to test alternative strategies on a global scale. As millions of people must mobilize to wage war, we are talking about the possibility of mobilizing the brains of millions of people to wage peace. The GLOSAS (Global Systems Analysis and Simulation) Project proposes gaming solutions on a very large scale to help decision makers deal with interwoven problems. It seeks to construct a "Globally Distributed Decision Support System" for a plus sum peace game. This system, with cooperative execution of autonomously managed simulation submodels at distributed locations, can provide a "meta-language" for improved communication among users of submodels. Progress in the study of distributed systems has produced a new scheduling algorithm—the Virtual Time concept—which allows for the organization and exchange of information among dispersed locations (Utsumi, 1985).

In less technical terms, we are talking about combining the power of global multimedia communication networks, global teleconferencing and computer conferencing, simulation and gaming methodologies as in war games and economic modeling, electronic data banks and indexing, expert systems, computer bulletin boards and "situation rooms." We are not talking about computers that would do our thinking for us, taking over to guide a missile, or perhaps even deciding when to shoot it. We are talking about mind-empowerment tools to help people do better thinking. Society has vast amounts of data that are not adequately brought to bear in solving many kinds of problems because the information is scattered, uncoordinated, and not available when needed. We need tools to put this data together in what Shubik (1983), in an article on "Computers and Modeling," calls pictures and wholes. He describes four kinds of models: verbal, mathematical, pictorial, and digital. All of these might be used by people who are seeking to build up more comprehensive models of alternatives to war. Pencil and paper will be as important as computers.

Importance of Modeling

Schank (1984) of the Yale Artificial Intelligence Lab points out, however, that from now on it will be essential to use computer modeling for making important decisions—models which incorporate more and more knowledge about people and institutions. Until recently, he says, it has not been possible to make large conceptual computer models of governments, of the work of politicians and other complex systems. Now, however, such models can be increasingly complex, integrated, and can be more and more useful and trustworthy for testing ideas, theories and possible actions. Computers will not make good decisions but can be used to help human beings make better ones. Licklider (1983) says that computer modeling and simulations are already beginning to play an important role in government research and planning as these expand and multiply beyond space and military projects to other national planning efforts. The Soviet Union, he reports, is planning to create a 3000-computer nationwide network with data bases for planning. The Russians were, after all, the first to attempt to apply linear programming optimization to their national economic planning, albeit premature at the time.

Gilpin (1983), in discussing war games, says that the economic and military changes which result from the use of computer and other advanced technologies are bringing human society into an age wherein more is to be gained through cooperation and an international division of labor than through strife and conflict. For, in the electronic global village all people will either lose or win together. To survive in a global society, Shubik (1983) suggests, we must develop tools to control pollution, fight inflation, provide justice and welfare, and to warn of new dangers and threats. This requires the building of more and more sophisticated models of an emerging global system in which computers and communication networks are to the twenty-first century what roads were to the first century's Roman empire.

Need for Tools

The problem is not technology, but what mind-tools we need and how to develop and use them. Their value, to paraphrase Seymour Papert (1980), will be determined by their success in helping us ask the most fundamental questions and solve the most desperate of human global problems. Some of the preliminary thought about waging peace through simulations was begun by Carroll (1983) as he explored the idea for a Catholic Peace Center. We must use these powerful new tools, he said, to understand how the human mind functions in matters of peace and war. Peace is not being achieved through weapons technology alone, so he proposed a system of "war control" wherein strong and weak nations could cooperate much like the system of ground control which regulates air traffic. As yet, he said, people do not even know how to define peace except as the absence of war, therefore sophisticated systems analysis is needed to experiment with peace systems.

Collective intelligence is needed for theory and practice. Hinds (1983) of the Peace Research Network says that computers and computer communications can make highly significant contributions to two fundamental tasks which are at the heart of peace and world order: trust and community building, and conflict resolution. New tools can now make it possible for more and more people—even millions and tens of millions—to get more involved in these explorations, and thus also in fundamental, the so-called grass root, decision-making.

To Do What?

A great deal of modeling experience is available in political science and economic models, and in strategic decision modeling as in the work of the Club of Rome. Kaplan (1979) says that although great individual minds may have been responsible for spectacular human advances at times, from now on human progress will require a community of minds in which theories are collectively developed, criticized, applied, and tested. Until that happens, he says, human thought in the areas of war, peace, and international relationships will continue to be too simplistic and inadequate.

Individuals can continue to make significant and often exciting contributions, especially as their research and thought is empowered with fifth generation computer tools. They can as individuals and in small groups explore, as Alexrod (1984) describes, strategies such as those necessary to solve the "prisoner's dilemma" game. Already, across international lines, people begin to confer through computer conferencing.

What are some of the games or simulations that might be undertaken? The list is endless; and many groups in different situations may explore different possibilities, separately or through computer connections. Some might begin with the United Nations, exploring alternatives for revising its structure or procedures. It will be possible to try out ideas, through simulations, that nations are unwilling to consider officially. For example:

- What might be done by a global congress—sometimes teleconference and sometimes computer conference in which delegates did not need to leave home—that represented neighborhoods instead of nations, with expanded town-to-town horizontal relationships? Suppose these were regional assemblies?
- What might be accomplished by "conflict anticipation groups" that went in to monitor any potential area of conflict?

- What kind of international police forces might be developed, perhaps to use non-violent methods?
- What kinds of important cases that are not allowed to come to the World Court might be simulated to see what the outcome would be (e.g., a simulation effort on Law of Sea, Sebenius, 1984)? Suppose, for example, a world leader who uses armed force in a situation were required to justify his actions (e.g., as logically presenting the quantitative results of gaming simulation) before a global tribunal. Hearings might especially be held to examine cases of torture.

Licklider (1983) says that it is technically possible now to give international politics much greater depth, wider scope, with much more citizen involvement. Millions of people, in fact, can be active participants, which makes it increasingly difficult for dictators to control or subvert the process. It will be a long time, he feels, before computer networks and conferencing can be used for the official work of legislatures, but simulations—large-scale unofficial experiments—can begin at any time.

Who Will Do The Gaming?

Official governmental and university projects will require special funding, but it is unlikely that "peace games" will be monopolized by government and official groups. War games, the nations feel, must be secret and official, whereas their quest for peace is nearly always an open process, involving anyone who may be interested. Student groups, church groups, peace groups, and informal groupings of interested people can begin to work on peace simulations right now—indeed, some have already started. Ordinary people, with computer facilities, are dreaming and experimenting. Some of them are in the Third World, where computer networking can help them reach out to work with those who may be more technically advanced.

Such groups can begin to examine the models they have in their minds—the usually unexamined political models which have led too often to war. As any given experiment enlarges to the point of complexity, dimensions of it can be divided up with groups in different places keeping in touch with each other via computer bulletin boards. As data banks and systems are developed, more and more groups can involve themselves in a continuing computer conference. This is not so much a new process as it is a way for more and more people to put their heads together. The advantage here is that people can work at different locations and times, as they prefer. Schank (1984) tells how nearly every experiment fails in his artificial intelligence lab because the participants set impossibly different goals for themselves. Yet each failure, when examined, reveals the next steps for experimentation in a continuing process of learning and development. In a similar way, instead of pessimism and discouragement about continuing failures in disarmament and peace processes, many more people need to use emerging mind tools to learn from political failures. There is a safeguard in that gaming simulations do *not* destroy anything in our real world.

Achievements and Current Status of the GLOSAS Project

During the past dozen years, thanks to the assistance of various U.S. Governmental agencies and to the support letters provided from various experts in the United States, a number of goals have been accomplished to advance computer telecommunications and information exchange between the U.S.A. and Japan:

- The extension of U.S. VANs to various overseas countries,
- Japanese deregulation to allow the interconnection of multiple host computers in the U.S. to a U.S./Japan leased data communication line; and to allow the use of electronic mail and computer conferencing via the U.S./Japan packet-switching line,
- Liberalization of the procurement policy of the Nippon Telegraph and Telephone Corporation, de-monopolization of telecommunication industries in Japan, and the proliferation of private and public VANs there.

These steps towards the establishment of infrastructure, the first stage of the GLOSAS Project, made possible the next step: focusing attention on the substance and content of global telecommunication networks. For example:

- Experimentation with the extension of American education to Japan and other countries, with the use of electronic mail and computer conferencing. This has included a TELEclass from the University of Hawaii to a dozen schools in Korea, Japan and other Asian countries.
- There also has been an extension of "connected education" from the New School for Social Research in New York to students and faculty in Singapore, Scandinavia, Europe, Canada, and Japan with the use of Electronic Information Exchange System (EIES) at New Jersey Institute of Technology.

Japan/United States connections are the places GLOSAS seeks to begin because of the high tech status of Japan in electronics and computers. Then after experimentation has proven the possibilities and value of what can be done with global VANs, an effort will be made to reach out to people in various countries.

Such experiments provide a foundation for the second and grand developing stage of the GLOSAS project, PEACE GAMING by the users of global communication media. Large-scale experimentation could begin by using and expanding Onishi's FUGI model (1983, 1984) which has a data basis in many countries and has already been used by the United Nations and various governments for economic and other simulations. It has been suggested, for example, that negotiators could work with greater success if they could use the same information and make continuing input into enlarging data

104

banks, as they use computer simulations to try out alternative solutions to a crisis. The bringing of many minds together, using interconnected computers as research tools to explore new alternatives for solving global problems and for the management of complexity can bring a new "collective intelligence" to bear upon issues of war and peace.

As demonstrated in the past decade, even preliminary experimentation can improve international relationships far beyond the enlargement of telecommunications and information technologies, as an effort is made to reach out to people in many countries for the promotion of mutual understanding and cooperation in search for new strategies for peace.

Summary

A long-range, gradually developing process is being initiated. People in Europe and America have become increasingly frustrated at the failure of their leaders to look far ahead, to plan alternatives to solve crucial problems before it is too late. It is difficult to get political leaders to look beyond the end of their terms of office, to do more than improvise patchwork solutions for each crisis that arises. More powerful collective intelligence tools can now enable simulations and research to look further ahead into the future, and deeper into the morass. These tools are the "sleeping giant" which can make it possible for problems to be examined and solved on a larger and larger scale.

"Games" and "simulations" can be undertaken to explore new alternatives for the United Nations, for regional associations of nations, for world law and courts, for global economic development, for trust-building, negotiation, conflict-resolution, police-peace forces, citizen action and preparation, for negotiations in dealing with terrorism and to discover the consequences of proposed unilateral actions.

In contrast to massively-funded global projects which can be encouraged by foundations and governments, the process of computer simulations of new alternatives for waging peace can begin locally in many small ways, then information and experience can be shared—as networks and data banks are gradually developed and enlarged. In time there can be global data banks and global game plans which groups large and small, global and local, can plug into and use. War games must be kept secret, but peace strategies can involve the participation of any qualified person, and can be used to educate, train, and democratically involve large numbers of people in many countries

The proposed global peace gaming system, when fully developed, can become an educational tool for students of international affairs and political science. Moreover, such a system can be at the heart of a global university, or a consortium of institutes in many countries. This can promote mutual understanding among the world's people, and hence advance peace-keeping. Education of young people and adults on a global scale can be one of the best future investments for world peace and progress.

References

1. Axelrod, R., *The Evolution of Cooperation*. Basic Books, New York, 1984.
2. Carroll, A.D., "Can Computers Be Used for Peace?" *Media Development*. (U.K.), 2, 1983.
3. Gilpin, R.G., "The Computer and World Affairs," *The Computer Age: A Twenty Year View*. Edited by M.L. Dertouzos, and J. Moses, M.I.T. Press, 1983.
4. Gleick, J., "The Man Who Restored Geometry," *New York Times Magazine*. December 8, 1985.
5. Hinds, J.A., "Communications and World Order," *Breakthrough*. Global Education Associates, Summer, 1983.
6. Kaplan, M., *Toward Professionalism in International Theory*. Free Press, New York, 1979.
7. Licklider, J.C.R., "Computers and Government," *The Computer Age: A Twenty Year View*. Edited by M.L. Dertouzos, and J. Moses, M.I.T. Press, 1983.
8. Nightingale, B., "Michael Frayn, The Entertaining Intellect," *New York Times Magazine*. December 8, 1985.
9. Onishi, A., "A Macroeconomic Study on the Future of Global Interdependence," *Proceedings of the 4th IFAC/IFORS/IIASA Conference and the 1983 SEDC Conference on Economic Dynamics and Control*. Washington, DC, June, 1983.——"A New Approach to Global Modeling," paper presented at the United Nations Inter-Agency Technical Working Group, Twelfth Session, Geneva, Switzerland, June, 1984.——"Alternative Simulation on the External Debt of Developing Countries: 1984-1990," paper presented at the Project LINK Meeting at Stanford University, 1984.
10. Papert, S., *Mind Storms*, Basic Books, New York, 1980.
11. Rossman, P., "The Coming Great Electronic Encyclopedia," *Global Solutions*. Edited by E. Cornish, World Future Society, Bethesda, MD, 1984.——*Computers: Bridges to the Future*. Judson Press, Valley Forge, PA, 1985.
12. Schank, R., "The Cognitive Computers. Addison Wesley Publishing Co., Reading, MA, 1984.
13. Sebenius, J.K., *Negotiating on Law of Sea*. Harvard University Press, Cambridge, MA, 1984.
14. Shubik, M., "Computers and Modeling," *The Computer Age: A Twenty Year View*, Edited by M.L. Dertouzos, and J. Moses, M.I.T. Press, 1983.
15. Utsumi, T., "Global Gaming—Simulation with Computer Communication for International Cooperation," paper presented at the 1972 International Conference on Computer Communication, Washington, DC, October, 1972.——"Joint USA/JAPAN Project on Global Systems Analysis and Simulation (GLOSAS) of Energy, Resources and Environmental (ERE) Systems," *Proceedings of the Conference on Energy Modeling and Forecasting*. Berkeley, CA, June 28 to 29, 1974.——"Peace Game," *Simulation*. November, 1977.——"Need for a Global Information System," *Proceedings of Conference on Information Societies: Comparing the Japanese and American Experiences*. International Communication Center, School of Communi-

cations, University of Washington, Seattle, December, 1977.——"GLOSAS Project: GLObal Systems Analysis and Simulation," *Proceedings of the 1980 Winter Simulation Conference.* Vol. 2, *(Simulation with Discrete Models: A State-of-the-Art View),* Orlando, FL, December, 1980.

16. Utsumi, T. and J. DeVita, "GLOSAS Project (GLObal Systems Analysis and Simulation)," *Computer Networks and Simulation II.* Edited by S. Schoemaker, North-Holland Publishing Co., Amsterdam, 1982.

17. Utsumi, T., A. Ishikawa, and J. DeVita, "Computer Simulation of International Crisis Management," *Proceedings of the Conference on Computer Simulation in Emergency Planning.* San Diego, CA, 1983.

18. Utsumi, T., P.O. Mikes, and P. Rossman, "Peace Games with Open Modeling Network," paper published in *Computer Networks and Simulation III,* Edited by S. Schoemaker, North-Holland Publishing Co., Amsterdam, 1986.

19. Utsumi, T., *Open Modeling and Simulation.* (Papers to be published in the near future.)

PROVOCATIVE VERSUS NON-PROVOCATIVE USE OF THE NEW SMART WEAPONS: ORGANIZATION MAKES THE DIFFERENCE

by

Alvin M. Saperstein

Introduction

Sticks and stones may break my bones but names will never harm me.
—Children's Rhyme

"Sticks and stones" are ways of impressing the wielder's will upon, or destroying, those who have fewer sticks and stones. The ability to impose your will upon another is not equivalent to the resolving of a conflict; unless destroyed or incorporated, the loser will seek revenge, prolonging and exacerbating the conflict. "Names," though not necessarily friendly, impose no will. Negotiation, or simple passage of time may lead to a resolution of the conflict if both sides are compelled to stick to names, barred from sticks and stones. If only one side has access to sticks and stones, it will be tempted to threaten their use, thus intensifying the conflict. If both sides have them and the first to use them deprives the other of the ability to use them and thus escapes unhurt, there will again be great temptation to do so in a squabble, meaning that neither dares wait for the conflict to be resolved. Such a situation is very unstable—any tension may discharge into violence.

> I didn't want to hit him though I had the means and motivation, which I thought he knew about, and so I thought that he thought that I was going to do so and therefore was planning to hit me, disabling me, before I could hit him, because I know he had the means, and so—in order to prevent that—I hit him.

On the other hand, if he who goes first is likely to lose, both may hold back, resorting to "names" instead. Eventually, the conflict may be bypassed or resolved.

For the foreseeable future, nations are going to be hostile to each other, afraid of each other in the absence of any superior "adult" or law, and so—like ungoverned small boys—inclined to resort to sticks and stones or names. Given that a nation's sticks and stones may

Alvin M. Saperstein, Physics Department and Center for Peace and Conflict Studies, Wayne State University, Detroit, Michigan.

be nuclear weapons, there is strong reason to attempt to restrict usage to "names."

A nation without means of defense, in the presence of hostile others, is subject to the will of others. Conflicts are not resolved. A nation with defense may provoke the hostility of others, again exacerbating conflict. Thus we must distinguish between provocative and non-provocative defense, only the latter encouraging conflict resolution. A cautious or frightened nation deploys some traditional military means of defense. Being traditional military, these imply the ability to wreak damage on the lives and properties of its neighbors. These neighbors, becoming disturbed and cautious, introduce their own traditional military defenses. This increases the threat perceived by the first nation, which becomes more frightened and deploys further military forces. The neighbors, reacting to the perceived military deployments and not to the unperceived fright and caution of the first nation, become more disturbed and deploy more military of their own. And so it goes, each nation (or group) provoking the others into a military response, leading to an escalating cycle of arms deployment and brandishing—independent of the initial motivation of any of the parties. A great deal of historical evidence indicates that such "arms races" often run away from the intended control or desires of the parties, leading (in a crisis) not to conflict resolution but to conflict exacerbation, war and mutual disaster. The escalating military capabilities lead to war in a crisis because each side thinks that the other will act first to use his capabilities to resolve the crisis in his favor. (I hit him before he hit me to prevent me from hitting him to prevent him . . . !) If we wish to give time, or other means, the opportunity to resolve conflicts, such mutually provoking defense cycles must be avoided. Since, for the near future, defense can not be avoided, means for non-provocation defense must be adopted by one or both parties to a dispute in order that there be a non-destructive resolution of the crisis (in the super-power context, in order that the dispute not lead to mutual annihilation).

A non-provocative defense is a means of preventing an opponent from "harming" you without being able to harm him as long as he makes no attempt at harming you. In the context of the conflict between the NATO and Warsaw Pact nations, the "harms" are either nuclear devastation of one or more nations or the occupation of the opponent's territory by military means. There is no way of preventing nuclear attack except the threat of retaliation (MAD). Hence an invulnerable "second strike" capability is the non-provocative defense in the nuclear realm. Since the threat to use nuclear weapons to deter aggression and occupation of territory contradicts the desire to keep nuclear defense non-provocative, nuclear weapons have no place in propelling or repelling a conventional attempt at seizure of territory. Hence, non-nuclear non-provocative means must be found to deter or defeat trans-border incursions by the opponent. If the threat of defeat for any and all invading forces is great enough, this should deter the invasion. Hence defeat and deter are equivalent in

Europe and a non-nuclear, non-provocative defense is a prerequisite for conflict resolution in Europe (and for the damping of the spread to Europe of conflicts which start elsewhere).

A non-provocative territorial defense allows you to throw an opponent off of your territory (defeat and destroy his forces while on your territory) without giving you the means to mount an offensive onto his territory. A modern, professional army (implying relevant ground, air, and naval forces) is highly mobile. Given the ability to destroy an enemy on your territory, it has the ability to destroy him on his own territory. The buildup of such an army is inherently provocative. (Both sides are currently engaged in such buildups in Europe.) A militia defense, a defense carried out by citizens, permanently tied to their home communities, acting as part-time military, is incapable of rapidly moving into, and wreaking havoc upon, an opponent's territory. Hence it is inherently a non-provocative defense. Can it be made to be an effective defense as well?

In the past, technology gave small groups of professional soldiers the means to impose their will upon the much larger groups of civilians which make up a society. For example, armored knights on horseback terrorized the medieval peasants and burghers. German panzers overran Europe, and, in their turn, Soviet tanks overran Eastern Europe; they still hold much of Europe in fear today. Today's new technology offers the possibility of the citizen standing up to the soldier. Whether he will do so, successfully, and hence inaugurate an era of non-provocative, rather than provocative, defense in Europe, depends not upon the technology (which can contribute to either) but upon the socio-political organizations which are set up to use the technology. As is usually the case, in matters of war or peace, destruction or survival, the question—and blame—is not technological but political, a matter of collective human will.

The Threat

The non-nuclear threat, brandished by each side in central Europe against the other, is armored force—large groups of tanks, backed up by mobile infantry and artillery, supported by attack aircraft and helicopters. The tanks can destroy the resistance of people in groups (civilians or infantry) but their utility is limited for flushing out dispersed, hidden individuals; this is best done by the follow-up mobile infantry. For their part, until now, individuals couldn't touch the tanks; the only defense was other tanks. Defense depended upon a battle between groups of tanks, a duel between professionals (analogous to the dogfight between airplanes; the ground based anti-aircraft fire, or the analogous light anti-tank fire of the infantry bystanders, was usually of little consequence). Thus this mode of defense requires at least as many defending tanks as aggressing tanks. Building up such a large body of defensive armor is indistinguishable from the buildup of an aggressive force—it is expensive and provocative.

110

The Precision Guided Missile (PGM)

New Technology—in the form of light but powerful rocket motors, shaped explosive charges and precision detonators which can generate armor penetrating jets, and compact solid state electronics which can generate and direct radiation toward armored targets, receive and analyze the reflections and direct missiles toward the target—have shifted the force balance between man and tank. Though still vulnerable, the individual—man or woman, youth or aged—is no longer powerless. Such an individual can now hand-carry and fire a missile which has a large probability of destroying a tank upon impact and which can reliably be guided to impact over distances up to several kilometers. Such "precision guided missiles" (PGMs) have been in existence for several years and were used with great impact in the tank battles in the Sinai (October 1973). The first such missiles were guided by signals sent via thin wires unrolled from the rear of the missile as it propelled itself toward the target. Later missiles received their guidance instructions via other forms of signalling from the launchers. In any case, the person launching the missile had to keep his sight on the target during the entire time of missile flight, computers in the launcher calculating the difference between the target's position in the sight and the missile's trajectory and sending appropriate corrective signals to the missile.

Since the initial launching of the missile produced significant smoke and flame, the target tank could become aware that it was being attacked and direct suppressive fire at the evident source of the attack, forcing the missile launching party to duck. Ducking could break the required continuous visual contact between target and attackers, thus saving the intended target tank. Nevertheless, sufficient numbers of Egyptian infantrymen were sufficiently brave and disciplined to stand up in the face of oncoming Israeli tanks and so wreak considerable destruction upon Israeli armor in the Sinai battles.

The individual could have even more effect upon advancing armor if he didn't have to be so brave, if he could "fire and forget," release his missile and duck, allowing the missile to guide itself to the preselected target. Much research and development has been put into such missiles and several now exist. Some are "passive"—homing in on the infrared radiation emitted by the tanks' engines or the ambient microwave power reflected from the tanks' armor. Others are "active"—radar guided. (The latter warheads are considerably heavier, more complex, and expensive.) Unfortunately for the defender, it is too easy for the invading tank to avoid such non-humanly guided missiles, quickly releasing smoke, decoy rockets, chaff. Human sight and guidance is less easily fooled, if it is not distracted by suppressive fire.

It is now technically possible to separate the person launching the anti-tank missile from the person guiding it. The former quickly ducks after revealing his position to the target tank (or its mates) upon firing. The latter, a large, safe distance away from the launcher continuously illuminates the target with a laser pointer beam using invisible radiation. The pointer person can stay relatively safely hidden during the process. The missile, once launched, homes in on the pre-selected radiation frequencies reflected from the target. Such weapons systems, once developed and deployed, should considerably enhance the effectiveness of the agile, unarmored individual in his battle against the massive tank. (Similar systems can also aid the individual in his defense against low-flying attack aircraft and helicopters.)

These remotely guided PGMs, in the hands of professional mobile infantry, attached to regular armored divisions, can aid these divisions significantly in their battle against other armored forces. Hence they can make major contributions to the repulsion of armored invasion. But they may also accompany the invader, contributing to his success in routing defending armored forces. Hence, this new technology, though designed to be defensive, is not inherently non-provocative: it can be deployed to defend the attacker.

PGM Militia Squads

The new technology which enables a dispersed group of individuals to stop an attacking tank column allows those individuals to be citizens—tied to their homes—instead of professional soldiers—tied to their regular mobile divisions. Such civilian groups, organized into community-based militia squads, could consist of reservists who have finished their regular compulsory military training service as well as neighborhood women, teens, and older people. They would train regularly in their neighborhoods, becoming familiar with the existing protective hiding places—cellars, caves, woods, etc., perhaps building additional ones—bunkers, tank traps, etc. Being instantly mobilizable in their own neighborhoods, they would not be victimized by surprise attack; fighting for their own homes and communities, they would have ample motivation for standing their ground as well as the technological means to destroy invaders in the process. (Even if they wished, as civilians, to evacuate the area, allowing the professional military of both sides to battle over it, the pace of modern warfare makes such evacuation highly unlikely. They would either remain, passively in their shelters, to be injured or killed by the collateral damage of the professionals' battle, or participate effectively themselves—without much greater probability of suffering injury.)

Though ordinary, economically productive citizens in peacetime, these PGM militia squads would be dispersed across the entire countryside, hidden and in place, upon warning of attack. As the invading armor crossed the territory, they would be subject to effective PGM fire from all sides. They would suffer great attrition in numbers, their organization would be disrupted, and their timing thrown off. Meanwhile, the regular professional defending army would have ample warning, time to mobilize and prepare its counterattack, at times and places of its own choosing, upon the weakened aggressors.

Thus the new PGM technology offers a nation the option of two defense components. In one, the new technology is grafted onto a conventional military structure, increasing its effectiveness but not diminishing its inherently provocative nature. In the other, a corresponding new social organization is created, based upon civilian life and hence providing a much more efficient use of a nation's human and economic resources. Less expensive for a given measure of firepower, it is also inherently non-provocative. The actual mix, between the two, to be adopted, will depend upon many factors, not the least being the political power of a nation's "military-industrial complex," who would naturally prefer the ceremony, prestige, jobs, power and profits of the conventional approach. Numerical estimates do indicate, however, that a mixture of purely non-provocative defense measures offers the prospect of a very effective defense of the conflict line between East and West in central Europe.

Conclusion

The "dark ages" saw the rise of the mounted, armored knight. It was a time when military considerations were paramount in all aspects of life and society, when the professional soldier sat at the pinnacle of the social structure. Civilization could not resume its progress until the hold of the military upon society was broken. One of the factors leading to the fall of the knight was the Swiss pikeman (soon emulated throughout Europe). The pike itself—the new technology, just a long spear—represented no great threat to the mounted knight. The threat—eventually successful—came from the human organization: groups of Swiss farmers, disciplined to move their pikes in unison, a mobile hedgehog upon which overly aggressive horsemen impaled themselves. It was the mixture of technology and organization which unhorsed the feudal military and hence started the decline of feudalism.

Similarly today, a "Swiss style" defense—a new combination of people and technology—an ever ready people having instant access to "smart weapons" in their homes and communal places—can significantly change the nature of the East-West confrontation in Europe, leading to an era of "common security" rather than "sticks and stones." Such a change, releasing the human and material resources currently devoted to mutual fear and hostility, could again lead to a further burst in the progress of our common civilization.

NORMS IN CONFLICT AND CONFUSION

by

Donald N. Michael and Walter Truett Anderson

Although Americans habitually describe political conflicts in economic terms, there are really very few controversies that can be reduced to the simple calculus of need and greed; most of politics involves the conflict of norms, in which different parties have different ideas of what is real, what is of value, what is to be done. And when such conflicts are resolved it is because the disputants share some norms about how conflicts are resolved or why they should be resolved.

This means that the present state of global politics is much more precarious than any economically-based analysis—whether of the right or the left—would reveal. The world has become a normative tower of Babel in which people hold different systems of value and belief, and live by different stories about where things are going.

The social construction of reality that once provided a certain coherence to Western society has been unraveling for decades. It was a worldview that valued progress, economic efficiency, science and technology—and saw a world composed of separate entities such as atoms, individuals, academic departments, corporations, cities, and nations. Causes were separate from effects, present from future, variable from variable, and "we" from "they." This worldview was in many ways highly productive: It generated a great burst of progress and change that is now bringing into being a postmodern world which, as Stephen Toulmin put it, "has not yet discovered how to define itself in terms of what it *is,* but only in terms of what it has *just-now ceased to be."[1]*

Many people have recognized this, and some have been led to the conclusion that a "new paradigm" will supplant the old worldview. We see no reason to believe that this is so—or, at least, that the new worldview will inevitably contain all the features—such as

Donald N. Michael is professor emeritus at the University of Michigan, Planning and Public Policy Department. Walter Truett Anderson is an author, political scientist, and environmentalist.

114

feminism, ecology and esoteric spirituality—which are commonly cited in the "new paradigm" literature.[2] The "new paradigm" story is only one of many candidates or aspirants to supplant the old world-view. However, there is one regard in which the "new paradigm" ideology is clearly correct—that is, its holistic emphasis. The most striking feature of the postmodern world is its systemic character, its astounding proliferation of linkages among once-separate cultures, governments, economies and ecosystems. So when people speak of a new worldview they can—really for the first time in history—consider the possibility of a worldview that is in some way or to some extent the common property of all cultures.

However, we are not at all willing to assume that the divergent peoples of the world are about to embrace a mystique of oneness. Rather, we foresee a host of developments creating objective *conditions* of connectedness that people will *have* to deal with at the same time that they continue to maintain vastly different normative systems and also continue to hold on, perhaps more tenaciously than ever, to ideas of separateness—ideas of separateness which are reinforced by those different normative systems.

In the postmodern world everything is connected to everything so that cause and effect, present and future, we and they are utterly ensnarled; even separating them for analytic purposes becomes far less convincing than it was in the heady recent times when academics talked with great confidence of factors and variables. But at the same time that this global connectedness sweeps through human affairs there is tremendous divergence and conflict, reaction and violence: Many political movements—particularly fundamentalist and separatist ones—are organized efforts to disengage from the snares of globalism. Many of the political problems that trouble Americans—like international terrorism, with its ability to manipulate communications media and make overnight worldwide news— are signs of the emergence of the postmodern global system.

The belief in progress, which served throughout the just-ending modern era as a unifying framework within which people of vastly different political persuasions could agree to disagree—socialist revolution vs. capitalist growth, for example—no longer commands the same respect. Opinion polls consistently report widespread erosion of confidence in the future. There is a strong strain of primitivism in the West today, a forceful rejection of the myth of progress; it is expressed in some ecological and spiritual movements, in groups attempting to imitate American Indian culture, in the crusade against biotechnology. You can use the word "progress" in such circles, but you had better smile when you say it. At the same time, however, the old myth still has its adherents in many parts of the world, in both its left-wing and right-wing versions. Progress is no longer *the* story, but one of many.

In the United States, conflict between left-wing and right-wing versions of progress still commands attention, but is often over-shadowed by the larger and far more perplexing normative conflict that arises when progress itself becomes the issue. Many of the skirmishes in this newer conflict have to do with the environment; they are differences of opinion between those who favor greater productivity and efficiency and economic growth, and those who stress other values such as biological sustainability. These conflicts often *unite* elements of the old left and right—such as developers and labor unions—against environmentalists, who are characterized as advocates of "no growth." There are usually tangible economic differences—which are relatively amenable to resolution—but there are also deeper normative issues for which no solution has yet appeared. People who want to build a housing development or a dam or a freeway—who were enculturated into a value system which celebrated such accomplishments—are often frustrated and profoundly confused to come into contact with people who oppose them. They believe their opponents to be against progress itself, and in a way they are right: No postmodern view of progress has yet emerged. There are bits and pieces of an alternative story of progress, present in embryonic form in the works of such writers as E.F. Schumacher, but its adherents form a subculture and a very small one at that. It is another candidate. A new postmodern idea of progress may well come into being as part of a prevailing worldview, but we suspect that such an idea is best described by Michael Polanyi's concept of an "emergent"—that is, something greater than the sum of the events that give rise to it, and by definition unpredictable.[3]

In the meanwhile, the claims and complaints of different groups in the population come from very different cultural bases—groups that have not only different interests, but different perspectives and norms. This became apparent in the 1960s when society began to rumble with conflict of a sort that was not only rich against poor but square against hip, young against old, culture against counterculture. Many people do not like the word "lifestyle," but the language needs some such term to describe the contemporary cultural landscape in which people occupy different stations in society which are not precisely classes but more properly subcultures, with individual and sometimes highly unusual sets of values and beliefs.

Societies have always had divergent subcultures, but they also had over-arching normative systems that dictated what the members of any group could expect and that provided a framework for the resolution of conflicts between them. In pre-modern societies rigid social hierarchies and established religions performed those functions. Throughout the modern era the older normative system steadily gave way to the new mythos of progress and growth, while ideas of upward mobility and an ever-expanding economy offered an attractive set of expectations and drained the energy from many class conflicts. The mythos of progress is still the "official" normative system of Western society, but it is beginning to show signs of age. So today we find demands coming from different claimant populations—younger/older, rich/poor, First World/Third World, educated/maleducated/uneducated, violent/nurturing, short view/long view, cosmopolitans/

locals, participative/alienated and so on—that have their own value and belief systems and sometimes only the most slender allegiance to the old myth of "keeping your station" or the modern one of success.

The situation appears random, fragmented, anomic—and in some ways it is. But there is pattern to the postmodern world—a pattern of people searching for a pattern. Many psychologists have commented on the importance of meaning in individual life, and it is no less important that there be social meaning: some idea of where society came from, and where it is going. These larger constellations of meaning are the major political driving forces in the world, the source of humanity's deepest conflicts and also the repository of its highest hopes; they are what we call stories.

We use the word "stories" here as a simple and common-sense way to talk about the human urge to create order in life, to assemble the events of individual existence within the framework of some larger structure of meaning and purpose. We mean by "story" about the same thing that other writers mean by "myth" or "paradigm," and use it instead because it emphasizes progression through time; the essence of a story is that it provides some explanation of where things came from and where they are headed. A story provides a cause for the activist, a sense of the flow of history for those more inclined to passive acceptance. A story may—or may not—be about the same thing as an ideology. Some stories are very ideologically sophisticated, with elaborate intellectual structures to explain precisely how and why things are headed in a certain direction (Marxism is the best example) while other stories may be nothing more than vague hopes that this or that will happen.

A story is not—certainly not for the person who lives by it—the same thing as a scenario. Futurists may create all kinds of scenarios in a playful exploratory way with no need to make any personal commitment to one or the other; a scenario becomes a story when one begins to believe it. And the person who has managed to find, amid the chaos of personal existence, a believable account of the direction of history and his or her own role in it cannot afford the flexibility of the futurist. A Christian fundamentalist who awaits the coming of God's kingdom on Earth is not interested in hearing about all the other possibilities. There is only one possibility. This is something the aspiring conflict resolver would do well to understand.

Several major stories are competing in the new postmodern world, the world that is in the process of trying to define what it is to become. Some of these stories have deep historical roots and elaborate ideologies, some are tenuous upstarts.

First among them, from the American perspective, is the progress story. Faltering a bit now, it still commands the allegiance of the American mainstream and the political establishment—both Republican and Democratic. It has been mythologized in the arts and literature, articulated in the works of many theorists; Herman Kahn has been perhaps the most dogged spokesman in recent decades. Its main prop in domestic policy is the GNP and the ethic of growth;

its main contribution to foreign policy the theory of development, with all its elaborate concepts about how primitive societies become Western-style industrialized democracies.

A competitor to the progress story in American society is the fundamentalist story of return to a society governed by Christian values. The true fundamentalist is suspicious of foreign influences, fiercely protective of national sovereignty, and deeply pessimistic about rapid change. Although fundamentalism is not new, its current manifestation as a potent political force does have a definite late twentieth century character: It is largely a reaction to the increasing pace of global connectedness. And although many conservative Americans manage to fit both the myth of progress and Christian fundamentalism into their personal worldviews, there is a basic conflict between the two. The Republican party's internal schism between progressive internationalists and Christian fundamentalists shows how serious this conflict can become—serious enough that many political analysts believe it to be an insurmountable obstacle to a period of Republican domination of American politics.

There are other fundamentalist stories that have the same emotional dynamic even though their outward form is entirely different. The most prominent of these in contempoary global politics is Islam. In many parts of the Third World, most notably Africa, it is Islam that stands as the real adversary of the Western-style story of progress. Islam offers to oppressed peoples a compelling political and economic ideology rooted in cosmology, and the basis for a pox-on-both-your-houses rejection of both capitalism and Marxism.

Meanwhile the classic Marxist story of revolution still gives form and purpose to political life for many people. It holds out the promise of the overthrow of the capitalist state, the creation of the socialist state, all wealth reallocated, a final end to class conflict. The Marxist story is the official ideology of a large part of the world; it is also the inspiration of guerrilla groups, a strong although somewhat waning force in the intellectual world, and (in one of the more historically ironic developments of our time) part of a radical new religious movement, liberation theology.

Most of the peoples of the world live out their lives according to one or another of the above four stories. Each story has its "establishment," its official version and revealed truths—but there are many variations, sects and combinations. People are highly creative about such things.

All four of the major stories took form during the modern era. Both the myth of progress and the ideology of Marxism are products of the Enlightenment and the Industrial Revolution, and contemporary fundamentalist stories (whether Christian or Islamic or any of the other versions) are reactions to them. Fundamentalist stories are never merely simple returns to the beliefs of the past, but rather new ideologies created out of old material in response to current conditions. And now postmodern stories are emerging: New candidates are in the field, and others will probably appear in the decades ahead. Here we will take note of two: the green story and the new paradigm story. Many people see these as one, but we think there are significant differences that make it worthwhile to distinguish between them.

The green story is identified with environmental values, with the mystique of solar energy and organic farming, with the animal rights movement and of course with the Green party of West Germany and similar political groups in other countries. It is, like fundamentalism, a reaction against the Industrial Revolution's myth of progress—but a postmodern and highly sophisticated one that finds adherents among idealistic young people, intellectuals, and some feminists. The green story tells of bringing a halt to the destructiveness of industrialized progress and returning to a simpler time of reverence for Earth and life focused on the local bioregion.

The new paradigm story is super-progress: a sudden leap forward to an entirely new way of being, and a new way of understanding the world. Although some new-paradigm thinkers draw heavily on the green mystique, others embrace big business and high technology and are enthusiastic about future exploration of space. The new paradigm story is a postmodern version of ancient millennarian cults that predicted the imminent coming of a new order, a paradise on Earth. But where old millennarian stories were derived from religious prophecy, new paradigm advocates like to support their expectations by reference to scientific theory such as Ilya Prigogine's work on dissipative structures. Evolutionary ideas, usually more of the Teilhardian than the Darwinian variety, also figure prominently. New paradigm thinkers tend to be convinced that the bright future they predict will inevitably come to pass; this is another point of distinction from the green movement, which is often pessimistic, alarmed and militant.

All of these stories—and others as well—compete for credibility in the postmodern world. All of their adherents say: This is where the world is going, this is how it must be. Clearly we are in for much conflict—not only the bipolar conflict between West and East, the myth of progress versus the ideology of revolution—but also fundamentalists against Marxists, Moslems against Christians, Greens against industrial progress, and many other permutations.

The question that naturally occurs to anyone who hopes for world peace is: What are the possibilities for reconciliation and conflict resolution among peoples who are traveling such divergent paths in a world that is becoming in many ways a single society?

Undoubtedly it will be possible to resolve many specific, limited conflicts and perhaps even to circumvent large ones, but—and this is something that must be understood—*Western society has no concept of any approach to reconciling the different cultural worldviews which are the source and legitimator of such conflicts*. To reconcile them is to persuade people to change their most fundamental values and beliefs. Furthermore, we can not even be sanguine about the ability to resolve limited conflicts. The various stories that people believe in carry a hard core of moral conviction, of good and evil. Westerners see evil in obstructing progress. Marxists see evil in the capitalist system. Fundamentalists see evil everywhere outside of their own religious culture. Greens see evil in progress as we have known it. New paradigm thinkers see serious moral deficiency in Newtonian physics, fundamentalist religions, and various other modes of non-Aquarian thought—enough to yearn for the immediate collapse of all of them. People of all persuasions believe that vigorous action is justified to bring about the eventual triumph over whatever they see as evil, and the percentage who believe violence equally justified is unfortunately quite high. Such convictions do not readily lend themselves to conflict resolution.

There is also the question of whether conflict resolution itself has any strong transcultural meaning. Western society shares certain ideas about what conflict resolution is—or at least, should be—but these are not necessarily universal ideas. And there is a deeper problem: Many of the world's stories are conflict stories in which the battle between good and evil is the very pivot. A person who anticipates Armageddon does not take much interest in the brisk "win-win" talk of the modern mediator.

The increasingly systemic, interconnected character of the post-modern world also creates new kinds of conflicts even among people who have some degree of a shared worldview—conflicts of a sort for which we find little normative foundation for resolution. The currently available ethical standards grew out of vastly different—and usually simpler—patterns of relation among different persons, groups, organizations or states. In the postmodern world it is extremely difficult for people to go about business as usual without suddenly being told that they are impinging upon the activities of someone else. Accountability, blame, allocation of gains and losses, are extremely difficult to establish where the systemic structure of the situation was not fully recognized and agreed to at the time key decisions were made. Consider, for example, the knot of arguments about the enormous national debts of many Third World nations. The Third World debt situation is perhaps the clearest evidence of a global economy. The problem is in a sense everybody's problem—a monumental crisis of the emerging world society—and a conflict resolution challenge of a scale and kind that is without precedent and consequently without an adequate body of normative guidelines. Several "world class problems" of different kinds—economic, ecological, social—are already on the table, and others can be expected to surface. These global issues are the markers of entry into the postmodern world, unexpected signs that the rules have changed. The global debt problem was not anticipated, and neither was the acid rain problem. They surfaced suddenly, as what had been business as usual turned out to be something entirely different.

We do not present these observations for the purpose of arguing that the situation is hopeless, but rather in the hope that developing a proper respect for the enormity of the problem is the best preparation for attempting to deal with it. The present world situation is a formidable one, and it is worth reminding ourselves frequently of the simple truth that it has not existed before. We can and must learn from the past, but this is not the same thing as believing that the solutions of the past will apply in the future.

The overwhelming need of our time is the emergence of a global culture containing some norms, values, beliefs, myths, concepts, that can—if only in the most tentative way—thread through the multifold worldviews and provide some basis for accommodation among them. To put the matter somewhat differently, we will have to have some *information* that is common to all people. There are many kinds of information, of course. Money is information. Myths and symbols, music and poetry are information. The very idea that there is such an entity as the planet, with people of different kinds living upon it, is itself a piece of information. In order for people to recognize the presence of global problems and move toward solving them, there will have to be some common foundation of *data* and *concepts*—about such matters as population and how it increases. The global culture will have to manifest itself as an ability of people of different worldviews to communicate about such things—at the very least, to know what it is they disagree about. Information will inevitably be both a cause of conflicts and a means of resolving them. And if we are to think about this with any clarity we need to develop some awareness of our own—that is, contemporary Western—attitudes toward information itself.

One of the most basic premises of progress-oriented Western culture is that more information leads to more knowledge which, in turn, leads to more power to control outcomes. This is the assumption that is beginning to turn on itself, and its collapse is the driving force behind most of the anti-progress movements that have recently arisen. Such movements are fueled by a deep and furious emotional reaction—as strong as a child's reaction when it discovers its parents are not truly omnipotent—against the traditional faith in information. The reaction tends to focus on the twin temples of that faith, science and technology.

Ironically, more information has led to an ever-increasing sense that things are out of control. Information about environmental deterioration, economic disarray, toxic wastes, national security, the failings of educational and health-delivery systems—all this points toward the feeling that we are unable to control society, to guide or regulate it into performing the way we (any group of "we's") would like it to perform. With more information people become *less* likely to find legitimacy in the institutions or organizations or officials described by the information. For one thing, information keeps revealing ineptitudes in practice and fumblings of purpose—if not downright immoral or illegal actions. For another, information provides the raw material for contending interpretations of what is going on and what should be done; such contention often deepens the conclusion that nobody really knows what to do or has any idea of how to control the situation. This compounding distrust and de-

121

ligitimation undermines efforts to gain control for the purpose of attaining desirable ends or for maintaining what Geoffrey Vickers called reliable "norm settings"—clear points of demarcation between what is legitimate or acceptable and what is not.[4] Finally, information in the form of future studies gives little reason to expect that things are likely to become more controllable in the years ahead.

Technical information will play an ever-greater part in the conduct of human life—but it will always be value-laden. Facts may well be facts, but it takes money and intent to collect, interpret and use them. Data may well be correct, but it is always fragmentary and selective when applied to reality. The pure objective neutrality that champions of science once claimed—and the public expected—is not really characteristic of scientific truth as scientists now understand it, or of the information that is so central to our political existence. Yet that kind of objective neutrality is still often inferred or demanded in the media and in agencies of government.

If the human species is going to make the transition from the modern to the postmodern world without absolute disaster, people are going to have to develop a different understanding of scientific truth and technical information. A failure to learn how to use information—and communicate it across cultural boundaries—will be fatal to the future of life on Earth. The challenge is in every sense of the word a matter of human survival.

When people cease to believe in the modern myth of infallible objective information, they can easily turn to a belief that there is no objective reality at all—that science and technology are pernicious, that the only trustworthy kind of information is intuition or mythic truth, that the future can be salvaged only by a atavistic return to the dark wisdom of the past. And clearly, some people are indeed forming that kind of belief. It is expressed in the new primitivism, in the fashionable disdain for "linear" or "left brain" thinking, in the environmentalists' suspicion of the "technological fix." What people really need to do, however, is not give up on information but begin to understand its limitations *and* learn how to use it.

This is the real challenge for the reconciliation of conflict, the avoidance of global disaster. Somehow, amid the din of normative chaos and divergent worldveiws, we need to find the ability—world-wide, species-wide—to deal with such matters as the debt crisis, overpopulation, acid rain, species extinction, toxic chemicals, and nuclear weaponry. This means dealing with information—and not only dealing with it, but developing a global "information culture" that embodies *both* information and the truth *about* information.

The challenge that the human species now confronts is essentially a learning challenge. We might more accurately call it a meta-learning challenge, since it involves something more than taking in information.

People who are deeply attached to a story will resist—often violently, often with great tenacity and political sophistication—information that threatens it. The best example of this in American society is the conflict over the teaching of evolution in the schools. There are many such conflicts. The reaction against information is a familiar feature of modern life; furthermore, the reaction does not come only from backward-looking fundamentalists.

Followers of the progress story tend to believe smugly that information is on their side, but in fact *all* stories are threatened by information. Every story is a response to present circumstances and a selective, creative ordering of information available at the time. As soon as a story takes form, it achieves a certain sanctity and becomes a vehicle of power. New information compels revision and inevitably threatens those who have built their psychological identities or political careers upon the story as it stood. The mythos of progress has been severely battered by the increase in information about environmental disruption, toxic wastes, economic crises and other malfunctions. Marxists are tired of hearing the data about the low productivity of Marxist economies. Fundamentalists are hostile toward much of modern science. Greens are against biotechnology and any information that might lead to other solutions than those they propose. New paradigm thinkers erect barriers against the evidence that neither science nor societies change by the rapid attitudinal flip-flop that the paradigm shift literature describes. If information is the common currency of the human species, resistance to it is the most common observable behavior.

Yet information has a momentum of its own, and people seek it out even when they fear it. The trend of the present era is not only toward a global society that is more connected, but toward a global society that possesses more information and is continually generating more yet. Information, like global connectedness, will impinge upon and inevitably transform the various subcultures and their stories, and create *some* basis for global culture.

Whatever its ultimate characteristics, that culture will not come into being without conflict. We have identified one kind of conflict—that is, conflict between subcultures, lifestyles, stories—but another kind of conflict will come out of the growing amount and importance of information; there will be, inevitably, struggles over interpretations of partial information and attempts to manipulate, disseminate or resist it. Whoever would seek to resolve conflict will have to develop a high sensitivity toward such informational and meta-informational issues.

Both of us have written in other places about the centrality of learning to contemporary life, and about the social and political values that social learning requires—different notions of leadership, competence, accountability and organizational performance.[5] The norms that would guide such a "learning society" are not really part of the cultural resource of any modern society or expressed in any story. And consequently the world faces a crisis—one that will be experienced as psychological stress by individuals, as social upheaval and conflict by societies—as people come to terms, often under conditions of great pressure, with the need to take in new information and also to use it effectively.

We could construct any number of scenarios about what forms this crisis might take: disturbing ones of disastrous consequences from information unheeded or misused, or from inquisition-like efforts to resist it; and favorable ones of a wise new global culture emerging out of the present chaos of normative conflict and informational confusion.

Some disruption is inevitable. But there is every reason to believe that the human capacity to learn is immense and untapped, and includes not only an ability to take in information but to learn *about* it, and to learn about learning.

We venture no prediction about the future of the stories we have identified here. Each is a partial view of reality, and none is adequate to serve as the cultural structure for a global society. But each is a human creation, and perhaps the human imagination will rise to the level of comprehending that they are things of its own making, and—like other kinds of information—most useful when we know their limitations. Thomas Berry has written that the human species is "between stories:" that the old social construction of reality has outworn its usefulness and that a new story must emerge.[6] Our hope is rather that, in the pressured and precarious milieu of the global information society, people may begin to tell one another, however uncertainly at first, a story about stories.

Notes

1. Stephen Toulmin, *The Return to Cosmology* (Berkeley: University of California Press, 1982).

2. Fritjof Capra, *The Turning Point* (New York: Simon and Schuster, 1982).

3. Michael Polanyi, *The Tacit Dimension* (London: Routledge and Kegan Paul, 1966).

4. Geoffrey Vickers, *The Art of Judgment* (New York: Basic Books, 1965).

5. Michael, *On Learning to Plan—And Planning to Learn* (San Francisco: Jossey-Bass, 1973); "Neither Hierarchy nor Anarchy: Notes on Norms for Governance in a Systemic World," in Anderson (ed.) *Rethinking Liberalism* (New York: Avon, 1983); Anderson, *To Govern Evolution: Further Adventures of the Political Animal* (Boston: Harcourt Brace Jovanovich, 1986).

6. Thomas Berry, "Comments on the Origin, Identification and Transmission of Values," *Anima,* Winter 1978.

PEACE BY REVOLUTION:
CIVILIAN-BASED OFFENSE

by

W. Warren Wagar

Perspectives on War and Peace

For various reasons mainstream futurists have seldom paid more than passing attention to the prospect of a third and terminal world war.[1] One problem is that the agenda of the contemporary futures movement was set in the early 1970s, during a period of detente in East-West relations, when public alarm centered not on Armageddon but on threats to the environment from unlimited economic growth. More to the point, futurists are reluctant to consider seriously a future that ends abruptly, giving them little chance to display their knowledge of the social and natural sciences. Delineating futurible alternatives and identifying workable solutions in the field of peace/ war studies has been left, for the most part, to scholars and activists without strong ties to the futures movement. When a peace/war scholar, such as the late Herman Kahn, does have such ties, he tends to compartmentalize his thinking, charting the future of human security as if it belonged to a different time-stream from the future of human society.[2]

This sort of schizophrenia serves futures research badly, and the cause of peace worse still. Comprised of scores of armed sovereign states, several deploying arsenals of apocalyptic force, the present-day global political system can be depended upon to collapse, sooner or later, in a system-wide spasm of mass destruction. Although it has obviously not collapsed yet, in more than forty years of repeated crises and confrontations, it has also failed to make even a modest beginning toward the fundamental overhaul of its structures, premises, and procedures that might make a lasting peace possible. The weapons accumulate and improve. The Superpowers continue to joust, following the age-old formulas of international politics. Their chief nuclear-armed allies and rivals, the Superbabies, pursue goals of their own, following the same formulas. Local wars around the

W. Warren Wagar, professor, department of history, State University of New York, Binghamton, New York.

planet have cost twenty million lives since 1945 alone.[3] Nothing has changed, except the capability of armed forces to inflict destruction, and here the changes are all for the worse. No practical assessment of the human prospect can fail to make World War III the centerpiece of its analysis.

It is my purpose in this essay to review the range of current thinking on how World War III may be prevented, and to argue that of the many remedies discussed, only the most extreme is likely to work, although it may never be tried. I say "the most extreme," because it is the only attainable remedy that will lower the likelihood of a third world war to zero. Nothing less, under the circumstances, will do. Any full-scale world war, whether fought in 1997, 2050, or 2222, would almost surely conclude the human experiment. Reducing arms, minimizing tensions, strengthening the United Nations, and all the other nostrums advanced by good-hearted liberals for postponing the inevitable may (or may not) buy us a little time; but in the nuclear epoch the logic of piecemeal reform dissolves. What in earlier times would have seemed realistic, now becomes utopian, or merely foolish. Today, only utopia is realistic.

Before addressing the central issue, a little must be said about the assumptions that undergird this essay, and in particular the assumptions about world history. My starting point is the observation, developed fruitfully by Immanuel Wallerstein,[4] that mankind in the twentieth century inhabits a single world system, which consists of an integrated global economy and a tangle of independent polities. This system first began to take shape in the sixteenth century and serves uniquely well the needs and interests of international capital. In a sense, it is the product of capital, the political expression of the dynamics of world capitalism. Most previous civilizations, as Arnold J. Toynbee long ago explained,[5] gave rise to universal states. But capitalism requires the freer atmosphere for business enterprise made possible by a plurality of competing states, and so has half-consciously, half-unconsciously thrown its considerable weight against efforts to unify the *ecumene* throughout the whole course of modern history. The price exacted is great international wars to maintain pluralism and the balance of power. Indeed, since 1689, there have been nine systemic wars involving most of the so-called Great Powers of Europe together with various European colonies, ex-colonies, trading partners and rivals overseas.[6]

Clearly, the world system in which we live is highly idiosyncratic. It may seem like the only possible system, because it has been around for almost five centuries, and because it has spread from its native ground in Western Europe to engulf the whole planet, but nothing could be further from the truth. Like capitalism itself, the modern world system is unique, characterized by an unprecedented unleashing of productive forces, unprecedented progress in technology, and unprecedented expansionism. No other world-system has so thrived on growth. Its invention of unprecedentedly destructive weapons should come as no surprise, and we may be certain that we have not yet seen the worst it can do in this department. Ironically, how-ever, the present world system also thrives on the tribalism that sustains its plurality of nation-states. The intellectual brilliance and business acumen of modern civilization are accompanied by an inter-national political morality hardly more sophisticated than the poli-tical morality of the Huns, the Vandals, and the Goths. The Roman Empire which many modern critics paint as degenerate and corrupt, was in this respect light-years ahead of the modern world.

Nevertheless, the present world system is firmly in place. Nothing has shaken its grip more than briefly, including the bloody antics of Napoleon and Hitler. Even the arrival of nominally anti-capitalist societies such as the Soviet Union or the People's Republic of China has made little difference. These countries may profess socialism, but they are part and parcel of the capitalist world-economy just the same, their socialism is mostly a sham, and the managers of their state industries and trading corporations behave very much like Western capitalists in the world marketplace. Although no one should let himself imagine that the system is all that could ever be, or has been, no one should forget that it is also deeply entrenched at this point in world history. All its structures fit together beauti-fully, like the parts of a smoothly running engine. The problem of peace and war, therefore, cannot be studied or solved in isolation from the rest of life; and the future of human security and the future of human society are one.

The perspective adopted in this essay, I should add, conforms to conventional wisdom in one major sense. It assumes that the problem of peace and war is fundamentally structural or historical, not per-sonal or spiritual. Some futurists, and some peace/war scholars, argue in a quite different and perhaps still more utopian vein. They suggest, for example, that structural thinking is a male characteristic (as is war-making itself). Until the more typically female characteris-tic of interpersonal thinking is wedded to social analysis, they see no hope for real understanding of how to effect change in the struc-tures of world politics. In short, men and women cannot be expected to behave peacefully in organized groups if they have not first learned to behave peacefully within and among themselves, which requires an infusion of female consciousness into the peace process. As Betty Reardon contends, there are deep-rooted connections between sexism and warfare. Only when interpersonal relations grounded in equity and mutuality prevail over the exploitative ethos of male-dominated culture can humanity live in true peace. "For me transformation involves a profound cultural change of such consequence and dimen-sion as to constitute a different world." In such a world, order would flow from "changing relations rather than coming prior to them . . . If we cannot change ourselves, I doubt we can change the world."[7]

There is surely more than a grain of truth in Reardon's argument, even if one cannot accept her theory of fundamental differences between male and female consciousness, just as there is truth in the assertion, often made by Toynbee, that the prerequisite of lasting

127

peace is a transvaluation of values made possible by some sort of universal religious revival.[8] In *The City of Man,* I insisted that the key to the preservation of mankind was the evolution of a new world culture, with its own distinctive religious outlook, ideology, and symbolic forms.[9] In the long term, cultural change is essential, and there cannot be an enduring global order without it; but the real question is which comes first, transformations in consciousness or in material conditions? Does culture, which extends to the innermost depths of the self and to relations between persons, create society, or does society create culture?

Obviously the two are interactive. Yet in the final analysis the scholar must answer this question one way or another; and for adherents (as I am today) of a materialist philosophy of history, the choice is clear. Society, meaning in this case a capitalist system of modes and relations of production, creates culture, specifically a capitalist culture that extols individual freedom and exploitative behavior, including the aggressions of states in a pluralistic political cosmos. Capitalist culture reinforces capitalist social relations at every turn, but the culture emerged in response to revolutionary changes in the socio-economic order centuries ago, and continues to follow, not anticipate, the further evolution of that order.

The difficulty, therefore, with arguments such as Reardon's or my own in *The City of Man* is the premise that world transformation can be initiated by invention at the level of ideas, values and mores. If the materialist conception of history is correct, this is to put the cart before the horse. All ideational systems, including feminism itself, become possible only when the development of material conditions in the society creates a soil and climate favorable to their growth. The trick is to know when those conditions are indeed favorable, and not to act too soon or too late.

Meanwhile, the reality that confronts us is a thriving capitalist world system with a single global market and a multitude of sovereign, armed nation-states influenced by but never entirely under the control of the economic actors in the system. The world-economy is like a basket, in which all our eggs are gathered, but the eggs—the politics—are not what they seem. They are in fact time-bombs, ticking away. Sooner or later, if we cannot and do not act decisively, one or more of the bombs will explode, and through the long, silent eternity that follows it will not matter a damn which clock ran out of time first.

The Range of Remedies

Although most of the world's best minds are currently engaged in activities that make World War III inevitable, or that contribute nothing to its prevention, some time and effort have been invested in the search for peace. The literature, if modest next to the mountains of documents heaped up by the war-makers, is still big enough to defy easy classification. But most of the remedies for the war system can be encompassed under six heads: peace by strategic deterrence, peace by strategic defense, peace by diplomacy and disarmament, peace by federation, peace by civilization-based defense, and peace by civilian-based offense. The first two remedies require the warriors to prevent their own wars. The second pair require states to fetter their own sovereignty. The last pair transfer initiative to those who have for so long been "defended" by warriors and "governed" by states—the people themselves. When this taxonomy is followed, notice, the remedies for the war system are arranged in ascending order of difficulty, from the most attainable to the least. Most writers on the subject do not even bother with the last pair. Most of the few who do, entirely ignore the sixth remedy, civilian-based offense.

For that matter, some writers ignore the first two, on the grounds that it is a contradiction in terms to speak of making peace by deploying weapons. Political liberals and internationalists are always ill at ease when discussing such remedies. They have no use for the old Latin saw, *si vis pacem, para bellum* ("if you want peace, prepare for war"). This is unfortunate, because weapons have prevented more wars than all the diplomats and peace activists combined. The current nuclear balance of terror, which holds the Superpowers in thrall by its assurance of swift and lethal retaliation in the event of a first strike, is clearly a stabilizing force in world politics. Beyond strategic deterrence lies the hope of the Reagan administration that a layered system of ground-, air-, and space-based defenses can be engineered to foil any nuclear attack by any future adversary. It is even arguable that if all countries possessed nuclear weapons with which to retaliate against an enemy or if all countries possessed or were protected by impermeable shields, the world would become safe again. In the first instance, the unacceptable risks of a conventional war escalating to nuclear conflict would deter conventional warfare, just as the Superpowers today never engage in direct armed combat with each other at any level. In the second instance, local conventional wars might still be fought, but could never degenerate into world-smashing nuclear holocausts.

The case for strategic deterrence and strategic defense is in many ways quite sound, yet fatally flawed by two irrefutable lessons of history: the certainty that the actors in the system will eventually fumble and go to war in spite of all constraints, and the certainty of destabilizing technological progress that will render the "perfect" offense somewhat less than overwhelming or the "perfect" defense somewhat less than impermeable. There is no limit to the ingenuity of technology, as arms enthusiasts always say. But such ingenuity is not confined to one side or another in a struggle, nor is it confined to those who engineer offensive systems or to those who engineer defensive systems. Sooner or later the sharpest swords break against stouter shields, and the stoutest shields fall to sharper swords. In short, the stability now present in the world system is more illusion than reality. It cannot last indefinitely, because the human actors who manage the system are fallible and because every advantage conveyed by technology is a temporary advantage, soon countered by other technology.

What, then, of our third remedy, peace by diplomacy and disarmament? In this category, I include efforts by states to resolve or minimize conflict through agreement among themselves. Here the great bulk of peace literature centers, and here most peace efforts founder and sink. The roll call is impressive: unilateral nuclear disarmament, treaties for strategic arms limitations, proposals for deep cuts, the freeze movement, a comprehensive test ban, the nonproliferation regime, graduated and reciprocated initiatives in tension-reduction, noncoercive inducements, the campaigns against Trident II, MX, and SDI.[10] They are all exercises in rational futility. Each makes a measure of sense, but whether they enjoy public support, or governmental support, or both, they miss the point. No such effort can ever give us more than a little breathing space, if that, no matter how many votive candles are lit or how much ink is applied to how much paper.

When advocates of peace cry out for disarmament, they are asking the wielders of sovereign power, which requires the possession of armed force, to place hobbling limitations on the force that sustains their authority. Governments will not do it. No sane leader of a modern state could, or should. On the contrary, it is the responsibility of governments to pursue the "vital" interests of their nation relentlessly. Negotiations for arms control are perceived—quite properly, under the rules of the game—as another form of warfare, in which victory consists not in mutual sacrifice but in propaganda advantage, the swaying of allies and neutrals, and, *summum bonum,* forcing the other side by trickery or guile into accepting limitations that will weaken its military establishment while, in effect, leaving one's own intact. To ask nation-states to disarm is to ask wolves to guard sheep, or cats—recalling Aesop's fable—to bell themselves.[11]

I do not mean, of course, that no good can ever conceivably come out of intergovernmental negotiation to curtail the arms race. The high cost of modern weapons systems tempts governments from time to time to seek agreements that may place less strain on national budgets. On occasion it may also be advantageous to make small concessions in order to please allies or curry the favor of electorates. But for the most part governments only feign an interest in arms reductions; and they will never—if they are Superpowers—allow their military preparedness to fall below the level they think necessary to insure the defeat of foes in any war they might some day need to fight. Lesser states, such as the Superbabies (France, Great Britain, China), may rely on the threat of nuclear vengeance or alliance systems, and states lesser still on the shield of neutrality; but it is the essence of Superpowerdom to remain armed for any eventuality, and to trust no one.

The fourth remedy is not to reform the war system, but to transform it by vesting the responsibility for the military defense of nations in a transnational agency. In the classic form of this remedy, proposed by Grenville Clark and Louis B. Sohn, the nations of mankind will agree to pool their sovereignties and create a federal world government.[12] In more recent years, peace activists who incline to the fourth remedy have abandoned the notion of world government or a world state in favor of eclectic "world order models," as in the thinking of Richard Falk; or an "alternative security system," as proposed by Robert C. Johansen; or a "world authority," following suggestions by Silviu Brucan.[13]

To some extent, the changes that have occurred in world order thinking between the heyday of world federalist agitation and the present are merely cosmetic. Falk, for example, deplores the either-or mentality of federalists and discovers "intermediate world-order options" that "involve simultaneous dialectical movements toward centralization and decentralization of authority within and among states."[14] In part he is trying to be more "realistic." The consensus of scholars, after a period of early postwar euphoria (from 1945 to 1955 or thereabouts), has long been that world government is a pipedream, because the various national regimes show no interest at all in establishing one. Falk is also responding to the widespread view, traceable to the fierce anti-utopian tradition of Zamyatin, Huxley, and Orwell, that a world state would turn out to be a monstrous tyranny or, at best, a stultifying global bureaucracy on the gray pattern of "Eurocracy." Thus, to make a new world order system more feasible and more palatable at the same time, latter-day publicists feel constrained to clothe their ideas in an alternative rhetoric, liberally seasoned with populist, decentralist, countercultural, and other humane values. Such values conceal the main point of their proposals, Falk's included: that governments must set up some kind of world security authority to keep the peace, an authority that would deprive governments of the essence of their sovereignty, the right and power to make war. As Michael Mandelbaum writes, in a different context, the abolition of nuclear weapons is unthinkable without the abolition of national sovereignty.[15]

But even if the new models of world order are substantively different from those of the now-discredited world federalism, they merit the same criticism. At their core, they are schemes for persuading wolves not to eat sheep. They invite the complicity of national states in dismantling their own power. Such complicity will never be granted, so long as the present world system endures. The vested interest of corporate elites, career bureaucrats, party politicians, military top brass, and all their millions of hangers-on in the society at large dictates that the responsibility for state security can never be surrendered to a transnational authority. The war-fighting option is the last option that governments will voluntarily relinquish, and anyone who thinks otherwise is dreaming.

Which leaves us with the last pair of remedies for war: civilian-based defense and offense. If generals and statesmen are unable to give us peace, what about the people? What about ordinary citizens, whose consent would go unsought in the hour of decision before the outbreak of World War III, and who might die by the tens or hundreds of millions later the same day?

There is a growing sentiment among peace activists for programs of civilian resistance, not in the older sense of resistance to military conscription, but programs to set up an alternative mode of national defense that would render armed forces obsolete. Supporters contend that if a civilian population is trained to resist any invader by non-violent defiance of its authority, the would-be invading power may be deterred from attacking in the first place. Even if it does invade, it may still be thwarted and in effect defeated by organized non-cooperation on the part of the invaded populace. In some versions of civilian-based defense, limited forms of violent resistance are also sanctioned, such as sabotage of enemy facilities. But the heart of the idea is for all civilians to withhold obedience from their conquerors. By work slowdowns, deliberate malfeasance, and obstructive tactics of all kinds, a citizenry can make the occupation of its country more trouble than it is worth.

Clearly the part of the world where civilian-based defense seems to offer the greatest advantage is Europe. As Gene Sharp notes, such defense can bring down repressive regimes, as almost happened and may yet happen in Poland, and it can deny to any potential foreign aggressor from East or West the fruits of its victory, without igniting a third world war that would destroy the countries being "defended." "With effort, risks, and costs," Sharp concludes, "it is possible for Europeans—and all peoples—to make themselves politically indigestible to would-be tyrants."[16]

Possible, surely. Against certain kinds of repressive regimes and foreign invaders, civilian-based defense could work, if the entire citizenry were mobilized and deeply committed to systematic resistance. The applicability of the program to countries remote from the probable battlefields of World War III, to countries such as the United States, Canada, and Australia, is less apparent, if only because their people are more likely to be attacked by missiles than by invading troops.

But a larger issue is what to do about the already existing military forces and governments resolved to deploy them in war. The United States is committed to the defense of Western Europe, and so are France and Britain. The Soviet Union is committed to the defense of Eastern Europe. How can generals and statesmen in the countries that have adopted civilian-based defense programs be dissuaded from resisting with armed force, and how can their Superpower allies also be dissuaded from joining the fray? The obvious answer is that national military establishments must not only be bypassed, they must be dissolved. This brings us back to our starting point. For civilian-based defense to have a chance to show what it can accomplish, states must abandon their sovereign power. Theorists of civilian-based defense, in effect, agree. Many believe that only through the "full transarmament"[17] of nations, meaning the transition (phased or immediate) to total reliance on civilian defense, can such a defense system offer true security.

I cannot quarrel with that. Full transarmament is indeed the only kind of civilian-based defense that has any possibility of preventing World War III, although a judicious mixture of military and civilian defense systems might be helpful in preventing local wars. But full transarmament is a benign phrase that conceals a stern truth: it means stripping governments of their war-making function, and this will not happen without revolutionary changes in the wielding and distribution of political power. It is no less "utopian" than the idea of world government. At the same time it lacks some of the manifest advantages of world government, chief among which are the establishment of a world rule of law embracing all nations and the elimination of national military forces everywhere, not just in those enlightened countries that have adopted a civilian-based defense program.

There is also a certain naivete, reminiscent of many Jewish leaders in Europe before and during World War II and also of Mahatma Gandhi (who advised those leaders not to resist the Nazis with force), in the assumption that all tyrannies and all invaders will be daunted by civilian resistance to their authority. Some, no doubt, would be daunted. Others would not. So long as there exists anywhere on earth the means to inflict mass destruction, and an assortment of sovereign states equipped with such means, mankind is not safe from war, massacre, and oppression. Failing a simultaneous universal transition to civilian-based defense, the whole scheme may simply be a formula for mass enslavement or genocide. Yet if the transition does occur simultaneously, it removes the need for any defense at all.

I conclude that civilian-based defense, although more attractive in its methods than other remedies for peace, cannot and will not prevent World War III. Yet in its theory of full transarmament, it brings us within range of an idea of far greater promise in the long run: the idea of civilian-based offense.

Civilian-Based Offense

The phrase "civilian-based offense" is used here, so far as I know, for the first time. It sounds like a rhetorical riposte to proposals for civilian-based defense, but it is much more than a trick of rhetoric. It brings into play concepts and methods that have been known for many years and yet are seldom associated with the search for world peace.

On one point the two approaches—civilian-based defense and offense—agree. Little can be expected, their supporters insist, from the initiatives of armies and states. The key to unlocking the secrets of world peace is held by the rest of us, by citizens acting on their own authority. Such a premise is dangerous, because it asserts that the lawful world at peace desired by virtually every citizen can be won only by struggle that may violate present-day law. Armies and states routinely punish citizens who act outside the parameters of national or international law, even if armies and states often act in the same way themselves. On ethical grounds, some may also find an inherent contradiction between the goal of world order and resort to the techniques of disorder. Do good ends justify bad means?

Both objections to civilian-based initiatives can be removed in only one way. If the legitimacy of the present world system is successfully challenged, if it is understood that the people—from whom all rightful power flows—are no longer protected or served by that system, then (in the terms of classical political theory) mankind as a whole has returned to a state of nature. The body politic has lost its *raison d'etre,* and the only surviving authority is the general will of the body social, which must create new polities through revolution.

Schemes for civilian-based defense envisage such a revolution, but only in a limited and negative sense. They call for the withholding of cooperation and obedience, but, as argued above, they do not supply ways and means of forging a new global order, or of dismantling the one that already exists. In this situation, defensive measures are not enough and, taken alone, not efficacious at all. The need is for a civilian-based strategy of active, revolutionary offense.

In another context, I have examined one possible mode of civilian-based offense: the seizure of global political power by a consortium of multinational corporations.[18] In a formal sense, at least, the MNCs are aggregations of private citizens, and citizens with exceptional opportunities to infiltrate and either paralyze or gain control of the greatest armies and states. As long ago as the 1920s, H.G. Wells was calling for an "open conspiracy" spearheaded by international corporate leaders.[19] In the business climate of the 1980s, his proposal for the erection of a new world order that relies on the MNCs to help bypass the established system of sovereign nation- states appears more relevant than ever. The MNCs are many times more wealthy and powerful than in Wells' day. Their moguls move freely in and out of government service. The multi-trillion-dollar arms industry ensures the most intimate collusion between these leaders and all the political formations of the First World. Meanwhile, in the Third World, MNCs control many weak regimes dependent on their largesse, and strike deals with their counterparts in the centrally planned economies of the Second World. A "managerial revolution" of top corporate executives and Soviet planners to terminate East-West rivalry and impose a global directorate is no longer (if it ever was) an exercise in political fantasy.[20] The means lie ready at hand. All that is needed is the imagination and the will.

The emergence of a worldwide managerial technocracy that could prevent World War III may indeed be the next stage in the evolution of capitalism. What more logical end for a system that thrives on the devouring of smaller, weaker competitors than the triumph of global monopoly and its absorption of the bourgeois state? In earlier times, a rigid imperial bureaucracy would have stifled capitalism. But in times yet to come, when only a few corporations control nearly all capital, the neutralization of the separate states and their super-session by a managerial technocracy may suit the purposes of capitalism far better than the existing order. It is hardly in the self-interest of monopoly capital to support a system hell-bent on demolishing everything on earth, including all capital.

I view this scenario as entirely credible. It could be the "big story" of the twenty-first century. But various developments must take place before it can happen. The managerial elites themselves must become politicized to an extent so far achieved by only a few individuals. They must break free from the sticky web of national loyalties and ideologies that hold most of them captive. They must also cut the vicious circle of the arms race, by which businessmen lobby govern-ments to buy more weapons and governments reward businessmen who invest more capital in weapons production. The strategy of economic conversion to a peacetime economy will need careful hand-ling, from the point of view of the MNCs, to prevent even a temporary erosion of profits and power. It will be something like taking athletes off drugs, to make them more effective in their sport.

In the end, if the MNCs are successful, the separate national states would remain, but only as facades, like the monarchy in Britain today. A world directorate of MNC executives and planners would dictate high policy. A rapid deployment force nominally responsible to the United Nations or to some other intergovernmental authority would snuff local dissent and keep the vestigial nation-states dis-armed in all but name. In such a world order, freedom and democracy would survive as hollow abstractions, forever invoked, forever ignored.

Clearly, mankind would be well advised to choose even global managerialism in preference to World War III. Just as clearly, global managerialism is a strategy for civilian-based offense, whereby civilians—a small number of private citizens—occupy the command-ing heights of business, government, and armed forces to re-volutionize the twentieth century world system. But it is a strategy suited to the needs of a sclerotic late capitalism that would inflict structural violence on most of the human race. It would enshrine social inequality and attack civil liberties at their heart, by a system-atic program of behavioral engineering modelled not so much on the terrors of the Gulag as on the banal wisdom of Madison Avenue. It is a remedy only marginally less hideous than the disease it would cure.

But can there be a peace initiative by civilians that ends the risk of world war without turning us all into the clockwork oranges of a monolithic technocracy? The answer is yes! Such an initiative is possible, although it entails its own risks and costs.

Let me speak quite simply and frankly. In the nuclear age the appropriate response to the official terrorism of armies and states is the replacement of both by a revolutionary world republic of work-ing people. Such a vision may seem almost quaint, in light of the many failures and disasters of revolutionary politics during the past two centuries. For decades little serious attention has been given by radical thinkers to the possibility of revolution, outside the Third World. But the time has come to reopen the question.

In three ways, any new revolutionary politics must differ from earlier efforts. First, as Rudolf Bahro and many others have argued,[21] it no longer makes sense to contemplate a movement limited to the proletariat as defined by Marx and Engels in the last century. The ranks of the proletariat, of unskilled and semi-skilled manual workers, have not grown in our own century. They have dwindled. Thanks to the dynamics of mature capitalism, a new work force exists today, which consists of farmers and farmhands, salaried employees and wage earners, affluent and poor, brain-laborers and hand-workers, "middle" classes and "lower" classes, thrown together willy-nilly by the demands of an increasingly high-technology economy. Except in the Third World, the differences between these groups tend to blur over the course of time. The outcome is likely to be a more or less homogeneous, superficially bourgeois work force, reasonably well educated, with skills and comforts, who are nevertheless dependent for their employment on the vicissitudes of the capitalist marketplace, just like the proletariat of Marx's day. The hope of a new revolutionary politics lies in whatever success activists may gain in awakening the consciousness of this new work force. If they can persuade it to see itself as a single working class, deprived of real power and a full good life by those at the top of the socioeconomic ladder, well and good. If not, capitalism will have won a great victory.

The second difference is that a new revolutionary politics must be planet-wide. In the modern capitalist world-economy, the phrase "socialism in one country" is an oxymoron. Experiences such as those of Soviet Russia and People's China show how difficult—indeed, how impossible—it is to carve out authentically socialist polities in an otherwise capitalist world. The market forces are too strong. Even if socialism could be achieved in one country, the goal of the new revolution must be a world at peace, and peaceful republics cannot coexist with warrior states any more (recalling our zoological metaphor) than sheep can coexist with wolves.

In this context, strategists of civilian-based offense must be particularly concerned not to exchange warfare among the industrialized great powers for a new round of wars between rich and poor nations. Under global capitalism, it is well recognized that an international class system has evolved, with the role of the bourgeoisie played by the peoples of the "mature" economies and the role of the proletariat played by those of the "developing" economies. North American and European working people are in this sense exploiters of working people in Asia, Africa, and Latin America. If the new revolutionary politics should be confined to the First and Second Worlds, or confined to the Third World, it might simply exacerbate international class struggle, with catastrophic results.

Finally, civilian-based offense will differ from the older revolutionary politics in its methods, above all in the First and Second Worlds. The power of the modern state in "mature" capitalist and so-called

136

socialist countries is too formidable to challenge directly at the barricades. This power includes not only the full array of modern police and military forces, but also the subtler power of behavioral engineering through propaganda, advertising, state-controlled education, welfare programs, and many other instruments of co-optation and persuasion. It will take a long, disciplined, relentlessly patient effort to wean even a significant minority of the population in the developed countries from its unthinking loyalty to the prevailing system. Resort to terrorism, guerrilla warfare, and the like would be counterproductive. So, at the other end of the spectrum, would full participation in the games of parliamentary and cabinet politics.

All that remains to us is a strategy of gradual non-violent disengagement from the structures of established power. Some of the tactics employed would be the same as those urged by planners of civilian-based defense, such as strikes, slowdowns, and civil disobedience. Others would be more overtly political, including the creation of workers' councils and political parties alternative to the institutions of the old order. All these initiatives would be taken in what Richard Falk terms the "third system" of politics, the system beyond national governments and international agencies, "represented by people acting individually or collectively through voluntary institutions and associations."[22] Examples of third-system formations that might be recruited for the revolution are labor unions, church groups, student societies, cooperatives, free schools, ad hoc political action movements, and associations of professionals.

But the single most critical ingredient in civilian-based offense would be a planetary political party, not unlike the Green parties active in Western Europe in the 1980s,[23] with cadres working in concert throughout the world. The world party would ensure a revolutionary presence in national political campaigns and legislative assemblies, but would not under any circumstances accept a share of power in the executive branch of government until such time as it could assume full power. It would have the responsibility of coordinating the new revolutionary politics at all levels and in every corner of the world. In the advanced capitalist countries, the work of revolution would be carried out above ground, at least until it became a serious enough threat to established power that normal civil liberties were suspended. In the so-called socialist countries, much of its activity could take place only underground, perhaps following the model of civilian resistance in Poland.

The Third World presents a special case. Here the obvious weakness and unpopularity of many regimes often makes it feasible to conduct armed revolutionary struggles, just as the absence of civil liberties leaves revolutionists with few if any alternatives. But the Third World is not monolithic. In some parts of it, patterned after First World societies, the new politics can proceed much as in the First World. In other parts, patterned after the U.S.S.R., the new politics must adopt tactics appropriate to activism in the U.S.S.R. or Eastern Europe.

At all odds, it will be essential for the strategists of revolutionary civilian-based offense to avoid entanglement in the prevailing system. They may be tempted to act within the system, working up through the ranks of power and rocking as few boats as possible in the process. But this is not revolutionary civilian-based offense. As soon as anyone becomes a cabinet minister, a judge, a general, or a corporate tycoon, he or she is beholden to established power. Compromises are struck, bribes are taken, and the goals and purposes of world-revolutionary politics gradually fade from view. This does not mean that selective infiltration of the system by agents of the world party in various special circumstances should not take place. But infiltration by a few trained operatives and full-scale collaboration are quite different matters.

How might all this come together to produce a democratic world revolution? When could we hope to proclaim a people's world republic liberated from militarism, capitalism, and state tyranny?

Not soon. Although we must think forward to such a day, and begin working now for its arrival, it cannot come in the near future. In all likelihood the capitalist world system has many years of vigorous life remaining in it. The material conditions that will make possible its overthrow may not fully develop for many more. Perhaps a democratic world republic will be attainable only after the integration of mankind by managerial technocracy, defined as the highest and last stage in the history of capital. In any case, the process sketched above will require generations of struggle. Long before it is finished, World War III may deliver the final judgment on our species, without chance of appeal.

But only a civilian-based peace initiative, technocratic or democratic, can open avenues of escape from the toils of the modern world system. The present-day international order is little more than institutionalized slaughter and anarchy. After centuries of mayhem, it has now reached its *reductio ad absurdum* in a nuclear Tower of Babel erected by governments and supported by the blood and sweat of all its people. Every part of the Tower, including every one of its 50,000 nuclear weapons, makes a certain grim sense, but taken as a whole, it is a monument to lunacy. The human race is held hostage to the collective homicidal paranoia of its ruling classes. We have no choice but to mount a civilian-based offensive to end the terror. Because we must, we will. Whether our offensive will succeed, no one can possibly know.

Notes

1. See, for example, Herman Kahn et al., *The Next 200 Years: A Scenario for America and the World* (New York: Morrow, 1976); Willis W. Harman, *An Incomplete Guide to the Future* (New York: Norton, 1979); W. Jackson Davis, *The Seventh Year: Industrial Civilization in Transition* (New York: Norton, 1979); Paul Hawken, James Ogilvy, and Peter Schwartz, *Seven Tomorrows: Toward a Voluntary History* (New York: Bantam, 1982); and Barry B. Hughes, *World Futures: A Critical Analysis of Alternatives* (Balti-

more: Johns Hopkins University Press, 1985), well respected general studies of the future that ignore or touch only briefly on the future of human security.

2. The only sustained discussion of military futures in Kahn's *The Next 200 Years* appears on pp. 219-221, where it functions as a kind of awkward afterthought; yet Kahn was best known to the general public as an analyst of nuclear war strategies, a role to which he returned in his last book, *Thinking About the Unthinkable in the 1980s* (New York: Simon and Schuster, 1984).

3. I extract this figure from Ruth Leger Sivard, *World Military and Social Expenditures 1985* (Washington: World Priorities, 1985), pp. 9-11.

4. See Immanuel Wallerstein, *The Capitalist World-Economy* (New York: Cambridge University Press, 1979), and various other works.

5. See Arnold J. Toynbee, *A Study of History,* 12 vols. (New York: Oxford University Press, 1934-1961), especially Vol. VII.

6. The nine world wars since 1689 are the War of the Grand Alliance (1689-1697), the War of the Spanish Succession (1701-1714), the War of the Austrian Succession (1740-1748), the Seven Years' War (1756-1763), the American Revolutionary War (1775-1783, a struggle among the European Great Powers as well as a war of national liberation), the French Revolutionary Wars (1792-1802), the Napoleonic Wars (1803-1815), World War I (1914-1918), and World War II (1939-1945).

7. Betty Reardon, *Sexism and the War System* (New York: Teachers College Press, 1985), pp. 83-84. Cf. Helen Caldicott, *Missile Envy: The Arms Race and Nuclear War* (New York: Morrow, 1984).

8. See Toynbee, *Civilization on Trial* (New York: Oxford University Press, 1948), pp. 39-40; cf. *A Study of History,* XII: 535; and Toynbee, *Surviving the Future* (New York: Oxford University Press, 1971), pp. 40 and 66.

9. W. Warren Wagar, *The City of Man: Prophecies of a World Civilization in Twentieth-Century Thought* (Boston: Houghton Mifflin, 1963).

10. Two convenient recent anthologies of peace literature are Richard Falk, Samuel Kim, and Saul H. Mendlovitz, eds., *Toward a Just World Order* (Boulder, Colorado: Westview Press, 1982), and Burns H. Weston, ed., *Toward Nuclear Disarmament and Global Security* (Boulder, Colorado: Westview Press, 1984).

11. In the foregoing, I have borrowed some of the views of the so-called realist school of international relations theory, typified by the writings of Hans J. Morgenthau; but not all realists would agree with the analysis I have presented.

12. See Grenville Clark and Louis B. Sohn, *World Peace Through World Law,* 3rd ed. (Cambridge: Harvard University Press, 1966).

13. See Richard Falk, *A Study of Future Worlds* (New York: Free Press, 1975); Saul H. Mendlovitz, ed., *On the Creation of a Just World Order: Preferred Worlds for the 1990s* (New York: Free Press, 1975); Robert C. Johanse, "Toward an Alternative Security System," *World Policy Paper No. 24* (New York: World Policy Institute, 1983); and Silviu Brucan, "The Establishment of a World Authority: Working Hypotheses," *Alternatives: A Journal of World Policy,* 8:2 (Fall 1982), 209-223.

14. Falk, "Toward a New World Order: Modest Methods and Drastic Visions," in Mendlovitz, ed., *On the Creation of a Just World Order,* p. 223.

15. Michael Mandelbaum, *The Nuclear Question: The United States and Nuclear Weapons, 1946-1976* (Cambridge: Cambridge University Press, 1979), pp. 5-6.

16. Gene Sharp, *Making Europe Unconquerable: The Potential of Civilian-Based Deterrence and Defence* (Cambridge: Ballinger, 1985), p. 193. See also

such works as Alternative Defence Commission, *Defence Without the Bomb* (London: Taylor and Francis, 1983), and Adam Roberts, *Civilian Resistance as a National Defense* (Baltimore: Penguin Books, 1969).

17. Sharp, *Making Europe Unconquerable,* ch. 3, "Transarmament."

18. See Wagar, "Technocracy as the Highest Stage of Capitalism," in Frank Feather, ed., *Through the 80s* (Bethesda, Maryland: World Future Society, 1980), pp. 210-215.

19. See H.G. Wells, *The Open Conspiracy: Blue Prints for a World Revolution* (Garden City, NY: Doubleday, Doran, 1928), and cf. Wells' novel, *The World of William Clissold,* 2 vols. (New York: Doran, 1926), the story of a world-minded business magnate, suggested to Wells by the career of Lord Melchett.

20. See James Burnham, *The Managerial Revolution* (New York: John Day, 1941). A possible forerunner of global managerialism is the Trilateral Commission, analyzed in Holly Sklar, ed., *Trilateralism: The Trilateral Commission and Elite Planning for World Management* (Boston: South End Press, 1980). For fictional images of global managerialism, see H.G. Wells' *When the Sleeper Wakes* (New York: Harper, 1899), and Norman Jewison's film, based on a story by William Harrison, "Rollerball" (1975).

21. Rudolf Bahro, *From Red to Green* (London: Verso, 1984), pp. 219-220.

22. Falk, "Normative Initiatives and Demilitarization: A Third System Approach," *Alternatives: A Journal of World Policy,* 6:2 (July 1980), 343.

23. On the Greens, see Fritjof Capra and Charlene Spretnak, *Green Politics* (New York: Dutton, 1984). The idea of a world revolutionary party was also broached in my *Building the City of Man: Outlines of a World Civilization* (New York: Grossman, 1971), pp. 57-67.

Roots of
Potential Conflict

FIRST YOU PET YOUR REPTILE

by

Robert P. Weber

Fever; crying; pain; alcoholism; municipal boundaries; national defense systems. What could these have in common? Basically, they are all behaviors, practices and structures which have been developed or adopted by, or within, the human race to achieve the welfare of the species. Additionally, as is becoming increasingly clear, they are examples of habits or policies which can produce more problems than benefits when they outlive their purpose for existence or become too generally employed.

To be more specific, fever is a mechanism whereby the human body raises its mean temperature in order to kill off bacterial infection which is posing a threat to the welfare of the organism. Even slight elevations in temperature have proven successful in accomplishing this goal. Only recently has fever gained respect as an effective and economical technique for eliminating infection.

Likewise, pain is a perceptible experience designed to alert the body to an existing threat to its well-being. Its warning signals are meant to be noticed so that the business of the body is difficult to maintain until the problem is corrected.

Human emotions have emerged, with all their hormonal prerequisites and consequences, to facilitate the "fight or flight" response, and in general, to promote the maintenance of survival amid perils and status among peers. At the risk of simplification it can be said that our emotional life is engineered to effect social equilibrium.

As useful as these systems have been throughout history, it can be seen that such reactions as fever, pain and emotions can "overdo it." Tending to excess, they often create more problems than they solve. Body temperature can become elevated so high that it actually threatens the health it is suppose to protect, even though threatening bacteria are eliminated in the process.

Robert P. Weber is a Catholic priest who has been looking for a way to integrate insights from two or more sources. He is the coordinator for the Philadelphia Chapter of the World Future Society.

143

Pain, when it typically persists after its message is acknowledged by the brain, sometimes produces more medical problems elsewhere in the body. The energy for "fight or flight," or any of the other special requirements needed when survival or status are under seige, are becoming counter-productive in modern encounters with other people or with other understandable natural events. Additionally, the heightened hormonal activity associated with obsolete energy levels tends to do damage to one's own organs, as well as to the recipients of actions taken in fits of anger, jealousy or fear.

The examples taken from human physiology illustrate what is a common principle in many areas of human life, namely, that reflexes and behaviors which have served mankind well throughout history may no longer be practical in the task of promoting survival and welfare. They continue to be employed, however, mainly because, due to their historical record of success, they have become deeply reinforced—apparently in the inner, more ancient part of our brain—a part that does not communicate intelligibly to the rest of the brain.

Other aspects of human behavior pose the same paradox. Consider the disciplining of children. A parent may experience great success in protecting the welfare of his or her child during the child's formative years by frequently saying to the child, "Stop that, that's bad! I don't want you doing that anymore." But as the child grows into adolescence, such parental comments can actually lessen the chances that the child will learn or grow. Instead, resistance, or even resentment, may result as reasons are not given and the child seems to think that freedom has been curtailed. What had been a helpful, succinct mode of communication at one stage of the child's life, becomes not only no longer appropriate, but actually counter-productive.

Think about crying. Crying may be a very successful attention-getting device for young children, but this and similar vocal expressions of malaise lose their effectiveness after a certain age and, in fact, may reduce the chances for complaints being taken seriously.

Resorting to the use of alcohol and other drugs to reduce anxiety or to remove oneself mentally from a stressful situation can be shown to be very effective in achieving these objectives. Short-range success, by this method, is noted and imprinted in the brain. The continued use of substances, however, reaches a certain point when the dis advantages outweigh any previous short-term benefits. Eventually, with recourse to drugs, anxiety levels begin to increase, not decrease. It is then time to change behavior in order to achieve the same goal of stress reduction. However, by this time the inner brain is committed to "proven" technique.

"Be a winner," we are told. Striving to win, whether in a contest or in some economic endeavor, has been regarded as a praiseworthy attitude. Not only have individuals and their families thrived with this attitude, but it can be argued that civilization as a whole has progressed dramatically where the value of winning has been respected. Those who have won have succeeded where others have failed. Their progeny is alive today because they have triumphed. Looking at the contemporary scene, with the athlete's access to blood-doping and steroids for the sake of money or fame, and the salesman's temptations to deception, misrepresentations, and other self-serving behavior, the time may have come when a winning attitude might, on balance, work contrary to the welfare of the human community.

Moving to a larger scale, societies have been developed with national and local boundaries, the identification of four basic racial groups, economic systems, defense systems, and social ideologies such as human rights. Presumably for most of human history, due to ethnic constraints and transportation limits, national and municipal boundaries may have been the most manageable context for fostering human welfare, but can these divisions be reasonably maintained in our present "global village," considering the proliferation of adjacent municipalities, each with its own bureaucracy and budgets? Duplication of services is costly and generative of narrowness of concern and loyalty.

While the facile identification of four basic racial types within humanity may have been proper, from understandably limited knowledge for many years, the reality of universal gradations of skin pigment and interracial breeding seems to represent a more accurate understanding of human ethnography. There are no pure racial types. Economic systems have been developed to address a single question: accepting the inevitable scarcity of what is needed for survival and prosperity, upon what basis should society determine who will be the privileged group? Who should have primary access to the limited resources? This privileged group has been designated as the nobility, the royalty, the workers, the clever, the landowners, the mighty and the inheritors of the gain of one's forebears. But what if, only in our time, the concept of inevitable scarcity of needed resources is reasonably determined to be fundamentally incorrect? This was one of the key contentions of R. Buckminster Fuller. Have our economic systems meanwhile become so firmly entrenched that we are incapable of perceiving this new reality, much less initiating appropriate changes in our economic philosophy?

Individuals and national defense systems enjoy a long history of success in allowing persons and societies to survive as well as they have. Facing real threats, people have always budgeted heavily—to the point of moderate sacrifice—for the purpose of defense. The question of today, however, is whether personal and national defense systems are making us more or less secure. Do handguns in handbags and nuclear warheads in silos increase or decrease our opportunities for survival and general welfare? Our collective consciousness is strangely deaf to this alternative. It basks in its successful reflex of keeping us well-armed with whatever weapons are available.

The ideology of human rights, so highly valued in relatively affluent countries where the possibility of ensuring these rights exists, may be impractical in less affluent areas, and, even in more wealthy nations, may lead to heightened expectations, backlogs in courts, and a more dissatisfied, self-seeking populace. Does the theme of human rights, which gave spirit to many progressive movements, including our own American Revolution, serve the best interests of all the people today?

To look deeper at all of the above structures and behaviors, and a great many others, certain characteristics appear to be common. They have developed early within the human individual or species. They have been reinforced through success. Once reinforced,they are resistant to change and tend to outlast their purpose. They over-generalize or saturate when a smaller dose would be more appropriate.

There is currently accumulating evidence, notably in the research of the socio-biologist Edward O. Wilson, and the brain physiologist Paul MacLean, that the human brain plays an active role in the resistance to change. The ancestral, inner brain which we have in common with reptiles and lower mammals, is still present and active within every human being. Though our understanding of the inner brain's activity and power is still meager, it is likely that this part of the brain, with its exclusively tailored agenda of survival, actually filters out new information and new behaviors. This "reptilian" brain is not concerned with interpersonal relationships or with long-term solutions; it is in place to contribute to survival. Any change or threat of change, whether of input (information) or output (decision) is opposed at the preconscious level. People cannot "get into their own heads;" they "don't get around to doing" what is appropriate. In command are old ideas and behaviors imprinted on the inner brain through a long history of success and reinforcement. The problem is not merely motivational or educational. It seems to have a much deeper physiological basis than we would have suspected prior to current research into the living brain.

All of the above, while interesting to students of human nature, would not be crucial except for this: the examples cited pose real threats to survival and well-being, not only for individuals, but also for the entire human race. When people had nothing but angry words, sticks and stones, they did not pose mortal threats to the future of humanity. But now we have nuclear weapons. The question today is this: are the instincts, behaviors, strategies and ideologies, despite their record of success, part of the solution or part of the problem at this stage of human history? If they have begun working against us, how can the demands of the present age be effectively integrated into the mentality of all, both strong and weak? And how can new practices be realistically implemented? There would appear to be no getting around the old part of the brain which perhaps controls the channels to and from the "higher" brain. Knowing that survival has been maintained thus far, with whatever the body has been doing, its intuition is that nothing should change. What can be done to wean the inner brain from instinctively promoting the most formidable of weapons?

Perhaps the first step out of this impasse is our increasing ability to understand the barrier we face. More attention must be paid to the power of the inner brain. Current and future research upon the human brain will serve as reconnaissance. The work of MacLean and others has discovered the active ancient agenda of the so-called "reptilian" and "limbic" parts of the human brain. Undetermined yet is whether this inner brain has "veto power," strictly speaking, over the agenda of the cortex. What brain research uncovers, however, must be taken very seriously. We dare not try to encourage change in people with complete disregard for this silent, but powerful presence.

At the other end, lessons can be learned from the experience of educators who have had success in facilitating the assimilation of new information behaviors. These can be applied carefully to those areas of human life in which change is vital—particularly in such crucial and timely areas as the nuclear issue and world hunger.

Appreciating the barriers to imperative change, one could identify four steps that must be taken in order for appropriate change to occur. First, the agent of change should labor to understand thoroughly why present behaviors and structures were developed initially. (Appreciate how tenuous survival was throughout most of human history. Understand how necessarily narrow our vision has been.) Secondly, the agent of change must respect the success achieved by those behaviors and structures during their history. Both internal and external structures were remarkable and success-fully tailored to the urgency of typical situations. Thirdly, the agent of change should have ready access to examples in which the first two steps have been successfully incorporated. Healthy changes in style and structure have occurred. How has this happened?

Finally, methodologies should be developed that will "stroke" the inner brain *throughout the process of change*. The red light can flash at any point in the process. The inner brain must never fear that its own precious values and agenda are being undermined. Respect must be paid constantly.

In practice, what would this actually look like? For one thing, there would be more study and dialogue in an attempt to foster better understanding of the urgency that led to the formation of current behaviors and structures. There would be a heightened empathy for individuals and cultures, for the desperation and the fragility that they experienced in facing their perceived threats. Presumably the agent of change would be less judgmental, and might even cele-brate the record of success achieved by established practices. Whether the problem is alcohol or weapons systems or styles of child-rearing, there should be a communicated appreciation for accomplished short- and long-range gains. There should be a recog-nizable continuity between the goals of the old behaviors and those of the new. If any bias exists in the mind of the agent of change, it should favor the idea that individuals and groups try to do the best that they can with what they have to work with in confronting the realities around them. What may be vital today, whether it be disar-mament, health foods, discussion or global consciousness, may well have been unthinkable or highly unprofitable during the previous eras of human history. If the inner brain is to be stroked sufficiently to allow enlightened ideas and practices to happen, it has to recognize that the agent of change is working in harmony with its own agenda of survival as the most pressing business of life.

To ease the hunger, to cool the nuclear threat, to restructure political boundaries, more is required than appeals to reason, ethical exhortation, and, when these fail, hand-wringing despair. Appropriate changes do not come as easily as we would like. Our brain is more than an "enlightened" neo-cortex. There are physiological realities "up there" which we could not have suspected until recently. Trying to "be sensible" is not enough when the human brain has a long evolutionary history.

To implement what is suggested here, there is obviously a need for much more research on the composition and the history of both the human brain and the world in which we live. In addition, there is a crucial need for input from scholars and practitioners in all fields of human endeavor to contribute corroborative (and antithetical) examples relative to the thesis that yesterday's solutions tend to become today's problems. Especially from the wealth of educational experience, where personal interaction, gentleness and conducive atmosphere are recognized as crucial, wisdom can be gained in ascertaining what contributes to and works against healthy, necessary changes in outlook and resolve.

Much of the opposition is located, not "out there," but within us—each of us—in our remarkable brain, respect for which we are being increasingly called to affirm.

VALUE CONFLICTS AND THEIR RESOLUTION IN THE WORLD OF WORK

by

David Macarov

Although it is both customary and comforting to believe that values, whether individual or societal, are relatively fixed and act to guide behavior toward certain goals, examination and experience indicate the fallacy in this assumption. Rather than being clear guides to behavior, most values are ambiguous, short-lived, and full of internal contradictions, with little effect on actual behavior. Nowhere does this seem more clear than in the world of work. Fortunately, it is in this very confusion that there lies the possibility of a relatively peaceful transition to the almost-workless world which lies in the future.

The Work Ethic and Work Behavior

In the early days of civilization, and at least up to the Middle Ages, work was seen purely as an instrumental activity whose only role was to provide the necessities of life. The hunter, herdsman or farmer saw no merit in working to produce more than he or his family needed, with perhaps a bit to barter with others. In the absence of storage facilities, refrigeration, roads, transport, marketplaces, and a money economy, surplus products just rotted. Consequently, it has been estimated that workers had over a hundred free days a year (Buckingham)—days which the state and the Church hastened to fill with national and religious holidays, lest the free time be used for secular or subversive purposes (de Schweinitz).

One evidence of this human disinclination to work beyond the fulfillment of immediate need is found in the very abundance of commandments, admonitions, maxims, fables, tales, instructions and sermons designed to encourage work. Were there a natural desire or innate need to work such pressure would not have been necessary. Nowhere, for example, do we find any exhortations to engage in sex—that which people want to do needs no urging. There

---

Dr. David Macarov is a professor at the Paul Baerwald School of Social Work, The Hebrew University, Jerusalem, Israel.

is no lack, however, of stories, poems, songs and sayings concerning the beauty and importance of work. Unfortunately for beliefs about the joy of working, most of these were written by non-workers. When workers sang, recited, or spoke, it was usually for and about shorter hours, better conditions, more money, less onerous tasks, and better employers (Foner). As Galbraith puts it: "All who do not themselves work with their hands or with expenditure of physical effort (should) stop talking about the work ethic for those who do."

History is replete with evidence that people did not, and do not, work if they can get out of it. The institution of slavery, for example, was based upon the desire to get someone else to do the work—or, at least, the difficult work. Diocletian ordered sons to continue in their fathers' occupations, since they tended to seek easier work (Kranzberg and Gies). To nomads, including today's Bedouin and Aborigines, one who settles down to farm or to work is an object of pity and ridicule. The ancient Athenians, who lived in a complete welfare state based on booty captured abroad, the tribute paid them, and the work of slaves (Gouldner), clearly and publically abhorred work. Socrates said that work made people bad friends and bad patriots (Kranzberg and Gies). Plato thought of work as of no great importance, and Aristotle saw work as corrupting citizens, making their pursuit of virtue more difficult (Anthony).

Jewish life in the Middle Ages, and in some places today, viewed work as an occupation only for those without the intelligence or intellect to study Torah. The begging bowl of Buddhist monks indicates that even today work, for them, is not the virtuous way of making a living. Jesus rebuked Martha for wanting to carry on with her housework, rather than taking time off to listen, as Mary had done (Luke). He also fed the multitude with loaves and fishes, rather than telling them to go to work. Even as late as the eighteenth century laborers did not desire income beyond a certain level—commentators are unanimous in the view that workers preferred leisure to increased income (Kuman).

This is not to say that rulers and governments of various kinds did not make tremendous efforts to find or provide jobs for their citizens. The building of the later pyramids were probably job-creation projects (Mendelssohn). Herod started a road around the Temple Mount to create jobs for the workers who had just finished rebuilding the Second Temple. Vespasian forbade the use of rivers for transporting building materials in order to create jobs (Garraty). But all of these activities were instrumental, so that people would have incomes, rather than based on the value of work as such.

It was not until the advent of Protestantism, with Luther declaring that one served God by working, that work began to take on an affective value. Calvin's admonition that one was forbidden to enjoy the fruits of one's labor—since the act of working was important, and not the result thereof—added impetus to the idea of work as a value in itself. This religious aspect of work had superimposed on it a patriotic aspect as nations vied with one another for commercial

150

supremacy, and the philosophy of mercantilism became predominant (Macarov, 1977). The goal of mercantilism was to make the nation (and not necessarily the citizens) rich and therefore powerful, not only by conquest and exploitation as previously, but by exporting at a profit. Cheap labor, working as hard as possible, was a requirement for success, and thus work took on a patriotic value—those who did not work hard were betraying their country's interests. Incidentally, this view has not faded with time: There are still countries that urge workers to join the export industries and to work hard in order to acquire or ensure a favorable balance of trade.

The economist Adam Smith added another element to the world of work with his "invisible hand," which balanced the economy for the benefit of all, with high quality and low prices, provided everyone would seek his or her maximum economic benefit—"each against all"—which, for most people, meant working hard. Those who slacked off, or didn't try, weakened the whole fabric, and thereby their friends and neighbors. Work thus became a communal duty, and the non-worker was seen as a drag on everyone else's welfare.

Sigmund Freud added another value overlay to work when he declared that happiness consists of the ability to love and to work. For subsequent generations steeped in or affected by Freudian psychology, one who did not work, work hard, or like to work was somehow not normal, not mentally healthy, and probably not happy.

These values with which work became endowed penetrated deeply into the basic fabric of the Western world. All of the instruments of socialization were brought to bear to inculcate this view in everyone. The family and the school; the church and the marketplace; the media and entertainment all played their role. Children on the see-saw in kindergarten sang that Jack shall get but a penny a day because he can't work any faster. At the other end of life concentration camp inmates were told that work would make them free.

The success of this socialization is not only evident all around us, but has been enunciated: "Workers feel that the condition they find themselves in is determined by some kind of predestination and that they should accept their fate" (Schrank). As Pym puts it, we are slaves to employment and its institutions no less than medieval man was to church, baron, and manor. This is why Wilson says that the avowed, conscious pursuit of leisure has become a genuine test of personal courage.

Yet, despite this thoroughgoing brainwashing that has continued for generations, the deeper instincts of man continue to make themselves felt. Although the need for and value of hard work continue to be emphasized in speeches and articles, in editorials and feature stories, in presidential pronouncements and economic programs, the doubts and ambivalences remain. For example, everyone knows that people work in order to satisfy deep instinctual and bodily needs, and are unhappy to the point of illness if denied such opportunity. At the same time, everyone knows that people are inherently lazy; that no one wants to work or does so unless he or she has to; and

151

that if they weren't both paid and monitored, people would stop working immediately. Many other such paradoxical feelings have been identified (Macarov, 1970). Indeed, the same Sigmund Freud who held that happiness required the ability to work also said that as a path to happiness, work does not seem highly valued by human beings, and that, further, there seems to be a "natural human aversion to work."

In addition to the ambivalence which people feel about working, there is also the gap between values expressed and behavior practiced. In almost all attitudinal surveys of worker satisfactions which simply ask whether, or to what extent, workers are satisfied, the results are overwhelmingly positive. People tend to say that they like to work, like their work, like their jobs, and like their work conditions (with the exception of salary, which invariably ranks low). Given the opportunity to work less for the same salary, however, the shortened work hours are not only eagerly grasped, but often are the major demand in bargaining situations. The recent protracted steel strike in Germany, for example, was purely around the demand for a 35-hour week. There is no example in the recorded annals of labor negotiations where workers as a group refused the opportunity for less work at the same income. As Jallade says, "A reduction of working time is considered by everyone to be a step forward both socially and economically." In Olmsted's study, a solid majority of workers said they would give up at least 2 percent of current earnings for more free time, and one-fourth said they would forego ten percent or more of their income for more free time. Despite the lip service paid to the value of work, workers would be seen as insane by the rest of society if they insisted on putting in more time than that paid for.

Nor is the demand for shorter hours per week the only evidence of a gap between work values and work behavior. More and more workers are retiring early. In the United States, given the choice of retiring at age 65 on full Social Security payments, or of foregoing three years' salary and 30% of subsequent payments for life, well over half the retirees opt for the earlier retirement date, and the proportion rises every year. Neither is retirement the hell that the establishment attempts to portray. Most people who retire on a decent income are enjoying their retirement, glad they retired, and wish they had done so earlier (Barfield and Morgan). Those people who take a deep cut in their standard of living due to retirement suffer, but from economics, not ideology. Unfortunately, few studies of retirees' satisfactions control for the money factor. Further, the desire to retire is not necessarily related to either health or policy. Parnes found that 62% of retirees were voluntary retirees, and healthy. Some workers are healthier after retirement (Eisdorfor and Cohen).

Given the opportunity to continue working beyond age 65, all of the eligible employees at Northwestern Life Insurance retired on reaching that age (*World of Work Report*, 1972). When a steel manufacturer offered early retirement in the expectation that not more than 400 employees would accept, there was surprise when 650 retired (*World of Work Report,* 1983). When Peugeot, in France, made it possible for workers to retire at age 56 on 79% of their last salary, they were amazed when 79% of engineers and senior personnel, 86% of technicians, and 91% of shopfloor workers put in for retirement (*World of Work Report,* 1981).

Finally in this connection, underlying patterns of work which are at variance with the mythology of the value of work are found in the amount of time which employees waste on the job. Variously called "unproductive work time," "time theft," and just plain loafing on the job, the amount of time wasted is both enormous and growing. One estimate holds that such time theft cost the United States $125 billion in 1982 (*Working Woman*), while other studies show a constant growth in this phenomenon (Kendricks; Cherrington)—a 10% growth between 1965 and 1975 (Yankelovich and Immerwahr). Nor is management exempt: The average white-collar management staff wastes four hours out of eight (Olson). Yankelovich found that 78% of his sample said they could work harder than they do, and all of Macarov's kibbutz sample said the same (Macarov, 1982). Only 12% of Americans have been found willing to give the fullest effort, intelligence and creativity to their jobs (Gyllenhammer, et al). When women working in the Jaeger factory in Caen were told to work at their natural speed, they responded that their natural speed was not to work at all (Gorz)—a response identical with that given by two of the original experimental groups in the Hawthorne experiments, who were forthwith replaced (Carey). Cherrington studied building workers and found that 49% of their time was used for purposes other than the task at hand. Finally, Walbank estimates that the average worker expends about 44% of his potential on the job.

Thus, the value of work as projected by opinion pollsters, and obediently repeated by workers, is quite at variance with the actual behavior of those condemned to work. Ponce holds that the relationship with work gets weaker and weaker all the time, and Jenkins and Sherman sum up concerning workers' real feelings about their lot: "If religion was the opium of the masses, then work is the castoroil of the population." It is this clear conflict between values expressed and behavior enacted which gives rise to the hope that the crises and conflicts which will arise from the current shift from human labor to technology will not be as deep, divisive, or devastating as they might otherwise become.

The Transition to the Almost-Workless World

The modern world of work is characterized by two major contradictory trends: The continual growth in per-person productivity, and the concurrent reduction in real work times.

It has been estimated that despite short-term fluctuations, productivity throughout the West grows at the rate of about 2.5% per year, which aggregates to over 30% in ten years. At the same time, hours of work are decreasing. In Australia, for example, they slid from 53 hours per week in 1900 to 44 in 1946, to 40 in 1948, and were 39.5 hours in 1979 (*Technological Change in Australia*). In the United States, labor hours per unit of output have been reduced by about 3% per year, and the average hours worked per year have been reduced close to .5% per annum (Kendrick). Hours of work in the United States declined from 53 hours in 1900 to 35 hours in 1980. Full-time employees worked an average of approximately thirty minutes less per week in 1975 than they did eleven years earlier (*World of Work Report*, 5). Vacations are longer, too. For workers with 11 to 35 years seniority, five week vacations are provided for in 53% of contracts, as compared to only 2% in 1966 and 42% in 1975. 16% of contracts provide for six week vacations, as compared to 5% in 1971 and 10% in 1975 (*World of Work Report,* 4). Retirement is also earlier: In the 1950s, nearly 9 out of 10 men aged 55 to 64 worked. Thirty years later, less than 3 in 4 did (Levitan and Johnson). Even the number of legal holidays constantly increases.

In addition to shorter hours, there is greater unemployment. Whereas the father of the welfare state, Lord Beveridge, saw 2% unemployment as inevitable; and in 1951 the British government announced it would not tolerate an unemployment rate higher than 3%; and the Humphrey-Hawkins bill in the United States was intended to bring unemployment down to 4% by 1983; currently 6 + % unemployment is seen as built into the economy (Thurow). If one adds to these official unemployment figures the discouraged workers who are excluded; those people working part-time only in the absence of full-time jobs; those sent on training programs and thus re-designated students; and other definitional and statistical artifacts (Field), the actual unemployment rate has been estimated by a number of authorities to be 50% to 300% higher than the published rate (Levitan and Taggart; Kogut and Aron; Field; Macarov, 1980).

Taking all these facts into consideration, it is clear that despite relatively large reductions in the total amount of human labor used, productivity continues to rise. The reason, of course, lies in the continuing growth of technology which makes human labor less necessary. There is very little reason to believe that technological growth will cease, or even slow appreciably, particularly since such growth is synergistic, each change calling forth and making possible further changes.

Although there is the viewpoint that technology will make possible new products and require new services, thus providing employment, it is equally true that many new products replace, rather than augment, old ones. Further, most of the new products are simpler to manufacture and to service than are their predecessors. An electronic telex machine, for example, uses one microprocessor in place of 936 moving parts (Norman). Finally, it has been found that services are no less vulnerable to the inroads of automation than is manufacturing (Monk and Wheelock; Rada). Thus, it is possible to foresee a

154

situation in which the need for human labor continues to diminish, and the problem of providing jobs for everyone will become more and more desperate.

There will probably be a transition period marked by social unrest of varying degres, temporary solutions, and—unless the wisest planning is brought to bear—human suffering. During this period the search for the few jobs available will take on the nature of that which Jackson terms "guerrilla tactics in the job market." Governmental efforts to provide enough jobs will include time-honored and vain programs to reduce working times, subsidizing labor-intensive industries, establishing national service schemes, and training and retraining programs of various kinds. Eventually, however, when the bankruptcy of these plans becomes evident, and the number of people without work substantially outnumbers those who are working, it will become obvious that a new method of distributing the technologically-produced resources of society is necessary—that holding non-existent jobs cannot serve the purpose. Many hold that this process of dislocation has already begun, and will worsen as time goes by (Williams).

A number of alternative methods for restructuring the distribution system have been suggested. These include redefining work to include activities hitherto unpaid; expanding social welfare programs to cover everyone, and to give them livable incomes; ownership of technology by cooperatives; equal division of resources; and support based on need (Macarov, 1985). Such changes have been both called for and predicted. Freedman speaks of meaningful alternatives to paid work; Mouly and Broadfield put this in terms of acceptable remunerated substitutes for work; Wiggans calls for no longer tying work to income; Werneke and Broadfield speak of an approach based on human needs; Marsden explicates the basis for a broader conception of work; several writers call for breaking the existing tie between work and welfare (Mitten, et al; Wiggans; Macarov, 1980). Rada outlines a new leisure society and ethic, while Gummer says, "After spending nearly 400 years in learning how to work hard, we may have to spend nearly as long learning how to relax."

The restructuring of the economic system will both require and create a new set of values regarding work—or in place of work. Fundamental changes in attitudes will need to emerge for the social and political system to survive under the new circumstances (Dineen). As the *Canberra Times* said recently, "All our current social indicators reveal . . . (present) values to be dangerously out of touch with reality. The curricula, teaching, training and job descriptions of staff reflect an orientation to a world we've left behind." In a situation where almost all of the human work needed is performed by a small minority of people, work can no longer be regarded as the be-all and end-all of life, the measure of a person's worth, the only method of structuring time, and the preferred method of seeking self-actualization. Other activities and characteristics will take their place in the pantheon of values, dethroning work as the central

155

activity. These may be cooperativeness, altruism, neighborliness, creativity, honesty, religiosity, or humor. Activities to be valued might include parenting, volunteering, performing, engaging in sports, certain hobbies, producing art objects, or a number of others. Which characteristics or activities will rank higher or lower is not yet knowable, but that a deep value-change must take place to fit and to facilitate the almost-workless world is certain.

Changing Values

There is a tendency to think of values as deep-seated and long-lasting, resisting change with tenacity. However, an examination of the history of some values, and the experience of others, casts doubts on this version. This can be seen in regard to many values—in childcare, care of the aged, regarding privacy, in connection with sex, and as regards families.

That parental care is more desirable for children than that available in institutions—even in good institutions—has been a widespread belief among professionals and laypeople alike, at least since the abolition of workhouses in which children were separated from their parents. This belief, often expressed in terms that there is no substitute for a mother's love, or that even a poor parent is better than a stranger, was not based upon research, experiment, or experience. It was, in fact, a value judgment. However, with the welfare programs in many countries, which require of welfare mothers that they take any job available, the need for extensive childcare facilities became necessary—primarily to counter the excuse that the mothers couldn't work because of small children at home. The need for such facilities was reinforced by the voluntary entry of more and more women into the labor force. At present, more than fifty percent of mothers with children under six are working (*The Working Woman*).

As a consequence of these developments, the provision of childcare outside the home became a growth industry, and in its wake there came a value change which now holds that contact with other children, even as early as age two or less, is healthy; and that care by professionally trained personnel is more desirable than that offered by amateur mothers. Indeed, even the working mother is seen as better for the child than one who doesn't work: "Women with outside interests may be far better capable of coping with child-rearing than those who are sheltered from the outside world" (Raichle).

The same thing may be observed, in reverse, as regards the aged and the mentally ill. As institutionalization became too expensive, the value of community care began to be touted, and inmates were sent back into the community on the basis of their own best interests. This has been termed "returning people to community care within a community that doesn't care." In any case, there are few, if any, valid studies that show that people are better cared for in the community than in institutions, but the value of community care is posited as self-evident.

Again, take the value of privacy. At one time it would have been unthinkable in America for the citizens of each town and city to agree to have their names and addresses published in a book and thus made available to anyone who was interested. With the invention of the telephone, however, such books became part of our culture (Brody). Similarly, the spread of automobiles, which were sometimes termed portable bedrooms, made unmarried sexual activity more accessible for many people, resulting in behavioral changes which were soon reflected in value changes. At a later date, the discovery of penicillin and the pill changed sexual values in one generation, while values regarding homosexuality—which were in the process of rapid change—suddenly reversed themselves with the advent of AIDS.

The concept of marriage as an unbreakable lifetime commitment— "for better or for worse"—and the value overtones which this included are challenged by the fact that one-half of first marriages of young adults in the United States today end in divorce, as do 60% of second marriages, and that three-fourths of young divorced persons are likely to remarry (Glick). The value is quickly becoming one of being free to experiment, to withdraw from mistakes, and to try again—and perhaps again. Individual freedom and fulfillment are becoming the value.

Finally, take the value of the traditional nuclear family. This has been one of the mainstays of American life for generations—the model to which young people were educated, and to which everyone was supposed to aspire. This model consisted of a working father, a non-working mother, and children living at home. Today that description fits less than 15% of American families, and over 20% of the families contain two working parents (Sheares).

Values, it is clear, arise from—and do not create—situations. Looking to the future, Gordon holds that "Values change to fit the world which technology presents." Rescher is more circumspect, but nevertheless clear: "Technology acts indirectly, shaping the way in which other forces have their effect on values." In any case, it is the relative ease with which values change, despite the mythology of their tenacity, that leads St. George to exclaim, "How shallow are our values!"

Avoiding Conflict

Although it is possible that the transition to an almost-workless world will involve the kind of turmoil outlined previously, it is also possible that sensitivity, consciousness, and planning can avoid the excesses of such a process. The chaotic transition has been termed and described in the "cataclysmic scenario" (Macarov, 1980). But there is also in existence a "peaceful scenario," in which the structural and value changes necessary come about with a minimum of disruption and suffering. Then there is the "passionate scenario," in which every effort is made to bring about the almost-workless world for the benefit of society as a whole and individual's in particular.

The fact that people, in the main, do not really like to or want to work, despite their socially acceptable responses to the contrary; and the fact that what were thought to be deep, fundamental and unchangeable values have changed so easily in the past in response to new situations gives reason for optimism that the inevitable shift to an almost workless world may—at least from a value-change point of view—be devoid of the conflicts that many foresee, dread, and try to forestall. Toffler says that a new civilization is emerging in our lives, but that blind men everywhere are trying to repress it. That civilization may be the most satisfying civilization yet created on earth, and we must be careful that outmoded values do not delay or distort it. Perhaps we should learn from Browning's Rabbi ben Ezra: "The best is yet to be."

References

1. Anthony, P.D. *The Ideology of Work*. London: Social Science Paperback, 1978.

2. Barfield, R.E. and J.N. Morgan. *Early Retirement: The Decision and the Experience and a Second Look*. Ann Arbor: University of Michigan, 1975.

3. Brody, J.A., J. Cornoni-Huntley and C.H. Patrick, "Research Epidemiology as a Growth Industry at the National Institute on Aging," *Public Health Reports,* 96(1981): 269-273.

4. Buckingham, W. *Automation*. New York: Mentor, 1961. *Canberra Times,* "'Dramatic Reformation' in Education Sought by Youth Organizations," August 29, 1985, p. 9.

5. Carey, A., "The Hawthorne Studies: A Radical Criticism," *American Sociological Review,* 32(1967): 403-416.

6. Cherrington, D.J. *The Work Ethic*. New York: Amacom, 1980.

7. Dineen, D.A., "Anti-Unemployment Policies in Ireland Since 1970," in Richardson, J. and R. Henning. *Unemployment Policy Responses of Western Democracies*. London: Sage, 1984.

8. Eisdorfor, C. and D. Cohen, "Health and Retirement, Retirement and Health: Background and Future Directions," in H.S. Parnes (ed.), *Policy Issues in Work and Retirement*. Kalamazoo: Upjohn, 1983.

9. Field, F., *The Conscript Army: A Study of Britain's Unemployed*. London: Routledge and Kegan Paul, 1977.

10. Foner, P.S., *American Labor Songs of the Nineteenth Century*. Urbana: University of Illinois, 1975.

11. Freedman, D.H., "Grounds for Pessimism," in Freedman, D. (ed.), *Employment Outlook and Insights*. Geneva: ILO, 1979.

12. Freud, S., *Civilization and Its Discontents*. New York: Paperback, 1958.

13. Galbraith, J., "What's So Ethical About the Work Ethic?" *Washington Post,* March 2, 1981.

14. Garraty, J.A., *Unemployment in History: Economic Thought and Public Policy*. New York: Harper and Row, 1978.

15. Glick, P.C., "Marriage, Divorce and Living Arrangements," *Journal of Family Issues,* 5(1984): 7-26.

16. Gordon, T.J., "The Feedback between Technology and Values," in Baier, K. and N. Rescher, *Values and the Future: The Impact of Technological Change on American Values*. New York: Free Press, 1969.

17. Gorz, A. *Farewell to the Working Class: An Essay on Post-Industrial Socialism.* Boston: South End Press, 1982.

18. Gouldner, A.W., *The Hellenic World: A Sociological Analysis.* New York: Harper and Row, 1969.

19. Gummer B., "All That Stresses Does Not Strain: Job Safety, Morale, and Turnover," *Administration in Social Work.* 3(1979): 489-494.

20. Gyllenhammer, P., S. Harman and D. Yankelovich, *Jobs in the 1980s and 1990s: Executive Summary.* New York: Public Agenda Foundation, 1981.

21. Jackson, T. *Guerrilla Tactics in the Job Market.* New York: Bantam, 1978.

22. Jallade, J.P., "Central Issues in Part-Time Work," in L. Bekeman (ed.), *The Organization of Working Time.* Maastricht: European Centre for Work and Society, 1982.

23. Jenkins, C. and B. Sherman, *The Collapse of Work.* London: Eyre Methuen, 1979.

24. Kendrick, J.W., *Understanding Productivity: An Introduction to the Dynamics of Productivity Change.* Baltimore: Johns Hopkins University Press, 1977.

25. Kogut, A., and S. Aron, "Toward Full Employment Policy: An Overview," *Journal of Sociology and Social Welfare,* 7 (1980): 85-99.

26. Kranzberg, M. and J. Gies. *By the Sweat of Thy Brow.* New York: Putnam, 1975.

27. Kuman, K., "Unemployment as a Problem in the Development of Industrial Societies: The English Experience," *Sociological Review,* 32 (1984): 189-233.

28. Levitan, S.A., and R. Taggart, quoted in Levison, A., *The Full Employment Alternative.* New York; Coward, McCann and Geoghegan, 1980.

29. *Luke,* 11:38-42.

30. Macarov, D., *The Design of Social Welfare.* New York: Holt, Rinehart and Winston, 1978. "Social Welfare as a By-Product: The Effect of Neo-Mercantilism," *Journal of Sociology and Social Welfare,* 4(1977): 1135-1144. *Work and Welfare: The Unholy Alliance.* Beverly Hills: Sage, 1970. *Worker Productivity: Myth and Reality.* Beverly Hills: Sage, 1972. "The Prospect of Work in the Western Context," in H. F. Didsbury, Jr. (ed.), *The Global Economy: Today, Tomorrow, and the Transition.* Bethesda: World Future Society, 1985.

31. Marsden, D., *Workless.* London: Croom-Helm, 1983.

32. Mendelssohn, K., *The Riddle of the Pyramids.* London: Sphere, 1977.

33. Mitton, R., P. Willmott and R. Willmott. *Unemployment, Poverty and Social Policy in Europe.* London: Bedford Square Press, 1983.

34. Monk, P.J., and J.V. Wheelock, "Technological Change and Employment Policy," in Didsbury, H.F., Jr. (ed.), *Creating a Global Agenda: Assessments, Solutions, and Action Plans.* Bethesda: World Future Society, 1984.

35. Mouly, J. and R. Broadfield, "Objectives and Policies: A Reassessment in the Wake of the Recession," in D. Freedman (ed.), *Employment Outlook and Insights.* Geneva: ILO, 1979.

36. Norman, C., *Microelectronics at Work: Productivity and Jobs in the World Economy.* Washington: Worldwatch Institute, 1980.

37. Olmsted, B., "'V-Time' Pleases Employees, Helps Employers Cut Costs," *World of Work Report,* 10 (1985):3.

38. Olson, V., *White Collar Waste: Gain the Productivity Edge.* Englewood Cliffs: Prentice Hall, 1983.

39. Parnes, H.S. (ed.), *Policy Issues in Work and Retirement.* Kalamazoo: Upjohn, 1983.

40. Ponce, M.A.C., "Work and Youth in Contemporary Industrial Society," *Work Times,* 16(1983):1-3.

41. Pym, D., "Towards the Dual Economy and Emancipation from Employment," *Futures,* June, 1980, p. 225.

42. Rada, J., *The Impact of Micro-Electronics.* Geneva: ILO, 1980.

43. Raichle, D.R., "The Future of the Family," in F. Feather (ed.), *Through the '80s: Thinking Globally, Acting Locally.* Bethesda: World Future Society, 1980.

44. Rescher, N., "A Questionnaire Study of American Values by 2000 A.D.," in K. Baier and N. Rescher, *Values and the Future: The Impact of Technological Change on American Values.* New York: Free Press, 1969.

45. St. George, A., *The Crazy Ape.* New York: Philosophical Library, 1970.

46. Schrank, R., *Ten Thousand Working Days.* Cambridge, MA: MIT Press, de Schweinitz, K., *England's Road to Social Security.* Philadelphia: University of Pennsylvania Press, 1943.

47. Sheares, L., "Changing American Family." *Parade,* September 1, 1985, p. 14.

48. *Technological Change in Australia.* Canberra: Australian Government Publishing Service, 1980.

49. Thurow, L.C., *The Zero-Sum Society: Distribution and the Possibilities for Economic Change.* Harmondsworth: Penguin, 1981.

50. Toffler, A., *The Third Wave.* New York: Bantam, 1980.

51. Walbank, M., "Effort in Motivated Work Behavior," in K.D. Duncan, M.M. Gruneberg and D. Wallis (eds.), *Changes in Working Life.* Chichester: Wiley, 1980.

52. Werneke, D., and R. Broadfield, "A Needs-Oriented Approach to Manpower," in D.H. Freedman (ed.), *Employment Outlook and Insights.* Geneva: ILO, 1979.

53. Wiggans, R., *Welfare State Developments and New Technologies.* Vienna: European Centre for Social Welfare Training and Development, 1984.

54. Williams, C., "The 'Work Ethic,' Non-Work and Leisure in an Age of Automation," *Australian/New Zealand Journal of Sociology,* 19(1983):216-237.

55. Wilson, R.N., "The Courage to be Leisured," *Social Forces,* 60(1981): 282-303.

56. *Working Woman,* September, 1983, p. 48.

57. *The Working Woman: A Progress Report.* New York: The Conference Board, Inc., 1985.

58. *World of Work Report,* 4(January, 1979):8; 4(September, 1979):72; 5(July/August, 1980):52; 6(April, 1981):6; 8(May, 1983): 40.

59. Yankelovich, D., and J. Immerwahr, *Putting the Work Ethic to Work.* New York: Public Agenda Foundation, 1983.

THE IMPLICATIONS OF FUTURE SCENARIOS FOR CONFLICT RESOLUTION IN THE UNITED STATES

by

Wallace Warfield

Introduction

As of this writing, the practice of predicting the future or "imaging" as it is sometimes called has become popular and almost trendy in its proliferation.

In the 1950s and 1960s the preoccupation was with describing American society. What comes to mind is David Riesman's *The Lonely Crowd,* John Kenneth Galbraith's *The Affluent Society,* Michael Harrington's *The Other America,* and Kenneth Clark's *The Dark Ghetto* which in their own unique ways, provided vivid portrayals of America.

It was not until the 1970s, however, that futurist writing broke out of its parochial mode and gained widespread public attention. Perhaps more than any, Alvin Toffler's *Future Shock* was one of the earliest attempts to merge the insights of artists, poets and writers in various fields with statistical analysis and operational research to yield a synthesis view of the future. Herman Kahn's *The Next 200 Years* attempted to provide us with a view of world-wide economic prospects.

Like other disciplines, the study of the future has begun to develop paradigms or schools of thought that reflect the learnings of futurist writers. Thus we have on one hand the Herman Kahn-Daniel Bell view of a relatively conflict-free, continued growth scenario based on new technology, where the only crisis is a crisis of will. On the other hand there is the Robert Heilbroner view of a need for a major transformation and systemic societal change that will not be met. Somewhat in the middle between nirvana and apocalypse is the paradigm represented by writers such as Lester Brown and Willis Harman who look at the world soberly and tell us that continued depletion of the earth's resources cannot continue. That acquisitive capitalism whether industrial or post-industrial must give way to a

---

Wallace Warfield is the Associate Director for Field Coordination for the Community Relations Service, Department of Justice.

system that is redistributive. Above all they tell us that a major change in values will be necessary to live a more spiritual life and conserve our scarce resources.

Interestingly, there is little emphasis on social tensions and conflict particularly as it relates to race or cultural relations. From this writer's perspective this is an area that should not be passed over lightly. Whichever futurist paradigm one adheres to, the status of race and cultural relations will figure prominently in its development. This paper will examine some future scenarios and attempt to depict what race and cultural relations will look like. It will be supportive of some paradigmatic components while rejecting others. Above all, the paper will suggest a process that should be engaged in if all groups within our society are to move equitably into the future.

Significant Social Conflict in the United States Demographic Impacts

Most of the major demographic changes in the United States have been accompanied by conflict between new arrivals and resisting indigenous groups. This has held true whether the conflict has resulted from intercontinental migration or population shifts within the country.

Conflict resulting from demographic impacts has marked the nation from its earliest beginnings. What comes to mind immediately was the intermittent conflict between white settlers and Native Americans in the 16th through 19th century, beginning in the new colonies and then spreading throughout the country as the emerging economic philosophy demanded the acquisition of new territory. This was the country's first racial conflict as well.

Towards the middle of the 19th century and on into the middle of the 20th, two significant and overlapping demographic changes were taking place that initiated strife of an often violent nature. One was the great migration into this country from northern Europe that took place between 1840 and 1880 and continued on in somewhat diminishing numbers into the early 1900s. This was augmented by immigration from southern and eastern Europe after the turn of the century. This immigration was created to sustain a burgeoning industrial economy, but it brought with it a collision between the values and life styles of an indigenous WASP population and a working class Irish, Italian and eastern European mix.

After the Civil War, the African diaspora took a new turn as former slaves with newly won freedom moved in large numbers from the rural south to the urban north and midwest. Here, some of the most violent racial conflicts this country has seen took place as blacks struggled with white ethnics for legitimacy on the same urban landscape.

Recent demographic changes and projections for future impacts suggest the climate is ripe for more upheavals. From 1930 to 1960 roughly 80 percent of the country's immigrants came from European countries or Canada. From 1977 to 1979, this proportion fell to 16 percent and Asia and Latin America accounted for about 40 percent each. In 1979, the nine leading "source" countries for legal migration were Mexico, the Philippines, Korea, China and Taiwan, Vietnam, India, Jamaica, the Dominican Republic and Cuba. The United Kingdom fell to three percent of the total.[1] At this rate, by the year 2000, California could very well become the first Third World state.

Important Impact Factors

Demographic changes in the approaching decade will have a profound influence on the issues of potential and actual conflict. Looking at the United States regionally (Northeast, Northcentral, South, and West) significant changes have already occurred. The average increase of the black population throughout these regions according to 1980 Census Bureau statistics has been 10.6 percent and while the South has retained its traditional position as the location for most blacks in the country (18.6 percent of the total regional population), it dropped 1.2 percent since 1970 while other regions increased an average of almost one percent. The Northeast/Northcentral sectors contain 39 percent of the black population, precisely those areas hardest hit by the recession, resultant unemployment, and decaying industries. Contrastingly, the Hispanic population growth is in the West and in the South.[2]

One piece of data that deserves highlighting is the relative youth of the black and Hispanic population. For percentages under 15 years of age, 28.7 percent of the black population and 32 percent of the Hispanic population is in this age group. The median age is 24.9 and 23.2 respectively. The difference in the average median age for black/Hispanic minorities and whites is 7.2 years.[3] According to Anthony Downs of the Brookings Institute, in 1980 one out of every four American children under the age of five was black or Hispanic. He concludes that "At that rate, within two generations, or about 60 years, most U.S. children could be black or Hispanic."

Earlier forecasts indicate there has been large, overall shifts in the population away from the Northeast/Northcentral sectors to the so called Sunbelt region. Indeed, the National Planning Association in a recent study concluded that by the year 2000, half the jobs in the United States will be in just 30 metropolitan areas, most of them in the South and West.

More recent studies note a parallel though less definitive trend emerging, however. Here, data compiled by the Bureau of Labor Statistics suggests the migration from the Northeast/Northcentral corridors may be ebbing if not actually reversing. The Bureau and other sources point to a transition in certain area economies (New York City and Northern New Jersey counties as an example) from a manufacturing base to one based on services and information.[4]

Whichever trend holds true, minority communities will remain in a precarious position. As I offer later in this paper, a number of

163

conflict scenarios present themselves as possible outcomes from these developments.

The Community Relations Services' Response to Racial and Social Conflict

In the 1980s, the Community Relations Service (CRS) section of the Department of Justice, set up to respond to racial conflict and community disputes utilizing the techniques of conciliation and mediation, has begun to witness certain kinds of conflicts that mirror paradigmatic changes taking place in the country. These conflicts and the responses to them hold both promise and foreboding for the future of race relations in the United States.

What holds promise is the expanding use of mediation or table negotiations to resolve disputes. As minorities gain in sophistication and political power, their ability to challenge apparent discrimination and inequities has grown. In some instances, minority groups are learning that negotiation is a continuum step beyond conflict to redress grievances. Accordingly, local public officials placed in adversarial situations recognize that minorities are wielding greater political and economic clout that can disrupt the established order and have shown an increased willingness to negotiate.

The Community Relations Service has successfully mediated disputes in education, housing, police-community frictions, equal employment accommodations and voting.

What is foreboding is that resistance to minority advancements seems to have been renewed in demonstrable ways. Since 1978, the Community Relations Service has seen a precipitous rise in Ku Klux Klan and anonymous hate group activity. In 1978, eight of these activities entered the agency's caseload. All of these related to demonstrations or other activities by the Ku Klux Klan. By 1980 these incidents had increased to 99 and were no longer centered in the South, but were occurring in every region in the country. A closer look at the data in 1980 revealed that not all these incidents were related to the Klan. Over 30 percent were of the anonymous hate activity.

Anonymous hate activity takes the form of cross burning, defacement of synagogues, destruction of property and other forms of harassment directed against blacks, Jews and other social or ethnic minorities. From 1981 to the end of fiscal year 1985, these activities formed the bulk of this caseload. In fiscal year 1985, for example, they were over 80 percent of all recorded incidents.

In another area, the Community Relations Service has noted a rise in concerns of police use of excessive force. Typically, these involve allegations of local police officers who are usually white, exerting unnecessary or deadly force against minority citizens who have been or alleged to have been in the commission of a crime. These incidents have inflamed minority communities and have served as the trigger for civil disturbances in the 1970s and in the beginning of this decade. With the exception of 1980, these incidents have risen steadily in the last few years, although data from other sources seems to suggest the number of shooting deaths have declined.

Examining Alternative Futures for Social and Racial Conflicts

Most futurists tell us there is no single future that we will move into but rather alternative futures depending upon choices that are made now. A collective work produced by the futures research group at SRI International provides an opportunity to examine how social and racial conflicts might take place in the context of various future scenarios. What is absent from these scenarios, except in a minimally implicit way, is the affect the stated events would have on race relations and racial conflict.

Seven Tomorrows: Toward a Voluntary History suggests seven alternative futures that could take place. These have been labeled: The Official Future, The Center Holds, Mature Calm, Chronic Breakdown, Apocalyptic Transformation, Beginnings of Sorrow and Living Within Our Means. Some of these are distinctive enough so that implications for race relations and the role of dispute resolution can be drawn.

Sociologists and human relations specialists often view society as a series of interactions taking place along a continuum. This can best be exemplified in the Laue-Cormick model of an interactive society which is illustrated below:

- *Cooperation* exists when elements of a society can agree upon the distribution of resources.
- *Competition* exists when the legitimacy of power is questioned or the allocation of resources is in question.
- *Conflict* arises when the existing power arrangements are seen as non-legitimate and resource allocation is inadequate. No quid pro quo exists. The status quo is challenged through a series of actions, i.e. strike, sit-in or work stoppage.
- *Crisis* occurs when conflicting groups undertake unusual action to make their desires or fears known. This is often violent action, or some method of inaction carried to the extreme that traumatizes the system. (The Boston school crisis would be an example.)[5]

Most communities exist somewhere along this continuum and indeed this is not a static situation. Communities frequently move back and forth along the continuum as they react to various internal and external events. It should be noted that it is the rare community that remains stabilized in cooperation. Given today's economy and scarcity of resources, a status of competition is the norm.

165

I have modified the continuum to add Heightened Tension as an interim stage between Competition and Conflict because it more accurately reflects the deterioration of dialog between parties in a community dispute.

Heightened tensions is distinctive because parties at this stage are in a posture of non-communication or abortive communication. Incidents have occurred and parties or adversaries are leveling charges and counter charges through the media.

All communities exist somewhere along this continuum. As an example, the Greater Washington Metropolitan Area, despite retrenchments in federal government and private sector employment, shrinking local revenues and a declining but still unacceptably high crime rate, can be depicted as being at the competition stage of the continuum. Various groups are competing with one another over scarce resources but alleviating mechanisms are being employed by public or private sector entities that prevent the situation from deteriorating into conflict.

In contrast, Miami during and for a time after the May 1980 riot could be depicted as being in a state of crisis. In the primarily black Liberty City area where the riot was taking place, the status had actually reached disintegration since for a time anarchy existed. For other segments of the city, life had become dysfunctional as normal alleviating mechanisms and checks and balances were drawn off to deal with the riot. The interactive society model then becomes a useful tool juxtaposed with the alternative future scenario.

The Official Future

The Official Future scenario is reflective of the Herman Kahn school of continued growth through technological improvements. Decreased government regulations tied to a free market economy dictates economic policy. Productivity rises as does savings, income and output.

Unfettered scientific advancement leads to medical discoveries and successful experiments with grafting body parts, implants and even cloning. Governmentally-approved experimentation with mood-altering drugs lends an uncomfortably Orwellian tone to scientific progress.

A conservative economic policy on the domestic front expands per capita income for a larger segment of the population that classifies itself as middle class. This same policy, however, continues cut-backs in social programs and the chasm between the haves and the have-nots produces a growing indigent population. Entire cities are designated as unhealthy or unsafe.

The national consumption euphoria, embraced by this scenario, extended logically from the free market paradigm that had guided it for more than 100 years. But this proves to be myopic because "What characterized America's approach to problems was its doggedness in looking for symptomatic cures while ignoring the longer term consequences of its actions."[6] An emphasis on productivity at all costs caused increases in carcinogenic and lung diseases. Growing economic disparity witnessed an increase in urban gangs and crime. The response is security forces and private armies with behavior modification becoming an acceptable modality of correctional treatment.

Implications for Race Relations and Social Conflict

The Official Future scenario does not tell us explicitly what the impact would be on race relations and social conflict, but it is possible to draw some inferences.

The urban centers that dominate the aging Northeastern, Midwestern and Southern industrial areas will continue to lose its white middle class, despite popular but small "gentrification" efforts. The results of this could very well have been previewed in a 1985 *Washington Post* article that suggests an economic separation with racial implications is already underway. The article cites Atlanta, Philadelphia, and the San Francisco Bay area as examples where offices, high tech firms, and other manifestations of a commercial boom are developing in suburban areas away from these cities' inner cores and largely minority population.[7] In the Bay area, this process has actually been underway since the mid to late 1960s as documented in Jeffrey Pressman and Aaron Wildavsky's book *Implementation*.

The February 1, 1983 edition of the Ford Foundation Newsletter had this to say about migrational shifts in America. "During the 1970s more than 500,000 people migrated to California's rural areas, two and a half times the number that moved to its cities. In North Carolina, blacks have left rural counties and whites have moved in, attracted by jobs offered by relocating Northern industries in search of a low-wage, nonunionized work force. In Vermont, rural growth has been propelled by tourism, education, health care, and other service activities. Two out of every three Vermonters now work in service-related jobs." Clearly minorities will be the indigent inhabitants of the unhealthy and unsafe cities.

Since a post-industrial information society is not dependent upon the aggregation of raw materials in an urban setting symbolized by the old industrial model, minorities will be left behind to fester in decaying inner cities while new housing starts will take place where the growth industries are located. From this can be inferred increased tensions over affirmative action between low skilled, younger blacks and older whites for remaining jobs.

Indigenous Hispanics will continue to grow as a population in the South and West. This at least places them in proximity to new high tech, service-oriented and communications industries. This is not a guarantee they will gain entry into this job market. The Community Relations Service should expect affirmative action and other work-related tensions between Hispanics attempting to gain entry into

167

this job market and whites anxious to retain control. Across racial and ethnic lines, disputants in this part of the country will be younger.

Interracial conflict between blacks and Hispanics will increase in the South and the West in competition over jobs, services and political control. An apartheid-like situation could result in rendering familiar affirmative action solutions meaningless. Civil Rights court suits will initially press demands for access to jobs that could be as far as 50 miles away from urban cores with publicly financed means of getting there.

The evolving legal perspective is previewed in the 1985 *Washington Post* article. In the Princeton, New Jersey area, Rutgers University sociologist David Popenoe says "we are essentially letting two large, old, established cities (Trenton and New Brunswick) fall into decay while building a new city between them." And Princeton Mayor Barbara Boggs foresees "A soulless, congested, harassing anti-city" with little or no mass transit, inaccessible to the poor. Princeton and Mercer County have taken the matter to court, hoping to get a ruling that will enjoin townships from issuing commercial building permits devoid of regional planning. The case was dismissed in a lower court and is now before the State Supreme Court. It is interesting to note that this same court in a 1984 decision ruled that New Jersey townships seeking to attract new industry must provide opportunity for low and moderate-cost housing for employees.[8]

It is dangerous to predict the mind-set of the United States Supreme Court. However, it is possible that a conservative Supreme Court would not support these suits or other attempts to force the construction of low-income housing in these more suburban environs.

Affirmative action suits will then switch from seeking symptomatic remedies to the underlying industrial policy itself. The demand will be for the equitable distribution of a new technology. There will be some civil rights leaders who will look upon this with consternation as a return to "separate but equal," but this will be overridden by sheer economic need.

It is doubtful whether a government cast in the Official Future mold will feel a need to negotiate either through the courts or a mediating institution. More likely, the response would be repressive and controlling rather than negotiating.

The question is who will be doing the repressing or controlling? The increase in minority populations in and outside of Northeast/ Northcentral urban areas will continue to influence the political make-up. Already there are 17 cities of 100,000 or more that now have black mayors and at least 5 large cities are represented by Hispanic mayors. This trend will continue into the 1990s.

The interactive society continuum in this scenario would be schizophrenic with the upwardly mobile middle class viewing itself somewhere between cooperation and competition and a large (perhaps larger) disenfranchised segment seeing itself in a state of conflict, even crisis.

This is not a hopeful scenario for mediating institutions or conflict resolution. Society and its ruling government would have to decide whether the cost of repressing the inevitable rebellions outweighed the cost of instituting equitable changes.

The Center Holds

If the governmental action in The Official Future seem vaguely Orwellian, the precepts that emerge from The Center Holds are grimly so. Events in this scenario begin as in The Official Future but the economy takes a downward turn as food and energy resources become scarce. Rather than think through and negotiate change, a frightened plurality votes into office an authoritarian president and cabinet that takes its mandate to exert strong central controls over society.

Dissent is not only discouraged but actively squashed. An accommodating Supreme Court allows the undermining of the First and Fourteenth Amendments to be the basis for destroying the checks and balance system. The House Unamerican Activities Committee regains its old prominence and the increase in lynching and harassment of Third World minorities by a socially prominent Klan and other hate groups receives the benefits of benign neglect from the Federal government.

Society is highly stratified with a technological elite at the top, a resigned but supportive "middle class" and a disaffected underclass composed of minorities, women and those who protest the new rules on moral grounds.

Implications for Race Relations and Social Conflict

It is not difficult to interject racial and social conflict into this scenario for the seeds of its growth have been sown in the present. As mentioned earlier, the Community Relations Service and other public and private entities who have an interest in racial tensions have witnessed a rise in Klan and hate group activity. This has extended to our most liberal centers of higher education, creating an aura of acceptability that paves the way for the kind of institutionalization described in the Center Holds.

Observers of social/racial conflict have noted the growing sophistication of participants in the most recent urban rebellions. In the April 1980 Miami disturbance, there was an increased use of sniping and other guerrilla tactics employed by black Viet Nam veterans.

As blacks and other minorities continue to represent a disproportionate share of American armed forces and as these armed forces engage in more military interventions around the globe, the government creates a potential guerrilla army. As increasing members of disillusioned minorities are returned to festering ghettos, they will seek each other out, forming a natural hegemony prepared to defend an imposed territoriality. Conflict will develop because of infractions of containment. When black armies conduct raids into surrounding

169

suburbs as a form of resource foraging, they will clash with national guard units that will have become virtual standing armies.

An improbable Orwellian nightmare? Perhaps. But it suggests the logical extension of the Herman Kahn paradigm gone awry. In his work *The Coming Boom,* Kahn envisions a revitalized work force where baby boom children, minorities and women will be better trained and therefore more productive. More people are gainfully employed simply because of a continued growth in the economy.[9]

Kahn seemingly dismisses or ignores continued trade deficits and proliferating economic competition from abroad and a workforce on the lower end of the economic scale with little marketable skills. Even if one surmises that renewed productivity provides plentiful jobs, a government that supports restrictive private-sector employment practices barring minorities and women from equitable training and pay will relegate this group to jobs where the hierarchy of need remains unsatisfied.[10] Current data does not support the view that this group will be satisfied with relativity.

The Implications of Immigration on Social Conflicts in the Future

The projection of an economic paradigm driven by a consumptive value system leaves little room to entertain the problem of how to accommodate escalating legal and illegal immigration. Obviously, a major influence in the 1990s will be the impact of any legalization program that goes into effect within the next couple of years along with an increasingly troublesome refugee problem. It is estimated there is anywhere between 2 and 6 million illegal immigrants in the United States today. When a legalization program goes into effect depending upon how it is constructed, it will carry enormous implications for indigenous minorities. Whether real or perceived, these potentially opposing groups will face off over competition for jobs, social services and political influence.

There are already 500,000 Salvadorans in this country and the political picture throughout Latin America shows continued destabilization into the 1990s. Nor is the Caribbean immune from such conflict. Continued recession, high inflation brought about by a cyclical climate of depressed export markets and unrestrained borrowing from international monetary sources will destabilize these governments as well. Florida as a "point" state will be further impacted endangering an already fragile human ecology.

The net effect for mediating institutions such as the Community Relations Service will be the probability of intervening or responding to increased tensions or conflicts of an intercultural nature. While the conciliation/mediation paradigm will remain largely intact, these new disputes will have implications for intervention techniques, e.g. styles of mediating, linguistic skills, and non-verbal body language.

The influx of southeast Asian refugees along the Texas Gulf Coast gave rise to serious tensions and conflict between refugees and indigenous white fishermen from 1979 through 1981.

170

As John Perez, Regional Director for the Community Relations Services' Southwest Region noted:

> Refugee resettlement of Indo-Chinese along the Texas Gulf Coast has reached a point where the whole problem may have resolved itself. According to native fishermen, Indo-Chinese have in effect taken over the industry and have relegated most natives to look for ways to cash in on the Viets' industry advances by cooperating in their efforts. There no longer seems to exist a struggle for who will control the industry. There appears to be only growth in sight for the Viets and diminishing returns for the natives.

He goes on to cite as an example:

> Along the Seabrook Coast area the Vietnamese now own eight of the ten largest commercial fishing houses formerly owned by Native Americans. Most boat docks have also been acquired by the Indo-Chinese. Native fishermen in this business survived only by forming partnerships with the Indo-Chinese. Natives predict a complete Indo-Chinese domination of the fishing industry along the entire Coast in the very near future.

The Population Reference Bureau provides an equally dramatic view. Beginning in the year 1980 and projecting through 2080, it has estimated the impact that net immigration will have on the United States—given current trends.

In its most conservative projection, by the year 2000 (just 16 years from now), the bureau suggests that the combined Hispanic, Asian and most likely other Third World immigrants will be almost as large as the black population. By 2080, this combined group will have grown to be more than one and a half times as large as the black population.

With a net immigration of 1.5 million, by the year 2080 they predict a combined Hispanic, Asian and "other" population three times as large as blacks with the white population a minority at 43.5 percent. The United States will be a Third World country.

An Alternative Future: A Role for Mediating Institutions

The rather foreboding previous scenarios are derivative of aspects of our current socio-economic paradigm. As Willis Harman notes, "The basic paradigm that has dominated the industrial era with its emphasis on individualism, free enterprise, production, consumption and materialism, has resulted in processes and states, e.g., waste and exploitation which end up counteracting human ends."[11] Harman states that higher human needs such as enriching work roles, environmental enhancement, and sharing are threatened by this value set.

What Harman offers is a counterparadigm based on a technology that is smaller in scale, decentralized, environmentally accommodating to the human need and as Naisbitt so adroitly puts it in *Megatrends,* combines "high tech with high touch." This counterparadigm would grapple with the growth dilemma through a redirecting of values. The emphasis would be on productivity in human terms towards a frugal society without sacrificing individual growth and development.

Some of Harman's recommendations to meet the coming transformation seem utopian. For instance, in *An Incomplete Guide to the Future* he notes that unemployment and worker dissatisfaction are buried triggers for social tension and racial unrest.[12] Since many educated and middle income workers are locked into repetitive and unrewarding jobs, he recommends that corporations and government invest in their talent through the provision of sabbaticals and other alternative reward systems. The return on investment would be a rejuvenated more highly productive worker. The unemployed could then be trained to take those jobs that are vacated.

Harman's solution overlooks the awesome attitudinal restructuring that would have to be undertaken to make this possible. At the heart of the difficulty lies a fundamentally racial and class consciousness. Even though this cadre of dissatisfied, middle-income workers may be willing to take various forms of leave for higher, cerebral opportunities, they might be opposed to the admittance into the mainstream of those people whose plight has been traditionally used as a measure of their own progress. Those on the other end would have to be infused with a desire for success and a willingness to take risks, a change in attitude that could only come about through a major training effort. It is also doubtful that enough opportunities could be found to make such a program quantitatively meaningful.

What is inviting about Harman's concept, however, is that it opens the door to negotiations and enhances the role of mediating institutions. The idea that a prevailing paradigm clashes with an emerging counterparadigm to produce a new society is in fact underway. The Civil Rights movement ushered in a new set of values that influenced and shaped the emerging counterparadigm. The quality of opportunity in the workplace for racial minorities forced employers to reexamine beliefs and values about hiring, promotion and work skills that paved the way for the women's movement. Despite recent controversy over affirmative action, a metamorphosis of the American workforce has taken place. Affirmative action law and employment practices that seek to redress past grievances have largely been brought about through a negotiating process. To assist in the transformation, mediating institutions such as the Community Relations Service have and will continue to play a role.

Inferential in earlier discussion, the refugee and immigration flows into the United States have challenged some of the prevailing paradigms about work (Texas Gulf Coast fishing), living (different, therefore clashing cultural styles), and social service educational infrastructures (welfare provision, educational instruction).

This metamorphosis will result in the United States being a much more heterogeneous society where the current ethic will be replaced by a multicultural, multiracial, mixed-gender decision-making atmosphere.

172

It would be a mistake to think of the counterparadigm as a monolithic movement that has achieved total consensus. Within it are contradictions and divergencies. The concept of educational equity has moved from "separate but equal" to the practice in the last 20 years to use of busing as a means to integrate schools and therefore achieve educational parity for minority children. But the realities of demographic shifts and suburban political power has made this an increasingly difficult and frustrating technique to employ. Busing has been largely a one-way burden for minorities with visible benefits evolving too slowly for parents who want satisfaction within their lifetime.

Black parents in the Hunters' Point section of San Francisco, despairing of the proposed court-ordered school desegregation plan that would have closed a school that had become a cherished neighborhood institution, demonstrated for its retention. They were successful and negotiated an agreement that it would remain open to serve black preschoolers.

Those in the vanguard of the counterparadigm who are negotiating for change would do well not to become so enmeshed in doctrinaire solutions that they do not hear the inner voices. The mediation function is integral to this process of transformation for it is essentially a humanist-optimist view of society that plays an "agent of reality" role to manage the accompanying conflicts. Whether we survive as a truly democratic society or head down the road towards repressive centralism depends upon the success of mediating institutions to demonstrate that solutions can be negotiated where everyone wins something.

Notes

1. James Fallows, "The New Immigrants—How They're Affecting Us," *The Atlantic Monthly,* November 1983, p. 46.
2. U.S. Bureau of the Census, *1980 Report.*
3. Ibid.
4. William K. Stevens, "Population's Rise in the Northeast Reverses a Trend," *The New York Times,* April 7, 1985.
5. James Laue and Gerald Cormick are well-known theoriticians and practioners in the field of dispute resolution.
6. Paul Hawken, James Ogilvy, Peter Schwartz, *Seven Tomorrows,* (New York: Bantam Books, 1982), p. 38.
7. Neal R. Peirce, "America Resegregates Itself," *The Washington Post,* August 25, 1985.
8. Ibid.
9. Herman Kahn, *The Coming Boom* (New York: Simon & Schuster, Inc., 1982), p. 15.
10. A.H. Maslow postulated that human needs arrange themselves in hierarchies of prepotency. One need usually rests upon the satisfaction of another.
11. Willis W. Harman, *An Incomplete Guide to the Future* (New York and London: W.W. Norton & Co., 1979), p. 53.
12. Ibid.

THE GROWTH OF PRIVATE DISOBEDIENCE

by

Randall L. Scheel

Both tyranny and democracy have long felt the impact of civil disobedience—nonviolent opposition to government policy. But there is now occurring in the United States a number of seemingly random and unrelated events exemplifying a new and unique phenomenon. It is similar to civil disobedience in many ways but very different in others.

Consider these recent events:

- In Pennsylvania a group of unemployed steel workers placed dead fish in their banks' safe-deposit boxes. The stench that resulted was to protest the banks' unwillingness to continue financial support of financially troubled local steel mills.
- Abortion clinics throughout the U.S. are being picketed and bombed; their employees and patients harrassed. These acts are not directed against medicine or the government—they are protests against abortion.
- In the rapidly growing direct mail industry, recipients of offers who feel their privacy is being invaded by "junk mail," are returning empty business reply envelopes. They do this knowing it costs the company postage to receive the empty letters.
- Environmental activists in the Northwest are pounding nails into trees designated to be harvested. This can ruin chainsaw blades as well as endanger the logger. It is proving to be effective.
- Disgruntled employees are sabotaging their employers' electronic information systems by causing computer programs to self-destruct at a later date. These "logic bombs" are usually activated after the employee has left the organization.

Taken together, these events indicate a new type of public militancy. It can be called private disobedience. It is different from civil disobedience in two ways. It is directed against the private sector, not the government as civil disobedience is, and it is sometimes violent.

Randall L. Scheel is president of R.L. Scheel and Colleagues, a consulting firm specializing in issues management.

Private disobedience, therefore, is characterized by deliberate acts of protest, sometimes violent, directed against the private sector.

Demographic Driving Forces

Research findings indicate that demography provides the longest range accuracy in forecasting—up to 15 years. Therefore, we can pretty much know the composition of American society between now and the year 2000, and we can speculate on how it may contribute to the growth of private disobedience. During the next 15 years the number of middle-aged Americans (age 35-44) will be increasing by 50%, reflecting the maturing of the post-World War II baby boom generation. As young adults, their large numbers created a surplus of new recruits that drove down entry-level wages and limited employment opportunities. Now, as growing numbers of this generation move into middle age, they will be moving into mid-career, with associated expectations for upward mobility. But, because of the rapid increase in the numbers of candidates for a relatively limited number of promotional opportunities, millions of baby boomers will be faced with what demographers call "mid-career compaction" due to "generational crowding." In 1975, there was an average of 10 candidates for every mid-career promotion opportunity in the U.S. There are currently 18 to 20 candidates for every mid-career vacancy, and by the mid-1990s, the ratio may be 30 to 1, or higher. Labor force analysts believe that as upward mobility is increasingly curtailed, there will be rising worker frustration, alienation and stress, leading to reduced productivity and higher turnover.[1] They have, however, largely neglected to include the probability of more incidences of private disobedience.

Added to these discomforting statistics is the recent slaughter of middle management ranks due, not solely to "generational crowding" but the realization that fewer managers de-bureaucratize the organization. This frequently means decisions are made more efficiently at a lower cost, a very attractive option in our challenging economic environment. Even those who are left unscathed must work harder and under stiffer demands for good performance. In this age of entitlements and rising expectations how long will the middle manager, not to mention the *unemployed* middle manager, take it?

Another more direct demographic influence driving private disobedience is the aging of American society. By the year 2000, over 13% of our population will be over 65 years old. This represents approximately twice as many as there were in 1940, and these retired people are active and taking an increased interest in social change. At the fourth biennial Gray Panthers convention, held in Washington, D.C. in 1981, resolutions on the following topics were adopted: Social Security, peace, mental and physical health, housing, legal services, long-term health care, nuclear energy, the Family Protection Act, hiring under the Older Americans Act, defense, the right to die with dignity, employment, and priority for those in greatest economic or social need under the Older Americans Act. Given this wide range of issues it is not insignificant that older people have, more than any other demographic cohort, the most discretionary time to act on these vital concerns. And it does not seem reckless to assume that in their opposition to perceived social injustices, private disobedience will play a part in their efforts to accomplish their goals.

Within a longer demographic time frame we can speculate what might occur as the baby boomers mature. The trend is clear—they have already stressed our educational institutions and are currently stressing our job markets. In the future they are going to place an enormous stress on pension plans, Social Security, medical and social care, and other institutions concerned with later life. As they approach retirement they will have to balance their own needs with those of their parents and even grandparents. The situation will be exacerbated by the low level of savings Americans tend to have as well as our increasingly longer life spans. In addition, as the boomers reach the oldest ages, they will have fewer family members to turn to for help because of the trend toward having fewer children. This crisis will grow rapidly as the population of the most frail elders increases. Now one third of all elders, those in need of more acute care will comprise 40% in only 10 years. This will be particularly true for older women, blacks, and Hispanics since these groups of elderly are growing even faster than the total 65-and-over population.[2]

Looking further into the future the dependency picture is even gloomier. The ratio of retirees to workers is expected to rise from around 20% in 1980 to 23% by 2000, to 33% by 2020, and to 42% by 2030. By 2055 the ratio would be more than 50%—just two workers for every pensioner. The anxiety and anger that may accompany this "granny crisis" is likely to result in as yet unimagined acts of private disobedience directed at equally unanticipated targets.[3]

Social Class Driving Forces

Due primarily to the prolonged economic recession and the pervasive shift from a manufacturing economy to a service economy, a case can be made that the American middle class is shrinking. U.S. Census Bureau statistics show that families with annual earnings of between $15,000 and $35,000 (using 1982 dollars as a basis) made up 44% of all families in 1982, down from 53% in 1970.[4]

The results are obvious in such cities as Johnstown, Pennsylvania, Akron, Ohio and Gary, Indiana. These cities are polarizing into two fairly distinct groups of residents. Relatively well off retirees and a growing number of the poor and recently unemployed. A similar situation is occurring in major cities such as New York and San Francisco where the middle class is being forced out by higher costs of housing.

Those who are employed in the newer high tech and service oriented industries tend, as a whole, to be paid substantially less than their manufacturing forerunners. In these companies the polarization is internal. Income distribution in high tech companies, for example, tends to be high for management and engineering and low for assembly workers. Certain consequences seem inevitable. The lower income workers, including secretaries, will be persuaded to unionize and increasing competition for high-paying jobs will lead to conflict, tension and frustration. For many, the only outlet will be direct and deliberate acts against the organization perceived as responsible for their plight.

Again, shifting our view further to the future we can identify other less obvious "vulnerable" groups, portions of society that may not necessarily share in its general well-being that could have a negative impact on the operation of U.S. business in the 1990s. These include the semi-skilled blue collar workers, many whose jobs will be replaced by automation, immigrants with few skills and little knowledge of English, and those youth in disadvantaged public schools where overall performance levels are well below national norms.[5] But, less obvious and perhaps more serious, is the large mass of people who will not derive the full benefit from the shift to the information/communications era. One aspect of the controversy is already heated as Congress debates, in the face of increasing rates, whether every American has the right to a telephone.[6] Phone companies report they are disconnecting more residential phones for nonpayment than at any time in decades, perhaps since the Great Depression.[7] To be unable to afford a telephone today may not seem extremely serious but with the coming of the wired household, without it one is denied considerble access to the rest of the world. With the explosion of on-line computer services are we pricing people out of education? Some contend that computers are already driving a wedge in our society, separating the country into classes of information rich and poor. A Louis Harris poll indicates:

- 68% of college graduates say they know how to use a computer; only 16% of those who didn't finish high school are computer-literate.
- 67% of those with incomes above $35,000 can operate computers, compared to 23% of those making less than $7,500.[8]

Even if Congress does decide that every American has the right to a telephone, it may eventually be asked to decide whether every American has the right to a home computer. Is the telephone and computer a right or a privilege? This is the question which will be at the center of one of the most critical issues of the next 10 years. The resolution of it will answer an impending question the government and the private sector is anxious to have answered: Which will contribute more to public militancy, greater access to information or more restricted access to information? Seventy years ago the Luddites consciously refused the modern world and chose to live a simple life in peaceful coexistence with those around them. Can we expect the techno-peasants of the future to do the same?

177

Special Interest Group Driving Forces

In spite of a seemingly conservative political shift in the U.S. we are witnessing a dramatic resurgence of environmentalism. Only this time it's different. Environmentalists are joining other groups for greater clout. Consumer, labor, and environmental groups are demonstrating a striking new ability to work effectively with each other. Furthermore, there has recently been a tremendous growth of grass-roots activism. Unlike the handful of national groups that led the environmental movement of the 1970s, thousands of small, local groups are currently springing up to put pressure on business. The strong public demand for a clean environment has resulted in intense pressure at the state and local levels. This sudden shift to local politics has caught business lobbyists by surprise; they have previously concentrated on Washington. The new laws tend to be tougher and costlier for business than those previously enacted at the federal level. It is easy to believe pollster George Gallup when he recently called the commitment to the environment the most deeply and widely held value his research has ever uncovered among Americans.[9]

When considered in the context of our technologically based environment and the role that microelectronics will continue to play in shaping society, these deeply held values take on more significant meaning. Microelectronics now has a world market of more than $19 billion and a direct workforce of more than 500,000 people. It has, until very recently, been thought to be a clean industry. Yet in a 1980 survey, the California Department of Industrial Relations found that the microelectronics industry has 1.3 illnesses per 100 workers, compared with 0.4 per 100 workers for general manufacturing industries. But it is not only the workers but the community at large that is falling victim to the health hazards of the industry. In 1982, the residents of Silicon Valley discovered that private water wells were being contaminated by toxic materials leaking from underground chemical storage tanks. Although this problem occurs at industrial sites throughout the San Francisco Bay area, Silicon Valley is the source of by far the largest number of leaks. Also, huge amounts of reactive organic gases which contribute to the formation of photochemical smog are being released into the air every day.[10]

The industrial and community health hazards resulting from the production of semiconductors are frightening, especially when one considers that the semiconductor is to the information/communications age what oil was to the industrial age. It can only be hoped that the zealousness of the activists mobilizing to address the issues will be tempered by this realization. It is still too early to know.

Workplace Driving Forces

Of the many issues impacting the workplace today, one of the most insidious is that of privacy. We typically hear about specific

178

acts whereby the corporation infringed upon the right of privacy of employee. Outrageously abusive cases have surfaced and unfortunately will continue to plague the workforce. Why the pessimistic assumption? It is due to the fact that we are in the midst of what the French call *l'informatisation de la société,* the informatization of society. It is forecasted that by the end of the century, approximately two-thirds of the U.S. labor force will be information workers. The real danger in this is due to an inherent characteristic of information—it is diffusive. It tends to leak and affect everything around it.[11] The result is often invasion of privacy—a violation most victims take very seriously.

American affluence has by itself contributed to the loss of privacy in a number of ways. Much buying today is done on credit. But to buy on credit, a consumer must agree to turn over information about his income, lifestyle, and other personal data to consumer bureaus. Increased affluence has also meant an increased demand for insurance. Insurance companies, too, demand to know a great deal about the people they are asked to insure before granting a policy.[12]

Information collected by the government and the private sector has been made more sinister by the development of modern computers and telecommunications. Data and information can be recalled almost instantly and sent anywhere with equal speed and low cost. The advent of this technology has also ushered in a whole new era of worker productivity monitoring. A new generation of technology is causing an upsurge in the electronic surveillance of workers, particularly in the service sector, the largest growing sector in the economy. The monitoring of workers is not new. What is new is the ease, speed and economy with which computers can report the production of people who were never monitored before. Researchers say it is now possible to envision a marketplace product that could instantaneously determine whether employees are concentrating on their job by analyzing their brain waves as they work.[13]

Not surprisingly, the Newspaper Guild, which represents news reporters and other newspaper workers, has joined the United Auto Workers, Communications Workers of America and 19 other unions in insisting on anti-monitoring clauses in their contracts. Among the several states with pending legislation to regulate VDTs, seven have included prohibitions against monitoring of private operators. No state has yet passed VDT legislation.[14]

Beyond the question of whether these techniques will ultimately raise productivity, is the question of worker acceptance. In other words, do the means justify the ends? A look at public attitudes will shed light on this. In December 1983 the Harris organization announced the results of a comprehensive public survey about surveillance and technology. Of the many findings, a few are especially noteworthy. Although 77% of all respondents said they were concerned about threats to privacy, only 59% of corporate executives shared the opinion. Furthermore, among all respondents, 8% felt we have already arrived at Orwell's *1984,* 26% said we are very close, 39% said somewhat

179

close, and 19% said we are not close at all. Yet 75% of the business executives responded that we are not at all close to *1984*.[15] Who is right? When putting these opinions in the context of increased public militancy it doesn't really matter. What matters is that, assuming the gap does not close significantly in the years ahead, we can expect a backlash of revolt against both real and perceived abuses of privacy.

There are at least two other workforce issues that are inviting increased social militancy. Both are in the emerging stage, a long way from being resolved. The first has to do with genetics. New research shows that our genes can influence our susceptibility to illness resulting from exposure to chemicals and other substances in the environment. U.S. manufacturers have become intrigued with the idea of using genetic screening to lessen the toll of occupational disease. Few companies are willing to admit interest which has critics claiming they are hiding from public scrutiny. History does show that the concept of inherited genetic differences among individuals and races has been used all too often to justify social and economic inequalities. The modern application of genetic screening could conceivably be used to justify denial of employment, job transfers, or even dismissal—none of which sets well with the public, even one fully aware of the hazards of chemically based manufacturing.[16]

A second volatile workforce issue is driven by rising concern about security. The fastest growing high tech security systems are biometric which compare some biological trait with the information about it stored in a computerized file of authorized users. Some are activated by fingerprints, others by voices, or the shape of one's hand. Perhaps the most exotic is one based on the retinal pattern in the eye.[17] The developers of these biometric devices concede that one reason for the heightened interest in high tech security is a feeling that employees are growing more hostile. But for some, the devices themselves are reason for rebellion. Probably out of a sensitivity to the presence of Big Brother, there have already been instances of sabotage—including cigarette packs and ashes jammed into the card slots of locks that read specially encoded cards.

Growing Alienation

A review of almost every poll and survey series that contains trend information on confidence in American institutions reveals an obvious pattern—confidence is on the decline, and has been at least since the 1960s. Survey analysts tell us their findings indicate that the public is quite clearly disillusioned with the leadership of our institutions, but so far as their private lives go, they are quite satisfied.[18] Therefore, the analysts reason, to threaten the satisfaction and sense of well-being obtained from one's private life in seeking redress of *institutional* grievances would be an extraordinary foolish act. For most of the population, after all, "institutions" are distant and alien things. That many of the people who run them seem incompetent or corrupt is thus more likely a source of bemusement than outrage. But this attitude may be changing. The increased incidences of acts of private disobedience are outward manifestations of outrage. Private citizens do not commit dangerous and felonious acts out of bemusement. They do so out of genuine anger and frustration.

Even more disturbing is the likelihood that declining confidence will make the public more susceptible to demogogic persuasions, creating support for movements seeking to change the system in a fundamental way. We are seeing this now by the plethora of activist groups comprised largely of people who view themselves as reformers with higher and more enlightened values than others. Opposition to their views are frequently considered to stem from selfishness, ignorance, bigotry, or even evil. Many see themselves as the "progressive" force overcoming the "oppressive" dominance of "selfish" profit-oriented business values, "dehumanizing" corporations, "blind" technology, "crass" materialism, and "commercialized" vulgarity. They tend to turn issues into ideological, spiritual, and/or moral imperatives or they treat them as so important, that they fail to subject them to compromise or cost-benefit analysis.[19]

A large proportion of people who become activists are those that easily find fault and do not adjust well to living and working with others. They lack the sense of compromise that successful life in our complex society requires. But as our world becomes increasingly complex, the art of compromise becomes more and more essential for progress, if not survival itself.[20] Many of the major driving forces that are, and will continue to shape our future, have serious negative implications. Even more serious, however, is the prospect of growing numbers of people practicing private disobedience, for in this type of militancy there is no room for compromise.

This, then, is the challenge that corporations must anticipate and become competent at dealing with—specific and deliberate acts of protest initiated by people with no intention of compromising. It is a new public militancy quite capable of undermining the spirit of compromise so valuable to the vitality of American business.

Notes

1. "Human Resources, Intellectual Capital & Education: The Strategic Context for Economic Development in Post-Industrial America," by David Pearce Snyder (The Snyder Family Enterprise, 8628 Garfield St., Bethesda, MD 20817).

2. Robert N. Butler. "A Generation at Risk: When the Baby Boomers Reach Golden Pond," *Across the Board,* July/August 1983.

3. "Pensions After 2000: A Granny Crisis is Coming," *The Economist,* May 19, 1984.

4. "Population Puzzle: Is the U.S. Middle Class Shrinking Alarmingly? Economists are Split," *The Wall Street Journal,* June 20, 1984.

5. "Forecast-1984," Institute for the Future, 2740 Sand Hill Road, Menlo Park, CA 94025.

6. "Reach Out & Crunch Someone," *Rolling Stone,* Sept. 15, 1983.

7. "Phone Disconnections Growing as Unemployed, Poor Lose Ability to Pay," *The Wall Street Journal,* April 28, 1983.

8. "New Poor: Computer Illiterates," *USA Today,* Dec. 8, 1983.

9. "A New Breed of Environmentalists Puts the Heat on Industry," *Businessweek,* March 19, 1984.

10. "The Not-So-Clean Business of Making Chips," *Technology Review,* May/June 1984.

11. Harlan Cleveland. *The Knowledge Executive: Leadership in an Information Society,* New York: E.P. Dutton, 1985.

12. Stephen Goode. *The Right to Privacy,* New York: Franklin Watts, 1983.

13. "Corporate Big Brother is Watching You," *Dun's Business Month,* Jan. 1984.

14. "Big Brother & Office Automation," *Privacy Journal,* Aug. 1985.

15. "Broad Public Support Found for R & D," *Science,* Dec. 23, 1983.

16. "Genetic Testing at Work: How Should it be Used?" *Technology Review,* May/June 1985.

17. "High-Tech Locks Keep Out Intruders—And Sometimes Those Who Are Welcome," *The Wall Street Journal,* May 14, 1985.

18. Seymore Martin Lipset & William Schneider. *The Confidence Gap: Business, Labor, & Government in the Public Mind,* New York: The Free Press, 1983.

19. Herman Kahn. *The Coming Boom,* New York: Simon & Schuster, 1982.

20. Philip Lesly. *Overcoming Opposition: A Survival Manual for Executives,* Englewood Cliffs, NJ: Prentice-Hall, 1984.

Economics:
Differing Perspectives

USING BRAIN SKILL ASSESSMENTS
TO INCREASE PRODUCTIVITY

by

Weston H. Agor

Introduction

Several developing countries have made significant strides in the last quarter century toward increasing their productivity under extremely difficult circumstances including rapid technological change, internal economic and political crises, and other major worldwide adjustments such as the terms of trade. Frequently, these productivity increases have been achieved by implementing highly quantitative management techniques such as the latest computer technology and integrated financial management systems (Heady, 1984).

Although we can expect developing nations to continue to employ these tools to help augment productivity, it is important to note that there are many circumstances when these management techniques are extremely difficult or inappropriate to apply. For example, often "hard data" necessary for analytical decision-making is either not available or cannot be gathered in time to resolve an impending crisis. Also, circumstances in many developing countries are changing so rapidly that attempts to project the future for management decision-making based on present or past data is likely to give a very inaccurate picture (Asher, 1978).

Recognition of this fact has led a number of developing countries such as Venezuela to explore the development of new management techniques to complement the use of traditional quantitative applications for decision-making. Research and field application there and in a number of other settings around the world indicate that productivity in developing countries can significantly be increased by implementing an integrated brain skills/management styles (BMS) program to guide organizational management decision-making and help solve national development problems (Newell-Garcia, 1983; *Leading Edge Bulletin*, 1983, p. 1).

Weston H. Agor currently directs the Master of Public Administration program at the University of Texas at El Paso, and is also President of ENFP Enterprises, Inc., a management consulting firm.

BMS Program for Management

A BMS program consists of identifying the human skills/management styles that exist in organizations, and matching these skills/styles to the management problem at hand where they can be best employed to enhance productivity.

Research indicates that there are basically three broad types of brain skills/management styles (BMS) in development administration (Taggert and Robey, 1981). The first which is often referred to as "left brain," has traditionally received the most attention in development administration training programs. This style stresses employing analytical and quantitative techniques (e.g., deduction, computer technology applications). So called rational and logical methods of reasoning are followed. There is a preference for solving problems by breaking them down into manageable parts, then approaching the problem sequentially relying on logic and data as tools in the process. Management settings are normally highly structured, hierarchical in nature, and methods of decision-making are carefully planned. Managers who prefer this style tend to work most productively in occupational settings which require detail, precision, and regular routines such as finance, engineering, and the military (see Table I).

An alternative and complementary management style employs "right brain" skills. This approach which has received considerably less attention and resource support until recently stresses quite different techniques for problem-solving. Here, reliance is placed primarily on feelings before facts when making decisions. Inductive techniques are employed. Problems are solved by first looking at the whole—often with inadequate information or data at hand. Decisions are then reached through intuitive insights or flashes of awareness that are received. The management settings in which "right brain" skills are normally employed tend to be more informal and collegial. Participatory and horizontal authority structures are employed, and decisions tend to be made in a somewhat more unstructured, fluid, and spontaneous manner. Managers who exhibit this style tend to work most effectively in crisis settings, rapid change environments, or in settings where brainstorming is employed to solve problems. They often work best in occupations requiring high person-to-person contact such as counseling, personnel, and nursing.

The third style which has often been called "integrated" employs both "left" and "right" brain skills interchangeably as the management situation demands. Managers who rely on this approach normally feel comfortable dealing with both facts and feelings when making decisions. They are "switch hitters" so to speak. But, they also tend to make their major decisions guided by intuition after scanning the available facts and receiving input from the management resources/personnel both on the "left" and the "right" in the organization. For example, Shigem Okada, head of Mitsukoshi, Japan's largest department store, states, "Our company's success was due to our adoption of the West's pragmatic management combined with the spiritual, intuitive aspects of the East" (Goodspeed, 1983, p. 42). Research indicates that this style is more prevelant at the top level of management where the executive needs to have a vision of the future, but also be able to implement that vision on a daily basis by integrating the input he or she receives from the "left" and the "right" within the organization into an effective ongoing development program (Bennis, 1982).

Table I

Level of Application	The Three Brain Styles in Organization		
	Left	**Integrative**	**Right**
Type of Organization Where Predominant	Traditional Pyramid	Dynamic	Open, Temporary or Rapid Change
Management Style Emphasized	Deductive, Objective	Deductive, Inductive used as Appropriate and Interchangeably	Inductive, Subjective
Example Settings where Most Effective	Quantitative Applications where Data Bases are Available	Problem-Solving Labor-Management Negotiations	Projection when new Trends are Emerging, Crises, Intelligence, Holistic Health
Example Applications	Model Building, Projection	Team Building, Synergistics	Brainstorming Challenge Traditional Assumptions
Occupational Specialty	Planning, Management Science, Financial Management, Law Enforcement and the Military	Top Policy Management and General Administration, Intelligence	Personnel, Counseling, Health, Organizational Development

How to Use a BMS Program to Increase Productivity

Managers responsible for the leadership of their organizations in developing countries are faced with the difficult task of achieving maximum human capital productivity which in turn requires a greater and greater understanding of what is required to satisfy and motivate their colleagues and subordinates. Even in authoritarian countries, this in turn requires an understanding of just who these people are. That is, what are their skills, attributes, styles, and preferences. It also requires some assessment of what their potential ability and actual performance can be. Implementing a BMS program which includes training can be useful toward this end.

Table II summarizes some of the human capital management problems in developing countries where a BMS program can be used to significantly increase productivity.

Table II

**Opportunities to Use BMS Assessments
for Human Capital Development**

- Recruit, place, and develop personnel by management level and occupational specialty including career changes, adaptation to organizational changes such as mergers, outplacement.

- Create teams that can function most effectively to solve problems on a situational basis (e.g., United Nations peace keeping).

- Assess future trends and implications for management.

- Assess, locate, and develop creative potential in organizations.

- Understand and overcome communication problems including sex role stereotypes and cultural differences.

- Stress assessment and management.

- Develop/implement training programs.

- Develop workable employee compensation/benefit programs.

The type of brain skills required in management vary by organizational type, by level of management, by problem or issue, and by occupational specialization. Accordingly, one of the very first practical applications of a BMS program is in the overall process of selection and placement of management personnel.

As part of this assessment process, testing can be done to not only measure a manager's inherent BMS characteristics, but also his or her capacity to actually use his or her skills to make decisions on-the-job. Following initial assessments, one of the most useful applications of an ongoing training program is to help managers not only learn more about the BMS skills they possess, but also to assist them to learn how to more effectively use these skills in practical management situations. Both organizational productivity and personal satisfaction can be significantly increased as a result.

Secondly, brain skills that are most productively useful will vary by problem and issue. Accordingly, selection and placement by brain type/style should be situational—based primarily on the brain style appropriate for each problem or situation. Therefore, BMS assessments can be used to construct teams for example that will enhance maximum performance by taking into account such factors as brain skills, the appropriate mix of brain types (left, right, and the integration of the two) depending on the problem at hand, and other personality characteristics. One specific example would be creating the most effective mix on a United Nations administrative team which includes managers from a wide variety of different cultural backgrounds (Briggs and Myers, 1980, p. 167).

Thirdly, it is becoming increasingly apparent that health (individual and organizational) is closely linked to (1) whether a person is "properly matched" on the job with the brain skills he or she possesses; (2) whether the person is in touch with his or her dominant brain style; (3) and whether the person is in fact using his or her dominant brain style on-the-job. Research has often indicated that managers who are dissatisfied with their present positions are so in part because they are mismatched, i.e., their brain skills/management style does not match well with those required for the position they are actually in. It is all too obvious that a more effective recruitment/placement/ongoing monitoring program within an organization which takes into account brain styles and position requirements would not only increase productivity, but would also decrease health costs that individuals and schools presently often bear.

Case Study Illustration

I have completed BMS assessments with over 2,000 managers in the last three years, and also implemented in-depth BMS programs in several countries in a wide variety of organizational settings (business, government, education, military, and health). Below is a case study illustration of how a BMS program can be used to increase productivity (Agor, 1984).

Recently, a group of key government managers were tested in a major developing country for their brain skill/management style. The goals of the assessment program were several. First, the top governmental leadership was interested in determining what the overall BMS patterns of their key managers were and where skills appeared to be located in the management structure. The purpose of this assessment was to determine if there appeared to be a good match between individual skills and job requirements in the bureaucratic structure. The top leadership was also interested in determining if there was any correlation between individual BMS assessments, job skill requirements, and health/other organizational statistics such as turnover rates and if there were more effective ways that they could use existing talent to solve organizational problems.

The BMS assessment turned up several patterns that served as a basis for designing a totally new way of using existing brain skills/management styles in the government bureaucracy. The assessment also served as a basis for designing an ongoing training program for the more productive use of BMS styles and skills that already existed in the governmental leadership.

Specifically, one of the key findings was that several top managers were not working in positions where their BMS skills could be most productively used. It was also frequently found that selected managers were totally unaware of key aspects of their underlying ability (e.g., creativity) that could be systematically "brought on line" to improve their performance—particularly in such critical management settings as crisis decision-making. Follow-up consultation with top management and the individuals in question resulted in several subsequent reassignments that appeared not only to improve performance but also job satisfaction as measured by such indicators as turnover and absentee rates, health data, and personal interviews.

Another significant finding was that top management was not using the most effective method for assigning personnel to deal with problem-solving issues. The normal pattern was to take key division heads who had several years of experience in the bureaucracy, put them together in a random pattern, and ask them to come up with new solutions to problems plaguing their respective divisions. Using BMS data, a more effective technique was designed. Managers who scored high on right brain skills were first put together cross-cutting normal divisional lines and asked to come up with a list of possible new solutions to the problems in question. This technique had several advantages. Right brain people tend to be more creative. They tend to be more insightful, and be able to identify new ways of doing things. They also tend to prefer a collegial informal style of decision-making that functions most easily across normal lines of responsibility—a style that often makes managers uncomfortable who prefer more traditional lines of authority for communication.

Following this first step, the list of potential solutions which the right brain management group devised was subsequently presented to a separate group of left brain managers. This approach also has several advantages. Left brain managers tend to be more analytical and critical. They also tend to be more skilled at assessing the practicality and relevant facts of another manager's proposal more effectively than being able to generate new ideas of their own. They also tend to throw cold water on new and creative ideas—often too quickly—which can inhibit the ability of right brain managers to function in tandem with them.

Table III

BMS Style	Focus	Methods Used
Right	Stage I possibilities	Personal, insightful enthusiastic
Left	Stage II facts	Practical and impersonal
Integrative	Stage III facts and possibilities	Personal, insightful and practical

▼

Results in
Effective total
Organizational team

The final step was to integrate the two management groups in a third meeting chaired by a manager who scored high on integrative skills. The integrative manager is best able to see the value of the alternative proposals suggested (i.e., whether from the left or the right) and fashion elements of each into a practical plan of action that can be implemented. Table III summarizes how each stage in this case study process actually works.

Conclusion

A central issue in administration is to find ways to achieve maximum productivity (effectiveness and efficiency) at the least possible cost. Maximum development and use of human capital potential is one of the most important options available to public administrators in the future. The use of BMS assessments holds great promise as one management technique that can be employed in a variety of practical ways toward this end.

Notes

1. Weston H. Agor (1984). *Intuitive Management: Integrating Left and Right Brain Management Skills,* Prentice-Hall, Inc., Englewood Cliffs, NJ.

2. William Asher (1978). *Forecasting: An Appraisal for Policy Makers and Planners,* Johns Hopkins Press, Baltimore, Maryland.

3. W. Bennis (1982). "Leadership: Transforms Vision into Action," *Industry Week,* May 31, 54-56.

4. I. Briggs and P. Myers (1980). *Gifts Differing,* Consulting Psychologists Press, Inc., Palo Alto, California.

5. Bennett W. Goodspeed (1983). *The Tao Jones Averages: A Guide to Whole-Brained Investing.* E.P. Dutton, Inc., New York.

6. Ferrel Heady (1984). *Public Administration: A Comparative Perspective,* 3rd ed., Marcel Bekker, Inc., New York.

7. Roberto Newell-Garcia. "Leaders and Leadership Styles in Developing Countries in Latin America: A Brief Essay" in S.S. Gryskiewicz, ed., (1983). *Selected Readings in Creativity,* Center for Creative Leadership, Greensboro, North Carolina.

8. W. Taggart and D. Robey (1981). "Minds and Managers: On the Dual Nature of Human Information Processing and Management," *Academy of Management Review,* 6:2, 187-195.

9. "Venezuela Boosts Basic Intelligence on National Scale" and "Network for Teaching Intelligence Spreads Throughout Latin America" (1983), *Leading Edge Bulletin,* July, 1.

THE FUTURE POTENTIAL OF INCREASED INTRA-DEVELOPING COUNTRIES TRADE

by

Stanley J. Lawson and Douglas O. Walker

Possibilities for World Development In the 1980s and 1990s

The question of the future possibilities for world economic growth and the potential for increased intra-developing country trade depends upon a host of factors including domestic economic performance and the international economic environment. To those factors that are rooted in economic circumstances must be added policy decisions and the commitment of national governments to support measures designed to improve their growth performance and re-orient their trade and economies away from present patterns of production and exchange towards those supporting mutual trade among the developing countries. In this paper, the host of economic factors affecting future growth have been summarized as historically estimated shares of investment expenditure in GDP and past incremental capital output ratios, expressed per person in the labor force. These investment shares and ICORs have been used in a modified Harrod-Domar production function to generate projections of economic growth corresponding to different scenarios of future world economic development.

Those factors affecting future patterns of trade among groups of economies have been summarized as historically estimated marginal propensities to import from different regions with respect to the importing country GDP. These marginal propensities have been used in a simple import demand framework to generate projections of the future pattern of world imports and exports. Factors reflecting a commitment to new domestic and international trade policies are proxied by changes to the rates of growth and incremental propensities that have been assumed under an adjusted historical trend extrapolation projection, called here the Medium World Growth Scenario. This section discusses the alternative sets of rates of growth

Stanley J. Lawson is with St. John's University, College of Business Administration, in Jamaica, New York. Douglas O. Walker is with the United Nations, New York.

of gross domestic product and the marginal propensities to import used to prepare three sets of illustrative projections of world trade. Section 4, below, presents the result of the trade projection exercise, and assesses the potential for increased economic cooperation among developing countries implied by the projections.

a. *Estimates of World Growth in the Early 1980s*

The most recent set of data relating to the direction of world trade are those for 1980. On the other hand, estimates of world economic growth are much more timely and forecasts can be used to bring them up-to-date. When preparing projections of world trade for 1990 and 2000, the world trade matrix for 1980 has been projected on the basis of rates of growth assumed for the period 1981-1990. These assumed rates are a composite of estimates and forecasts for 1981-1985, on the one hand, and postulated rates for the balance of the decade, on the other. Specifically, growth rates for 1981-1983 are historical estimates and those for 1984 and 1985 are forecasts prepared on the basis of results from Project LINK and other sources. These growth rates for 1981-1985 are used in conjunction with the three sets of assumed rates to produce a composite projection for the entire decade of the 1980s. Assumed growth rates for the rest of the 1980s and the 1990s under the different scenarios are discussed below.

With regard to the historical rates of growth and their implications for the future, it is clear from Table 1 that growth in the world economy during the decade of the 1970s slowed considerably from the pace set in the 1960s, and suffered a severe and protracted recession at the onset of the 1980s. Guarded optimism now prevails with regard to the possibilities of a recovery in economic activity in all of the developed economies; prospects for the developing world are assessed to be mixed, with a few bright spots, in particular, the newly industrializing economies in South and South-East Asia, but signs of continued weakness in Latin America, Africa and the rest of Asia and Oceania are evident. Whether this signifies that the long-term trend rate of world economic growth will continue to decline or, rather, that it will experience an upturn is a matter of conjecture, and dependent, at least in part, on policies followed by national governments and international institutions.

Given the uncertainties of the future, for the balance of the 1980s and for the remainder of the years to 2000 long-term world growth has been assumed in this paper to encompass three broad possibilities or scenarios: High World Growth, Medium World Growth and Low World Growth. Associated with these possibilities for economic growth are three sets of assumptions regarding the propensity of regions to import out of their growing gross domestic product.

b. *The High World Growth Scenario*

The High World Growth Scenario is designed to explore the implications of extremely rapid world growth and a shift toward significantly greater economic cooperation among developing countries in the levels and patterns of world trade. It is based on the assumption that national and international policies will be directed toward the

193

Table 1.

Growth Rates of World Production Assumed Under Different Scenarios

Scenario and Group	Historical		Historical & Forecasted 1981-85	Projected 1986-90	Composite Projection 1981-90	Projected 1991-2000
	1960-70	1970-80				
Scenario 1—High World Growth						
Developed Market Economies	4.9	3.1	2.0	4.0	3.0	4.0
Developing Market Economies	6.0	5.2	1.8	7.0	4.4	7.0
Latin America	5.8	5.4	0.2	7.0	3.6	7.0
Africa	6.1	4.7	0.9	7.0	4.0	7.0
Western Asia	8.7	5.4	0.3	7.0	3.7	7.0
South and South-East Asia	5.1	5.2	5.4	7.0	6.2	7.0
Centrally Planned Economies	6.7	4.9	3.7	5.0	4.4	5.0
World	5.3	3.7	2.3	4.7	3.5	4.8
Scenario 2—Medium World Growth						
Developed Market Economies	4.9	3.1	2.0	3.3	2.7	3.5
Developing Market Economies	6.0	5.2	1.8	5.6	3.7	5.7
Latin America	5.8	5.4	0.2	5.9	3.1	6.0
Africa	6.1	4.7	0.9	5.3	3.1	5.3
Western Asia	8.7	5.4	0.3	4.9	2.6	4.9
South and South-East Asia	5.1	5.2	5.4	5.9	5.7	5.9
Centrally Planned Economies	6.7	4.9	3.7	4.2	4.0	4.6
World	5.3	3.7	2.3	3.8	3.1	4.2
Scenario 3—Low World Growth						
Developed Market Economies	4.9	3.1	2.0	2.6	2.3	2.6
Developing Market Economies	6.0	5.2	1.8	4.8	3.3	4.8
Latin America	5.8	5.4	0.2	5.2	2.7	5.3
Africa	6.1	4.7	0.9	4.5	2.7	4.4
Western Asia	8.7	5.4	0.3	5.1	2.7	5.1
South and South-East Asia	5.1	5.2	5.4	4.1	4.8	3.9
Centrally Planned Economies	6.7	4.9	3.7	3.5	3.6	3.6
World	5.3	3.7	2.3	3.2	2.8	3.2

Source: Historical growth rates for the 1960s and 1970s and the projected rates for 1980s and 1990s are taken from "World Economic Development and the International Development Strategy: Projections of Gross Domestic Product and Related Investment Expenditures" PPS/QIR/REPORT 1 (April 1982). Historical growth rates and forecasts for the period 1981-1985 are taken from Conference Room Paper 1, "World Economic Outlook, 1984-1986: Highlights from the Expert Group Meeting on the World Economic Outlook," presented at the Twelfth Session of the Inter-Agency Technical Group of the ACC Task Force on Long-term Development Objectives (Geneva, 1984).

achievement of a substantial rise in growth in every developing country, an acceleration that reflects growth potentialities created by significant changes in domestic policies and in the international economic environment. When used as a basis for preparing trade projections, the high rates of growth assumed in the scenario allow for an elaboration of the maximum potential for trade in the world economy at large, and among the developing countries in particular. Corresponding to the assumption of rapid world growth is an assumption of significant changes in prevailing trade propensities.

Underlying all scenarios are projections of gross domestic product made for 124 individual countries. Growth acceleration in the individual economies in each of the gross project under the high growth scenario was achieved by specifying improvements in their performance in two areas, investment effort and investment efficiency, in a manner consistent with their past performance. For slower growing countries in all groups of economies, the high growth scenario assumes that investment shares and incremental capital/output ratios in these countries will attain standards already achieved by one-half of all the developing countries in their group. For fast-growing countries in all income groups, it allows for an improvement in these two areas where it is thought the prerequisites include a substantial economic and technical base and a potential for higher growth rooted in an expanding and diversified export market, especially through widespread regional cooperation. For the fast-growing developing economies, the high-growth scenario assumes a modest decline in their pace or expansion as these economies begin to attain characteristics more in line with other faster-growing economies. This overall acceleration of growth in the developing economies would be accompanied by faster growth in the developed economies as all groups of countries participate in a general expansion of the entire world economy.

In the area of international trade, the High World Growth Scenario explicitly postulates change in present trade relationships as policy measures designed to spur trade, particularly trade among developing countries, are introduced. Import demand is estimated on the basis of postulated propensities to import from different exporting regions. A basic set of propensities, used to project imports under the medium growth scenario, has been estimated on the basis of historical data for the period 1960-1980. Changes to the basic set of historical propensities used to prepare projections for the high growth scenario have been made on the basis of three assumptions: 1) when the propensity to import for the period 1970-1980 was higher than that for the medium-growth scenario, it was used as the import coefficient for the high-growth scenario during the period 1980-1990; 2) import propensities of the developed country regions for the period 1991-2000 have been increased by 10 percent; and 3) import coefficients representing the propensity to import of a developing country region from developing countries for the period 1991-2000 have been increased by 20 percent. It is also assumed that the developed economies will further their efforts aimed at import substitution and conservation. These changes are consistent with the extent of past movements in these propensities and the stable and supportive international economic environment outlined in the United Nations International Development strategy. Since the main objective of the scenario is to examine the implications of rapid growth and greater mutual trade among the developing countries on the pattern of trade that might prevail in the year 2000, the postulated higher propensities to import by developing economies from other developing economies policies introduced by the developing countries to promote that end. Export prospects for each region are equal to the sum of each region's demand for imports from that region.

c. *The Medium World Growth Scenario*

A medium World Growth Scenario is based on the general assumption that long-term historical factors determining growth and trends of international trade in the world economy will continue into the future largely unchanged. Projections of world trade patterns prepared under this assumption therefore represent hypothetical extrapolations of past national and international policies and economic relations, should these relations and policies be extrapolated into the future without significant change.

The scenario is based mainly on the growth and trade of the world economy during the periods of the 1960s and 1970s. As such, it should be regarded as medium-growth assumption of essentially unchanged long-term individual economy trends in the rate of increase in output per unit of labor, except as required to eliminate extreme trends. By postulating stable growth trends in output per economically active person, rather than in total output, prospective changes in labor force expansion rates have been taken into account in the extrapolation. It also assumes, like the high and low growth scenarios, that the external environment imposes no significant constraint on future growth since any projected internal or external imbalance is sufficiently small to be accommodated by reallocations of domestic resources or is assumed to be financed by concessional aid and/or private capital flows. It is important to stress that the extrapolations discussed here are intended neither as a forecast nor as normative policy projections but only as simple extensions of past trends, as modified by adjustments designed to eliminate extreme results and to take into account long-term changes in the growth rate of the labor force.

With regard to the trend projections, the propensity to import from each world region under the medium growth scenario is based on ratios of incremental import propensity coefficients, computed by source over the entire period 1960-1980. However, the overall level of the assumed total propensity to import is based on a continuation of the experience of these regions during the 1970s and 1980s. Because of the use of propensities to import when preparing the projections, an implicit assumption is made that the long-term elasticity to import will decline as the average propensity to import rises asymptotically to reach the estimated incremental propensity. Since the general historical tendency is for average propensities to exceed marginal propensities, the average projected elasticity to import, for the world as a whole and its regions, is probably underestimated in the projected period even as a trend.

d. *The Low World Growth Scenario*

The scenario for low world growth is intended to serve as a comparison projection of the experience of the world economy during the late 1970s and the general consensus that the period of the 1980s and 1990s will be one of slow growth in production and trade. It provides an indication of the longer-term consequences of economic disruptions and misallocations of resources which characterized the world economy during the late 1970s and early 1980s. Since it is based upon empirically-derived parameters computed from data describing growth in the latter part of the 1970s, it attempts to take into consideration the apparently latest changes that have taken place in recent years in the basic circumstances governing economic activity and international trade in different groups of economies. As in the case of the medium growth scenario, the rate of growth projected in this scenario refers to the increase in output per economically-active person in the population, and therefore represents a projection of growth in productivity rather than in the levels of gross output.

In general, the low growth scenario assumes that the extraordinary slow-down in the growth of the world economy in the first half o the 1980s will end, with some moderate improvement as the decade unfolds. During the 1990s, growth is assumed to continue at a rate substantially below that recorded in the 1970s. Although the scenario postulates a stable international economic environment for the world as a whole, this environment must be regarded as more adverse than that underlying the assumption of the continuation of past trends that is described above. Consistent with this adverse environment, the scenario assumes that past attempts by developing countries to increase their imports and exports, which have been to some extent based on their ability to borrow on international capital markets, cannot be accommodated over the long-term as present constraints on their ability to borrow continue over the longer-term. Given this situation, and because of the rise of protectionism and difficulties in structural adjustment, average coefficients of import demand corresponding to the entire period 1960-1980 have been used instead of those for the 1970s and 1980s. As a result of these assumptions, projections prepared under this scenario present a significantly more pessimistic picture of future growth than that given by an extrapolation of longer-term trends.

Patterns of Trade in 1980s and 1990s

Associated with a growing world economy are shifts in the pattern of world production and in the level, composition and direction of trade among the world's regions. As the industrialization of the developing countries continues, more capital- and more skill-intensive

197

lines of production will be established in these economies, with the result that the existing international division of labor based on the complementarity between primary producing developing countries and secondary-producing developed countries will be altered. Under conditions of high world growth it must be expected that these changes would take place rather rapidly and will alter perceptively the global economic landscape. Even the continuation of past long-term trends or prolonged slow world growth would involve changed output compositions and productive structures in all region groups, and with these changes would come changes in established patterns of world trade.

Some idea of the magnitude of change to the present pattern of world trade can be discerned from the estimates made for import demand and export prospects under the three alternative scenarios of world growth discussed above. The present section reviews these estimates in order to shed light on what the pattern of world trade might look like at the end of the century. These projections also allow an assessment of the possibilities for greater mutual trade among the developing countries inherent in rapid world growth. Possibilities under high world growth conditions can be compared with results from the other scenarios, and the extent of trade re-orientation that can be expected by significantly greater emphasis on enhanced economic cooperation among developing countries may be estimated.

a) *Some preliminary comments on the nature of projecting exercise.*

Before reviewing the results of the projections exercise a few words of caution are in order. Given the uncertain nature of future trends in the economic activity and trade performance of different groups of developing countries, particularly the contracts between and changing experience of petroleum-exporting and petroleum-importing economies, the preparation of long-term projections for the possible evolution of exports and imports must be regarded as less a problem of prediction than of defining broad trends consistent with alternative national and international policies and conditions. In the case of the import projections presented here, demands arise from postulated rates of growth and specified import propensities defined as a possible condition in a scenario of future world development. The assumption that import demand in a region is related to its level of gross domestic product means that the estimated growth of imports will move step by step with the pace of the region's economic growth. Furthermore, given the historical experience on which the import demand propensities are estimated, whereby imports into these economies tend to increase significantly faster than their gross domestic product, one would expect to see a tendency for the projected level of imports by these economies to rise rapidly and grow faster than their total production. With regard to export possibilities, the period used to estimate import demands from different regions is not necessarily indicative of the magnitude of expected import demand in the future, or, especially, of the strength of the demand for exports from the petroleum-exporting economies. Nor does the approach used here take into account factors which could affect the supply of exports emanating from an economy. For these reasons and others, the projections discussed here must be regarded as illustrative in nature. They have been designed to explore in a preliminary manner questions entailed in preparing long-term projections of trade consistent with policies promoting greater economic cooperation among developing, and are intended to provide order-of-magnitude estimates of changes in patterns of trade consistent with different world development scenarios. To this end, results presented here are of interest in themselves and provide a basis on which to consider improved approaches for resolving questions concerning the effect of different national and international policies on the longer-term evolution of world trading patterns. They should not be regarded as predictions of the future.

b) *Trade patterns under the high world growth scenario.*

In contrast to the continuing decline registered in the rate of increase in world economic activity during the last two decades, economic growth is postulated to rise under the High World Growth Scenario from now to the end of the century. Production in the developing countries, assumed to grow at an average rate of 7 percent per annum, rises at an especially fast pace in this scenario. Although quite high by present standards, these rates of economic growth are not unprecedented and have been recorded by the developing countries as a group in the past. For the groups of developed market and centrally planned economies, the rates assumed here are substantially below those attained by these countries in the 1960s, and for this reason should be regarded as feasible in the future under favorable conditions. It should also be noted that while the rates of growth specified for the developing countries are ambitious, both the absolute level of production generated and the average *per capita* income in the developing countries in the year 2000 would still be far below that attained by most developed countries today.

Historical and projected growth rates of exports and imports corresponding to the alternative scenarios are given in Table 2. It can be seen that the rapid expansion of world trade during the 1960s and 1970s stands in marked contrast to the troubling experience of the early 1980s, when the expansion of world trade stopped. From the early 1960s to the mid 1970s the volume of world trade grew by an average of more than 8 percent per annum. As the 1970s came to an end, however, its tempo had declined to less than 4 percent a year on average, and during the early years of this decade absolute declines in the volume of world trade were recorded in 1982 and 1983. The trade performance of all major groups of world economies, with the exception of the newly industrializing developing countries, generally deteriorated when seen in long-term historical perspective. Growth in the trade of Latin America, which has been adversely affected by large external debt problems and tightened international liquidity, has suffered the severest setback. This decline in world trade performance reflects the decline in the rate of increase in world productivity and production alluded to above.

199

Table 2.

Growth Rates of World Exports and Imports Projected Under Different Scenarios

Scenario and Group	Exports					Import				
	Historical 1960-70	Historical 1970-80	Historical & Projected 1981-85	Projected 1981-90	Projected 1991-2000	Historical 1960-70	Historical 1970-80	Projected 1981-85	Projected 1981-90	Projected 1991-2000
Scenario 1—High World Growth										
Developed Market Economies	8.3	6.4	2.3	4.0	5.7	8.7	5.3	4.6	3.5	4.8
Developing Market Economies	8.0	4.4	-0.2	4.4	6.3	6.1	8.5	2.1	5.1	7.8
Latin America	5.3	4.2	3.4	4.0	6.2	5.2	5.9	-5.0	4.0	7.8
Africa	9.3	2.8	-6.1	3.9	5.6	5.3	6.3	-2.5	4.9	7.2
Western Asia	10.4	3.1	-7.0	4.6	6.5	9.8	15.8	2.8	4.0	7.6
South and South-East Asia	6.9	8.0	5.7	4.8	6.6	6.6	8.1	4.2	7.2	8.0
Centrally Planned Economies	8.4	5.6	—	6.2	7.3	7.9	5.9	—	8.4	7.9
World	8.2	5.9	1.7	4.3	6.0	8.2	6.0	1.7	4.3	6.0
Scenario 2—Medium World Growth										
Developed Market Economies	8.3	6.4	2.3	3.2	5.0	8.7	5.3	4.6	3.0	4.2
Developing Market Economies	8.0	4.4	-0.2	3.4	5.1	6.1	8.5	2.1	4.1	6.7
Latin America	5.3	4.2	3.4	2.9	5.4	5.2	5.9	-5.0	3.2	7.0
Africa	9.3	2.8	-6.1	3.1	4.7	5.3	6.3	-2.5	3.2	6.9
Western Asia	10.4	3.1	-7.0	3.5	5.2	9.8	15.8	2.8	2.8	7.2
South and South-East Asia	6.9	8.0	5.7	3.8	5.3	6.6	8.1	4.2	6.4	6.2
Centrally Planned Economies	8.4	5.6	—	3.4	6.7	7.9	5.9	—	4.2	7.9
World	8.2	5.9	1.7	3.2	5.2	8.2	6.0	1.7	3.3	5.2
Scenario 3—Low World Growth										
Developed Market Economies	8.3	6.4	2.3	2.6	3.3	8.7	5.3	4.6	2.4	2.7
Developing Market Economies	8.0	4.4	-0.2	2.7	3.3	6.1	8.5	2.1	3.4	4.6
Latin America	5.3	4.2	3.4	2.3	3.5	5.2	5.9	-5.0	2.7	5.3
Africa	9.3	2.8	-6.1	2.5	3.1	5.3	6.3	-2.5	2.7	4.4
Western Asia	10.4	3.1	-7.0	2.8	3.4	9.8	15.8	2.8	2.7	5.1
South and South-East Asia	6.9	8.0	5.7	3.0	3.4	6.6	8.1	4.2	5.1	4.0
Centrally Planned Economies	8.4	5.6	—	2.9	3.5	7.9	5.9	—	3.7	3.7
World	8.2	5.9	1.7	2.7	3.3	8.2	6.0	1.7	2.7	3.3

Sources: Historical growth rates for the 1960s and 1970s are taken from "World Economic Development and the International Development Strategy: Projections of Exports and Imports, Factor Income, and the External Balance," PPS/QIR/Report II (July 1982). Historical and forecasts growth rates for 1981-1985 are taken from "Report on World Economic Prospects, 1984-1986," prepared by the Projections and Perspective Studies Branch of the United Nations Secretariat. Projected rates for the 1980s and 1990s are those prepared by the authors as discussed in the text.

With the return to rapid growth postulated under the High World Growth Scenario, a reversal of the deteriorating trade performance of the world economy can be expected in all regions. Rates of growth of exports and imports under this scenario correspond to the pace of the 1960s and 1970s. As is expected, the calculations for import requirements of the developing countries indicate a rapid rise in the import demand associated with their accelerated growth. Because of the greater degree of intra-trade among the developing countries themselves, the share of the developing countries in the market for their own imports is projected to rise from less than 30 percent in 1980 to about 35.5 percent in 2000.

However, this is not expected to be shared equally among all *developing country regions*. Under the high growth scenario, Latin America and Africa do not fully benefit from the general growth of imports into the developing country market, while the projected share of developing country intra-trade contributed by the exports of West Asia and South and South-East Asia rises by several percentage points. In terms of major export market re-orientations the changes are even more pronounced, with the share of exports from developing countries to their major market, the developed market economies, being reduced from over 70 percent of the value of their exports in 1980 to less than 60 percent in 2000; indeed, the incremental share of exports to both groups of developed economies—market and planned taken together—is only 58 percent, indicating that the assumptions of the scenario would lead to over 42 cents out of every additional dollar of export revenue earned by the developing countries being generated by exports to the developing countries. As in the case of import re-orientation, greater changes took place in the direction of trade in the cases of West, South, and South-East Asia than in Latin America or Africa.

The generally high but significantly different rates at which the exports of different major groups of countries expand under this scenario bring about important alterations in the relative significance of different groups of countries in world trade. In 1980, for example, by far the largest world market for imports was the group of developed market economy countries, which absorbed over 67 percent of all world imports. Less than one-quarter of all world imports were purchased by the developing countries in that year. As a destination for developing country exports, this latter trade area accounted for less than 7 percent of the value of world trade. Mainly because of the export surplus of the petroleum-exporting economies of West Asia, the developing countries, taken as a whole, recorded an export surplus in 1980 on the order of 5 percent of total world trade under this projection. In the year 2000, the largest world market for imports would be the developed market economy countries, but the share of this market has been reduced to 56 percent. Under the conditions assumed in the high growth scenario, the relative importance of the developing countries overall world trade has risen significantly. Although the flow of merchandise trade among the developing countries themselves increases rapidly under the high growth scenario, it is nonetheless projected to be only about 10.5 percent of total world trade in the year 2000. In contrast, exports from the developed economies to these countries may be expected to be on the order of 17 percent of world trade. Hence, it must be noted that despite the significant shift in the geographical source of developing country imports assumed for the scenario, the share of the developed countries in the developing country market remains high.

In another important change, by the year 2000, given the strong demand for imports inherent in the postulated rapid rates of growth, the developing countries are estimated under this scenario to have a trade deficit of 1.5 percent of world trade. In past, this reflects the fact that during the 1980s and 1990s, capital goods strategy for lifting capital formation for economic growth in the developing countries would have to be imported preponderantly from the developed economies. In past, it also reflects the fact that the demand for primary goods exported by the developing countries is inelastic and centered in countries where growth is not expected to be as high as attained in the past. Consequently, for the high rates of economic growth of the developing countries assumed in this scenario to be regarded as feasible, increased concessional aid and other types of capital inflows would have to be forthcoming.

c) *Trade pattern under the medium world growth scenario.*

Under the Medium World Growth Scenario, gross world product would grow over the course of the 1980s and 1990s at about the pace recorded on average in the 1970s. Some slight increase in the rate of economic growth can be noticed, particularly in the 1990s. For the most part, this is due to an expected increase in labor force growth rates in the developing countries. World trade as projected under this scenario, in contrast to that for GDP, expands at a rate slightly below that of the decade of the 1970s. This lower rate is attributable to the use of incremental propensities to import observed on average during the 1970s as the average propensities for projecting trade during the 1980s. Notwithstanding this slower rate of trade expansion the total world demand for imports still rises faster than gross world product, increasing the share of products entering world trade and continuing a clear trend toward increased international economic integration.

The nature of the dependency of the developing countries on the markets of the developed countries is also reflected in the projections made for imports by developing countries. Estimated increases in exports of the developing countries in this scenario rise at a rate slower than the projected increase in their gross domestic product. The sluggish expansion of exports originating in the developing countries may be traced to the slow growth of production in the developed economies, which is the main market for developing country exports. In contrast to exports, import growth in the developing countries expand faster than their GDP, and, since the developed countries represent the main source of these imports, much of the benefit from faster than average world economic growth is channeled to these countries. Hence, one main consequence of slow economic growth in the North combined with faster growth in the South is an increasing balance of payments deficit in the developing countries.

The integration of the developing economies into the world economy, as measured by the share of imports in their gross product, proceeds more slowly in this scenario than under high growth assumptions; moreover, the share of intra-trade in their own exports and in total world trade is also lower, indicating that the mutual integration of the developing countries is also less. As mentioned above, under trend conditions, the developing countries do not benefit substantially from the general growth of imports into their own region, and gain only 1 in every 3 additional dollars they spend on imports. This compares with the 3 out of 8 dollars earned under the high growth scenario. Consequently, the basic export and import orientation of the developing countries is not altered in any significant respect under the trend scenario as they continue to rely mainly on the markets of the industrial areas for both their export revenue and their import needs.

d) *Trade patterns under the low world growth scenario.*

The Low World Growth Scenario provides an indication of the longer-term consequences of the economic disruptions and resource misallocations now characterizing the world economy. For the developed economies, economic growth is postulated to rise from the extraordinarily low rates of the early 1980s to the rate of productivity growth experienced on average during the latter half of the 1970s. This assumption excludes the experience of the developing countries during the period of the early 1980s when their rate of growth fell precipitously; moreover, it incorporates the effects from rising growth rates of the labor force. Therefore, although low by historical standards, the rates of economic growth assumed for this scenario cannot be regarded as unduly pessimistic given recent trends in the world economy.

Should the slow growth trends of the late 1970s and early 1980s continue until the end of the century it is likely that the pace of trade expansion in the world economy will be very slow. Under this scenario, world trade is projected to increase at only about 3.3 percent in the 1990s, only 0.1 percentage point higher than the growth of gross world product. Given the large-scale fluctuations in economic activity that have accompanied slow growth trends in recent years, and even greater swings in export and import volumes and payment balances, it must be expected that the international economic environment will be one of instability and imbalance. For this reason, growth rates for GDP and trade in this scenario should be regarded as maximum that are consistent with the assumed conditions postulated in the scenario.

Projections for exports and imports prepared for this scenario indicate that no significant change may be expected in the relative significance of the developing countries in world exports. Although some improvements in the share of the mutual trade of the developing countries might take place, the incremental share of the developed countries in the markets of the developing countries remain high. Furthermore, the relative significance of the developing countries in their major export market (the developed market economies), would be reduced at a time when the pace of increase in other markets is reduced. In the case of imports, the market for exports provided by the developing countries increases but at the slowest pace of any scenario and with the least effect on the global pattern of trade. Projected imbalances between exports and imports for some of the individual regions of the developing countries, notably Latin America, are also greatest in this scenario, indicating that even slow growth trends in some regions of the world will not alleviate their balance of payments deficits. In short, the pattern of trade projected for the low growth scenario indicates the least change in the overall distribution of world trade and is still characterized by large scale and worsening balance of payments crisis.

e) *Some conclusions from the trade projections.*

Trade projections prepared for this paper correspond to three alternative scenarios of world development trends to the end of the century. All scenarios studied here assume that the key factors defining future trends in world trade are the rate of economic growth in different world regions and the propensity of these regions to import from each other. With the use of a trade matrix, we have calculated the export prospects of each region, as the sum of the demands for the region's exports stemming from all regions of the world. Using this approach, projected world exports are identically equal to projected world imports.

The future pattern of world trade projected under the alternative scenarios has also been influenced by adjustments made to the propensities to import. These adjustments proxy the effects of policy decisions intended to influence the geographic pattern of world trade, such as the effort to promote greater economic cooperation under the high growth scenario, or capture the secular rise that takes place in the propensity to import over time. In the case of the medium and low growth scenarios, the distribution of the import propensities among exporting regions is also intended to reflect the experience of the world economy during different periods of its history.

Some main conclusions that can be drawn from the trade projections are:

1. To begin with, the projections indicate that the developing countries will maintain or increase their importance in world trade under all scenarios. Increases, however, are centered on imports, which rise faster than exports, and almost no improvement in the share of exports from developing countries in total world trade can be noticed under trend and low world growth conditions. These results point to persistent balance of payments pressures in the developing countries in all scenarios,

Table 3.

Projected Pattern of World Exports and Imports
By Origin and Destination under Alternative World Development Scenarios

Year and Region Group	Developed Market Economies	Developing Market Economies	Latin America	Africa	West Asia	S & SE Asia	Centrally Planned Economies
Scenario 1—High World Growth, 2000							
Developed Market Economies	36.5	17.4	4.0	3.7	3.6	6.0	5.2
Developing Countries	16.9	10.4	2.8	0.9	1.4	5.2	1.5
Latin America	2.9	1.8	1.4	0.2	0.1	0.1	0.6
Africa	3.3	0.7	0.3	0.1	0.1	0.1	0.1
Western Asia	6.8	4.1	0.8	0.2	0.6	2.3	0.2
South & South-East Asia	3.8	3.6	0.2	0.3	0.4	2.6	0.4
Centrally Planned Economies	2.3	1.6	0.2	0.3	0.3	0.6	7.7
Total Imports	55.8	29.6	7.2	5.0	5.4	11.9	14.5
Scenario 2—Medium World Growth, 2000							
Developed Market Economies	39.5	17.8	4.3	3.6	3.8	5.9	4.3
Developing Countries	17.4	9.2	2.6	0.8	1.2	4.4	1.3
Latin America	3.0	1.8	1.3	0.1	0.1	0.1	0.5
Africa	3.4	0.7	0.3	0.1	0.1	0.1	0.2
Western Asia	6.8	3.6	0.7	0.2	0.6	2.0	0.2
South & South-East Asia	3.9	3.1	0.2	0.2	0.4	2.2	0.3
Centrally Planned Economies	2.5	1.7	0.3	0.3	0.3	0.6	5.9
Total Imports	59.5	28.7	7.3	4.9	5.5	10.9	11.6
Scenario 3—Low World Growth, 2000							
Developed Market Economies	41.2	17.8	4.5	3.6	4.0	5.5	3.6
Developing Countries	18.1	8.8	2.7	0.7	1.3	3.9	1.1
Latin America	3.2	1.7	1.3	0.1	0.1	0.1	0.4
Africa	3.6	0.7	0.3	0.1	0.1	0.1	0.1
South & South-East Asia	4.1	2.9	0.2	0.2	0.4	2.0	0.3
Centrally Planned Economies	2.6	1.5	0.3	0.3	0.4	0.6	4.8
Total Imports	62.0	28.3	7.6	4.7	5.8	10.1	9.6

Sources: Based on projections prepared by the authors as discussed in the text.

205

and the sets of growth rates for economic activity underlying all scenarios are feasible only if accompanied by large and increasing capital flows to the developing countries.

2. Under all scenarios studied here the preponderant amount of trade of the developing countries is still with the developed countries, both as an outlet for exports and a source for imports. Under the High World Growth Scenario, the share of total export from developing countries rises from less than 25 percent in 1980 to more than 33 percent in 2000. For the developing countries to significantly alter their present patterns an even greater re-orientation of their trade than that assumed here, and an even greater time span than that studied here, is required.

3. Market share gains in the intra-trade of the developing countries that are projected to take place are not spread evenly over all exporting developing countries groups. In the projections prepared here the importance of the markets of the developing countries for the exports of West Asia and South and South-East Asia are significantly greater than for the two other regions of developing countries, and gains from increased mutual trade are centered in these two regions.

4. The large increases of imports into the developing countries points to their increasing importance as markets for all groups of world economies. Exports to all regions of developing countries increase as a proportion of world trade under all scenarios. The main problem before the world economy relates to the financing of these imports, which, because export markets of developing countries grow slowly, are very dependent upon capital inflows from the developed countries.

AN ALTERNATIVE TO THE FREE TRADE SYSTEM

by

SHIGEKO N. FUKAI

By comparing the experiences of Japan and the West, this study explores the interrelationship between the "quality of life"—which includes noneconomic factors—and international trade. The analysis suggests that as noneconomic, qualitative goals become more important than maximization of material production and consumption, self-sufficiency may replace free trade as a guiding principle in the international socioeconomic order.

"Silent Revolution" in the West

In Western Europe, welfare became the dominant public concern during the 1960s when social democrats were elected to office in one country after another. Shorter work hours, longer vacations, better working conditions, and humanization of work began to qualify the drive for economic efficiency and productivity growth. In the United States, the Democrats pursued policies roughly parallel to those of the West European social democrats.[1]

In the late 1960s a growing awareness of environmental disruption combined with the Vietnam War experience to foster doubts about technological progress and counter-culture attitudes among some segments of Western societies. Analysts related the decline of the work ethic to growing affluence-cum-popular disenchantment with economic growth and a creeping suspicion that material abundance may ironically expand spiritual hollowness and induce social disintegration. A "silent revolution," a change in basic values from acquisitive to "postbourgeois" (i.e., nonmaterial values, such as intellectualism and aesthetic self-fulfillment), was presumably taking place in the affluent West.[2] The *Limits to Growth* anticipated world catastrophe unless we halt the economic growth that is aggravating the population explosion, world inequality, resource exhaustion, and environmental disruption.[3] Followed propitiously by the Arab oil embargo, these predictions triggered debate on the desirability of

Shigeko Fukai is assistant professor in political science at Auburn University, Alabama.

growth. Forecasts of postindustrial society were joined by a call for the return to a simpler life.

Surveys indicate that significant numbers of people began experimenting with simpler alternative lifestyles (ALSs). These people rejected *material* well-being and *economic* efficiency as criteria for evaluating action and policies. Instead, they attached a higher priority to *non-material* goals, such as social relationships and community life and the development of human faculties. Viewing work as a means of realizing these goals, they opposed excessive mechanization and fragmentation of work; they preferred human-scale technology and the preservation of traditional skills. They valued conservation and frugality and rejected conspicuous consumption and planned obsolescence. Many preferred soft energy paths. The ALS trend encompassed the political left and right from all walks of life.[4]

In short, from the 1960s through the first oil crisis, both popular opinion and public policy in the West shifted toward the "quality" vis a vis the "quantity" of economic life, focusing attention on equality, the amenities, the environment, and nonmaterial satisfaction. Economic growth was seen as meaningful only to improve the quality of life.[5] As economic vitality ceased to be a central concern, Japanese observers became interested in finding the reasons for what they saw as the declining vitality of the West.[6]

The 1973-74 oil crisis had contrasting impacts on the thinking of policymakers and the public in the affluent societies. On the one hand, it dramatized the North-South and resource issues and globalized their perspectives and analytical frameworks. It deepened the awareness in Western societies that both rules of economic activity and ways of life should be reexamined from the perspective of global human welfare. On the other hand, the oil crisis, along with competition from Japan and other newly industrializing countries, led to a reappraisal of economic growth and technological progress. Analysts often pinpointed social policy as the source of disincentives to work, save, and invest, and hence as a cause of underutilization of resources. In an attempt to revitalize their economies, policymakers and analysts increasingly support denationalization and decentralization of social policies.

Japan's Anti-Growth Movement

How did trends in Japan compare with those in the West? In the late 1960s, Japan also witnessed the emergence of "anti-growth" movements. While similarities in timing and goals are significant, differences in motivation are crucial in explaining Japan's economic vitality. Unlike the movements in the West, Japan's anti-growth movement was generated not by affluence but by the visibly deteriorating environment and inadequate policies for the welfare of urban residents. It was inspired by the disappointment suffered by urban workers with the poor quality of life resulting from their hard work and a sense of injustice regarding distribution.

208

The expansion of heavy and chemical industries in the 1950s and 1960s had enabled Japan to rise from a "semi-developed country" (in the OECD classification) suffering from a chronic balance of payments deficit (both lasted until 1964) to the second largest industrial economy in the free world; it had also created an alarming level of pollution, urban congestion, and rural depopulation and instituted a vastly inadequate social infrastructure. In large cities, the shortage of land for housing and land speculation caused a sharp price hike, making it impossible for many urban workers to buy a house. Social welfare programs remained nominal. Despite a rapidly growing GNP, insecurity and discontent were widespread, spawning massive public protests and demands for change in the nation's high economic growth policy. The Socialist and Communist parties captured governorships, mayorships, and majority seats in local assemblies in metropolitan areas.

The early 1970s witnessed some improvement in social welfare, but after the first oil crisis, the government called for a "reexamination of welfare," embodied by the catch phrase "welfare society Japanese style." That phrase implied that Japan's welfare system was commensurate with those in the West and that European welfare policies would have an adverse impact upon Japan's economic vitality. After a brief flirtation with the Western welfare state, Japan returned to her traditional approach based on self-help and private mutual support.

Consequently, Japan in the early 1980s still lagged significantly behind the West in social overhead capital stock and social welfare institutions. Because of the poor quality of housing, a shortage of city parks, and inadequate sewage systems, as well as the poorly funded social welfare system, opinion surveys indicate there is no real sense of affluence among the people, although Japan now accounts for 10% of the world's GNP. Some economists have observed the emergence of an asset-deprived "new poor" working class in Japan. Also, Japan's growth strategy has led to "an extremely uneven structure of productivity growth" during the postwar high growth period by sector and firm size. Leaving social welfare to private firms in the dual economy has meant widening "discrepancies between the welfare of employees of well-established large-scale enterprises and those outside" (about two-thirds of the labor force) and a greater need for personal savings during periods of slow economic growth.[7]

The government white papers explain Japan's high savings rate, which remains around 20% of disposable income, by the availability of housing and the high costs of education as well as poorly funded social security. This savings habit, or the mechanisms that support it, plays a crucial role in explaining both the international competitiveness of Japan's export industries and the slow improvement of the quality of life in Japan. By enabling "the most impressive investment performance ever achieved in any peacetime, democratic, market economy," this mechanism has enabled the high productivity growth rates of Japanese manufacturing industries.[8] Little effort has been made to use these savings to improve living-related social capital,

209

housing, or social welfare institutions. "Workaholic" lifestyles may well reflect the fact that the Japanese have been unable to build habits or skills to enjoy leisure. Until recently, public policy has continued to emphasize economic growth and export promotion. Under these circumstances, most Japanese workers have no choice but to maintain the "workaholic" lifestyle, inadvertently contributing to Japan's persistent trade surplus against Western partners, where the prevailing lifestyle incorporates leisure and essentially noneconomic activities as vital functions. What makes Japan's trade frictions with the West intractable is this collision of lifestyles.

"Quality of Life" vs. Economic Vitality

To a large extent, different lifestyles can be explained by the different needs and aspirations of the early industrializers and a newly industrialized society. Unlike its Western counterparts, the Japanese working class has never achieved governing power (except for a brief period) and Japanese policy has been "geared primarily to the maximization of private capital accumulation" rather than to quality-of-life investment.[9] The consequent gap in the social stock, in turn, has helped foster different values, attitudes, and behavior patterns in Japan and the West.

From the above, the interrelationships between international trade and the quality of life in Japan and the West may be summarized as follows. First, in the West, the public emphasis on social welfare and amenity has reduced productive investment ratios to the GNP; in addition, changes in popular values and lifestyles away from quantitative growth have weakened incentives for work and consumption. This change in incentives has been the basic factor in the declining competitiveness of Western industries vis a vis their Japanese counterparts, who have been supported by the government's emphasis on export-oriented economic growth and lifestyles that emphasize work and savings. Japan's international competitiveness and semi-permanent trade surplus are rooted in this structure of relationships, not in "unfair" trade practices or bureaucratic inertia.

Second, the impact of competitive pressure from Japan and other newly industrializing countries may be summarized as a revival of economism, the swing back from welfare to growth as a major policy concern for the latter. Western policymakers responded with a variety of policies which included intervention in the market with an increasing variety of subsidies to "rejuvenate" mature and declining industries, leniency in enforcing antitrust and antipollution regulations, regulating the money supply to control inflation, and cutting public spending at the expense of the welfare system. Finally, to improve their balance of trade, many have expanded the armament industry and its exports. This has accelerated the wasteful consumption of resources and Third World financial problems and armed conflicts.

From an ecological viewpoint, it makes sense for mature nations to shift priorities from growth to welfare, from quantity to quality.

The return to simpler lifestyles in developed countries also makes sense, from the viewpoint of conserving resources for Third World development. The free trade system, however, constantly exposes mature nations to competitive pressure from younger nations driven by the single-minded urge to catch up. The DCs, with a quarter of the world's population, continue to use 79% of the world's income and resources. In their effort to revive international competitiveness, they accelerate consumption while aggravating their social pathological problems, many of which are related to over-consumption. Despite the oil glut, depletion of oil reserves before the development of alternative energy sources remains a real danger, and certain by-products of industrialization are threatening the earth's life support system. Surveys provide ample evidence of personal disappointment in material affluence. To use a metaphor, slower growth in a mature economy may reflect nature's rule, which free trade disturbs.

Implications for the Developing Countries

Even if Japan "matures" and becomes less concerned with quantitative growth and softens her competitive edge in the world market, economic friction may not abate. As Japan's mercantilist policy took root in the free trade environment of the 1950s and 1960s, so are many late-comers to the world market, including the NICs in Asia and Latin America, running roughshod over qualitative issues in their pursuit of rapid economic growth. This growth often begins in a "free production zone," an enclave designed to attract foreign capital. To gain a trade advantage, many have become "pollution havens."[10] Often, their model has been Japan, despite the change in international circumstances since its industrialization.

Two examples may be cited to illustrate the important change that might aggravate today's development problems. Unlike Meiji Japan, which relied on domestic sources of capital, many LDCs today depend on international loans and suffer from serious accumulated debt problems caused by rapidly rising external loans. To service debts, they often concentrate their development efforts in the export-oriented sectors in relative neglect of domestic markets or the social infrastructure necessary for building a viable economy.[11] Demographic patterns have changed also. Japan has experienced a slow but sustained decline in mortality in line with its economic development, whereas contemporary LDCs have undergone sharp reductions in mortality.[12] Population pressures increase demands on resources and the environment. Continued poverty and intensive use of technology aggravate soil erosion, deforestation, desertification, and water pollution in the Third World.[13]

Compounded by these problems, many LDCs suffer from distorted development (concentrated on a few, mostly export-oriented, sectors) and structural dependence upon the industrial world, in spite of their pronounced goals of self-reliant economic development.[14] Without fundamental changes in the West's philosophy of foreign investment, capital inflow may only prop up wealthy overlords, contribute to oppression, or aggravate income disparity.

The situation in both the developing and developed worlds clearly points to the need for reexamining the validity of ideas and assumptions underlying the free trade doctrine in the light of changing conditions for technology, resources, environment and North-South problems.

The Future of International Trade

Why do countries open their markets to foreign manufacturers? One reason is the prevailing belief that self-sufficiency has become impossible, or, more precisely, that a living standard cannot be maintained without importing foreign goods. The national standard of living can be raised by using the comparative advantage, a desire to achieve a higher standard of consumption with a given income by purchasing cheaper, better quality foreign goods. A third reason may be the influence of the liberal doctrine, which associates protectionism with war and free trade with peace.

If qualitative standards of judgment replace quantitative ones, these reasons for supporting international trade may be invalidated. As we reexamine national self-sufficiency and our standards of living, we are faced with fundamental questions: why return to a world view that rejects a "materially simple but internally rich lifestyle" as lacking economic vitality? Why open our markets to countries that single-mindedly pursue economic efficiency? Why not limit trade to those nations with similar values and lifestyles? Under rising protectionist pressure, unemployment has tended to overshadow the public's interest in the standard-of-living, and liberalism's policy-guiding capacity has eroded noticeably in the DCs.

Liberalism as an ideology has lost much of its appeal and may lose more under a growing perception that uncontrolled competition accelerates resource consumption and environmental disruption. As regards Third World development, some policymakers and analysts are examining the theory of delinking, which argues that if less developed countries are to develop a viable economic structure, they must build self-sufficiency by dissociating themselves from the international economic system dominated by advanced capitalist economies.

Material Self-Sufficiency as an Alternative Principle

My hypothesis is that the twin concepts of material self-sufficiency and non-material interdependence may replace the free trade doctrine as a guiding principle of an alternative world order.

First, my proposal combines the goal of self-sufficiency in materials and goods for a nation or a group of nations (in some cases, regional economic integration may be necessary) and the international exchange of ideas, information, and services. Second, the key factor in promoting the new economic order is a new international business norm: foreign investment and technology transfer must promote

212

self-reliant development, that is, help the host country accumulate capital, generate employment, diffuse income, expand domestic markets, and launch self-sustaining technological developments and thereby reduce its vulnerability to world economic fluctuations. Direct investment motivated simply to reduce production costs of exports to third countries should be discouraged. It should produce the goods needed and ultimately consumed by the local people, using technology appropriate to local conditions.[16] The profits, except for an equitable return for the capital and technology supplied, should be retained and used in the host country. The concept of equitable return for investment needs to be articulated as a criterion for legitimate business conduct, and as a conceptual tool by which to transform the international business culture. Direct investment thus conducted may reverse the trend that economic development, accompanied by foreign goods and commercialism, tends to destroy indigenous culture.[17]

Also, home countries can avoid "deindustrialization" as well as indirect friction with a third country. Furthermore, changing from an export-oriented mass production system to a system slimmed down primarily to meet domestic needs would have resource-and energy-saving effects and facilitate the "humanization of work."

The transition from a free trade system to a self-sufficiency oriented system requires fundamental changes in our priorities and lifestyles. Measuring living standards by material consumption would be replaced by quality-of-life criteria, in which nonmaterial means of satisfaction would be balanced against the inconvenience of reduced material consumption. That transition would accompany a change in what might be called global collective consciousness from expansionism to self-contained internal growth, a change in which noneconomic factors are vital components.

Achieving self-sufficiency does not mean ending economic growth. Technological innovations in recycling, renewable energy sources, and new materials would be integral factors in gradually raising the level of self-sufficiency in raw materials, and the growth of knowledge and recreational industries would provide new areas of employment.

Japan, "a front runner in the population-resource-environment crisis," presents an interesting case for a feasibility study of an alternative social economic order. If Japan could achieve self-sufficiency by reorganizing its industrial structure, inventing efficient recycling methods and new materials and energy sources, and adopting materially simpler but healthier lifestyles, it would provide the world with an encouraging prospect for sustaining a growing population despite declining sources of natural resources and of mounting wastes and pollution.

Notes

1. I.L. Horowitz, "Economic Equality as a Social Goal," *Journal of Economic Issues,* Dec. 1980, p. 945.

2. R. Inglehart, "Silent Revolution in Europe," *American Political Science Review,* Dec. 1971, pp. 991-1017.

3. D.H. Meadows et al. *The Limits to Growth* (New York: Universe Books, 1972).

4. R. Dahrendorf, *After Social Democracy* (London: Liberal Publication, 1980).

5. R.D. Hamrin, *Managing Growth in the 1980s Toward a New Economics* (New York: Praeger, 1980).

6. S. Shishido et al., eds., *Senshinkoko mondai no tembo* (The Prospects of Advanced Countries' Problems) (Tokyo: Nihon keizai, 1973).

7. H. Kitamura, *Choices for the Japanese Economy* (London: Royal Institute of International Affairs, 1976), p. 51.

8. K. Ohkawa et al., *Japanese Economic Growth* (Stanford: Stanford UP, 1973).

9. Kitamura, op. cit., p. 69.

10. R.J. Barnet, *The Lean Years* (New York: Simon & Schuster, 1980), p. 312.

11. H.C. Blaney, *Global Challenges* (London: New Viewpoints, 1979) p. 90.

12. N. Ogawa et al., "Lessons on Population and Economic Change from the Japanese Meiji Experience," *Developing Economies,* 1982, pp. 196-219.

13. *OECD Observer,* no. 116 (1982) pp. 50-53.

14. R.L. Merrit et al., eds., *From National Development to Global Community* (London: George Allen & Unwin, 1981), Part III.

15. D. Sanghaas, "Dissociation and Autocentric Development," in ibid.

16. E.F. Schumacher, *Small is Beautiful* (London: Blond & Briggs, 1973).

17. W.E. Moore, *World Modernization* (Oxford: Elsevier, 1979), p. 22.

AVOIDING A CRASH:
PUBLIC INVESTMENT, PRIVATE REGULATION

by

Frederick C. Thayer

The annals of American history have recorded Herbert Hoover as the protector of *laissez-faire* economics, while remembering his successor, Franklin Roosevelt, as the champion of government intervention and the welfare state. But despite their presumably different economic philosophies, both depression-era presidents used strikingly similar language to describe the roots of the economic crisis of the 1930s. "Destructive competition," noted Hoover in 1931, had brought "demoralization" to such industries as coal, oil, and lumber—coal production in that year, for example, required the services of only half the available miners. Two months after taking office in 1933, Roosevelt made a similar observation: "We have found our factories able to turn out more goods than we could possibly consume," he declared, adding that "cutthroat" and "unfair" competition was punishing workers with "long hours and starvation wages."

Hoover—the Rugged Individualist—and Roosevelt—the New Dealer—both recognized, although belatedly, that the sustained revival of the U.S. economy depended upon the reduction of this excessive competition and overcapacity in both industry and agriculture. Hoover sought immediate revision of the country's stringent antitrust laws to permit firms to reduce competition by consolidating,[1] and Roosevelt promised to "encourage each industry to prevent overproduction" and to decrease the disastrous surpluses that had plunged the country's farmers into poverty.[2] One result of this pledge, the short-lived National Industrial Recovery Act (NIRA), permitted firms in individual industries to jointly plan output, wages, and prices—in short, to engage in industrial self-regulation with minimal governmental oversight.

The words and actions of these two presidents are worth recalling, for this nation and others now face problems very similar to those

Frederick C. Thayer is a Professor in the Graduate School of Public and International Affairs at the University of Pittsburgh and the author of Rebuilding America: The Case for Economic Regulation (New York: Praeger, 1984).

that Roosevelt and Hoover blamed on industrial overcapacity and agricultural overproduction. Many of the troubling conditions that accompanined the last depression are present today. Unemployment is at or near double-digit figures in most industrialized countries. Agricultural surpluses are multiplying, as are farm foreclosures. Mergers and bank failures have increased and trade wars loom on the horizon. All these trends indicate that overcapacity plagues major industries worldwide, including steel (which is now operating at less than 50 percent capacity), autos, textiles, copper, chemicals, electronics, and oil. Similar problems have begun to threaten those U.S. industries that have been substantially or wholly deregulated in recent years. Even America's youngest and most robust high-tech companies are burdened by increasingly large inventories and a slowdown in sales. With stiff competition from both domestic and Japanese companies, as many as 300 personal computer manufacturers are expected to go out of business within the next year.

The basic problem is this: many industries now produce, or could produce with existing capacity, much more than can be sold at prices that bring reasonable profits. This worldwide "glut" of products and services threatens to exert deflationary pressure on the global economy, increasing today's already high unemployment and pressuring industries burdened by overcapacity to make desperate attempts to dump their surpluses overseas.

Despite evidence to the contrary, most politicians and economists still tend to view unregulated competition as a sure prescription for prosperity and peace. This standard economic view reverses the true order of things, defining the problem—overcapcity and overproduction—as the solution, and the solution—economic regulation—as the problem. Because overcapacity is both the inevitable outcome of unrestricted competition and a recurring cause of depressions, we can avoid future worldwide depressions only by inventing mechanisms to restrict excessive competition and ensure full employment. No major industry can remain viable without some form of administrative machinery to regulate capacity, output, prices, wages, and, in many cases, imports and exports. Only permanent regulation—whether formal or informal—can prevent overcapacity and overprodution and thus ensure a smoothly functioning and growing world economy.

At the same time, massive quality-of-life programs are needed to provide useful jobs, which cannot be created by the producers of consumer goods who already have more capacity than they can utilize. These programs could build or rebuild the nonexistent or collapsing infrastructures—water, sewage, transportation, communications, environmental, and conservation systems—not only in the United States but also abroad. While the precise needs of each country may vary and must be determined by the country concerned, some efforts, such as major environmental, transportation, and conservation projects, must be instituted on a multilateral basis to be truly effective.

A two-part agenda of this sort might have prevented the two great depressions that have occurred within the past hundred years and perhaps the ravages of the wars that followed them. Now, if we are to head off another worldwide economic bust, we must rethink the conventional wisdom that guides most economists and the policymakers they advise.

Rethinking Depressions: Getting Rid of Overconfidence

To suggest that the global economy may be suffering from over-capacity and is thus headed toward a prolonged collapse is tantamount to economic heresy. Most economists and politicians believe that even if governments have not solved the problem of the business cycle, they have at least learned how to use "legislative and administrative tools . . . to prevent major depressions and serious unemployment on a scale that occurred more or less regularly in the good old days." In the words of the same economist, "1932 will not come around again."[3] At a time when the economy is still expanding, the possibility of another depression seems especially remote.

There are a number of reasons to be less sanguine. To begin with, the economists themselves do not even agree on what constitutes or causes a depression.[4] From the outset, then, one must be skeptical of cavalier assertions that depressions are now impossible. More important, the prevailing conventional view apparently overlooks the historical correlation that exists between double-digit unemployment and depression. Except for the 16 years associated with two great depressions—1893 to 1898 and 1931 to 1940—the United States has experienced double-digit unemployment in only one year since 1890: 1921, when unemployment temporarily climbed to 11.7 percent. By this standard, which is admittedly a somewhat arbitrary one, the industrialized world is today hovering close to depression. Unemployment in the United States averaged 7.5 percent in 1984, and in many European countries—France, Britain, the Netherlands, to name a few—well exceeds 10 percent. Although one might plausibly argue that double-digit unemployment is not necessarily an indicator of depression, such arguments provide no solid grounds for optimism when considered in light of other warning signs—commodity deflation, increased mergers, mounting bankruptcies, and numerous bank failures. Rising levels of unemployment should force a more serious reassessment of the nature of depression than the prevailing view now permits.

This raises an even more fundamental point. Conventionally-minded economists dismiss the possibility of a recurrence of depression partly because they do not even acknowledge that over-capacity, which both Hoover and Roosevelt cited as a cause of the last depression, can exist. Resistance to the notion of general over-capacity is particularly acute within the Reagan administration, whose supply-side economic policies are based on the blind faith that

217

supply can never exceed demand because the production of consumer goods always generates enough purchasing power to buy all that is produced. This attitude is simply a derivative of a widely acknowledged economic principle known as Say's Law, which holds that any economy generates sufficient demand to buy its own output. According to this principle, a temporary lack of buyers for the output of an industry, or even a few industries, will compel those producers to lower their prices; new buyers will quickly clear the saturated markets, and equilibrium will be restored. The most dedicated adherents to Say's Law, supply-siders, argue that so long as the government does not worsen the situation by intervening in glutted markets, all such fluctuations automatically "cycle" into a new balance. By suggesting that the "invisible hand" will keep supply and demand in balance and that overcapacity is therefore impossible, many economists dismiss the notion that the world economy is still susceptible to depressions.

Keynesian economists disagree with this formulation only to the extent of advocating short-term government "pump-priming" if any temporary lack of buyers ("underconsumption") does not quickly self-correct. Thus, the Keynesians contend that through the skillful use of macroeconomic policy, governments can increase purchasing power to correct underconsumption and stimulate renewed economic growth. Along with supply-siders and other schools of economic thought, however, Keynesians refuse to entertain the notion that because demand may not be infinite, overcapacity and overproduction can cause prolonged economic slumps or at least excessive economic instability. To be effective, government policy would have to be more or less permanent, both stimulating demand and regulating supply.

In addition to unquestioningly accepting Say's Law, most U.S. economists and politicians hold firmly to the principle of unrestricted competition, treating it both as the key to prosperity and as a sacrosanct and undeniable right of the consumer. From this perspective, competition can never be detrimental because it benefits "sovereign consumers" by permitting them to choose from the offerings of many producers. Over the years both Congress and the Supreme Court have codified this principle by passing and enforcing antitrust laws. As early as 1904, the Supreme Court commented that "the unrestrained interaction of competitive forces will yield the best allocation of economic resources, the lowest prices, the highest quality, and the greatest material progress."[5] What is often overlooked is how this firm belief in competition, which underpins the nation's antitrust practice as well as the current emphasis on deregulation, in fact contradicts the equally firm belief that overcapacity is impossible. Say's Law holds that supply *cannot* greatly exceed demand, but the belief in competition holds that supply *must* greatly exceed demand—otherwise the consumer would not be "free to choose," to use Milton Friedman's words. Such is today's economic theology: over-capacity cannot exist even though it is prescribed by this nation's antitrust laws. Yet there is considerable historical evidence—beyond Hoover's and Roosevelt's assessments—that suggests that overcapacity is the natural result of unregulated competition and that it can lead to depressions.

1893 and 1929

Historians are often influenced more by the broader perspective that the long term yields than by the theories and dogma that some social scientists use to analyze short-term events. The historians who have studied the depressions of the past, for example, have almost routinely attributed them to overinvestment and overspeculation in the private sector, which together spurred deflation and depression. Nowhere was the detrimental effect of unrestrained competition more evident than in the frenzied overbuilding of railroads during the 1880s. In a single decade, railroad companies laid 74,000 miles of track in their hasty attempts to prevent competitors from claiming the territories first. The establishment of the Interstate Commerce Commission in 1887 to regulate the industry was a case of "too little, too late." By that time, the nation's demand for rail transportation had already failed to keep pace with the rapidly increasing supply, and the weakest competitors were already being forced out of the glutted market.

As the railroads failed, so did those industries dependent upon them: within the first six months of 1893, 32 of the nation's steel companies went bankrupt.[6] The domino effect of failing industries set off a general panic and bank runs. But speculators had freely used the country's reserve capital to finance the overinvestment of the preceding decade. Unable to collect on their loans, the banks crashed, bringing down the stock market as well. Within the next five years, the ravages of overcapacity raised the nationwide unemployment rate to over 18 percent.

It was no coincidence that the first wave of U.S. corporate mergers occurred in the wake of this depression. When overcapacity is a problem, mergers provide one means by which industries can "streamline" and "reorganize," thereby reducing industrywide capacity. Such a strategy reflects a conscious decision by corporate managers that buying existing firms is economically more rational than building new facilities.

Congress balked, however, at the concentration of power that occurred because of these mergers and responded by strengthening antitrust laws to discourage both further mergers and industrywide planning. Unable to regulate their production or sell their output at home, many industries began to "dump" surpluses in foreign markets. In their search for additional markets, U.S. manufacturers were joined by their counterparts from England, Germany, and other Western countries that were also suffering from the effects of overcapacity. Through this modern-day imperialism, the Western nations essentially rounded up buyers at gunpoint. Writing in 1902, English economist J.A. Hobson linked domestic surpluses with imperialism; the competition for markets abroad acted as one catalyst for World War I.

In similar ways, overcapacity and overproduction played an important role in bringing about the Great Depression. During the 1920s, increases in worker productivity had been two to three times greater than increases in their real-wage purchasing power. As unsold inventories began to pile up in mid-1929, it should have been apparent that most industries were producing more than they could ever sell at a reasonable profit. The downward price-wage spiral then accelerated; wholesale prices in the United States fell 16 percent in 1931, simultaneously falling in Germany by 13 percent, in the Netherlands by 20 percent, in Great Britain by 18 percent, and in Japan by 21 percent. For those with money to spend, the low consumer prices promised by the principle of unrestricted competition were indeed available. But few Americans occupied such a privileged position: millions were unemployed, and for many of those who were fortunate enough to have jobs, wages had dropped to 35 cents an hour.

As the depression lingered and deepened, fragmentary proposals began to emerge. Some industrial managers recognized the problem of overcapacity and sought to remedy it by regulating competition and production. In 1931, soft coal operators suggested that the industry be regulated—a position *The New York Times* endorsed, arguing that a "public utility" approach might prevent overproduction. The following year, railroad executives repeatedly met in an attempt "to avoid preventable and competitive waste." These business leaders were joined in their efforts by politicians who similarly sought to mitigate the deflationary effects of industrial overproduction. In 1932, Senator David I. Walsh introduced legislation to authorize "curtailment of production." When Attorney General William D. Mitchell proposed a relaxation of antitrust laws, he cited "overproduction" as the reason. Hoover, in 1931, and Roosevelt, during the 1932 campaign, both proposed removal of the long-term "duplication" and "waste" from the national railroad system, as well as regulation of a new trucking industry that largely duplicated the railroads.

Roosevelt's response to the economic crisis of the 1930s included programs that reduced both the labor force and the productivity of the private sector. By strengthening the child labor laws, initiating the Social Security program for the nonworking elderly, and successfully implementing a plan for shorter working hours with no reductions in wages, Roosevelt began to curtail the excessive productivity of the private goods economy. Though fated to be only a temporary measure, the NIRA was also a small step in the right direction: by the time the Supreme Court ruled the NIRA unconstitutional in 1935, 557 industries had adopted "codes of fair practice" to restrict output and keep floors under wages and prices.

The effects of these programs were, however, doomed to be limited. While firms entered into cartel agreements under the NIRA in the hope of gradually returning to full production, nothing short of reorganizing entire industries could have achieved this goal. As it was, the agreements may have discouraged the mergers that could have streamlined the industries concerned. Moreover, government spending for Roosevelt's public works programs was far less than what was needed to rectify the unemployment problem. Until World War II, Roosevelt incurred annual deficits of only 4 to 5 percent of the gross national product (GNP)—about the same size as those incurred by Hoover in the last two years of his administration. Consequently, unemployment still hovered at over 17 percent as late as 1939. Only World War II, a likely by-product of economic conditions that spurred another wave of imperialism, ended the depression. The unemployment rate finally dropped to 9.9 percent in 1941.

Four factors, all of them war-related, accounted for the U.S. economy's eventual sustained recovery. The first, of course, was virtually full employment for the civilian labor force as 12 million other Americans became members of the armed forces. This military version of public works programs was actually an extreme form of Keynesian pump-priming that succeeded in stimulating purchasing power. As unemployment declined to less than 2 percent, many workers found their paychecks suddenly doubled or tripled. Livable wages were paid for the first time in more than a decade. Although those in the military and those producing military goods were technically on the welfare rolls— which according to today's economic logic should have deepened the depression—the war effort corrected one of the most disastrous ramifications of overcapacity: unemployment.

A second factor in the recovery was the truly massive governmental spending during the war years, which further ameliorated domestic economic conditions. Although economists today warn that deficit spending should never exceed 2 percent of GNP, the wartime deficits that contributed to recovery totaled 14.9 percent of GNP in 1942, 31 percent in 1943, 27.3 percent in 1944, and 21.9 percent in 1945. These extraordinary governmental outlays yielded much the same economic outcome that could have been achieved years earlier, and in a much more desirable way, by "crisscrossing the country with superhighways and building hospitals, schools, and underground urban parking facilities."[7] The government spending of the 1940s was a decade late.

Third, the recovery was also partly the result of comprehensive economic regulation. Even more important than the price and wage controls that held down inflation as purchasing power increased was the regulation, even the rationing, of private goods. Because of their limited supply, gasoline, tires, fuel, oil, sugar, coffee, meat, and other commodities were available only to those who had both money and coupons. Had industry been able to respond to consumer demands within the normal framework of unrestricted competition, the depression might well have continued. Although such extreme measures as rationing are clearly not necessary in peacetime, some form of regulation seems indispensable.

Finally, the war brought an abrupt end to the overcapacity crisis of the 1930s by putting some of U.S. industry's major competitors out of business. While much of Europe and Asia's industrial capacity was destroyed during the war, the United States was not only left unscathed, but actually expanded its own industrial capacity. This destruction of the world's excess capacity was, in a sense, an extreme form of economic regulation. The United States was left in a position that enabled it to preach the virtues of free trade without having to worry about a sudden invasion of exports from abroad. But wartime destruction did not itself account for the several decades of sustained recovery and prosperity enjoyed by the United States following the war. Another much less widely understood phenomenon also played a major role.

The Rise and Fall of Self-Regulation

From the end of World War II until the early 1970s, when the U.S. economy became much more vulnerable to international competition, a form of industrial self-regulation sustained prosperity by preventing runaway overcapacity. Paradoxically, the competitive constraints that antitrust legislation imposed on large U.S. corporations were responsible for this regulation. Like their predecessors at the turn of the century, the antitrust enforcers of the postwar era sought to prevent monopolistic control of industries and to stimulate competition. But in those industries ruled by oligopolies[8]—situations in which no more than four firms account for 60 to 70 percent of an industry's total sales—this antitrust fever produced an unforeseen side effect. By indicating that they would consider a large market share in a given industry to be a violation of the antitrust laws, the Justice Department and the Federal Trade Commission *inadvertently* forced the oligopolies to restrict output. Had the government actually been doing what it believed it was doing—stimulating competition—this self-regulation could not have succeeded. Former Solicitor General Robert Bork has outlined in hypothetical terms how self-regulation of this sort probably worked: if "the law announced a policy of dissolution of any firm that exceeded 50 percent of the market, [any firm approaching that size] *would have every incentive to restrict its output to avoid the penalties of law." Going further, Bork observed—as historian Richard Hofstadter had earlier—that in such an environment managers had to make all their decisions "with one eye constantly cast over their shoulders at the Antitrust Division."* [9]

There is enough evidence to suggest that Bork's hypothesis is not idle speculation. The history of antitrust proceedings in this century suggests that corporate managers had good reasons to fear gaining an excessive market share in a given industry. In 1945, Judge Learned Hand ruled that a large market share can itself be a violation of antitrust laws. U.S. Steel, International Harvester, Standard Oil,

American Tobacco, and, most recently, AT&T have all been hauled into court and, in the latter three cases, broken up. The courts have also enforced less severe measures to limit the size of market shares. When General Motors held a 50 percent share of the automobile industry in the 1950s, the courts compelled it to help competing bus manufacturers by sharing technology and to sell off the plants of a subsidiary road machinery company. A 1957 Supreme Court order forced DuPont to relinquish a 23 percent holding in General Motors, on the grounds that DuPont supplied too much of the automobile company's fabric, finishes, and antifreeze. And in the early 1970s, the Federal Trade Commission launched an unsuccessful ten-year effort to break up the "big four" of cereals—Kellogg, General Mills, General Foods, and Quaker Oats—accusing them of setting prices 25 percent higher than they should have been.

To limit their own market shares, the largest firms also had to be careful not to run their major competitors out of business. According to one widely circulated story, General Motors President Alfred Sloan once advised Walter Chrysler on how to better organize Chrysler Corporation, and later quietly arranged for some of General Motors' better managers to take jobs with the Ford Motor Company when the latter needed help after World War II. The demise of either Chrysler or Ford would almost certainly have resulted in governmental action against General Motors.

During the 1950s, several electrical companies took more direct action to ensure that all the firms would stay in business. In 1961, executives of General Electric, Westinghouse, and several smaller competitors were convicted of having illegally conspired to divide the electrical business according to prearranged market shares. The facts of the case are somewhat different from what one might expect. If General Electric and Westinghouse had competed as vigorously as possible by substantially reducing their prices, they might have driven their rivals out of business, which would have certainly provoked an antitrust action against them. But because government subsidies for reserve industrial mobilization capacity were then threatening to stimulate overcapacity in the electrical industry, the executives devised schemes to prevent a glut of capacity and thereby ensure that all the firms would stay in business. Ironically then, these giants were found guilty not of market concentration, but of deliberately losing business and ultimately profits—a classic antitrust anomaly.

Among the other industrial self-regulation schemes that produced better outcomes than strict adherence to antitrust laws would have were the much-maligned practices of "bid-rigging," "price-fixing," "dividing the business," and "collusion." Highway contractors have routinely engaged in such practices for many years because the rules for competitive bidding virtually compel them to do so. A contracting firm does not want to win all contracts, for fear of becoming a monopoly; therefore, it must occasionally submit artificially high bids. On the other hand, if the firm hopes to win even a single contract, it must sometimes understate projected costs. Long ago, groups of contractors concluded that they must plan among themselves in order to develop efficient schedules for hiring, buying, and moving large equipment from contractor to contractor and from job to job. Because of this practice, the Justice Department has targeted the construction industry for the largest single investigation in antitrust history.

Yet all of these forms of self-regulation, contrary to the principles underlying antitrust laws, contributed to widely enjoyed economic stability. With prices more or less "fixed" over relatively long periods of time, interdependent firms could negotiate long-term contracts with each other. More than anyone else, blue-collar workers enjoyed the benefits of this stability: job security and decent wages enabled these workers to establish roots, buy homes, educate their children—to become the solid citizens of Middle America.

On the other hand, these clandestine forms of self-regulation were hardly the most efficient or cost-free means of avoiding overcapacity. In order to convince the Justice Department and the Federal Trade Commission that consumers had enough alternatives, many big firms had to engage in clearly wasteful practices. Oil companies, for example, routinely cluttered intersections where a single service station would have been sufficient. Large firms typically spent billions on advertising: consumers ended up subsidizing the salaries of high-paid television newscasters. Price-setting also enabled firms to accumulate more profits than they could possibly use for expansion, thus setting the stage for expensive merger wars; this unofficial taxing system turned consumers into unacknowledged and unrewarded shareholders. Meanwhile, taxpayers were forced to spend untold sums on antitrust proceedings. All these hidden costs of self-regulation dwarfed those that taxpayers would have had to incur if an openly acknowledged system of regulation had been in place.

The era of prosperous self-regulation in the United States came to end in the mid-1970s with the rise of more "efficient" international competitors and the sudden influx of low-cost, high-quality goods from abroad. Foreign trade had been a relatively insignificant component of the U.S. economy until the late 1960s, but the postwar recoveries of European and Japanese industry eventually changed all that. The rapid development of industrial capacity in many Third World nations also contributed to the growing role of trade in the U.S. economy: during the 1970s alone, U.S. imports from developing countries rose from $3.6 billion to $30 billion. Thus, while in 1970 Americans imported only 9 percent of what they consumed, that figure has now risen to over 25 percent. With so many competitors now seeking to earn foreign exchange in the same markets, the greatest immediate impact of increased worldwide industrial capacity has fallen upon those countries, like the United States, that have erected relatively few trade barriers and that have failed to take other actions to rationalize new and existing industrial capacity. From the mid-1970s until the early 1980s, the rising tide of U.S.

imports swept many U.S. workers out of their jobs, bringing unemployment to levels occasionally approaching 10 percent.

One popular explanation for this increased U.S. dependence on imports is that U.S. firms were outcompeted by more modern and better managed firms in the "miracle economies" of Japan and West Germany. Adherents of this position argue that by not replacing aging factories and machinery with new technologies, the managers of many U.S. industries—steel, automobiles, and textiles, for instance—lost their competitive advantage to overseas rivals. While there may be some truth in this argument, it overlooks important factors. The recent failures of both *old* and *new* industries throughout the United States suggests that the failure to modernize is not the real problem. In fact, even those "sunset" manufacturers that dedicated themselves to modernization have had little success at warding off disaster.

The experiences of Wheeling-Pittsburgh Steel Corporation illustrate this point. In 1978, when it ranked as the nation's seventh largest steel manufacturer, Wheeling-Pittsburgh borrowed heavily to embark upon a $1-billion modernization program, the largest capital spending program in its history. Its union helped out by agreeing to lower wages and benefits until at least 1986. But having suffered $170 million in losses since 1982, having paid no dividends since 1979, and having become unable to repay its loans, Wheeling-Pittsburgh was recently forced to declare bankruptcy.

These valiant efforts to save Wheeling-Pittsburgh through modernization were in vain, primarily for two reasons. First, they overlooked the worldwide overcapacity that already existed and will continue to exist in the steel industry. Steel executives themselves estimate that the total steel-producing capacities of noncommunist countries—600 million tons per year—will dramatically exceed demand—400 million tons—for at least a decade. And these estimates do not take into account the approximately 700,000 tons of steel exported from communist countries to the United States in 1984.

Second, these efforts to save Wheeling-Pittsburgh overlooked the rise of lower-wage steel producers in the Third World. In recent years, U.S. steel imports have come more and more from developing countries. Annual shipments from South Korea, Brazil, Mexico, Argentina, and Venezuela jumped from 1.6 million tons to 5 million tons between 1979 and 1984, with some of the shipments displacing steel previously imported from modernized Japan and West Germany. Like the U.S. steel industry, steel producers in other OECD nations cannot outcompete these Third World exporters without lowering wages to Third World levels. As long as the newly industrializing countries are able to churn out steel at such relatively low costs, no amount of modernization will save the U.S. steel industry from the onslaught of imports. And as steel imports continue to pour in, the ability of the large U.S. steel producers to regulate the domestic industry will continue to decline. In this sense, any attempt to increase the productivity of the U.S. steel industry is counterproductive, as the worldwide steel industry is already suffering from more capacity than it can utilize.

Even the youngest and most modern U.S. industries are encountering economic difficulties. High technology, electronics, semiconductor, and computer industries are hardly "industrial dinosaurs." Yet these new and generally progressive industries are no more immune to the ravages of overcapacity than are the older industries. Until recently, for instance, the United States registered a $6.8 billion electronics trade deficit; this year's deficit threatens to reach $12 billion, equivalent to a full 10 percent of the total U.S. trade imbalance.

To be sure, the high value of the dollar is in part responsible for this expanding deficit, but excessive international competition also plays a role. The spread of technology throughout the world has produced such an immediate glut of electronics goods that many of the firms in California's Silicon Valley stand on the brink of disaster. In order to reduce costs, a good number of them have taken steps to move production abroad. But such a strategy is not without its costs. By relying on outsourcing to the point where many U.S. factories now merely assemble prefabricated parts, U.S. electronics companies are gradually losing much of their expertise. Unknowingly, U.S. manufacturers may be pushing themselves out of the world market.[10]

The overcapacity crisis in the computer industry has already, as noted previously, forced many firms out of business. Other firms are merging in attempts to rationalize capacity and output. In 1984, mergers and acquisitions in the U.S. software business were up 80 percent from 1983, for a total volume of $4.3 billion. As a result of this restructuring of the industry, many Americans are now "computer orphans," stranded with computers from firms that have stopped making them, have stopped supplying parts and programs, or have gone out of business altogether. Among these orphans are two million consumers who bought Texas Instruments 99/4As, one million who bought Commodore VC 20s, 700,000 who bought Timex Sinclair 100s, 200,000 who bought Coleco Adams, 135,000 who bought Franklin Aces, and even 250,000 who bought IBM PCjrs. These figures suggest that the benefits of unrestricted competition for the consumer may not be as great as many have thought.

Thus, even the best corporate managers in both "sunrise" and "sunset" industries are almost helpless during an overcapacity crisis. A 1982 bestseller, *In Search of Excellence: Lessons from America's Best-Run Companies,* highlighted 43 firms whose presumably outstanding managers had produced outstanding results between 1961 and 1980. But by November 1984, separate studies by McKinsey & Co., *Business Week,* and Standard and Poor's Compustat Services concluded that at least 14 of these "best-managed" firms no longer met the specified criteria for excellence, and that three others were experiencing severe problems. Among those companies that had fallen from grace were Delta Airlines, Eastman Kodak, Atari, Caterpillar Tractor, Digital Equipment, and Texas Instruments—a combination of both young and old firms.[11]

The economic problems encountered by these well-run firms—particularly those in high-technology production—make a mockery of the argument that the United States is in a difficult but promising phase of transition from old frostbelt industries to new sunbelt industries. Instead, it is evident that the problem lies in the existence of redundant worldwide capacity, as firms both in the United States and abroad are investing more and more in the same industries in hopes of expanding their own market shares. A significant amount of evidence indicates that this behavior will only lead this country, and the world, down the road to depression.

Indicators of Depression III

In the United States today, many of the indicators that accompanied the two great depressions seem to be signaling another economic crisis. Despite Reagan administration claims to the contrary, unemployment still remains at dangerously high levels, with at least 8 million Americans now out of work. In addition, the nation has recently been faced with mounting bankruptcies, another merger wave, and growing mountains of agricultural surpluses. On top of all of these historical signs of depression, the United States now faces a banking crisis that links domestic economic problems with those of the heavily indebted Third World. Taken together, these conditions—all products of unregulated competition and overcapacity—foreshadow a period of prolonged economic troubles. Each of them deserves closer attention.

Unemployment. Recognizing the deflationary pressures caused by high unemployment, the drafters of The Employment Act of 1946 charged the government to maintain "maximum employment, production, and purchasing power." But since the early 1960s, presidential economic advisors have whittled away at the responsibilities the Employment Act laid on the government by announcing their estimates of the "natural rate of unemployment," implying that the government need not concern itself with trying to bring unemployment below the rate accepted as "natural." These official statements have in a sense served to turn a new economic theory into an actively implemented policy. In theory, if unemployment were to fall substantially below the natural rate, workers would be able to demand wage increases that would trigger inflation—something the government can justify working to avoid. In practice, however, the natural unemployment rate policy is designed to ensure that the supply of labor will always greatly exceed the number of jobs available. The unemployed serve the presumably useful purpose of threatening to replace any workers who ask for "excessive" wage increases or, in some cases, who refuse to accept wage decreases in order to keep their employers in business. For the government to admit this aspect of its policy would of course be politically unacceptable; thus it continues to link the natural rate of unemployment with the need to control inflation.

The "natural" rate of unemployment articulated by the executive branch has steadily risen over the past 25 years, from 4 percent in the early 1960s, to 4.5 percent in the late 1960s, 5 percent in the mid-1970s, 6 percent in 1979, and now 7 percent—8 million U.S. workers unemployed as a matter of public policy. Few observers point out that 7 percent unemployment rates are extremely rare in U.S. history. Except for the depression of the 1890s and the 1930s, the United States suffered from these rates during only four years—1908, 1914, 1915, and 1921—until they became "natural" in the 1970s. Since then, over the past 10 years, unemployment has dipped *below* 7 percent only twice, in 1978 and 1979. Today, if we count "discouraged" workers—those who have given up looking for jobs they know they cannot find—the total may be as high as 14 million. And were it not for today's unprecedented peacetime military spending, unemployment would stand at around 15 percent. By historical standards, then, Depression III has already arrived in the United States, as it has in the West European countries whose unemployment rates now exceed 10 percent.

The question remains whether this depressionlike level of unemployment is only a moral or social problem, to be dealt with on those grounds, or whether it is an indicator of deeper economic malaise as well. Although that question cannot be answered definitively, it is clear that when 8 to 10 million members of the labor force are out of work at all times, the economy is functioning at less capacity than is economically desirable, if only because the society is less productive than it could be if unemployment were lower.

Bankruptcies. According to traditional economic thinking, a business failure indicates that the market is doing what it should—allowing the more efficient competitors to drive out the less efficient competitors. If no bankruptcies occur within a particular industry, economists are likely to conclude that there is too little competition. The advocates of airline deregulation, for example, argued that because in 40 years of regulation no airline had gone out of business, the United States needed more airlines. New airlines did indeed proliferate after deregulation in 1978, but so did bankruptcies—30 so far, half of them since January 1984.

The number of industrial and commercial failures in this country increased from 7,584 in 1979 to 31,334 in 1983. But it does not seem reasonable to conclude that this quadrupling represented simply a quadrupling of incompetent managers over a four-year period. Nor does a rash of airline bankruptcies back up the claim that before deregulation there were too few airlines. It is more likely that since deregulation there have been too *many,* or at least too many competing for the same high-volume routes. Overcapacity, not inefficiency, is the cause of these failures. An upsurge in bankruptcies is a sign of economic sickness rather than health.

Mergers. Firms in industries plagued by overcapacity know that investing their retained earnings in additional production facilities would make little sense, since the market is unable to absorb any more goods. Instead, they look for other firms to invest in. The proliferation of mergers in recent years attests to the overcapacity that exists in many U.S. industries.

Most mergers begin when a particular firm's stock appears to be "undervalued"—when the total value of all shares of its stock is less than the presumed value of all its assets. Most observers of the stock market take such "undervaluation" to mean that the market is giving a "false signal" of the firm's actual worth or that the firm in question is suffering from bad management. The prospect of acquiring a firm at a low price can lure many prospective buyers, who start to outbid each other. The price of the firm's shares can skyrocket as "hostile" and "friendly" buyers fight it out, or as the firm itself buys back much of its own stock in order to thwart a takeover attempt. By the time a merger war finally ends, the "winner" is often buying *overvalued* shares, having piled up mountains of new debt in the process. During the fight for control of Gulf Oil, for example, shares of Gulf stock doubled in price, even though the express purpose of the merger was to reduce surplus capacity. Phillips Petroleum, on the other hand, recently preserved its autonomy by buying out the "hostile" bidders who had promised to fire Phillips' managers. But to afford this, Phillips had to double its own debt, from $3.8 billion to $7.3 billion—75 percent of the firm's total worth, which is an entirely unacceptable level of debt for a corporation to sustain.

Such financial transactions seem to be getting more and more destabilizing. In a "leveraged buy-out," for instance, a public firm's managers use the firm's own assets as collateral in order to secure loans that enable them to buy the firm themselves. Investment banker Felix Rohatyn has complained about the damage that this type of deal may be having on the economy: "A public company, with say $100 million of debt and $900 million of capital, is turned into a private company with $900 million of debt and $100 million of capital . . . exactly the opposite of what our national objectives should be." [12]

Hundreds of billions of dollars are changing hands in transactions that often transform old equities into new debts and pay windfall profits to shareholders whose companies are actually closing down. The "undervalued" shares of stock that look so attractive to prospective buyers may be undervalued for a good reason: the firm's capacity represents a surplus, an excess of capacity within the entire industry, and hence the firm's assets are really not worth that much, since they are essentially useless. Obviously, entire industries need to be streamlined and reorganized. But because most economists and policymakers hold overcapacity to be impossible, the planning and coordination that this type of reorganization requires have not been passed into the necessary regulation. The clumsy device of mergers is the only recourse available to most firms—and we have seen what undesirable outcomes mergers produce.

Agriculture. More than any other industry, farming closely resembles the economic ideal of "perfect" competition: there are so many producers that no one of them can influence price levels. Under these conditions, what sort of industry has farming become in the United States? In 1955, one student of the U.S. economy concluded that all the problems farmers had faced over the previous 60 years could be summed up in one sentence. *"The supply of farm products as a whole has exceeded the demand for them at prices which cover the costs of most farm units."* [13] *Unless weather interferes, or the land simply wears out, U.S. farming tends toward overproduction and depression.*

The government, albeit somewhat reluctantly, has intervened to stabilize the farm economy. Until recently these interventions have been reasonably successful in preventing an all-out farm depression. But government policies are not widely understood. For example, price supports, which are now blamed for the crisis in the farm economy, do not in themselves cause surpluses, though they can be managed in ways that encourage greater production than is necessary or desirable. The real purpose and effect of price supports is to prevent the food shortages that would result if extremely low prices were to trigger-as they probably would—widespread farm failures and depression in the farming industry. Free-market farming would almost certainly yield not equilibrium but chaos and depression.

Other government policies are not just misunderstood; they lead to outcomes the government never intended. One long-term policy has been to preserve the family farm, a goal that conforms to the principle of unrestricted competition. But in the absence of cooperative planning, this policy has led to overproduction and to periodic collapses in the farm economy. Many family farmers have been forced out of business as a result. Similarly, for the past 75 years, the government has provided large-scale education and technical assistance to farmers, enabling them to become more and more productive. Not only has this program encouraged overproduction and surpluses, but it has led to the adoption of mechanized farming techniques that deplete the topsoil.

Most recently government policy has had tragic outcomes. In the 1970s, Washington encouraged farmers to produce as much as possible. Farmers complied, increasing their output and incurring debts to buy more land. True, the embargo on grain sales to the Soviet Union hurt U.S. farming, but even without the embargo farm surpluses would have mounted. Now prices are falling, interest rates are staying high, and the resultant decline in land values means that land is no longer suitable collateral for outstanding mortgages and crop loans. The Reagan administration, ignoring the history of U.S. agriculture and obsessed with reducing federal spending, is trying to restore free-market farming. Farmers are being blamed for the dire situation they find themselves in; they are being told to give up their farms and move to cities to look for jobs that do not exist. The rash of farm foreclosures spreading across the Midwest is painfully reminiscent of the last great depression.

Banking and Finance. The effects of overcapacity, overproduction, and unrestricted competition are multiplied many times over when they come together in the financial institutions on which public confidence in the economy ultimately rests. The Federal Deposit Insurance Corporation, created in the 1930s to restore confidence in banks and keep track of the banking industry, now lists more than 800 "problem banks"—more than at any time since the agency began counting them. The cause of "problem banks" is "problem loans" on which principal and interest are not paid on time, and these problem loans are often the result of the economic plight of firms in overcapacity-plagued industries, such as oil and agriculture. This situation cannot be blamed on incompetence or mismanagement either by the individuals, businesses, and developing countries that borrowed the money or by the institutions that made the loans. All parties have done exactly what economic principles instructed them to do. But the government, unfortunately, deregulated financial institutions in ways that are proving more and more detrimental.

For one thing, banks are increasingly allowed to cross state boundaries, which makes their activities less subject to supervision and control and encourages them to open up more branches. In addition, a federal loophole now permits banks and other institutions to open "half-banks"—branches that can either take deposits or make loans, but not both. With Sears, Prudential, and similar firms now operating "half-banks," the line between less speculative banking activities and more speculative brokerage and investment activities is increasingly blurred, and the effective capacity of the financial industry has been vastly increased. Thus more institutions are pursuing the business of the same number of depositors. Nationwide direct mail campaigns provide one indication of this increased competition.

The most far-reaching form of deregulation was the lifting of restrictions on interest rates: financial institutions are now free to offer depositors whatever interest managers think the bank can afford to pay, and to charge borrowers whatever interest rates the "free market" will bear. As a result, the United States now has the highest real interest rates in history.

To understand how these high interest rates have come about, one has to understand the peculiar way that supply and demand operate in the financial industry. When competition is unregulated, there is—theoretically, at least—no immediate limit to the availability of the resources that a producer would need to enter business. For instance, when trucking was deregulated, new and used trucks could be easily found; thus many individuals bought or leased trucks and set up new companies. Competition is in fact intended to produce this excess of supply over demand, which is supposed to drive down prices.

Banking is a major exception to this general rule. The total supply of the crucial resource—money—is always limited, or regulated, by the Federal Reserve Board. In general, when a vital resource becomes limited, countries may find themselves compelled to set aside traditional economic principles and ration available supplies at fixed prices, as the United States did during World War II. But instead of setting the price of money—interest rates—at a fixed level, the government has lifted virtually all controls on interest rates. Thus as more and more banks and other institutions have competed for this money, its price—interest rates—has climbed. The situation has been exacerbated by the tight money policy that the Fed, under Paul Volcker, instituted in 1979 in order to reduce inflation. The slightly more expansionist policy the Fed adopted in late 1982 lowered interest rates somewhat, but to reduce them as much as is necessary the Fed would have to vastly increase the money supply; this, however, would trigger inflation, which the government is reluctant to do. So the U.S. and international economies are saddled with high interest rates, whose primary cause is not, as many claim, the federal budget deficit, but rather interest rate deregulation.

This deregulation, by stimulating increased competition in the financial industry, has created other problems. Banks now find themselves in a two-way squeeze: they have to compete as vigorously as they can for both depositors and borrowers. Because there are more financial institutions competing for the same number of depositors, banks have had to increase the rate of interest they pay to depositors in order to attract as many of them as possible. But because competition for borrowers has also increased, banks have had to keep the interest rates they charge those borrowers as low as possible. Thus the margin between interest rates paid out—expenses—and interest rates charged—income—has decreased. To maintain their profits, banks must reduce their own costs of operation, employing the smallest possible number of loan officers, and they must make extremely quick decisions about lending money if they are to collect the interest they need to pay interest to their depositors. These pressures have led to a number of unwise loans, which are now becoming the problem loans that turn banks into problem banks.

Meanwhile, interest rate deregulation has drawn enormous sums of money from abroad. Good opportunities for industrial investment are as scarce in many foreign countries as they are in the United States; foreign depositors, attracted by high U.S. interest rates, have put money into insured U.S. accounts. Not only does this demand for U.S. currency drive up the dollar, worsening the U.S. trade imbalance, but it also compels U.S. banks, flooded with deposits, to make increasingly risky loans, both at home and abroad. It has become less and less realistic to expect that all these loans will be repaid at one time, especially since the interest charged on them has become astronomically high. Many small banks have already failed or been swallowed up by larger banks—and large banks no longer seem immune to these kinds of problems, as Continental Illinois proved in 1984. When we consider the central role of banking and finance in the U.S. and world economy, these developments must give us pause.

Yet the government is not taking steps to alleviate the current crisis; if anything, current policies threaten to make the situation worse. There is continued momentum for deregulation of industries. Nondefense public spending has repeatedly been slashed. And many policymakers argue that, in order to revitalize the U.S. economy, we must "outinvest," "outproduce," and "outcompete" every other nation in the world. To implement this strategy, many influential individuals and organizations have argued, the United States must redesign its tax laws so as to *increase* savings and investment and *decrease* consumption.[14] The "simplified" or "flat" tax, advocated by such diverse figures as liberal Senator Bill Bradley and conservative Congressman Jack Kemp, is billed not only as tax relief for a broad base of U.S. citizens, but also as a way of stimulating personal savings and huge new investments in industry. What no one points out is that these proposals resemble measures taken by Europe and Japan during the 1950s and 1960s as they struggled to solve the *undercapacity* created by World War II. Accordingly, they fail to address America's current *overcapacity* crisis.

In another attempt to strengthen the U.S. economic position, some business and education leaders have insisted that the United States must "meet the competitive challenge" by reversing the decline in American sales abroad—by "recapturing" lost U.S. export markets.[15] This call for renewed competitiveness is a response to the same pressures—the imports flooding U.S. markets, the problems of U.S. sunset and sunrise industries—that have forced U.S. policymakers to accept a 7 percent unemployment rate as "natural." The proposed tax reform would make renewed competitiveness seem like an even more urgent necessity: if investment in U.S. industry is encouraged but domestic consumption is discouraged, there is no place to sell U.S. products but abroad. Yet the United States cannot reasonably expect other countries to close their factories and buy U.S. goods. A drive for renewed competitiveness would probably result not in renewed U.S. prosperity but in trade wars, with disastrous results for U.S. industry, the health of the world economy, and international political stability.

Setting the Agenda

Given the overcapacity problems that exist today, what we need is a combination of industrial regulation—this time on a multilateral basis—and an extensive program of public works projects. Unlike increased private investment in the production of consumer goods, major public investment in our nation's infrastructure and environmental health could greatly increase employment, stimulate additional economic growth, and lay the foundation for America's economic future. But these efforts alone will not ensure the smooth functioning of the U.S. economy or the world economy. They must be accompanied by some form of permanent economic regulation, for the private sector remains the heart of the economy. Above all the United States needs a trade, industrial, and investment policy that is coordinated with those of other countries.

In some circles, public works are regarded as little more than a short-term and half-baked response to downturns in the "business cycle," or as make-work for the unemployed to keep them from resorting to thievery. But the evidence suggests that public spending, especially in quality-of-life programs, may be the most efficient means of stimulating the economy. Any investment in the economy is valued not only for the employment it generates by itself, but also for its "ripple effects"—the jobs it creates among suppliers of parts, transportation companies, and businesses that serve the newly employed workers. Public spending apparently outdoes private spending in terms of the ripple effects it creates. One study indicated that, in 1980, each $1 billion of private spending created 30,000 jobs, fewer than the 35,000 jobs created by $1 billion of defense spending and fewer still than the 50,000 created by $1 billion of nondefense public spending. Other estimates show that each $1 billion of spending on public works can create 70,000 to 80,000 jobs, which may mark it as the most economical method of increasing employment.

Public works are necessary not only to create employment and to stimulate economic activity, but also to rebuild our infrastructure, to prevent further environmental damage, and to lay the foundation for future economic growth. The quality of this nation's—and this planet's—life cannot be treated indefinitely as a trivial matter. Just a glance at recent assessments of the state of this country's infrastructure enables one to understand why some observers describe an *America in Ruins:*[16]

- Forty-five percent of 557,516 highway bridges are deficient or obsolete.
- The interstate highway system is still incomplete, and furthermore is deteriorating so rapidly that every year 2,000 miles of it need reconstruction. The outstanding backlog is four times that amount.
- In 10 of 28 major cities, leaking water systems lose 10 percent of the water they carry. Two of the worst systems—New York's and Boston's—have yet to be studied in detail.
- Half of all U.S. communities are already operating their waste—water systems at full capacity—they could not handle any more than they already do. Many sewer systems are badly deteriorated.
- The railroad system is in such a shambles that repair and renewal costs cannot even be estimated.

The nation's educational, communications, and environmental systems also need massive attention. Many Americans attack school systems for the reputedly widespread deterioration of educational standards, but few people advocate spending more federal and state funds to hire more teachers, reduce class sizes, and update school buildings and materials. To ensure our nation's economic future, more public spending on education is needed, not less. Similarly, communications systems will require immense and coordinated investments if they are to make use of the computer and telecommunications technologies now being developed. Comparable public investment is required to preserve the environment. Environmental programs should no longer be hampered by the conditions currently imposed—we tend to adopt no program until we know for certain that it will accomplish its objective—but instead should be designed to prevent any further environmental damage. Not just rail systems, but all transportation systems need extensive repair and expansion. This expansion should take place on an international level: one of the tragedies of the current famine in Africa is the difficulty of transporting food to those who need it. We should be constructing giant multinational and multicontinental projects that will facilitate the global transportation of resources like food, fuel, and water. These logistics networks, including offshore port complexes, could strengthen international linkages by establishing physical interdependencies that would make war less and less thinkable.

The Congressional Budget Office has estimated that the United States should be spending at least $50 billion annually on public works programs, double or triple recent levels. The type of program outlined above would require at least $75 to $100 billion per year. This may sound like a large amount—but consider that it is less than one-third of the projected defense budget, and would create 6 to 8 million jobs. Much of the funding could be raised by new taxes and disincentives for nonproductive investment. For example, when industrywide overcapacity prevents a corporation from investing its earnings in new domestic facilities, those earnings should be taxed away as windfall profits. This would discourage companies from retaining earnings they cannot use in creating new capacity and thus might reduce consumer prices. It might also discourage merger speculation—the financial activity that corporations tend to resort to when they have nowhere else to invest their profits. In addition, depreciation schedules should be extended over longer periods of time, to reflect more accurately the useful lives of plants, equipment, and office buildings. Capital gains should no longer receive special treatment but should be taxed as ordinary income. Personal tax rates should also be adjusted: contrary to most conventional economic prescriptions, taxes for those with higher incomes should be *raised* instead of lowered. Because of overcapacity, wealthy individuals, like wealthy corporations, tend to invest their surplus funds in financial speculation rather than in productive capacity. The country would profit greatly if some of these funds were taxed away and used for greatly needed public works.

Unfortunately, such changes seem unlikely to occur in the near future. In today's policy climate, public works are more threatened than ever. In an effort to reduce the federal deficit, many existing programs are being reduced or eliminated altogether. The supply-side strategy and conservative bent of the Reagan team are not the only obstacles, however. Just as traditional economic principles prevent most observers from correctly attributing depressions to overcapacity, so traditional economic and accounting practices reinforce most people's resistance to the type of public works program proposed here.

Consider, for example, the distinction made between private spending and public spending in our national accounts. The money that businesses borrow and spend on new plants and equipment is labeled "investment" and entered as such in our National Income Accounts (NIA). Theoretically, the firms spending this money will be able to sell their manufacturing output at reasonable profits and pay off their loans; in this sense, the plants and equipment, even though they are paid for with borrowed funds, are considered to be additions to the national "wealth." The total of this sort of new investment, as a fraction of GNP, is an accepted indicator of economic strength.

These evaluations depend on the assumption that overcapacity is impossible. But the facts do not bear out this assumption. The Wheeling-Pittsburgh modernization program is one example. Another is a $450-million brewery that the Miller Brewing Company built in Ohio last year. Analysts predict that the brewery will not open for at least five years, if ever, because even now Miller is capable of producing 42 percent more beer than it can sell. Still further examples of this trend are provided by the new and empty office buildings that have sprung up all over the country—a glut that has been encouraged by the shortening of depreciation schedules from 40 to 15 years. Again, it is clear that overcapacity is waste rather than wealth. Except in conditions of undercapacity, such as existed in Europe and Japan after World War II, substantial increases in rates of private investment can signal not prosperity but oncoming depression.

In contrast to private spending, public spending, whether to build roads and bridges or to protect the environment, is *not* considered economic investment. Charles L. Schultze, Jimmy Carter's chief economic advisor and a leading authority on income accounts, has described this misleading practice of the U.S. government accounting:

> Part of the federal, state and local government spending represents investment in productive assets (schools, highways, sewerage and water systems) which contribute to the capacity and efficiency of the economy. In the U.S. national income accounts, however, . . . such investment-type outlays are not included in the investment category of GNP, which is reserved for private investment.[17]

One might argue that this does not create a problem, since Schultze does acknowledge that public works can be "productive assets." Yet accounting practices greatly influence the way Americans assess investment in new factories versus investment in public works such as roads, bridges, environmental protection, and education. Despite the fact that these public systems and services are vital to the efficient functioning of the U.S. economy, they are considered to be of much less economic importance than private investment. Even the interstate highway system was justified on grounds of national defense, not economic necessity.

Other financial practices also contribute to the priority given to private investment. For example, new plants and equipment can serve as collateral for the money borrowed to construct them because of the erroneous belief that they will always have enough market value to back up any loans. But when the government builds a bridge, it has no intention of ever selling it; since the bridge is technically worthless, it cannot secure any loans to finance its construction. According to this logic, the government is guilty of "monetizing" its debt by printing worthless money; *all* government deficit spending, then, causes inflation.

Thus an accounting practice has encouraged widespread misunderstanding about the nature of government debt and the nature of corporate debt. In 1950, the federal debt was $217 billion whereas corporations owed only $142 billion. By 1976, the last year for which the Department of Commerce reported the data, the federal debt was $516 billion but corporate debt had skyrocketed to $1.4 trillion. The Federal Reserve Board has since released figures that set corporate debt much lower. But no matter whose data is used, it is clear that federal credit market debt is much less significant than it used to be. As a share of total debt, it dropped from one-third in 1950 to slightly more than one-sixth in 1982; as a fraction of GNP, it declined from two-thirds in the early 1950s to one-third in 1984.

Corporate debt, on the other hand, may be much larger than estimated. For one thing, corporations and government use different accounting practices. Albert T. Sommers, until recently the chief economist for the Conference Board, has pointed out that if business used government reporting standards, the "fastest-growing and most potentially successful businesses . . . would report deficits year after year." [18] Economist Alan Blinder has made a similar argument in reverse: if government used business accounting practices, it would have "run a budgetary surplus during most of the past 20 years." [19] This state of affairs becomes all the more disturbing when one recalls that much recent corporate debt has been incurred not to build new industrial capacity but to engage in speculation and mergers. Thus the popular notion that government borrowing crowds out legions of entrepreneurs seeking loans to build new plants and create new jobs is highly misleading. At this time, many of the measures designed to encourage investment in the private sector will only exacerbate the underlying problem of overcapacity. On the other hand, major public works projects can restore full employment and stimulate economic growth not only in this country but also abroad.

Sustained economic growth, however, will require new forms of public regulation, both domestically and internationally. We need to devise mechanisms that will reduce existing overcapacity, rationalize new investment, and coordinate trade and investment with other countries. Only occasionally, however, has the government made tentative steps in this direction. A rare example is the ad hoc protectionism that is occasionally instituted. But because import quotas are designed merely as temporary actions to give U.S. industries "breathing room" to modernize and not as part of a larger coherent policy, they fail to provide what industries really need—a basis for systematic long-term planning for domestic investment.

Take the case of the U.S. auto industry. During the 1970s, when steep rises in oil prices suddenly increased U.S. demand for fuel-saving small cars, the Japanese were well positioned to take advantage of the new market. The profits of U.S. auto manufacturers fell so much that capital for quick retooling was not readily available; the survival of Ford and Chrysler was increasingly threatened. Finally, in 1981, the government negotiated quotas with Japan and intervened to save Chrysler. U.S. auto firms did redesign their products and began to reap larger profits, although at lower levels of employment and output than in previous years. But now that President Reagan has lifted the quotas, in the hope that Japan would respond by opening its markets to U.S. goods, U.S. auto manufacturers may be in trouble again. For Tokyo has announced that it will set its own automobile exports at a level about 25 percent above the number shipped during the last year of quotas. This means that nearly half a million additional Japanese cars may be sold in the United States, eliminating possibly 90,000 jobs in the U.S. auto industry. Chrysler and Ford, worried about being able to compete without the quotas, have indicated that they may scrap all plans to build new plants in the United States and instead locate them in Mexico and South Korea, where wage costs are lower. Alternatively, they may enter into joint ventures with foreign firms to "get behind" whatever barriers may be erected during trade wars. As a result, the auto industry may come to resemble the electronics industry.

As more U.S. workers are laid off, as more U.S. corporations locate their operations overseas, as more U.S. industries become unable to compete in the international economy, the inadequacy of Washington's current hands-off approach to the economy should become more apparent. The only solution is increased government regulation of industry in order to discourage unproductive activity, decrease current overcapacity, and coordinate planning not only among U.S. industries but also among industries around the world.

An example from Japan may indicate why the Japanese have competed so much more successfully and have thus far been able to maintain high levels of employment. Recently, having decided that its chemical industry had too much capacity, the Japanese government asked the 18 producers of ethylene and its derivatives to collaborate on developing recommendations about how to eliminate excess capacity. The firms agreed among themselves that they should reorganize into three new consortia. Each consortium would reduce its individual capacity by 36 percent—a substantial but reasonable figure, considering that executives in the oil and steel industries have estimated overcapacity in the industrialized countries at 30 to 50 percent. The Japanese consortia respected the country's guaranteed employment policy and agreed to keep surplus workers on the payrolls during a period of underemployment, eventually shifting them to other jobs. Because this plan was officially labeled "advisory," it did not violate antimonopoly laws. Subsequently, the Japanese government enacted a government-industry partnership agreement to reorganize the chemical industry in light of world economic conditions.

The United States should take the lead from Japan and initiate this type of industrial rationalization. The program should include measures to reduce and allocate capacity and to develop long-term plans for necessary new capacity. (As part of this process, shares of stock in merging corporations should be amalgamated so as to reasonably compensate shareholders without giving them unjustifiably large windfall profits as unneeded plants are closed down.) Many Americans fear that attempts at this type of planning would lead to a series of ill-informed and secret bureaucratic decisions. That, however, is the situation that already exists: because of overcapacity and antitrust laws, financiers and managers now make overnight arrangements for one firm to buy out another, often putting managers in charge of a company in a different industry they have no expertise in. What is needed are *partnership* arrangements, bringing together those individuals from government, business, and labor who know the most about conditions in particular industries. This shared authority would enable governments to link industrial rationalization with quality-of-life public works programs. Such a system could result in the kind of stability that the United States enjoyed during the 1950s and 1960s, with an important difference: instead of the war-induced and hidden self-regulation of that period, there would be an open form of regulation directly connected to considerations of the public interest.

For such plans to be effective, however, they must be implemented on a multilateral basis and be linked, where appropriate, to import quotas as well as to quality-of-life programs. Mutually negotiated import quotas represent small steps in the right direction. After the 1981 U.S.-Japan automobile agreement, five other countries—Belgium, Canada, Luxembourg, the Netherlands, and West Germany—reached similar agreements with Japan. European nations have negotiated innumerable such agreements among themselves. Quota agreements also benefit many other U.S. industries, including meat, shoes, radios, televisions, and textiles, although electronics and textiles are increasingly threatened by imports. The problem with quotas as they are now implemented, however, is that they are viewed as temporary stopgaps instead of as the beginning of permanent and adjustable agreements. Too few people notice that quotas would rarely be needed if industries were not already saddled with overcapacity. Quotas can help to solve this overcapacity, if they are established on a more permanent basis and linked to broader schemes of industrial rationalization.

Clearly, this is an extremely tall order. The international economy is so complex and closely woven that any attempt to institute an extensive set of multilateral agreements will necessarily involve difficult problems of equity. Developing countries, for example, now need foreign exchange to service the debts they have incurred in recent years. Yet if they try constantly to increase their exports to the industrial countries, unemployment among the latter will continue to rise, diminishing their ability to buy the developing countries' goods.

These are, however, problems that must be grappled with and that require broad solutions. There seems to be a growing, albeit still limited, recognition of the need to rationalize industry on an international, multilateral level. In 1984, steel executives made it known that only a comprehensive multilateral agreement to regulate that industry could solve its overcapacity crisis. Subsequently, the American Iron and Steel Institute asked the White House to call a conference of steel producers to address the overcapacity problem and perhaps to take initial steps toward a broad agreement on a gradual division of the world's steel output among the various steel-producing countries. The Reagan administration responded to this request with the decision to negotiate voluntary agreements with foreign steel producers to limit themselves to 18.5 percent of the American market. These temporary quotas, however, will only continue the present uncertainty in the industry and prevent systematic long-term planning. Steel firms are now considering making arrangements to produce steel elsewhere. The administration's refusal to take needed action is tragically short-sighted. Other U.S. industries need the same attention that steel has asked for: the copper industry, which was recently denied its request for quotas; and the oil industry, which continues to face stiff competition from the refineries that are proliferating in the Middle East.

Multilateral industrial regulation would also address the current need for increased multicorporation research and development. Widespread cooperation in research and development now takes place most commonly among military allies pursuing joint military activities. But individual firms, and in some cases individual nations, are no longer equipped to pursue single-handedly their own research objectives. The fixed cost of R&D—especially the cost of developing new technologies—is rapidly becoming so great that only the very largest multinational corporations with assured markets can undertake these efforts. Thus rather than stymieing innovation, multilateral cooperative agreements that pool resources and share costs could actually promote it. Moreover, the secrecy imposed by vigorous competition among firms *or* nations actually retards the development of new knowledge: technological progress would be greater if cooperation were more widespread. In addition, the new technologies and products that are being introduced more and more rapidly need immediate regulation to prevent industrywide chaos. This will become even more important as new industries increase capacity while old industries are reducing theirs.

Opponents of cooperative research and such multilateral agreements are, to some extent, correct when they argue that the sharing of more standardized technologies, along with the increased use of multinational regulation, would probably cause some decrease in international trade. But this is a trend that should be accepted. In today's world of rapidly moving capital and technology, the Ricardian notion of comparative advantage has lost much of its meaning. The determining factor in many areas of competition is not natural resources, but lower wages. Thus some form of managed trade is necessary to ensure a better balance between supply and demand. Ideally, imports should be confined to goods that are indispensable and cannot be domestically produced in large enough quantities. The United States, for example, would remain a large net exporter of food, and countries with minerals would continue to export them. All this, of course, would take place within the framework of multilateral regulatory systems. Such a multilateral arrangement would have to include "socialist" as well as "capitalist" producers. Whatever ideologues of either stripe may believe, the problems of excessive competition and overcapacity are world problems, as growing steel exports from socialist countries demonstrate. Long-term market-sharing arrangements between East and West could not only facilitate economic growth but also create additional incentives for peaceful cooperation.

Finally, the health of our banking system, both nationally and internationally, requires immediate attention. The international economy is presently threatened by several disturbing trends, not the least of which is the mountain of Third World debt. Much of the money now being loaned to Third World countries merely enables them to keep up interest payments on debts they can never by expected to repay in full. Exercises in "debt restructuring" continue to take place primarily because banks do not want to register huge losses on their balance sheets and because it is not possible to "repossess" Mexico or Argentina. Many observers now suggest that, at the very least, interest rates on outstanding loans to developing countries must be reduced. But ultimately, some measure of debt forgiveness may be needed.

Any reduction of interest rates on foreign loans in the near term should be linked to *re*regulation of U.S. interest rates. The disastrous policy decision to deregulate financial markets must be reversed: depositors should be paid interest that reflects the rate of inflation. This step alone would help to alleviate the "strong dollar" problem by making U.S. banks a less attractive repository for foreign capital.

Reregulation of banking should stimulate reevaluation of other deregulatory actions that have been taken in recent years. Whatever its pitfalls and limitations, regulation of industry and commerce is preferable to the overcapacity and depression that result from unrestricted competition. During the 1930s, regulation was instituted only after free-market competition had failed. Before we are engulfed by another such crisis, we must implement the planning and controls that U.S. industry and the U.S. economy need. And we must concentrate on putting America back to work, through large-scale quality-of-life public works programs.

Today such programs seem to be opposed by both Republicans and Democrats, both conservatives and liberals. President Reagan condemns government's tendency to "tax and tax, borrow and borrow. and spend and spend," while Democrats warn of the dire consequences the federal budget deficit will have on future generations. But if we are worried about the legacy we leave behind us, we should concern ourselves with the debts associated with overcapacity at least as much as with those connected with public works. In the end, we must ask which will benefit our children more: a healthy environment and better schools, hospitals, communication and transportation systems,or a countryside littered with commercial and industrial ruins that were unneeded as soon as they were built?

Notes

1. *New York Times,* December 9, 1931; April, 3, 1932.

2. Ibid., May 8, 1933.

3. Robert M. Solow, "The Intelligent Citizen's Guide to Inflation," *The Public Interest,* No. 38 (Winter 1975), p. 60.

4. This is not surprising, given the current disagreement among economists about the lesser problems of recession and inflation. Economist Lester C. Thurow has compared the discord in the economics profession today to that of the early days of the depression: "The current intellectual disarray among economists is matched only by a parallel time of confusion during the early days of the Great Depression. Economists then could not agree on what caused the Depression or what to do to get out of it. Individual economists were supremely confident that their own theory would work, but without a decent consensus within the economics profession, policymakers didn't know how to proceed, so basically they did nothing." Lester C. Thurow, *Dangerous Currents: The State of Economics* (New York: Random House, 1983), p. xv.

5. Quoted in Mark J. Green (ed.), *The Closed Enterprise System: Ralph Nader's Study Group Report on Antitrust Enforcement* (New York: Grossman, 1972), pp. 5-6.

6. Harold U. Faulkner, *Politics, Reform and Expansion: 1890-1900* (New York: Harper & Row, 1959), p. 145.

7. Ross M. Robertson, *History of the American Economy* (New York: Harcourt & Brace, 1955) pp. 565-66.

8. Aluminum, copper, rubber, cigarettes, soap and detergents, cereals, liquor, glass, refrigerators, cellulose fibers, photographic equipment, cans, computers, and sugar long were examples of such market concentration; the "big three" of automobiles were the most famous of all.

9. Robert H. Bork, *The Antitrust Paradox: A Policy at War with Itself* (New York: Basic Books, 1979) pp. 3-4, 197.

10. *Business Week,* March 11, 1985.

11. Thomas J. Peters and Robert H. Waterman, Jr., *In Search of Excellence: Lessons from America's Best-Run Companies* (New York: Harper & Row, 1982); *Business Week,* November 5, 1984.

12. *Wall Street Journal,* May 18, 1984.

13. Robertson (fn. 7), p. 390 (emphasis in original).

14. See the statement of the Bipartisan Budget Appeal, a group of 600 business leaders, economists, and university presidents, assembled by five former Treasury secretaries and one Commerce secretary, *New York Times,* May 4, 1984.

15. *America's Competitive Challenge: A Report to the President of the United States from the Business-Higher Education Forum.* Washington, D.C., 1983. Foreword, Chapter 1.

16. Pat Choate and Susan Walter, *America in Ruins: The Decaying Infrastructure* (Durham, NC: Duke University Press, 1983.)

17. Charles L. Schultze, *National Income Analysis* (Englewood Cliffs, NJ: Prentice-Hall, 1964).

18. Albert T. Sommers, "The Federal Budget Should Be Rebuilt From the Ground Up," *Across the Board* (New York: The Conference Board, May 1981), p. 19.

19. Alan S. Blinder, "Vaudeville on the Potomac," *Washington Post,* August 27, 1982.

Continuous Education for a Changing World

LEARNING NEEDS IN A CHANGING WORLD: HUMAN RESOURCES IN A KNOWLEDGE CIVILIZATION

by

Mahdi Elmandjra

Change and Learning

The word "change" has been overused and often abused. We tend therefore to overlook the meaning and implications of its content and we rarely take the trouble to project into the future the consequences it may entail particularly with respect to learning. This is due first of all to our learning systems which are geared toward maintenance and pattern reproduction and are not therefore at ease with dynamic processes.

The world is changing. This has been so ever since the beginning of humanity. What is new however is the high rate of this change which has greatly reduced the time allowed for adaptation. We could almost say that the very concept of change has itself changed due to an acceleration of nistory.

What are some of the striking changes which need to be recalled to permit us to sketch out very broadly a few of the new learning needs? These changes are of a quantitative as well as of a qualitative nature although quite often the distinction between these two aspects is blurred and becomes almost a formal one.

- For the first time in the history of mankind, man is capable of eradicating his own specie not to speak of all other forms of life. The meaning of "survival" has thus radically changed. This has far reaching implications for our learning systems.
- The growth of the world population and the inability to cope with its socio-economic consequences has brought about new problems for national and planetary management.
- Remarkable breakthroughs in science and technology have led to a higher complexity and created a new "problematique"—to use an expression dear to the Club of Rome—that is an intermeshing of a large number of sectoral problems none of which can be properly handled on a purely sectoral basis.

Mahdi Elmandjra is president of the International Association of Futuribles.

- A real explosion of knowledge has ensued from these break-throughs and has contributed to an overflow of information.[1] It is estimated that the total knowledge of mankind doubles now every 7 or 8 years. Over 2,000 titles of new books are published daily. It is not only the amount of information which has grown. The speed of its processing (1.2 billion operations per second in Cray 2 computer), the stocking capacity (the equivalent of 275,000 pages on a small compact laser disk which fits in a pocket) and the ease and rapidity of access through telematics have totally transformed the servicing of knowledge.
- The information revolution and the developments in the other high technologies such as artificial intelligence, biotechnology, new materials and space technologies have come about and flourish on one main ingredient: knowledge and with much less emphasis on natural resources or even capital. This transformation of society from a civilization based on raw materials, capital and production to one based on human resources and knowledge is of course at its very beginning and does not yet affect all parts of the globe with the same intensity. It is however an irreversible development with huge consequences for our learning systems.
- One of the economic indicators that help to measure these changes is the increased weight of "services" in national economies and in international economic relations. In international trade, services amounted to $30 billion in 1970; in 1985 this figure went up to $400 billion.
- Change has also affected the ethical norms of the international system but not always for the better because our societal learning processes did not enable it to capitalize on the positive aspects of these transformations. Maintenance learning has prevailed in spite of the decolonization of the 1950s and 1960s. Although the planet has become a village, inequities have been reinforced and social justice slighted to the point where we could speak of the development of an international feudalism.
- Things have changed and are changing but not in the same way and the same place for every one. Hence the emergence of a completely new paradigm of social justice and human rights and the need to learn how to reverse the increasing gap between the "two humanities" and to reduce the schism between the "two cultures." Over one third of humanity is living below the poverty line, famine is still the lot of tens of millions of people not to speak of the devastations of ignorance and disease.
- On the eve of the 21st Century almost one out of four inhabitants of the globe is still illiterate, over 400 million people are under-employed or unemployed at a time when human resources have become the key factor of development. With 20% of the world population, the industrialized countries account for 85% of the world expenditures on education and 95% of those on research. These disproportions are further accentuated when one takes into account the fact that over one-third of the world population

is under 15 years of age and that 90% of them live in the Third World.

Major Obstacles to the Rational Use Of the Human Potential

One could go on with a long list of positive and negative changes which affect our life but this paper is not about change per se but rather on the learning needs which are called for by these changes. One of the problems is that the development models which have made these changes possible have tended to and continue to exclude man from the equation. It is only in recent years that we began to hear, in "developmental" circles, about the role of the "human potential."

In the early 1960s the World Bank made its first soft loans to education as a social sector rather than as a "productive" one. One had to wait until the Bank's report of 1985 to discover a formal and official stand about the importance of human resources for development. The report of the Executive Director of UNICEF of this year highlights more clearly than ever before the place of the "human factor" in socio-economic development.

The United Nations Development Program has come a long way from the stand it took twenty years ago about the financing of literacy projects. It is therefore most encouraging to read in the letter of invitation which the Administrator of UNDP addressed to invitees to its April 1986 meeting in Tokyo that "the time has come for bold new ideas to improve the use of the human factor in development and to formulate practical plans for practical action . . . "

We note here another change and a welcome one. But there are at least five important things which have not yet seriously changed and which constitute major obstacles for the assessment and satisfaction of the new learning needs:

1. The development models—especially those of Third World countries which are the product of an almost blind imitation, either voluntary or imposed by external expertise;
2. The learning systems in the North and the South alike;
3. The mental structures which these models and systems produce and maintain;
4. The insufficient weight accorded to socio-cultural values in the elaboration of educational systems and the programming of their content;
5. A resistance and/or an incapacity to analyze and seek solutions within a long-term perspective, i.e. an absence of vision due to the short-sightedness of politicians, government officials and most decision makers who are usually more preoccupied by the short-term.

These are also the major causes of what we have called the "human gap" in the Club of Rome report *No Limits to Learning*.[2] The human gap being the distance which separates the level of our attainment in the areas of knowledge and resources from our capacity to master and solve the problems engendered by this knowledge. This gap can also be seen as a learning failure. For Aurelio Peccei, the founder of the Club of Rome, one of the major problems of society is the great gap—if not divorce—between man as a creator and man as a manager.

The above constraints must be taken into account whatever measures are envisaged at the learning level. One of the first needs of learning is how to overcome them. In my view this can not be done through mere adjustments, mild reforms, increase of financial resources and adaptation. What is needed is an overhauling of the learning systems and their transformation so as to make them socio-culturally relevant and capable of facing the challenges which change has brought about.

In the above-mentioned report to the Club of Rome, the authors advanced a relatively simple thesis. The present learning systems like all those which preceded them have one basic historical function: maintenance—the reproduction of norms and values from one generation to another. In the past, change was slow enough to allow these systems to evolve and adapt. This is no longer possible, hence the need for "innovative learning" instead of "maintenance learning." Innovative learning calls for two prerequisites: participation (solidarity in space) and anticipation (solidarity in time).

The issue in question here is of a universal nature and we should avoid, at all cost, bi-polarizing it into a "North" and "South" perspective; the problems of the learning systems are quite similar especially if, in addition, we bear in mind the fact that the learning systems of the South are very poor photocopies of the northern ones. The qualitative needs are the same and so are the challenges ahead even if quantitatively the problems of the South are enormous in scope. We are, of course, speaking here about the purpose and objectives of the systems of learning not about their specific content.

To be brief and in order to facilitate the discussion let me simply sketch out in telegraphic style a list of issues which ought to be considered in any exercise aiming at the reassessment of learning needs and the optimalization of human resources in a changing world.

- The greatest element of waste in our contemporary society is to be found in the area of human resources. We are obsessed by the concept of productivity and efficiency when it comes to land, mines, machines, products, industrial processes and management. At the same time we find about 1 billion illiterates a very minimal rational use of the human potential including those who have received an education. According to some specialists we do not, as individuals, even use 10% of our learning potential. We have a fairly exact inventory of the natural resources of the planet and we are surveying the composition of the universe but we do not seem to be sufficiently preoccupied by all of the untapped human resources which could greatly improve the quality of life and enhance creativity.

- In spite of the great strides which have been achieved in science and technology, including artificial intelligence, neuro-physiology and psycho-pedagogy, we still know very little about how our learning process functions. A part of the small knowledge we have acquired is not available to the scientific community at large and is kept in the laboratories of the military and the pharmaceutical industry.
- The main characteristic of a society of knowledge is the increasing proportion of resources devoted to research (in the advanced technologies, industry spends between 7% and 11% of its turnover on R&D). In the area of learning the amount spent on R&D is not only infinitesimal but it is almost impossible to identify and much less so to measure. We do not even have international norms and standards to collect comparable statistics. Statistics on R&D in the educational sector are not available in any international yearbook. So not only do we not know much about the learning process, we know even less about what we are doing to find out more about it.
- The role of socio-cultural values in the learning process and the role of the latter in their orientation is vastly underestimated.
- Learning is in essence a process of internalization which necessitates endogenous models of development and does not successfully lend itself to excessive imitation or non-imaginative borrowing; its main ingredients are innovation and creativity. At the risk of being totally misunderstood and misinterpreted, let me say that learning is the area of international cooperation in the truest sense of the term; it is also the least suited for massive flows of external technical assistance or financial aid. The key part of the learning process and of national educational policies is self-reliance. You cannot build up self-reliance through dependency. There is not a country in the world today that does not have the local ways and means to eradicate illiteracy and to develop its human potential. What most countries lack is the political will and the courage to do so—in spite of or because of the great socio-political transformations which education brings about.
- Because of an acceleration of history, learning has become, more than ever before, a long-term process. Any reform of learning systems ought to be worked out in terms of generations to be able to achieve a thorough change from preschool education to postgraduate studies, including the training of teachers and the production of new teaching materials. A period of 15 to 20 years is the minimum time required to transform an educational system.
- The unemployment crisis in the world has introduced new preoccupations which have distorted the relationship between education and employment. A fair proportion of this unemployment is due to structural causes of change and lack of foresight and long-term planning and not to the basic functions of education which go beyond the mere provision of a work force for the economy. For

251

over half of the jobs which will be needed by the year 2000 there are today no suitable courses in the universities and higher training institutes throughout the world.

Some Learning Needs of a Society of Knowledge

What are some of the learning needs of the society of knowledge which is in the making and which will sooner or later engulf all the parts of the world?

1. A re-centering of the development models around man and his creative capacities.
2. National programs for the eradication of illiteracy within the shortest time possible and with the highest priority with very little or no reliance on external financial assistance.
3. A reshaping of the learning systems so as to favor innovation, participation and anticipation so as to facilitate the tackling of the growing complexity which a society of knowledge entails.
4. A greater emphasis on R&D particularly in areas which have a direct bearing on the understanding of the learning process.
5. A concentration on the high technologies especially in the case of the less developed countries leaving aside what has been euphemistically called "appropriate" or "adapted" technology.
6. The development of new criteria and parameters as well as statistical norms and standards to monitor achievements in the fields of education and learning.[3]
7. The building up of national, regional and international information networks on learning.
8. The launching of an international multi-disciplinary research project on the learning process involving industrialized and developing countries alike.
9. A greater integration of science and technology in national development plans of Third World countries so as to facilitate the integration of national qualified manpower and to reduce the brain drain phenomenon.[4] Third level university students from the developing countries represented around 20% of the world total, the proportion moved to about 40% in 1985 and will exceed 50% in the year 2000. India alone had 2,500,000 scientists and technologists in 1983. The brain drain problem needs to be tackled in a more imaginative manner through the building up of policies, facilities and an environment conducive to a constructive use of the qualified manpower in Third World countries.[5]
10. Special attention needs to be paid to the rural world bearing in mind the fact that no developmental policy of any kind is capable of stopping the process of urbanization in the developing countries. About 40% of the working population of the world in the year 2000 will still be in the agricultural sector and this is where illiteracy is concentrated.
11. The learning systems still have to ascertain how to make the best use of the advanced technologies, such as informatics, robotics

and telecommunication sciences, which present a great potential for the enhancement of knowledge and its application to the solution of contemporary problems.

12. A new understanding of the concept of "work" is needed and a more intimate connection between employment, learning and leisure is required.

13. A novei approach to equity and social justice which would provide equal learning opportunities within and between countries as well as a learning justice and a cultural justice with full respect for cultural values.

Conclusion

The report of the 1985 Annual Conference of the *Grandes écoles* in France states that "the basis of the profession of engineering tomorrow is to be a technician, a financier, an organizer, a psychologist, an economist and a philosopher." In the United States the great new academic concern is the insufficient number of philosophers to deal with the paradigms and the algorithms which are required for research work on artificial intelligence.

A society of knowledge is one in which the frontiers between disciplines gradually crumble and where substance is sought at the interconnecting nodes. One of the challenges of the learning tasks is how to unlearn and how to reduce the resistance to change of those involved with the learning profession.

A society of knowledge is also one which manages to overcome the technological fix and the supremacy of technocrats so as to democratize the production and the use of the fruits of science and technology for the betterment of life.

The survival of the human race, in a society of knowledge, will depend on its ability to bridge an ever increasing human gap between knowledge and the manner in which it is used. Let me conclude with the following quotation from *No Limits to Learning,*

> We have become aware of just how deeply the human gap cuts across all cultures, values, ideologies, races, and religions. Debate and discussion about the human gap and its relation to the world problematique necessarily calls for an international dialogue on the need for commitment to and practice of innovation if we wish to ensure the universal vision required to enhance both the diversity of cultures and the common global requirements for survival and dignity.

The question that remains is why is it so hard to convince decision makers that human resources are the greatest asset of humanity?

Notes

1. According to an MIT study of 1983, the number of words distributed by the media in the United States increased by around 9% annually whereas the number of words absorbed by the American public increased by less than 3% annually.

2. J. Botkin, M. Elmandjra and M. Malitza, (Pergamon Press, 1979).

3. In March 1986, the French Ministry of Education announced the creation of a "Centre de prospective et d'evaluation" which will elaborate new "efficiency indicators" to measure the returns of the investments and activities within the education sector (*Le Monde,* March 9, 1986).

4. In 1983, 51% of the engineers with a Ph.D. degree who entered the U.S. labor market were non-Americans (1226 out of a total of 2391), see A. Zahlan, *The Brain Drain,* mimeo, London (September 1985).

5. UNDP launched, in 1977, a program known as "Tokten" (transfer of knowledge through expatriate nationals). Over 1000 assignments were made under this program and it may be useful to learn from UNDP what lessons they have drawn from this experience.

GLOBALIZED MEDIA: TOWARD COMMUNITY
OR CATASTROPHE
ON THE PLANET?

by

Harold G. Shane

The most remarkable paradox of our time is that, in proportion as the instruments of communication have increased in number and power, communication has steadily declined. Mutual intelligibility is probably a rarer phenomenon than at any time in history.
—Robert M. Hutchins[1]

The current flood of publications, many dealing with the deplorable condition of the media, strongly confirms Chancellor Hutchins' prescient statement written as humans stood on the threshold of the information society some thirty years ago. Before we begin an in-depth look at the present status and role of the media, however, let us look at some of the meanings associated with the term.

What does "the media" mean? There are at least ten dictionary definitions associated with the term "medium." The two most relevant here are (1) "an intervening thing through which a force acts" and (2) "any means, agency, or instrumentality such as radio, television, or printed materials which serves as a medium of communication." Patently, computers, and networks built around them, certain types of robots such as "Topo," satellites, newspapers, indeed most of the systems which support our microelectronic surround, may be classed as means of communication.

A sampling of America's media giants. During 1985 Standard and Poor's Corporation compiled basic data with regard to the income of the 12 biggest media corporations as of the previous year. The accompanying table indicates the revenues totalled over $25 billion dollars.

The information is provided to suggest the status of the fiscal empires of a few of our media corporations, their financial power or clout, and the enormous amount of money spent by companies seeking to sell their products or causes through commercials—sometimes more elegantly described by announcers as "messages from our sponsors."

Harold G. Shane is a professor of education at Indiana University, Bloomington.

In the pages that follow, some of the power of the media—political, social, economic, and educational—will be described and assessed. Especial heed is given to the media's permeation of childhood and youth, the family, and the larger society of which they are a part.

Table 1

Revenues of the Twelve U.S. "Media Giants" (1984)*

1) CBS, Inc	4.93 billion
2) ABC	3.71 billion
3) Time, Inc.	3.07 billion
4) Times Mirror Co.	2.80 billion
5) Dun and Bradstreet	2.40 billion
6) Gannett Co.	1.96 billion
7) Tribune Co.	1.79 billion
8) Knight-Ridder Newspapers	1.66 billion
9) New York Times Co.	1.23 billion
10) Washington Post Co.	984 million
11) Dow Jones and Co.	966 million
12) Capital Cities	940 million

*Data from Standard and Poor reported in *U.S. News and World Report,* April 1, 1985.

Media Frontiers, 1978-1990

Wonders ever new. In view of the broad definition for "media" presented above, the list of "wonders ever new" with which we are being well-nigh overwhelmed needs to be compressed a bit in the interests of conserving space! An impressive example of media power was provided in 1984 when communications networks provided millions of persons with "free tickets" to the Olympic Games at Sarajevo. The non-print microtech deluge provides a first-rate example of the level of sophistication attained by the mid-1980s.

One of the media giants, ABC, 1) initially designed its "wonder coverage" in Los Angeles, 2) assembled and tested it in New York, 3) packed its equipment on 30 trailers which went to Yugoslavia's Winter Games aboard ship, and 4) were hauled to what the ABC insiders dubbed the "Little Olympic Village" at Sarajevo.

Once installed, the array of equipment and personnel involved were mind-swirling! Seventy TV monitors provided widespread input, 36 videotape machines recorded the contests and interviews while 150 miles of cable and various satellite connections were involved.[2]

The Olympic Games at Los Angeles later in the year also demonstrated how times have changed since a runner bearing a torch opened the Games in ancient Greece. The excitement transmitted

256

to our homes electronically by the media-covered events in California spread over 4,000 square miles.[3] Further to complicate Olympic coverage, contestants speaking 83 languages had come from 51 nations, hence interpreters had to be kept on hand. All told, 1,700 terminals were installed with 14 computers to run or to monitor the terminals.[4]

While the Sarajevo and Los Angeles Olympics epitomized the scope and cooperation of the media, other marvels constantly are being described in the literature; marvels making their debut so frequently that it is virtually impossible to keep up with them. A few intriguing examples include:

1) "Living wallpaper" made possible by huge TV screens thin enough to hang on the wall and which can be used to display a variety of electronic "wallpaper graphics" when no program is being watched.

2) The Lexicon 1200 Audio Time Compressor/Expander which enables three out of 60 minutes to be salvaged for commercials or news breaks without losing any dialogue or action from a TV program.[5]

3) The fusion of computer and portable telephones plus "cellular radio"—a mobile telephone network that came into use during 1984-1985.[6]

4) Elimination of costly installation and maintenance of phone lines in developing nations by means of satellite phone linkages.

5) Deployment of the Intelsat VI satellites which *simultaneously* handle 33,000 phone conversations as well as carrying programs on two TV channels between Europe and the U.S.

6) Recent developments in fiber optics which permit 240,000 simultaneous phone conversations to be carried on between Washington and New York by means of half-inch cable. (This is twice as efficient and costs a small fraction of traditional copper wiring.)[7]

7) Satellite navigation for automobiles with dashboard print-outs of a map showing the drivers' precise location.

8) Electronic translation of an English manuscript into Arabic, Chinese, etc., and vice versa.

9) Already established are the electronic newspaper, electronic banking, and electronic mail.

10) Successful production of a $180 million Infrared Astronomical Satellite (IRAS) or robot observatory with detectors so delicate that they can spot a small light bulb's glow on the planet Pluto—a distance of over 3 ½ billion miles.

Something to be watched in communications futures is one of the possible outcomes of the $5 billion bet General Motors is making on the new Saturn automobile. Among the goals of the venture is to link together robots and computers who can "speak" to one another! If this two-way machine-to-machine communication can be evolved successfully:

> ... exact specifications for an engine valve, once devised and tested on a computer can be transmitted to a computerized machine tool on the shop floor and manufactured. Flaws would be detected after just a few parts had been made, not after thousands had been installed.[8]

One final educationally relevant item that merits inclusion in our listing of innovations in communications is the news that the Grolier Publishing Company announced that it would begin marketing in October 1985 a compact disk (CD) encyclopedia. A single CD will contain the 9-million word, 21 volume contents of Grolier's printed encyclopedia.[9] The CD operates on personal computers. For purposes of comparisons in communications it is of passing interest to note that a single disk of this type can store the contents of 540 copies of the King James Bible.

The Media: Commercialism, Gilded or Biased News, Politics, and Self Evaluation

While the media frontiers mentioned above are important for educators to understand, it is in our elementary, secondary, and post-secondary programs that the emerging role of the media is probably of consummate significance. This seems especially true with respect to TV. Furthermore, the curriculum in many schools has yet to adapt itself to the micro milieu which is engulfing it.

An in-depth review of the literature, particularly fugitive material,[10] suggests the need for teachers and their students to become increasingly better informed with respect to the commercialism, gilded or slanted news, and the political aspects of television and the press. Each is considered in turn before we examine the effects of the ways in which the media are infusing society, and creating dilemmas for the family, childhood and youth.

The multi-billion dollar marketplace. As Table 1 demonstrates, the financial stake the media have in capturing audiences is enormous. The financial "take" also is growing as our microelectronic milieu becomes more and more a part of the global scene.

Hype, Hype, Hype! The high-powered promotion, commonly called "hype," goes back to the days of P.T. Barnum. It differs from conventional advertising because of its sheer intensity—the effort of the media to overwhelm the viewer with promotional messages.

The motion picture field appears to be the outstanding example of applied guile and know-how insofar as carefully designed marketing plans are concerned. Major studios spend millions to publicize films and, in the case of *The Return of the Jedi,* for example, the sum exceeded $10 million. The pay-off can be enormous as certain film hits such as the Jedi opus can gross in the millions per week.

An interesting example of the monies involved is illustrated by a scene in *E.T.: The Extra-Terrestrial.* The charming little visitor, E.T., was lured from his hiding place by a young lad who used "Reese's Pieces," a brand of candy, as bait. Hershey's modest sales of the sweet zoomed upwards by 65% in the month following the release of *E.T.* as youngsters who spotted the orange candy wrappers hastened to candy counters to help fill Hershey Food Corporation coffers.

Other examplars of deliberately planned promotions range from the ABC network's meticulously planned build-up of *The Day After* (which described for 100,000,000 viewers the aftermath of a nuclear exchange), the debut of "Mr. T" at the January 1983 Super Bowl, and Coca-Cola's launching of diet coke by renting the Radio City Music Hall for 4,000 guests—at an estimated $100,000! The 1984-1985 Coke/Classic Coke hoopla, whether by accident or design, has been even more spectacular.

Selected news. What we believe, and why we believe it, serve in many ways to govern our thinking and our behavior. Because of the growing infiltration of global society by the media input unleashed by the microelectronic surround it has become of increased importance to help learners, both young and old, to understand such phenomena as "selected news," so-called docudramas, and the artfully "enhanced truth" sometimes purveyed by the media to suit the purposes of commercial or political sponsors or the bias of those in seats of power which press, radio, and TV provide.

Even Pope John Paul II was moved to comment on the evils of bias and innuendo. An AP dispatch from Vatican City quoted him as saying:

> Cleverly placed emphasis, slanted interpretations, even loaded silences, are devices which can profoundly alter the significance of what is being communicated.

It is important to note that representatives of the media themselves as of the 1980s have begun to criticize sharply the practices of certain of their colleagues! Virtually all of the material cited or paraphrased below, readers will note, are from persons associated with the media.

A major problem, "selected news" (as distinct from outright misrepresentation) was called to my attention during an interview with a distinguished scholar, Lawrence Cremin. He pointed out that on a TV newscast or in newspaper quotes that someone had the prerogative of choosing, let us say, two or three statements from among 20 or more taped or photographed items. The items that are broadcast often are selected more for the pathos, the threat voiced, or the bias of the individual who selects items that often turn out to be "enhanced truth" to capture for a TV anchor's program the largest horde of listeners or newspaper's readers possible.

Thomas Griffith[11] at the time of the 1984 political conventions in Dallas and San Francisco commented on the arrogance and condescending coverage of the media which assumed that "its own maunderings are more interesting than what is being said on the platform." His most barbed remark was that CBS assumed that the audience would rather hear Dan Rather speak smugly in San Francisco than hear the hoarse Irish Oratory of Tip O'Neill.

Endemic concern over the press also is prevalent.[12] One of the 70 ombudsmen for U.S. daily papers, Donald D. Jones, averaged 40 complaints a day directed at the Kansas City *Star* and the *Times*. Public mistrust, he said, resided in what was deemed to be: 1) inaccuracy, 2) arrogance, 3) unfairness, 4) disregard of privacy, 5) newspaper chains regarded as the "equivalent of fast food joints," 6) insensitivity with respect to race, religion, and sex slurs, 7) overemphasis on criminal and bizarre happenings, and 8) bad writing. Jones also cited a Gallup Poll (1983) reflecting greater hostility to the press than in any previous poll conducted by Gallup.

S.M. Lipset,[13] in the same vein, adds that TV, by broadcasting bad news as it happens, "has helped maintain public negativism," and Bishop James Armstrong of the National Council of Churches felt impelled to request time to rebut a segment of "60 Minutes" which contended that some NCC funds supported Marxist causes overseas.

Perhaps the kindest remarks I could find with regard to "limited" or "selected" news was written by David Marc[14] who noted that, "Like the menu at McDonald's and the suits on the racks, the choices on the dial—and thus far the cable converter—are limited and guided."

Overexposure provided by the media. In addition to "guided" programming the media also have been berated for providing too much coverage. A memorable example, is provided by the horde of 1,800 journalists who poured into Ballyporeen during President Reagan's visit to the Ireland of his ancestors. The newscorps outnumbered the village's entire population by more than five to one!

Perhaps because of public resistance to "overkill" by the press and TV, John Chancellor's criticism of the President's temporary Grenada invasion press ban resulted in 500 phone calls to NBC supporting the ban by five to one. The ABC anchor, Peter Jennings, said that 99% of his mail was from persons supporting President Reagan's decision to delay press coverage! As former *Washington Post* ombudsman Robert McCloskey saw it, "It may well be that the public reacted cumulatively with a judgment that the press had it coming." The explosion of home TV delivery gear such as cable and the home taping of programs promises to "turn off" more and more viewers as sources of infoglut—information overload—increases.

In a recent prophetic HBO release, a movie entitled "Wrong is Right," Sean Connery portrayed a TV newscaster who made entertainment out of disasters. Connery's role assumed added significance because of the TV coverage, and perhaps meddling exposure, that occurred during the 17-day Beirut hijacking of a TWA 747! Zbigniew Brzezinski[15] contended that the media, particularly TV, operated to the detriment of the country when hijacking or hostage taking are involved. He explained his conclusions succinctly:

1) An essentially political confrontation, because of excessive media coverage, transmitted into a personal drama which interferes with our government's ability to cope.
2) The bargaining capacity of the kidnappers is enhanced and the U.S. government forced to seek some way of accommodating them.
3) The enemy is "humanized" by audiovisual contacts and victims are subject to manipulation.

Henry Kissinger went so far as to urge a news media blackout in Beirut rather than give persons such as Nabib Berri, a spokesman for the kidnappers, direct access to means of moulding public opinion in America.

To sum up, uninhibited media access to and selection of presumed "news" is a price we pay for the free communication channels in our information society—but ethical conduct codes need further development by the media if we are to cope with selected news and crisis situations in the U.S. and around the planet. To avoid what has been labeled "Ignorance Abroad" it is essential, too, that seasoned, thoughtful personnel be chosen for the coverage of international news.

In our school environments students must be helped to develop the insights needed to enable each of them to interpret and to respond intelligently to the complexities of their micro milieu.[16]

Power politics: the need for a symbiotic ethic. Ward Just is among a substantial cohort of writers who, in recent years, have expressed concern about the role of the media in politics. Events often are arranged by television for television he tells us, noting that " . . . the symbiotic relationship between the politicians and electronic mediators is so close as to resemble the chummiest of marriages: scratch one and the other bleeds."[17]

While a close working relationship per se cannot be disparaged the nature of the relationship should be ethical. In Barry's metaphor, "The only thing people make in Washington is policy or gossip, and you usually don't know where one leaves off and the other begins."[18] This suggests that educators need to help students to identify and analyze bias, propaganda, and the loaded words that creep into interviews. The problem insofar as loaded words—or selected pictures and taped excerpts—are concerned is that they are designed to persuade an audience to accept a prefabricated opinion! As S.I. Hayakawa phrased it in *Language in Thought and Action,* there are "purr-words" and "snarl-words." We need—as the media's influence grows—to recognize that the terms used by reporters (and politicians!) can short circuit our thinking.[19] The need for our insights on the part of learners young and old is increasing.

How the media's interpretive treatment of the news is changing. Freedom for the press and other media has long been an axiom taught in U.S. schools. There appears to have been a subtle shift since the 1950s when the media, particularly during international crises, began to lose the erstwhile simple patriotism of earlier eras. An examination of records, radio, film footage on TV, and reports in the press tend to reflect a shift from "cooperative patriotism" to skepticism.[20]

To illustrate, American media in 1962 helped to make an exceedingly ominous international development one of the most carefully concealed secrets in our history. The press withheld news of the U-2 plane flights which had established the fact that the Russians were building nuclear-tipped missile installations in Cuba until an official announcement was made by the U.S. government on October 22, 1962. The so-called missile crises was one of our few well-kept secrets of recent years. President Kennedy had known about Russia's knavery for six days before the information was presented for publication to the media.

What subsequently was published was based on U.S. government handouts as of the 1962 crisis. Furthermore ten suitably located radio stations permitted themselves to be taken over for three weeks so that Spanish "Voice of America" programs could explain to Cubans the dangerous situation that Fidel Castro, with Russian weaponry, had created.

TV coverage of an extremely portentous potential problem was an exemplar of restraint according to the MIT News Study Group which charted the media's switch since the 1950s "from patriotism to skepticism" in reporting.[21] Without attacking our traditional freedom of the press the MIT Group notes that ABC, NBC, CBS coverage has been marked because of three key differences that have surfaced and which show " . . . how far TV News (freedom) has come in two decades—and how much Government has had to adjust to this changed media reality."[22]

1) The attitudes of journalists have changed with respect to cooperating with the government.
2) The press, including networks, have much greater access to more information and a concomitant complexity in presentations of events—more diverse versions of reality have been spawned.
3) New technologies in the micro milieu for which we are educating our students have increased enormously. In 1962, CBS News got news from Cuba by means of hiring a plane to fly close enough to the island to get within range of Havana TV. Now, with "microwave instantaneity" news and images circulate among such places as Washington, Mexico, El Salvador, Guatemala, and New York City.

Clearly, we once again in the microelectronic surround have a need to achieve greater clarity of understanding with respect to microtrends and coping strategies for ourselves as educators and for our young charges.

Facts and fiction. An added caveat embedded in the emerging role of the media was voiced recently by Reed Irvine, head of Accuracy in Media, Inc.[23] After recognizing the good job that some broadcast commentators are doing, Irvine adds that the real problem crises are increased when journalists "start with a premise and then shape the evidence to fit that premise." "Documentaries," he added are "very definitely designed to manipulate public opinion." Clearly, educators and learners of every age need to be made aware of the implications of such developments in the realm of propaganda.

Although my data generally persuasively support the good intentions and integrity of personnel in the media arena, some cautions are needed lest the audience find itself bemused or even confused by facts and fiction. Here student guidance in interpreting what is presented is of supreme importance. As our former director of the National Security Council, Richard Allen, said:

> Competition among the Washington press for air time and space is so great that sometimes an inadequate respect for the facts takes over. This willingness to publish leaks and views of "anonymous" sources leads to particularly vicious situations that are grossly unfair to the object of the leak.[24]

David Shaw, author of *The Best and the Brightest,* also has expressed concern about programs which confuse or obscure the *truth* of "docu" and the fiction of "-drama." Selecting the program, "Robert Kennedy and His Times," Shaw shows respect for the man but contempt for the media "distortion and sanitization" of the foreign policy during a turbulent era. For instance, no mention is made in the docudrama, Shaw points out, of the U.S.-sponsored invasion of the Bay of Pigs or of the U.S. role in the 1963 assassination of Ngo Dinh Diem, then president of South Vietnam.

Other numerous points similar to those cited, if more were reiterated, would transport readers from pessimism to ennui! I choose to close this section on "the need for a symbiotic ethic" to govern politics and the media with a candid statement from Henry Kissinger.

> Did I sometimes use the press? Yes. There is absolutely no doubt that when an official deals with the press, he is trying to "use" the press. And there is no doubt that when a reporter deals with an official, he is trying to "use" the official . . . the press must understand that the official is not there to please them but to achieve his objective.[25]

Stars of eventide: the TV anchors. Our substantially abridged resume of the growing power and influence of the media as technologies multiply would have a major gap if passing comment were not made on the anchorpersons who, along with commercials, dominate our TV screens.

The first evening network news program went on the air, under the aegis of CBS, on August 15, 1948. Historically "number one" anchor was Douglas Edwards.

By February 1949, John Cameron Swayze subsequently was introduced by NBC under the sponsorship which nostalgic viewers may remember as the "Camel News Caravan."[26]

As a devoted multiple evening newscast viewer I was a dedicated Walter Cronkite ("The man trusted by most Americans") fan as well as an enthusiast for others in my "personal news pantheon."[27] Their faces stand out in my mental images like the presidential carvings on Mount Rushmore!

However, and this is an important reason for educators to understand in our increasingly sophisticated micro milieu, some of the implications of our powerful, proliferating evening news programs must be more thoroughly understood by both U.S. teachers and learners. In part this is due to the stakes that are involved—billions from product sponsors and other sources—that have helped networks to become desperate to recruit and to keep on their rosters top-flight *journalists* who project well as *newsreaders,* too! According to Matusow,[28] "networks are giving away salaries and editorial prerogatives that could not have been fantasized a decade ago."

The point I seek to make is that with anchors' package deals sometimes pushing toward, or beyond, the $20 million dollar level there is the possible danger of power grabs deals, and a further increase in some of the various forms of hype.[29] Tomorrow's youth, while recognizing the value of access to news and the general integrity of the media in various forms, also needs to understand, as Lewis H. Lapham put it, that journalists don't necessarily know how the world works and—if history resembles architecture—the media can sometimes bear comparison to a tent show.[30] Art Buchwald's classic April 1982 comment provides a punch line, too! Under the caption, "My Latest Nightmare," he explains his Falklands-and-Beirut era panic of the week. "I'm frightened," he says, "because the next big war is not going to be started by two countries but by an anchorman from one of the major TV networks."

Our students must be taught how to interpret what they see and hear and how invisible sources—greed, ambition, power quests— sometimes can be invisible ingredients behind the TV cyclops' eye in our homes.[31]

While the news may sometimes be gilded,[32] while we may be increasingly exposed to injections of opinion in TV news,[33] it is important to recognize that some of our anchors also want a system that permits them a better job. Tom Brokaw is on record with specific suggestions, made in 1985; "Network News: How We Can Do It Better." His thoughtful comments suggest certain areas in which American "eventide anchors" and televiewers could join forces for their mutual benefit.

A sampling of points made in Mr. Brokaw's essay follows:

1) Network news will never be an adequate replacement for a first-rate daily newspaper, a weekly news magazine or a periodical specializing in a specific subject. Instead, think of network news as a part of the information spectrum.

2) We need a wider stage. The time constraints on the evening news programs are suffocating. A one-hour network evening news program is an inspiration if television news is to fulfill its potential and its obligation to its audience.

3) Our most glaring shortcoming: we don't adequately examine the many sides of complicated subjects in a sufficiently broad context. An hour format should attract those who now avoid broadcast journalism with a 22-minute time limit after commercials are run.

4) Our coverage should focus on subjects that receive scant attention on many local news programs. We need to provide depth and breadth to the bits of information that bombard viewers all day.

5) It is television's role to do what print cannot do in conveying light and sound and unfiltered emotion including being bold enough to report stories where there are no pictures. New graphics technologies are making this possible.[34]

Concluding Comment

I found this paper singularly difficult to write. There are, perhaps, three factors that contributed to the difficulty. For one thing the torrent of current literature to be reviewed ages rapidly and is both varied and highly scattered. Second, the sweep of change—both technological and sociological—is tremendous in the realm of the media. Finally, the micro milieu has cast the media with its varied forms in so many pervasive roles in our lives that it is difficult to extricate and examine media apart from our total microelectronic surround.

Notes

1. Robert M. Hutchins, *The Conflict in Education*. New York: Harper and Brothers, 1953. p. 102.
2. For more details see Richard Stengel's report, "Your Ticket to the Games," *Time,* February 13, 1984, pp. 65-66. Also see George Plimpton, "Here's One Man's Meet," *Time,* August 20, 1984, pp. 76-79.
3. See *Chicago Tribune,* Sunday, March 18, 1984, Sec. 6, p. 1.
4. Each of the computers had a 300 megabyte disk drive, and each megabyte contained 1,024,000 bytes. (See glossary).
5. John Leo, "As Time Goes Bye-Bye," *Time,* July 19, 1982, p. 78.
6. "What Next? A World of Communications Wonders," *U.S. News and World Report,* April, 1984, pp. 59-63.
7. Ibid., p. 61.
8. Cited by *U.S. News and World Report,* August 5, 1985, p. 24.
9. Cited in "Business Notes," *Time,* July 29, 1985, p. 64. Grolier also is developing an unabridged CD dictionary and a thesaurus. Also see Parker Rossman, "The Coming Great Electronic Encyclopedia," *The Futurist,* 16:53-57, August, 1982.
10. Fugitive materials (magazine and newspaper sources) were the primary source of the information summarized here. Not only were books on the topic rare, they quickly became obsolete because of the speed with which media-related events occur.
11. Cited in *Time,* August 20, 1984, p. 105.
12. *Time,* May 9, 1983, p. 94.
13. Distinguished Chair Professor of Political Science and Sociology at Stanford University.
14. David Marc, "Understanding Television," *Atlantic Monthly,* 254:34, August, 1984.
15. National Security Adviser during President Carter's administration.
16. For stunning examples of the apparent excesses of docudrama, readers are referred to scathing commentaries on the CBS docudrama *The Atlanta Child Murders.* See 1) Julian Bond, "Television Toys with the Truth," circulated by the Newspaper Enterprise Association and printed in various newspapers; e.g. *Bloomington Herald-Telephone,* February 23, 1985, p. 5, and 2) William A. Henry III, "The Dangers of Docudrama," *Time,* February 25, 1985, p. 95.
17. Ward Just, "Politics: We Are the Hostages," *The Atlantic Monthly,* 245:100, April, 1980.
18. John M. Barry, "Washington's Powerhouse Press Corps," *Dun's Business Monthly,* 124:26, July, 1984.
19. There are, by the way, between 8,000 and 10,000 people in the

Washington media corps. Over 4,300 have Congressional accreditation! (See John M. Barry, ibid., p. 27).

20. For a detailed review, see Edwin Diamond (and others in MIT's News Study Group), "The Turning of TV News," *TV Guide,* 30:4-8, August 7, 1982.

21. Edwin Diamond, ibid., pp. 6-9.

22. Ibid., p. 6.

23. Cited in an interview published by *U.S. News and World Report,* February 21, 1983, p. 50.

24. Mr. Allen was cited in *U.S. News and World Report,* March 22, 1982, p. 56.

25. Neil Hickey, "Henry Kissinger on Politics and TV Journalism," *TV Guide,* 31:3, April 2, 1983.

26. For a history of "anchored programs," one written with a touch of gossip and sizzle, see Barbara Matusow, *The Evening Stars.* New York: Houghton Mifflin and Company, 1983.

27. Among communicators I've especially enjoyed, often for divers reasons: Chet Huntley and David Brinkley, Dan Rather, Roger Mudd, Peter Jennings, Barbara Walters, and Tom Brokaw.

28. Barbara Matusow, Op. cit.

29. As far back as 1975 Dan Rather had a $2 million ABC agreement. NBC had to match ABC's hefty seven-year package proffered to Tom Brokaw. (Cited in the *Milwaukee Journal,* Monday, August 15, 1985. "Green Sheet," p. 2).

30. Lewis H. Lapham, "Sculptures in Snow," *Harper's Monthly,* 263: 8 August, 1981. (Paraphrased).

31. *Time* Magazine's complimentary roster of "Five who Dominate TV News," as of April, 1985, included: Sam Donaldson, Ted Koppel, Dan Rather, Mike Wallace, and George Will. (See p. 75.)

32. Lewis H. Lapham, "Gilding the News," *Harper's Magazine,* 263:31-39, July 19, 1985.

33. Thomas Griffith, "Don't Tell Us What to Think," *Time,* May 24, 1982, p. 71.

34. Tom Brokaw, "Network News: How We Can Do It Better," *TV Guide,* 33:4-7, July 6, 1985.

EDUCATING FOR THE INFORMATION SOCIETY

by

Harlan Cleveland

Shortly after the attempted assassination of President Reagan in 1981, Secretary of State Alexander Haig announced on television from the White House that "I am in control here . . . . " That statement produced neither reassurance nor anger from the American people: rather, the response was nervous laughter, as in watching theater of the absurd. We, the people, know by instinct that in our pluralistic democracy no one is, can be, nor is even supposed to be "in control." By constitutional design, reinforced by the information-rich conditions of work, we live in a nobody-in-charge society.

In a nobody-in-charge society, where decisions are made by consensus and committee, policy is made by an upside-down version of the traditional pyramid of power. Russell Baker, probably the best satirist currently practicing, captured the essence of this anomaly in an ironic dialogue with himself several years ago:

"What does this country need today?"
"Leadership . . . The country yearns for new leadership for a new era."
"If led, will the country follow?"
"If given the right kind of leadership, the country will surely follow."
"But what kind of leadership is the right kind?"
"The leadership that leads the country in the direction it wants to take."
"And what specific direction does the country want to take?"
"Who knows? That's for the leader to figure out. If he is the right kind of leader, he will guess correctly."
" . . . Am I wrong (Baker asks) in concluding that it isn't leadership the country wants in a president, but followership?"

Russell Baker was not wrong. High policy—that is, major changes in society's sense of direction—is first shaped by an inchoate consensus reached by the people at large.

Harlan Cleveland, Dean of the Hubert H. Humphrey Institute of Public Affairs at the University of Minnesota since 1980, is a political scientist and public executive.
This article has been adapted from The Knowledge Executive: Leadership in an Information Society *by Harlan Cleveland.*

If you find this upside-down pyramid hard to visualize, you are in distinguished company. The classic expression of this wearied cynicism is still Walter Lippmann's brooding book *The Phantom Public,* in which he announced his conclusion that "we must abandon the notion that the people govern. Instead," he continued, "we must adopt the theory that, by their occasional mobilization as a majority, people support or oppose individuals who actually govern. We must say that the popular will does not direct continuously but that it intervenes occasionally." The task, Lippmann thought, was "to find ways for people to act intelligently but in ignorance."

Walter Lippmann was the most brilliant pundit of his time—but he never ran for office or even ran an organization. No political leader or corporate executive could operate on his premise and survive.

Tick off in your mind some major shifts in U.S. policy these past twenty years:

- The federal government was the last to learn that the war in Vietnam was over.
- Richard Nixon and his immediate staff were the last to tumble to the fact that the president had fumbled his way out of office.
- The tidal waves of social change in our time—environmental sensitivity, civil rights for all races, the enhanced status of women, recognition of the rights of consumers and small investors—were not generated by the established leaders in government, business, labor, religion, or high education. They boiled up from people (and new leaders) who had not previously been heard from.
- The nuclear power industry was derailed by the very large numbers of plain people who concluded that the experts had not done their homework on nuclear safety, on nuclear proliferation, and on the disposal of radioactive waste—yet were, nevertheless, pushing this new source of energy down their throats.
- American women had stopped having so many babies long before school boards and government planners adjusted to no-growth or slow-growth assumptions.
- People were opting for smaller cars well before Detroit caught on.
- There was a grassroots movement toward an ethic of qualitative growth while government and business leaders were still measuring "progress" by quantitative aggregates.
- Americans became interested in energy conservation and solar energy while the ranking alarmists on energy policy in and out of government were still pooh-poohing sun-based alternatives to imported oil, driving around in gas-guzzling limousines, and failing to practice conservation in their own organizations.

Sprinkle on your own illustrations, to taste.

What seems to happen is that if the question is important enough, people-in-general get to the answer first. Then the experts and pundits and pollsters and labor leaders and lawyers and doctors and business executives and foundation officers and judges and professors and public executives—many of them chronically afflicted with hardening of the categories—catch up in jerky arthritic moves with all deliberate speed.

Journalists and educators serve as gatekeepers, moving all this information from its specialized sources to the general public, where it is then circulated through powerful but informal interpersonal networks. Only then, when the policy decision is long since made and the experts have finally done the programming, written the editorials, raised the money, painted the directional signposts, and staged the appropriate media event, the publicity heroes and heroines come forth, the people that *People* magazine thinks are our leaders. They climb aboard the train as it gathers momentum and announce for all to hear the new direction of march—speaking by television from the safety of the caboose.

It's more and more obvious: those with visible responsibility for leadership are nearly always too visible to take the responsibility for change—until it becomes more dangerous to stand there than to move. It is not a new idea: "I am a leader," Voltaire wrote, "therefore, I must follow."

The Informatization of Society

This state of affairs has been brought about by the two interdependent macro-trends of our time: the sudden emergence of new information technologies, and the sudden emergence of a new *attitude* toward new technologies.

It is still shocking, forty years later, to remember that the Manhattan Project, the huge secret program that produced the atomic bomb during World War II, did not employ on its staff a single person whose full-time assignment was to think hard about the policy implications of the project if it should succeed. Thus, no one was working on nuclear arms control—though I.I. Rabi says he and Robert Oppenheimer used to discuss it earnestly over lunch. We have been playing catch-up, not too successfully, ever since.

The Manhattan Project was not, however, an exception; it was the rule. For three hundred years, until the 1970s, science and technology were quite generally regarded as having lives of their own, each with an "inner logic," and an autonomous sense of direction. Their self-justifying ethic was change and growth. But in the 1970s, society started to take charge—not of scientific discovery, but of its technological fallout. The decision not to build the SST or deploy an ABM system even though we knew how to make them, the dramatic change in national environmental policy, and the souring of the nuclear power industry, bear witness.

The most prominent and pervasive consequence of the people's concern about the impacts and implications of new technologies is characterized by a French coinage, "l'informatisation de la société," which we will Americanize to "informatization." It will serve as well as any to describe what is happening to some of our key concepts

269

and conceptions as information becomes the dominant resource in "post-industrial society." (The new word is certainly better than "post-industrial," which describes the future by saying it comes after the past.)

The revolutions that began with Charles Babbage's "analytical engine" (fewer than 150 years ago) and Guglielmo Marconi's wireless telegraphy (not yet a century old) started on quite different tracks. But a quarter of a century ago, computers and telecommunications began to converge to produce a combined complexity, one interlocked industry that is transforming our personal lives, our national politics and our international relations.

The industrial era was characterized by the influence of human-kind over things, including nature as well as the artifacts of human-kind. The information era features a sudden increase in humanity's power to think, and therefore to organize.

The "information society" does not replace, it overlaps, the growing and extracting and processing and manufacturing and recycling and distribution and consumption of tangible things. Agriculture and industry continue to progress by doing more with less through better knowledge, leaving plenty of room for a knowledge economy that, in statistics now widely accepted, accounts for more than half of our workforce, our national productivity, and our global reach. (*The Economist* recently estimated the information sector at 56 percent of the U.S. economy.)

The actual growing, production, and extraction of things now soaks up a good deal less than a quarter of our human resources. Of all the rest, which used to be lumped together as "services," more than two-thirds are information workers. By the end of the century, something like two-thirds of all work will be information work.

If information (organized data, refined into knowledge and combined into wisdom) is now our "crucial resource"—that's how Peter Drucker describes it—what does that portend for citizenship, and for the education of citizens? The answer has to start with a close look at the inherent characteristics of information considered as a resource. These provide some clues to the vigorous rethinking that lies ahead for all of us:

Information is Expandable. In 1972, the same year *The Limits to Growth* was published, John McHale came out with a book called *The Changing Information Environment.* It didn't sell three million copies in sixteen languages, but it may prove to have been the more prescient of the two studies. McHale argued that information expands as it is used. Whole industries have grown up to exploit this characteristic of information: scientific research, technology transfer, computer software (which already makes a contribution to the U.S. economy that is several times the contribution of computer hardware), and agencies for publishing, advertising, public relations, and government propaganda to spread the word (and thus to enhance the word's value).

Information is not Resource-Hungry. Compared to the steel- and-automobile economy, the production and distribution of information are remarkably sparing in their requirements for energy and other physical and biological resources. Investments, pricing policies, and power relationships that assume the more developed countries will gobble up disproportionate shares of real resources are overdue for wholesale revision.

Information is Substitutable. Information can, and increasingly does, replace capital, labor, and physical materials. Robotics and automation in factories and offices are displacing workers and thus requiring a transformation of the labor force. Any machine that can be accessed by computerized telecommunications doesn't have to be in your own inventory. And Dieter Altenpohl, an executive of Alusuisse, has calculations and charts to prove that, as he says, "The smarter the metal, the less it weighs."

Information is Transportable. Words and numbers can be transmitted at close to the speed of light. As a result, remoteness is now more a matter of choice than geography. You can sit in Auckland, New Zealand, and play the New York stock market in real time—if you don't mind keeping slightly peculiar hours. And the same is true, without the big gap in time zones, of people in any rural hamlet in the United States. In the world of information-richness, you will be able to be remote if you want to, but you'll have to work at it.

Information is Diffusive. Information tends to leak—and the more it leaks the more we have. It is not the inherent tendency of natural resources to leak. Jewels may be stolen; a lump or two of coal may fall off the railroad car on its way from Montana; there is an occasional spillage of oil in the ocean. The leakage of information, however, is wholesale, pervasive, and continuous. In the era of the institutionalized leak, monopolizing information is very nearly a contradiction in terms; that can be done only in more and more specialized fields, for shorter and shorter periods of time.

Information is Shareable. Shortly before his death, the great British communications theorist Colin Cherry wrote that information by nature cannot give rise to exchange transactions, only to sharing transactions. Things are exchanged: if I give you a flower or sell you my automobile, you have it and I don't. But if I sell you an *idea* or give you a *fact*, we both have it.

An information-rich environment is thus a sharing environment. That needn't mean an environment without standards, rules, conventions, and ethical codes. It does mean the standards, rules, conventions, and codes are going to be different from those created to manage the zero-sum bargains of market trading and traditional international relations.

The Erosion of Hierarchies

The historically sudden dominance of information resources has, it seems to me, produced a kind of theory crisis—a sudden sense of having run out of basic assumptions. And somewhere near the center of the confusion are the difficulties caused by thinking about infor-

271

mation (which is to say symbols) using concepts developed for the management of things—concepts such as property, depletion, depreciation, monopoly, "inevitable" unfairnesses, geopolitics, the class struggle, and top-down leadership.

The assumptions we have inherited are not producing satisfactory growth with acceptable equity either in the capitalist West or in the socialist East. As Simon Nora and Alain Minc wrote in their landmark report to the president of France: "The liberal and Marxist approaches, contemporaries of the production-based society, are rendered questionable by its demise."

The most troublesome concepts are those which were created to deal with the main problems presented by the management of things—problems such as their scarcity, their bulk, their limited substitutability for each other, the expense and trouble in transporting them, the paucity of information about them (which makes them comparatively easy to hide), and the fact that, being tangible, they could be hoarded. It was "the nature of things" that the few had access to them and the many did not.

Thus, the inherent characteristics of physical resources (natural and man-made) hastened the development of hierarchies of *power based on control* (of new weapons, of energy sources, of trade routes, of markets, and especially of knowledge), hierarchies of *influence based on secrecy,* hierarchies of *class based on ownership,* hierarchies of *privilege based on early access* to valuable resources, and hierarchies of *politics based on geography.*

Each of these five bases for discrimination and unfairness is crumbling today—because the old means of control are of dwindling efficacy, secrets are harder and harder to keep, and ownership, early arrival, and geography are of dwindling significance in getting access to the knowledge and wisdom which are the really valuable legal tender of our time.

Suppose you and I were living in a large wooden structure, without noticing that termites have eaten away its supporting pillars from the inside. Any day now, we may lean against a pillar and it will turn out to be a hollow shell. Something like that is happening to the hierarchies we have grown accustomed to in a civilization based on industrial production.

Let's examine more closely, as a "for instance," just one of these five eroding hierarchies: the familiar pyramid of power based on control, which has been the building block of bureaucratic, corporate, and military organizations.

Power and Participation

Knowledge is power, as Francis Bacon wrote in 1597. Therefore, the wider the spread of knowledge, the more power gets diffused. For the most part, individuals, corporations, and governments don't have a choice about this; it is the ineluctable consequence of creating—through education—societies with millions of knowledgeable people.

272

We see the results all around us, and around the world. More and more work gets done by horizontal process—or it doesn't get done. More and more decisions are made with wider and wider consultation—or they don't "stick." If the Census Bureau counted each year the number of committees per thousand population, we would have a rough quantitative measure of the bundle of changes called "the information society." A revolution in the technology of organization— the twilight of hierarchy—is already well under way.

Information was always the basis of human organization, of course. Those with better or more recent information (Moses with his tablets, generals with their fast couriers, kings with their spies and ambassadors, speculators with their quick access to markets for gold, diamonds, or ownership shares, security forces with their sources of rumor and gossip) held sway over the rest of humankind.

But, once information was capable of being spread fast and wide— rapidly collected and analyzed, instantly communicated, readily understood by millions—the power monopolies that closely-held knowledge used to make possible were subject to accelerating erosion.

In the old days when only a few people were well educated and "in the know," leadership of the uninformed was likely to be organized in vertical structures of command and control. Leadership of the informed is different: it results in the necessary action only if it is exercised mainly through persuasion and by consulting those who are going to have to do something to make the decision a decision. When people are educated and are not treated this way, they either balk at the decisions made or have to be dragooned by organized misinformation backed by brute force. (Examples of both results have been on recent display in Poland.)

In an information-rich polity, the very definition of control changes. Very large numbers of people empowered by knowledge—coming together in parties, unions, factions, lobbies, interest groups, neighborhoods, families, and hundreds of other structures—assert the right or feel the obligation to make policy.

Decision making proceeds not by "recommendations up, orders down," but by the development of a shared sense of direction among those who must form the parade if there is going to be a parade.

Collegial, not command, structures become the more natural basis for organization. Conferring and "networking," not "command and control," become the mandatory modes for getting things done.

Planning cannot be done by a few leaders, or even the brightest whiz-kids immured in a systems analysis unit or a planning staff. Real-life planning is the dynamic improvisation by the many on a general sense of direction—announced by the few, but only after genuine consultation with those who will have to improvise on it.

More participatory decision making implies a need for much information, widely spread, and much feedback, seriously attended—as in biological processes. Participation and public feedback become conditions precedent to decisions that stick. That means more openness, less secrecy—not as an ideological preference but as a technological imperative. (Secrecy goes out of fashion anyway, because secrets are so hard to keep.)

Education for Citizenship

Let's consider now the implications of "informatization" for the education of a society. In the upside-down pyramid, where the people really do make the policy, leadership is continuous dialogue—not an act, but an interaction between leaders and followers. The preparation of self-selected leaders is an important piece of the puzzle. But the whole puzzle is much larger: it is how citizens at large learn to make policy on issues that affect their destiny.

Education is the drivewheel of citizenship in the informatized society. With information now America's dominant resource, the quality of life in our communities and our leadership in the world depend on how many of us get educated for the new knowledge environment—and how demanding, relevant, continuous, broad, and wise (not merely knowledgeable) that learning is. Our task as educators is to make sure that during the half-century or more that our average student will live, he or she will also be *alive*. How are we doing?

We now have a national system of post-secondary education to which more than two-thirds of our high school students aspire. Such a system will obviously serve multiple purposes: education as an investment (for the poor), education as a consumer good (for the affluent), education as a device for avoiding decisions about what to do next (for the unattached, the uncertain, and the unemployed). But whatever the individual purpose of "going to college," the social contract in American higher education is clear enough: colleges and universities, and especially the public colleges and universities, are the egalitarian means for making an aristocracy of achievement acceptable in a democratic society. It is now part of our democratic ethos that if you apply the merit principle to a large enough body of students with a fair enough representation of previously disadvantaged kinds of people, the resulting discrimination is permissible. This double ethic suits the students fine: they want an equal chance to go to college, but they also want a job when they get out.

Of course, no one is much good at forecasting the job market: the science of what people will be doing for a living is still the most primitive part of a still adolescent discipline.

The critics of higher education are judging by a simpler standard: if a job isn't awaiting the student as soon as he or she acquires credentials, then the system of higher education is not working the way it should. Most educators, by contrast, think their most important task is not to train for a meal ticket the week after graduation, but to educate for fifty years of self-fulfillment: to help students develop a capacity for learning that will be a continuing asset, and a joy, for decades to come. Our egalitarian target is not an equal crack at a first job, but an equal chance at a full life.

In this longer time perspective, the attempt to quantify human resource requirements is bound to produce nonsense. In a society of increasing information-richness, the content of many, perhaps most, jobs a generation hence is unknowable today—just as the children of yesteryear were unable, through the ignorance of their parents and guidance counselors, to dream of being astronauts, nuclear physicists, ecologists, computer programmers, television repairmen, or managers of retrieval systems. (It was not until quite recently that the category of "guidance counselor" was added to the roster of our school systems.) Already a decade ago, the U.S. Department of Labor was guessing that by the year 2000, two-thirds of 1974s kindergarten students would be filling jobs which did not yet exist.

I have set down elsewhere my skepticism of the forecasting racket. Do not suspend your own skepticism as I now try, with an impressionist's broad brush, to project the kinds of work that are bound to be especially valued in a knowledge-rich society.

There will be more "information" and "services" work, and proportionately fewer "production" jobs, to be had. Machines will keep on eating up routine and repetitive tasks; the jobs left for people to do will require more and more brainwork, and more skill in the people-to-people relations, which machines are no good at.

"Computer literacy" will be part of knowing how to read, write, compute, and communicate. (That doesn't mean more than a rudimentary understanding of the architecture and electronics of microprocessing; it does mean understanding what computers, linked to telecommunications, can do for us—just as most of us understand an automobile's functions without being able to repair it.)

Despite tenure systems and retirement benefits, people will move around even more than they do now—from place to place, from function to function, from career to career.

Work, and therefore education for work, will become less competitive and more organized around cooperation.

There will be a growing market for education as a non-polluting leisure-time "consumer good." Already some union contracts entitle workers to time off for education; Italian metal workers, for example, are entitled by contract to 150 hours of education a year.

A growing proportion of the demand for higher education will be for "recurring education"—the 1980s international in-word for what used to be called "adult" or "continuing" education.

Education for leadership in varying forms will be a growth industry, because the proportion of the population that performs some leadership function will keep growing.

More and more people will work at the management of international interdependence—in the federal government, multinational corporations, private voluntary agencies, and international organizations both public and private (if you can tell the difference). International travel for work and for leisure, and the expansion of global telecommunications will also keep spreading, therefore swelling the demand for people with training in cross-cultural communication.

This is a vision of full and fulfilling employment. Will there be enough jobs to go around? No one knows. What Howard Bowen said in the 1970s still seems a good guess in the 1980s: that "two centuries of history have revealed no secular trend toward greater unemployment as technology advances." There is no finite amount of "work" to be divided up among a given number of "workers." Work, along with capital, expands with our capacity to use what is new in new ways for new purposes. The United States did not get to be a great nation by redoing in each generation what it used to do well in the one before—like making propeller aircraft or mechanical adding machines or oversized automobiles. It got there by constantly thinking up new things to do—like linking computers to telecommunications—before others did.

Education for Integrative Thinking

How are we doing in teaching wisdom—the get-it-all-together way of integrative thinking?

The academy's students, and its outside critics too, notice that the vertical academic disciplines, built around clusters of related research methods, are not in themselves very helpful in solving problems. No real-world problem can be fitted into the jurisdiction of any single academic department. As every urban resident realizes, we know every specialized thing about the modern city—but we seldom "get it all together" to make the city livable, efficient, safe, and clean.

As they awaken to problem solving, students therefore gravitate to those of the academy's offerings that seem to promise an interdisciplinary approach. These offerings are sometimes disappointing. A course on environmental issues may be taught by an evangelist less eager to train analysts than to recruit zealots. A workshop on a "problem" may mask a research contract for a client (the government, a corporation, a wealthy donor) who knows the answer and is looking for ammunition and an academic seal of approval for a predetermined course of action.

We all know that the only truly interdisciplinary instrument is not a committee of experts, but the synoptic view from a single integrative mind. In university education, what is too often lacking is an interdisciplinary role model up front by the blackboard.

Even so, many students prefer offerings that promise to cut across the vertical structures of method and help them construct homemade ways of thinking about the situation as a whole.

The revolt against methodology is also powered by the quickening interest in ethics—which started even before Watergate. A growing number of students come to college after some life experience—in the army or on a job or in a commune. They are groping for purpose, for effective ways of asking "Why?" and "Where are we supposed to be going, anyway?" Disciplines that seem neutral about purpose, modes of analysis that are equally applicable to killing people or building low-cost housing, make these students uncomfortable.

The students' intuition may not be wrong. Yet, they face an impressive phalanx of opposition to their instinct that the vertical disciplines should be stirred together in problem-solving, purpose-related combinations. Access to academic journals, collegial admiration, and promotion and tenure are not achieved by having lunch with colleagues in other departments. In addition, the external critics are for once on the professor's side: the division of knowledge into manageable compartments enabled the alumni to develop self-esteem and earn a decent living, so they don't understand why the curriculum has to be controversial.

But doesn't the new knowledge environment place a much greater premium on integrative thought? Won't we have to take a new look at higher educational systems that award the highest credentials for wisdom to those who master the narrowest slices of knowledge?

We are born, aren't we, with naturally integrative minds. I suspect that a newborn baby knows from the start, by instinct, that everything is related to everthing else. Before a child is exposed to formal education, its curiosity is all-embracing. The child hasn't yet been told about the parts, so it is interested in the whole.

The more we learn, ironically, the less tied together is our learning. It's not situation-as-a-whole thinking, it's the separation of the specialized kinds of knowledge that (like racial prejudice) "has to be carefully taught."

Holistic learning comes especially in grades K to 4; the fourth-grade teacher is perhaps the premier generalist in our society. (Think of the variety of subjects on which she—it usually is "she"—has to be able to answer the question "Why?") Farther up the ladder of formal schooling, we do manage to persuade most children that the really important questions start with "When?" and "Where?" and "How?" and especially "How much?" Fortunately for the nation and the world, some young citizens persist in asking "Why?"

Jasmina Wellinghoff, a Twin Cities scientist and writer, writes about her first-grader:

> When my six-year old learns that we heat the house with forced air, she immediately wants to know who is forcing the air, where natural gas comes from, and how it got stuck underground. After I have done my best to explain all this, comes the next question: "If we didn't have natural gas, would we die in the winter?" There you have it. Geology, engineering, physics and biology, all together in a hierarchy of concepts and facts.
>
> However, a few years from now my daughter will be studying the structure of the earth's crust, combustion, hydraulics and the classification of living beings—all in different years and quarters, neatly separated, tested and graded.

It is a well known scandal that our whole educational system is geared more to categorizing and analyzing patches of knowledge than to threading them together. Yet the experts obviously don't have the answers, and we are exposed to daily and dramatic demonstrations of experts in the service of expertise rather than in the service of values. What we've been neglecting is education for breadth.

Now the good news. Just in time, new instruments that can be used for thinking in breadth are at hand.

The computer, the complex simulations it makes possible, and its hookup to a worldwide network of electronic communications, now make it possible for individuals and small groups to analyze enormously complex natural systems (global weather), economic markets (the international monetary system), technologies not yet deployed, decision "trees," models of voting behavior, crisis management, and conflict resolution. Tools such as these empower those who learn to use them to make complex judgments in the more mindful knowledge of alternative futures. Systems thinking has created new ways to help encompass in a single mind some approximation of "the situation as a whole," as it relates to the problem being studied.

Don't get me wrong. There are dangers in excessive dedication to systems analysis. Part of the body count in Vietnam is certainly traceable to quantifying the tactics of war while neglecting the impressionistic strategies of peace. Still, it is useful for decision makers to be able to count what can be counted—as long as they remember that if it can't be counted, that doesn't mean it doesn't count.

The machines that are so useful in processing information are, of course, stupid beyond belief. Despite the attribution to them of "intelligence" (in the much misunderstood phrase "artificial intelligence"), they can still only count (very fast) from zero to one and back again, and transmit the results (at nearly the speed of light, in large and increasing volume) from place to place around the world. People have to do all the rest—define the human needs and purposes, select and analyze the relevant data, fix the assumptions to be made, stir in the inferences and insights and imagination, form the organizations, make the decisions, issue or implement the instructions, and above all, deal with other people.

Time for a New "Core"

The people who will perform these functions will be mostly college men and women. What should they be learning for this purpose, during the years they are students?

It would be nice if the dilemma were simple. But the ancient clashes between "training" and "education," between "vocational" and "general," between honing the mind and nourishing the soul, divide the outside critics, the professional educators, and the students, too.

Just now our favorite way to resolve the dilemma is to delegate it to the individual student. We "maximize the student's options" by creating a bewildering proliferation of courses and programs of study, a cafeteria of the intellect using what the food service people call the "scramble system."

For the limited numbers of students who know just what they want and why, the new freedom doesn't work badly. But most students expect and need some guidance in creating an intellectually nutritious trayful of reading, discussion, writing, computing, and work experience.

My guess is that if U.S. colleges and universities continue to proliferate courses, external pressure groups and the state and federal governments will sooner or later impose social, economic, and even political criteria, on curriculum-building in higher education. At the graduate level such coercion is already felt to some extent, as governments bribe the universities with research funds to teach what political leaders think is important—and know is safe. At the undergraduate level, if our ultimate curricular principle is the cop-out called "maximum options," the outsiders will, in the end, tell the academics what to teach and the students what they can learn at the public's expense.

The answer, as usual, is not to settle the argument by choosing one of the dilemma's horns or the other. Honing the mind and nourishing the soul are both functional in the new knowledge environment. What we need now is a theory of general education that is clearly relevant to life and work in a context of the information age—a rapidly changing scene in which uncertainty is the main planning factor. Perhaps, in the alternating current of general and job-oriented education, it is time for a new synthesis, a new "core curriculum"—something very different from Columbia's World Civilization, Syracuse's Responsible Citizenship, or Chicago's Great Books, yet still a central idea about what every educated person would know, and have, and try to be.

I had a chance, not long before his untimely death in 1982, to consider with Stephen K. Bailey the make-up of a new "core." Bailey had been vice president of the American Council on Education and president of the National Institute of Education, and had thought long and hard about curricular reform in higher education. We concluded that such a core would not have much to do with learning "facts." It is said that each half-hour produces enough new knowledge to fill a twenty-four-volume edition of the *Encyclopedia Britannica*. Our world of indiscriminate erudition turns out millions of new books and articles and pamphlets in a year's time. Most of the facts we learn in school are unlikely to be true for as long as we can remember them.

(The last time I took physics, in the mid-1930s, my instructor told me that atoms couldn't be split. When I studied Keynesian economics with a young Oxford tutor named Harold Wilson, I learned that inflation and recession were periodic, but occurred at opposite ends of the business cycle; the idea that they might be glued together in persistent stagflation was not mentioned. This remembered learning has not been very useful to me, of late; it didn't seem to work very well for Prime Minister Wilson, either.)

If, however, we think hard about the requirements of the new knowledge environment, and consult the instincts and perceptions of our own future-oriented students, I think we could construct a new "core curriculum" from such elements as these:

- Education in integrative brainwork—developing the capacity to synthesize, for the solution of real-world problems, the analytical methods and insights of conventional academic disciplines. (Exposure to basic science and mathematics, to elementary systems analysis, and to what a computer can and cannot do, are part, but only a part, of this education.)
- Education about the social goals, public purposes, costs, benefits, and ethics of citizenship—to enable each educated person to answer for himself or herself two questions: "Apart from the fact that I am expected to do this, is this what I would expect *myself* to do?" and "Does the validity of this action depend on its secrecy?"
- A capacity for self-analysis—through the study of ethnic heritage, religion and philosophy, and art and literature, leading to the achievement of some fluency in answering the question, "Who am I?"
- Some practice in real-world negotiation, in the psychology of consultation, and the nature of leadership in the knowledge environment.
- A global perspective, and an attitude of personal responsibility for the general outcome of public life—passports to citizenship in an interdependent world.

The fusion of computers and telecommunications, and developments in bio-technology, are the basis for a legion of new activities, new things to do, new "jobs," on Earth, in the oceans, in the atmosphere and outer space. The number and quality of "jobs" will be a function not of physical constraints but of the human imagination. Will we use our imagination to create full employment at fulfilling work? In the words of Barbara Ward: "We do not know. We have the duty to hope."

There are two predictions to which I would assign a high probability value. The first is that people who do not educate themselves—and do not keep re-educating themselves—to participate in the new knowledge environment will be the peasants of the information society. The second is that societies that do not give *all* their people an opportunity for relevant education, as well as periodic opportunities to fine-tune their knowledge and their insights, will be left in the jetstream of history by those that do.

280

Wider Boundaries for More Effective Management

REGIONAL COUNCILS:
TODAY'S GOVERNMENTAL TOOL
FOR THE 21st CENTURY

by

Thomas J. Christoffel

Revenue sharing may soon become deficit sharing, as the crisis of the U.S. Federal debt causes the national government to retrench from its fiscal assistance to state and local governments. With programs being eliminated or severely cut back, state and local governments are getting financial and program responsibility for their own self-help for urban, suburban and rural development. This decentralization is occurring at a time when the shift to a global economy is causing havoc in many industries and likewise in the tax base of local government. As they seek to broaden the tax base to help take up the federal fiscal slack, they find themselves in competition with other regions of the country or their own state, for existing as well as new development. Since no industry is safe from downturns, greater diversity is being sought in the local economic base. Economic development is the goal of the day for most state and local governments.

An important reality that governmental officials are learning is that " . . . business owners select locations primarily on the basis of regional characteristics, not local attributes."[1] The structure of the economy does not follow governmental boundaries at the local level any more than it does at the global level. While this is not startling information to futurists, it is news to those elected officials who have not caught up with the changes in the global economy. Local officials must look at economic development in the context of their geographic region and attention must also be paid to the governmental services that create the environment in which productive economic activity can take place. In *The Third Wave*, Alvin Toffler correctly identified the trend to decentralization in government. To deal with it he said, " . . . the institutions of government must correlate with the structure of the economy, the information system, and other features of the civilization."[2] State and local governments now need such an organization of the future to deal with these changes.

Thomas J. Christoffel is Executive Director of the Lord Fairfax Planning District Commission in Front Royal, Virginia.

Organizations of the Future

Toffler said organizations of the future, " . . . have flatter hierarchies . . . are less top-heavy . . . (and) consist of small components linked together in temporary configurations . . . capable of assuming two or more distinct structural shapes as conditions warrant. . . . "[3] Furthermore, these organizations:

> . . . need managers who can operate as capably in an open-door, free-flow style as in a hierarchical mode, who can work in an organization structured like an Egyptian pyramid as well as in one that looks like a Calder mobile, with a few thin managerial strands holding a complex set of nearly autonomous modules that move in response to the gentlest breeze."[4]

Surely there is no "module" more autonomous than a local government. Do local governments have such an organizational structure and managers available to help them deal with the crises of the future as the demands on and cost of governmental services increase? They do, since most local governments belong to:

> " . . . a public organization encompassing a multi-jurisdictional regional community . . . founded, sustained and directly tied to local governments through local and/or state governmental laws, agreements or other actions."[5]

Although the local name may be council of governments, planning district commission, or planning and development district, the generic name is "regional council." There were 534 councils in the U.S. at last count and they exist in all but four states: Alaska, Hawaii, New Jersey and Rhode Island. Their governing bodies are composed of elected and/or citizen members appointed by the local governments and states.

Although formed in response to federal programs and state enabling legislation, they each now work essentially as a tool of the local governments within their region, and as an advocate of the region to the state and federal levels. Staff size and budget vary with the nature of the region served, ranging from under 5 employees in some rural areas to over 50 in large metropolitan areas, but generally ranging between 6 and 15. Budgets similarly run from $150,000 to over $5 million, a very small share of the total local government cost.[6] In Virginia in fiscal year 1982 for example, regional council budgets totaled $6.9 million compared to $4,313.2 million for cities and counties. This does not include towns or special districts.

Besides an executive director, councils employ what are essentially information workers; planners for community assistance, economic development, environmental concerns, human services, and transportation; engineers, data analysts, cartographers, and computer specialists. By providing ad hoc coordination from a regional perspective, they help the local governments correlate their local plans within the structure of the regional economy. They are also capable of dealing with specific sets of localities on various issues, being for example, the transportation planning organization for the urbanized areas of the region or the service provider for programs for the elderly. They are entrepreneurs providing data services to local governments and the private sector, regional training for agencies and ride-matching services for commuters. Unlike local governments, they can easily expand and contract their staffs to meet program needs.

Changes in Local Government

According to the International City Management Association (ICMA), 1960 was a benchmark year for " . . . the beginning of rapid growth in the federal aid system, the closely related expansion of local government responsibilities, the creation of substate regions, and the modernization of state governments."[7] In contrast, 1980 is the benchmark year for the decline of the federal aid system, but the roles it helped fund still remain for local government to carry out. In 1960, local governments raised 70.6% of their revenue and their budgets totaled $32,424 million. In 1983, their $178,994 million local share was 60.7% of their $294,651 million total budgets.[8] Although the percentage share declined by 10%, the total increased 909% in 23 years. The Federal government share of state and local government revenues peaked at 22% in 1978, and declined to 18.5% by 1983. The difference of 3.5% was absorbed 1.7% by the states and 1.8% by localities.[9]

This has created conflict at all levels of government, since citizens want better services without further tax increases. Quality governmental services are, in fact, a prerequisite for the economic development sought to balance the tax base, so more investment is necessary. Local governments will be forced to seek greater efficiency and look for economies of scale in service delivery to deal with the impact of the federal fiscal crisis, the changes brought by technology, and the global economy now and on into the 21st century.

How has the structure of government changed to correlate with that of the global economy? Local government has gotten more complex and fragmented. Since 1962, at the local level, decreases have occurred in counties, declining in total from 3,043 to 3,041; townships and towns from 17,142 to 16,734; and school districts from 34,678 to 14,851. Municipalities have increased from 18,000 to 19,076 and special districts from 18,323 to 28,588.[10] Thus in spite of the consolidation of almost 20,000 school districts, the total number of local government units has increased by 10,931 since 1962.

Consolidation of local government units is often proposed as a means of dealing with the cost of government, but is generally rejected by local politicians and even by the voters in referendums, if the idea gets that far. The report of the Governor's Commission on Virginia's Future in 1984 called for a bold realignment of local government boundaries to consolidate many rural counties, but the idea has not moved any local governments to action. It also recommended more aggressive state leadership in the promotion of regional solutions to regional problems and state aid to reward regional cooperation and encourage consolidation among local jurisdictions.[11] The rapid pace of change may in fact make people cling to the local identity provided by governmental boundaries, even as they understand that they work, shop and play within a greater region than the single jurisdiction in which they live. State aid to reward regional programs is more likely to help achieve coordination among the autonomus modules of local governments, since it offers something in return for local control shared in a regional program. Likewise, the state agencies must share decision making with these regional programs.

Kent Mathewson, Counsel on Urban Affairs from Ray Associates, Inc., recently told city and county managers in North Carolina that, "Fiscal restraints are reshaping Federalism."[12] He quoted Andrea Beatty, a former Vice President of ICMA, on the benefits to local governments of this situation: "As the Feds opt out the locals are given the opportunity for greater control and decision making and . . . enlarge the opportunity for regionalism as a cost necessity, e.g., water resources and economic development."[13] What tools do localities have for working regionally?

Primarily there are the special districts, the majority of which are single purpose. They deliver services such as transportation, sanitation, parking, etc. As a reflection of the complexity of governmental services, they have grown by 56% between 1962 and 1982. While they can be efficient in delivery of a limited range of services, Kent Mathewson says his boss, Jim Ray, " . . . foresees the awful prospect of impotent general purpose local government elected officials (city and county) as special purpose politics move power and service options out of their hands and into special purpose districts, independent local commissions or boards, and regional single-purpose authorities."[14]

The Regional Council Alternative

Regional councils are a type of special district, but they can be comprehensively multi-jurisdictional and multi-purpose in terms of the scope of their services. By their representation from local governments, they can avoid some of the tunnel vision that limits single purpose authorities. Although regional planning commissions have existed in metropolitan planning areas since the 1920s, they were composed primarily of citizen representatives. It wasn't until the 1950s that informal meetings of city and county elected officials became structured as councils of government, as a response to local interest and encouragement by the Federal Housing Act of 1954.[15] Georgia, in 1957, created a statewide system of planning and development districts. Other states investigated the idea and followed suit. With the 1968 Intergovernmental Cooperation Act, the federal government encouraged the concept by establishing the A-95 review process which called for a regional review of applications for grant funding to determine the regional impact of projects. The Department of Housing and Urban Development supported the concept by funding councils for regional planning.

Regional councils, as early networks, put local governments into a situation where they had to share power in decision making. Under this system, applications for Federal and sometimes state grants, had to be reviewed by a regional clearinghouse for its impact on local and regional plans. Thus to get local approval of a grant application, a central city may have had to deal with growing suburbs or visa versa. These early regional forums were either controversial or tiresome as they dealt with the allocation of assisted housing or abstract issues of regional planning. The reaction of local officials to the concept of the regional council in many cases was that it was an unnecessary level of government and a threat, fearing that they would be eliminated at some time in the future. State administrations often oversold the early regional councils, such as in Virginia, where the enabling legislation even included an option for a directly elected multi-purpose regional service district.

What are the roles of regional councils today? That depends upon the size and characteristics of the region served. There are three basic categories, depending upon the size of the metropolitan area within the region: large, medium and small or rural if there is no city/suburban area of over 50,000 population within a metropolitan statistical area of 100,000. In a 1985 meeting of regional council executive directors, all levels saw economic development as a functional concern of their member governments. This reflects a growing understanding by all involved in the process that companies pick regions in which to locate, since single jurisdictions can seldom offer all the amenities sought. Also the high cost of marketing encourages cost-sharing approaches. The rural/small metro and medium metro councils saw their roles as providing specific types of technical and operational assistance for localities, while promoting, brokering and assisting in financing/grantsmanship deals to bring about economic development. The large metros operate as information/data resources with increasing private sector ties to facilitate better management of a broader region.[16]

As tools of local government, regional councils can be shaped by the member governments to handle programs for one or more member government as desired, though authority may have to come from state legislation. In southwest Virginia, two regional councils are involved in implementation of a variety of programs, including development of a regional industrial park, operation of solid waste disposal programs, and job training. In southeastern Virginia, for the Norfolk-Portsmouth-Virginia Beach metropolitan area, the regional council serves as the ad hoc coordinator for a variety of regional services through a network of appointed and elected officials. The states can use these councils to promote regional cooperation through an application of incentives, however if they are to function in concert with state agencies, the agencies must share power.

Conclusions

Looking back at the 1950s, the leaders in the regional council movement envisioned the benefit of local governments working cooperatively to benefit themselves and each other. Within the past

287

thirty years, the regional council has grown from a "meet and eat" affair for local officials, to become a valuable tool for local and state governments to deal with complex issues which are now faced by the various substate and interstate regions of the country. A tremendous amount of consciousness raising was necessary on the part of local officials to get them into the 20th century. Now that many have arrived, using the local planning tool, it is now time for them to shift to a tool for the 21st century, the regional council.

The ultimate decentralization in the current political structure is to the local government, those boundaries set up in the horse and buggy days. The identity local governments provide is as important to American democracy today as it was then, so it is unlikely that the public will voluntarily reorganize in the name of efficiency. At the same time local government will face crises as impacts are felt from (1) the shortage of public dollars, (2) the shift to a global economy, and (3) technological changes. A viable option for local governments is the continued evolution of regional councils consistent with the needs of the regions they serve. The regional council is a tool for today and tomorrow.

Notes

1. National Association of Towns and Townships, "Harvesting Hometown Jobs: A Small-Town Guide to Local Economic Development," Washington, D.C.: 1985 National Center for Small Communities, p. 11.

2. Alvin Toffler, *The Third Wave,* New York: William Morrow and Co., Inc., 1980, p. 449.

3. Ibid., p. 280.

4. Ibid., p. 281.

5. National Association of Regional Councils, "Directory of Regional Councils 85-86," Washington, D.C., p. 3.

6. National Association of Regional Councils, Report No. 107, March, 1985.

7. Wayne Anderson, et al., *The Effective Local Government Manager,* Washington, D.C.: International City Management Association, 1983, p. 172.

8. U.S. Bureau of the Census, *Statistical Abstract of the United States: 1986,* (106th edition). Washington, D.C., 1985, p. 274.

9. Ibid.

10. Ibid., p. 262.

11. Governor's Commission on Virginia's Future, "Toward a New Dominion: Choices for Virginians," Charlottesville, Virginia: Institute of Government, University of Virginia, December 1984, pp. 37-38.

12. Kent Mathewson, "Perspectives on Council-Manager Government: American Federalism," remarks to the 25th Annual City and County Management Seminar, Institute of Government, University of North Carolina, Chapel Hill, text copy, p. 6.

13. Ibid., p. 7.

14. Ibid., pp. 11-12.

15. Richard C. Hartman, "The State's Role in Regionalism," February, 1973, p. 163, *The Regionalist Papers,* Kent Mathewson, ed., Southfield, Michigan: Metropolitan Fund, Inc., 2nd edition, 1978.

16. National Association of Regional Councils, "Directors' News," Vol. 6, No. 10, October 25, 1985.

"GOOD FENCES MAKE GOOD NEIGHBORS:"
THE LIMITS OF THE TERRITORIAL SOLUTION

by

Leigh S. Shaffer and Samuel F. Moore

Environmental problems do not stop at national boundaries.
—Jimmy Carter

The history of mankind is strewn with habits and creeds and dogmas that were essential in one age and disastrous in another.
—James Reston

Robert Frost, in his well-known poem "mending wall" (in Latham, 1969), takes the persona of a Maine farmer to tell of meeting his neighbor for a spring ritual—the mending of stone fences dividing their properties. "Something there is that doesn't love a wall;" the two men have gathered to mortar stones of a wall they didn't build and whose purpose is far clearer to the neighbor than the poet. Musing about the aimlessness of the fence in his mind, the poet finally gathers the courage to confront the neighbor with his questions about their activities. The query elicits from the neighbor a line which may be the most familiar line in American poetry: "Good fences make good neighbors."

The wall is a symbol and a testimony of a timeless strategy of conflict resolution that, to our knowledge, has no explicit name. We have chosen to call this strategy "the territorial solution." As social scientists can readily attest, mankind has not made great strides in conflict resolution; more often than not we have settled our differences with wars. But territory has provided a historical alternative. People have long recognized that geographical features such as mountain ranges and oceans have provided social and political insulation for groups. When the balance of power between two groups has been so uneven as to encourage one group to impose itself upon another, groups

Leigh S. Shaffer and Samuel F. Moore are with the Department of Psychology at West Chester University.

This article is an extensive revision of a paper presented by the first author at the Newagen Conference on the Psychology of Peace, Boothbay Harbor, Maine, July 1984. The authors wish to thank Mary Anne O'Donoghue and Adma D'Heurle for their comments and suggestions on the previous draft.

have "voted with their feet" and sought the security of isolation. New England's history is enriched by the presence of many such communities. But the major trends of recent demographic history—population growth, urbanization, and industrialization—have greatly curtailed the possibilities of geographic, political, and social isolation. As Thomas Carlyle remarked to a friend in the United States, "You won't have any trouble in your country as long as you have few people and much land, but when you have many people and little land your trials will begin." (quoted in Ennis, 1969).

When groups with great social, political, religious, or ethnic differences are forced to coexist with one another, or when groups have historical grievances or current disputes, they have been faced with the choice of armed conflict or settling their differences and resolving their conflicts. The drawing of boundaries while one of the most pervasive strategies of intergroup relations, has been successful in avoiding armed conflict in the past, but its overutilization has postponed the learning of true conflict resolution skills required in contemporary times. Historically, parties threatened with conflict in the face of breakdown in negotiated settlements have turned to the solution of declaring territorial boundaries, and "settling" the dispute by segregating the parties and avoiding provocation of hostilities by isolating one another from direct contact with their counterparts' objectionable practices, beliefs, or simple physical presence. This practice of defining a boundary in order to escape or avoid armed conflict we have called the "territorial solution." The wall is both the symbol and, if it is sturdy and imposing enough, the means of enforcing the territorial solution. "Good fences make good neighbors!"

Until now, the territorial solution has been a tacit doctrine; from a social psychological perspective it is an instance of "implicit social relations theory" (Wegner and Vallacher, 1977). By making manifest what has been tacit, it is possible to make rational its character and make manifest its limits. And our principal concern is with its limits. Once the logic of the territorial solution is stated, it is obvious that this strategy is based on a simple, but crucial assumption: for the territorial solution to work, both the members of each party *and the products or the consequences of their activities must respect the boundaries* drawn between the antagonists. Historically this assumption has easily been met; as long as the groups acted within the legitimate limits of their territory, they were unlikely to provoke their neighbors in any way. However, the growth of industry and technology has changed the situation drastically. There is now a distinct set of products of industrial activity and consequences of collective behavior that violate the assumption of intergroup insulation. *These products and consequences define a set of problems—environmental problems—which cannot be solved by the territorial solution! They cannot be solved because these effects of group behavior cannot be confined to a territory.*

This paper has a simple thesis, but one that should be profoundly disturbing. To paraphrase the words of James Reston at the head of the article, the territorial solution is a habit which was essential in ages past, but disastrous in our age. Attempts to invoke a territorial solution on environmental problems are doomed to failure, because the air, the oceans, the soil, radiation, and other agents will not respect territorial boundaries. This point may seem so simple as to be trivial until it is realized that cities, states, provinces, nations, and international organizations are currently trying to devise and implement territorial solutions to air and water pollution problems, acid rain, soil erosion, toxic wastes, noise pollution, and problems of rights to pursue environmentally based activities such as smoking. We will illustrate the pervasiveness of the territorial solution presently, but we must first state the implications of our current situation.

We (the human race) are trying to solve environmental problems with the territorial solution—and such solutions cannot work.

We are postponing the task of learning the skills necessary to negotiate real and lasting solutions to such problems; these are skills that we do not now possess.

In the meantime, we continue environmentally destructive behavior. This situation both exacerbates the problems themselves and increases the danger that any one of these problems will become so intolerable as to provoke armed conflict.

Finally, by letting these problems exacerbate and mutual provocation increase, we are diminishing the time that we have available to develop the skills of real conflict resolution.

The territorial solution must be recognized as a barrier to conflict resolution and not a reliable tool in service of forging such resolutions. But as we will illustrate shortly, the futility and danger surrounding reliance on the territorial solution is not currently realized by governing bodies. Therefore, the message of the limits of the territorial solution must be clearly and forcefully proclaimed.

A Small Example: Smoking

A simple and current example of our thesis is the attempt to regulate smoking in public places. Scientific and medical concern about the insidious effects of breathing tobacco smoke in the air has coincided with widespread social activism concerning the recognition of the rights of nonsmokers to breathe clean air. The result has been a spate of local and state ordinances regulating smoking, but all such legislation that we know about has invoked a territorial solution! In dealing with the respective rights of smokers and nonsmokers, the ordinances have not negotiated a settlement of the relative rights of each group and developed a code of smoking behavior that takes into account the pretenses of both groups. Rather, the approach has been to create territories designated as "smoking" and "nonsmoking" areas which segregate the two groups. An early piece of legislation taken widely as a model by other states is the Minnesota Clean Indoor Air Act which requires, for example, the creation of designated smoking and nonsmoking areas in all restaurants and mandates that at least 30 percent of the seats be reserved for nonsmokers

("Showdown on Smoking," 1983). But the problem with such a territorial solution is that it cannot work because of the simple fact that smoke diffuses and will not confine itself to the designated smoking area!

In a series of field studies of smoke diffusion in public buildings, Repace and Lowrey (1980) demonstrated that the levels of respirable suspended particles in nonsmoking areas were a health risk to nonsmokers and that both existing and foreseeable ventilation systems are inadequate to remove the risk to nonsmokers. They pointed out that most establishments possess filtering systems that are relatively ineffective at removing smoke from the air; they also pointed out that simply increasing the rate of mechanical ventilation yields "exponentially diminishing returns" in terms of energy and cost, making increased ventilation a hopeless option for solving the problem. Simply stated, the diffusion of cigarette smoke completely violates the assumption on intergroup insulation made when applying the territorial solution for the problem of indoor air pollution, and unless buildings have ventilation systems strong enough to lift the lint off the carpet, the net result of invoking the territorial solution is to remove the nonsmoker from proximity to the source of smoke but not to protect the nonsmoker from the dangers presented by unwanted smoke.

Respirable suspended particles constitute the health hazard from smoking, but the *smell* of smoke to the nonsmoker more properly fits the legal category of nuisance, and it is "nuisance law" that gave impetus to the territorial solution of similar problems in the past with the creation of the institution of *zoning*. At the interpersonal level, zoning is the most familiar example of the territorial solution and, in tracing its history, Babcock (1966) points out that zoning was invented in New York City in 1916 as an explicit extension of nuisance law. Babcock contends that the practice of zoning caught on because of its ease of application: "It was a simple matter to draw lines on the municipal street map showing the boundaries of the districts" (Babcock, 1966, p. 5). Similarly, it is easy to divide up the floor plan of a public building into smoking and nonsmoking areas. But the problems of the 1980s are a far cry from the problems confronted by judges in the early days of nuisance law. Babcock reports one early judge's characterization of a nuisance as an object or activity out of its "proper place": A pig in a farmyard, he said, is not a nuisance, but a pig on a residential street is a nuisance. At last report, New York City has mastered its problem with barnyard animals, but problems like nonsmokers' rights, air pollution, noise pollution, toxic wastes, radiation and the like will never be controlled by zoning laws.

Four Big Examples: Grasslands, Oceans, Antarctica, Outer Space

While the previous instances of the territorial solution are at the level of local government and interpersonal relations, there are examples to be found at the national and international level. While each of these is complex, we will sketch each only briefly in order to demonstrate in the application of the territorial solution in each case, the limits of the solution for the problems raised in each case, and an historical trend to be discerned in the application of the territorial solution to environmental problems.

Grasslands: The "Land Grab"

Happiness is exclusive access to a valuable resource.
—R.J. Miller

The tragedy of the American grasslands is a frequently cited example of Garrett Hardin's concept of the "Tragedy of the Commons" argument (Coggins and Lindeberg-Johnson, 1982). Briefly, a commons biologically is an ecosystem which is considered as a renewable natural resource serving as the chief means of life-support for a population. A commons economically is a resource which is not subdivided into private property but serves as a common resource for all prospective parties: open range land, known by the British term "commons" stands as the prototype of this arrangement (Hardin, 1968). The "tragedy" of the commons is a scenario Hardin believes likely (even in some cases inevitable) when the commons becomes overexploited. When the number of organisms subsisting on the commons begins to reach a number where their collective demands meet and begin to exceed the natural resource's ability to renew itself (a level referred to as the "carrying capacity" of the ecosystem), a crisis occurs. The tragedy is that humans who exploit the commons will probably respond to the crisis by choosing to pursue a course of maximizing short-term profit (and thereby push the commons into ruin by preventing it from renewing itself) rather than maximizing long-term interests which includes the preservation of the commons as an ecosystem. This contest of short-term versus long-term interests is called "the commons problem," and is currently believed to model a wide variety of environmental problems (see Edney, 1980; and Fox, 1985). The collapse of the American cattle industry and the ruin of the grasslands during the time of the so-called "land grab" is a clear historical example both of the tragedy of the commons and of the limits of the territorial solution.

The public rangelands were created by act of Congress from the free grass of the Great Plains. In the early years of the cattle industry, the rangelands were treated as a commons by the cattlemen as an economic necessity; they were undercapitalized for buying land (even if it were locally available) but even more so for the practice of ranching which would have required capital to finance a costly payroll of cowhands to mend fence and look for strays, and, most importantly, to buy the feed necessary to sustain livestock confined to the owner's property. So long as the numbers of livestock remained relatively small and there was no practical means of fencing the land, the cattlemen were willing to treat the grasslands as a commons. But between 1820 and 1870 the number of cattle and sheep on the grasslands increased exponentially (for a description of the growth see Hough, 1953; Kraenzel, 1955; Osgood, 1929; and Worster, 1979), and barbed wire—the practical means needed to fence a property claim—was invented in 1874. When it was clear the size of the herds were crowding the range, cattlemen initiated a frantic, sometimes violent, scramble to obtain control of desirable land—especially land with water resources (Riegel and Athearn, 1971). Not all of the lands were fenced, but almost all of the valuable land was taken. Since "water controlled the range," the usual pattern of acquisition was staking claim to land adjacent to a reliable water source; when one made *two* such claims it was usually possible to annex all of the land in between because it was worthless without access to water (Hough, 1958; Osgood, 1929). By a combination of tactics such as fraudulent acquisition of land ceded to the railroads, abuse of the Homestead Act, control of water rights, and claims based on shaky legal principles such as "prior use," "range rights," and "squatter's rights," the cattlemen sought to protect their investments by assuring themselves exclusive access to some land for their exploitation. This period of our history has been called the great "land grab."

The land grab is a good example of the territorial solution because it reduced provocation of range wars through the division of the land. And it appealed to all of the parties because no one was forced to give up their right to self-determination over ranching practices or productivity. But the limits of the territorial solution are graphically illustrated here because the exploitation of the individual rancher's lands had consequences for neighbors across the barbed wire fence: even when a resource ceases to be treated as a commons economically and politically, it never ceases to be a commons ecologically. Despite increasing acres of stripped grassland bringing soil erosion with rain and blowing dust with drought, the cattlemen continued to push the rangeland to ruin. The carrying capacity of the land steadily decreased: a steer that needed only five acres of grazing land to sustain itself in 1870 needed as many as 30 to 50 acres by 1880 (Osgood, 1929; Worster, 1979). The collapse of the grasslands inevitably brought the collapse of the cattle industry as well. The years 1889-1890 are remembered as "the Great Debacle" when millions of head of cattle and sheep perished by starvation, drought or winter cold. While cattle-ranching eventually reestablished itself with different practices, the boom and bust of the cattle industry has permanently altered the rangeland. Today approximately 80 percent of the lands controlled by the Bureau of Land Management produce less than half of the forage they produced in 1800 (Coggins, 1984). And, of course, one by-product of the exploitation of the land was the great dustbowl (Worster, 1979), a sobering symbol of pushing an ecosystem beyond its limits. "The meaning of dust storms," wrote Archibald MacLeish (1935), "was that the grass was dead."

The Oceans: "Sea Grab"

I am proclaiming today an exclusive economic zone in which the United States will exercise sovereign rights in living and nonliving resources within 200 nautical miles of its coast.
                                                                    —Ronald Reagan

294

With that statement, President Reagan announced that the United States would join whith the majority of seafaring nations in declaring a 200 mile Exclusive Economic Zone in addition to the 12 mile claim of Territorial Waters. This trend which began in earnest in the 1970s was precipitated prospectively by belief in the potential for exploitation of minerals in the continental shelves of the world and retrospectively by realization of declining harvests of many species of fish. An event that dramatized the latter development is the so-called "Cod War" between Iceland and Britain.

The doctrine of the freedom of the seas was undergirded by belief in the limitlessness of the ocean's resources. But in the fishing industry, decreases in yields in the face of more intensified fishing efforts had occurred for the major food species in waters in the North Atlantic including cod, haddock, herring, and ocean perch (Holt, 1969). Indeed, overfishing led to a marked decline in the world fish catch in 1972 for the first time in a twenty year period where average annual increases in yield of 5 to 6 percent had been the rule (National Academy of Science, 1975). In 1972, Iceland, which was heavily dependent on fishery exports, unilaterally extended its territorial jurisdiction to 50 nautical miles, resulting in a serious conflict with British fishing fleets which had long fished in those waters. In 1975, Iceland extended its limits to 200 nautical miles. The resulting increases in tensions between British and Icelandic fishing fleets was finally marked by an incident in which an Icelandic gunboat fired on a British ship. Although the matter was ultimately resolved by the United Kingdom's agreement to reduce its codfish quota in the area under dispute, it has remained an uneasy settlement (Hollick, 1984; Pabst, 1976).

During the 1970s the world's interests in the oceans were formally debated with the convening of the United Nations Conferences on the Law of the Sea (UNCLOS). The treaty-drafting initiative began as early as a conference convened in 1958; while this conference led to no formal treaty, most of the parties were agreed that nations could protect only narrow territorial seas and that the open oceans should be viewed as a common resource for the benefit of all mankind. But by the third UNCLOS in 1974, the hope of maintaining the open seas as a commons seemed empty. During the 25 years of UNCLOS, unilateral jurisdictional claims increased from three, to six, to twelve, and finally to 200 miles. In 1977, Ehrlich, Ehrlich, and Holdren observed that, despite the original intent of UNCLOS, the parties to the negotiations had switched their primary emphasis to getting their share in "dividing up the pie" (p. 941). As nation after nation declared 200-mile Exclusive Economic Zones, nearly 40 percent of the world's oceans came under the sovereign jurisdiction of individual coastal states. And since the vast majority of known mineral resources and fishing stocks are on the respective continental shelves, the resources have by now been effectively territorialized.

But will the territorial solution work any better in the oceans than it did in the grasslands? We argue that it will not. Overfishing within a 200-mile zone will have the same environmental consequences as overgrazing had on the ranches of the plains. It is interesting to note here, however, that nothing analogous to barbed wire exists to divide the sea. Cattle would not respect boundaries but could be retained by barbed wire fences. The World Court has finally resolved the conflicting territorial claims made by the United States and Canada for the prime fishing areas of the Maritimes: it will be interesting to see if both nations try to issue passports to the perch!

Territorial solutions will do nothing to halt the spread of water pollution either. David Epel in 1970 warned about the dangers of pollution in a speech entitled "The Death of the Oceans." In talking about the threat posed by pesticides, he used the apt, if inelegant, metaphor of waste disposal: "The oceans are the toilets of the world," he said. While fresh water bodies have mechanisms for cleansing themselves, the ocean has "no plug at the bottom of the sea," and toxic wastes can only accumulate. In talking about the waste disposal practices of nations, Epel reminded his listeners that " . . . global pollution respects no national borders" (Epel, 1970, p. 412).

The Future: "Ice Grab" and "Sky Grab?"

Outer space is not a new subject, it is just a new place in which all the old subjects come up.

—Senator Albert Gore

The trends discussed in the historical development of territorial claims in rangelands and the oceans can also be discerned in two new emerging areas of environmental resource management— Antarctica and outer space. If it was possible to talk about a recent "sea grab" as a parallel to the infamous "land grab," it is possible to foresee an "ice grab" and a "sky grab" as well! As the quote from Senator Gore suggests, many of the issues that we highlighted in the case of the grasslands and the oceans are already repeated themes in the case of outer space, but also Antarctica.

In the case of the latter, effective exploration of Antarctica has been very recent. Nonetheless, the tensions between those who wish to territorialize versus those who wish it to be viewed as a commons have already emerged. Between World Wars I and II, many nations were involved in exploration of Antarctica. While the United States and the Soviet Union refrained from making territorial claims, seven other nations did assert claims, usually claiming "effective occupation" as the rationale. Using a tactic previously applied to the Arctic, nations began to make claims extending to the South Pole using the "sectoring principle" which extends territorial claims between settlements on the coast to the Pole itself. By 1940, only one section representing approximately one-sixth of the continent, remained unclaimed (which is still the case today; Luard, 1984). A treaty in 1958 representing nations most involved in scientific research provided for common access to Antarctic for scientific research and put territorial claims aside without invalidating them. The treaty worked well until the 1970s, even adding new nations to the status of consultants to the Treaty. But the situation changed when it began to be clear that Antarctica held significant mineral deposits, especially oil. According to Luard (1984), the political issues among signers and consultants to the Treaty mattered very little until the issue of resources was salient:

> The Treaty system is under attack now because the Treaty powers are increasingly involved in discussion of another matter in which a large number of countries feel that they have a vital interest: the question of what system should be introduced to regulate the exploration and exploitation of the potential mineral resources of Antarctica (Luard, 1984; pp. 1180-1181).

Current debate centers on the theme of tempering the territorial claims of individual nations against providing the "have not" nations opportunity to share the wealth of Antarctica. Malaysian Prime Minister Mahathir bin Mohamed expressed this theme succinctly:

> The days when the rich nations of the world can take for themselves whatever territory and resources that they have access to is over. Henceforth, all the unclaimed wealth of the earth must be regarded as the common heritage of all the nations of this planet (cited in Luard, 1984, p. 1183).

The nonaligned nations have backed the principle of treating Antarctica as a commons, and debate on restructuring the treaty goes on now. One of the complexities in the Treaty negotiations is that many of the resources lie on Antarctica's continental shelf, and the question of whether those riches can be annexed by declaring an Exclusive Economic Zone by a continent with no sovereignty has been debated.

Effective exploration of outer space is even more recent than that of Antarctica, but its pace over the last thirty years has been remarkable, and the potential benefits, but also problems, represented by that exploration are profound.

Until recently, the greatest concern for outer space has been that of preventing its use for military purposes. Since the first United Nations Assembly Session in which this issue was the focus, both formal (e.g. the 1966 United Nations Space Treaty) and tacit agreement, however vague, have been directed at preventing what President Kennedy foresaw as the potential for space becoming "a new terrifying theater of war" (cited in Lay and Taubenfeld, 1970, p. 9).

Although the use of surveillance satellites, the U.S.S.R.'s testing of "killer satellites," and the recent U.S. "Star Wars" initiative stretch the limits of existing agreements and threaten the possibility for new agreements, there has been a consistent effort to reach agreement to preclude military exploitation of outer space. The trend in other areas of agreement is not as clear. In fact, formal agreement in the form of space law is "like space itself . . . a vacuum waiting to be filled" (Fisher, 1985). What is clear, however, is that the "vacuum" of space law is being filled through the process of unilateral initiatives and claims.

This process is clearest in an area of outer space termed the Geostationary Orbit (GSO). The GSO is that band of space immediately above the equator in which satellites can maintain twenty-four hour orbits and thus remain stationary in relationship to the earth. GSO placement for a satellite offers clear telecommunications advantages, an advantage currently enjoyed primarily by developed Western nations and the U.S.S.R. Available transmission wavelengths in the GSO are rapidly diminishing to the point that developing nations are concerned that none will be available to them as they reach the capacity to launch their own telecommunications satellites. These concerns on the part of developing nations were a major impetus for the convening of the most recent United Nations Space Conference— UNISPACE '82 (Corcoran, 1982). The final conference report on UNISPACE '82 represented the best compromise that could be achieved between developing nations' hopes for reserving access to the GSO and the developed nations' already claimed advantage in the GSO. That report, while acknowledging that a problem of over-crowding was foreseeable, carefully avoided endorsing any proposed solutions including one suggesting that the developed nations should relinquish their established claims to preferred transmission bands in the GSO (Dickson, 1982). In short, existing "divisions" or claims will prevail.

For now, regulation of military activities in space and the problem of overcrowding in the GSO are the predominant concerns about outer space. A rapidly emerging concern is that of the exploration of mineral resources of celestial bodies. At present, the 1966 space treaty defines celestial bodies as a commons to be used in free competition for the benefit of all (Lay and Taubenfeld, 1970). As White (1970) suggests, until more is known about what of actual value can be extracted from such bodies, it is in the interest of individual states to advocate an open commons, or the *Res Commons Principle,* in application to distant celestial bodies. What will happen as the feasibility and derived value of exploitation increases?

The circumstances of the moon as the closest celestial body provides a probable answer. A "moon treaty," established by the United Nations in 1979, proposed an international regime (similar to the international Seabeds Authority) to manage the commercial development of the moon for the benefit of all nations) (Mereson, 1984). Only fourteen nations have signed the treaty, and among the more notable non-signators are the U.S. and the U.S.S.R., the two nations with the greatest technological and economic potential for exploring the resources of the moon! (In fact, Art Dula who is a space law authority employed by private industry indicates that it is the U.S. which is most likely to take the lead in establishing mining and scientific outposts on the moon. When asked what the U.S. response would be if other nations encroached on American claims, he responded "I suspect we'd blow them away before we'd let them in there." (Fisher, 1985).

We can only conclude that the brief history of activity in outer space and on Antarctica suggests that old themes, already played to regrettable conclusions in the grasslands and the oceans, are the predictable themes which will predominate in the new frontiers of Antarctica and outer space.

The Historical Trend: Claims to Commons to Territorial Solution

The preceding examples, both large and small, have offered retrospective accounts and prospective scenarios concerning the pervasive use of the territorial solution. We suggest that in the case of the four large examples—grasslands, oceans, ice, and space—there is a recurrent pattern. The pattern has three stages of development toward a territorial solution. The first stage is that of *individual claims* made by persons (or even nations) to sovereign control of territory within an environmental resource. The second stage is the pressure from those without prior claims to declare the resource to be a *legal commons* for the benefit of all concerned. But the third stage has been an ironic response: the movement for cooperation and common exploitation has led or seems now to be leading to invocation of *the territorial solution,* where individuals or independent sovereign nations make exclusive territorial claims to the resource for private exploitation. A possible fourth stage, seen so far only in the case of the so-called "land grab," is *the tragedy of the commons.*

Stage one, the appearance of individual claims, whether latent or manifest, informal or formal, illegitimate or legitimate, can be illustrated in all four of our major cases. In the historical example of the land grab of the open rangeland of the United States, this stage involved a variety of mechanisms including claims of "squatter's rights," the passing of local "range rights" laws, claims over water rights that led *de facto* to exclusive use of the land between water claims, and illegal fencing with barbed wire. In the oceans, this first stage involves the claims to territorial seas and fishing rights made both formally and informally. Currently, this first stage is illustrated by the sectoring of Antarctica and the filling of the geostationary orbits for satellites.

The second stage occurs when parties previously uninvolved in making claims begin to press for the resource to be made into a legal commons. In the land grab, Congress legislated that the range lands be public land not to be privately held, and stockmen's associations were formed to protect the open range. In the oceans, Grotius' articulation of the law of "open seas" was both a repudiation of the Papal Bull dividing the ocean between two claimants, Spain and Portugal, and an affirmation of the sea as *res communis*—a common heritage of all mankind. More recently, the UNCLOS deliberations included third world nations resisting individual national claims to press for the declaration of the oceans as a commons. Antarctica, in the 1950 Treaty, was made a commons for scientific exploration and current debate includes the imperative of forming a new treaty which allows all nations to share in exploitation of fishing and drilling possibilities. The so-called "Moon Treaty" includes a comparable statement for outer space.

299

While this second stage is typically precipitated by concerns of exclusion by parties without prior claims on the resource, there are instances in which parties with existing claims also find it in their interest for the resource to be defined as a commons. For example, nations with a technological lead for the exploitation of outer space resources such as potential valuable mineral deposits on celestial bodies currently find it to their advantage to have such bodies considered as a commons open to exploitation through free competition until the actual value of the potential resource is more fully known (Lay and Taubenfeld, 1970; White, 1970). Then, as the actual value and prime locations for mineral deposits are identified, technologically advantaged nations will undoubtedly establish "past practices" claims for the most valuable locations in preparation for the third stage of the territorial solution.

The third stage of the territorial solution has been documented in the case of the land grab with the fencing of the range lands and in the ocean with the race for nations to declare 200 mile Exclusionary Economic Zones. And while these stages have not been reached for Antarctica and outer space, we presented scenarios which depicted the appearance of the territorial solution as being likely. The fourth stage, the "tragedy of the commons" where the environmental resource was ruined by the pursuit of self-determined exploitation within individual territories has happened with the failure of the cattle industry in the United States and the ruination of the rangeland. We have argued that it may be happening in the ocean, both with respect to world fishing, but also with pollution. Finally, the rapid utilization of the geostationary orbit illustrates the same type of development in space. It is the belief that the third stage of territorial solutions makes more likely the fourth stage of the tragedy of the commons that is the impelling motive for writing this paper, and it is to that theme that we turn to now.

The Limits of the Territorial Solution

We hope that we have made clear the limits of the territorial solution, even with the brevity of our documentary presentation. There are, of course, other examples of past and current environmental problems that have been created or exacerbated by the drawing of boundary lines. (Need we remind readers of the motivational intractability of the problem of acid rain, where the consequences of activities of one region or nation are visited across a boundary on the territory of others?) We hope that we have conveyed our sense of urgency in proclaiming this simple observation because of the ubiquitousness of the territorial solution displayed in these problems. The territorial solution once worked; it will not work now on these problems. Time is getting short, the situation is getting worse, and progress in learning to solve these problems is obstructed by what must now be viewed as an anachronous and self-defeating strategy.

Lest we leave you with despair, we will spoil our Jeremiad with an optimistic conclusion and a caveat. The caveat concerns the positive

300

use of territory: while the territorial solution cannot work, it may be useful to have territorial designations and responsibilities in workable solutions. That is, for purposes of monitoring environmental quality, of determining the compliance of individuals or groups with negotiated solutions, and of holding individuals and groups accountable for their actions, it may be necessary to draw territorial boundaries and respect them. In asserting the futility of the territorial solution, we do not mean to advocate a return to a literal commons as an answer!

The optimistic conclusion comes from applying the work of Carolyn and Muzafer Wood Sherif in their famous field studies of the origins of conflict and conflict resolution (Sherif, 1958; Sherif, 1964; Sherif and Sherif, 1969). They believed that their most important contribution was the concept of *superordinate goals*—goals that were salient and attractive to many groups, and that were sufficiently motivating to encourage intergroup cooperation. The reason that these goals worked toward building cooperation and reducing conflict was that *the goals were unattainable through unilateral effort but attainable by cooperation*. All of the individual problems we have mentioned may become superordinate goals—indeed, their magnitude may some day make them superordinate for the global community. That's the good news, the bad news is that the time clock measuring the opportunity to manage these problems before we suffer disastrous consequences seems to have been started.

Walter Weisskopf (1983) recently wrote: "An ethic for our technological age is a task for prophets and not intellectuals. What intellectuals can do is to remove the mental rubble that has been amassed during the last four centuries of Western history" (p. 99). The territorial solution is such a piece of mental rubble: figuratively it lies in our path toward learning how to negotiate answers to our pressing environmental problems. When people are presented with compelling problems whose nature is unclear, whose parameters are undetermined, and whose solutions are "blowing in the wind," it is characteristic that the level of activity is high, but the direction is diffuse. If we may be so bold, let us concentrate on removing the territorial solution as an impediment on the road to peace before we dissipate our energies in seeking new paths. Let's spread the word on the limits of the territorial solution! We must inform politicians of these issues and support those who would exercise the political courage to advocate that nations negotiate treaties of mutual self-restraint.

References

1. Babcock, R. F. (1966) *The Zoning Game: Municipal Practices and Policies*. Madison, WI: University of Wisconsin Press.

2. Coggins, G.C. (1984) "The Law of Public Rangeland Management V: Prescriptions for Reform." *Environmental Law,* 14(3), 497-645.

3. Coggins, G.C., and M. Lindeberg-Johnson (1982) "The Law of Public Rangeland Management II: The Commons and the Taylor Act." *Environmental Law,* 13(1), 1-101.

4. Corcoran, E. (1982) "Unispace 82." *Space World, S-e-9-224-225* (August/September), 18-19.

5. Dickson, D. (1982) "U.N. Space Conference Ends in Compromise." *Science,* 217(3), 915-916.

6. Edney, J.J. (1980) "The Commons Problem: Alternative Perspectives." *American Psychologist,* 35, 131-150.

7. Ehrlich, P.R., A.H. Ehrlich, and J.P. Holdren (1977) *Ecoscience: Population, Resources, Environment.* San Francisco: W.H. Freeman.

8. Ennis, H. (1969) "Human Ecology: Creation of Public and Professional Awareness." *Vital Speeches,* 35(7), 210-215.

9. Epel, D. (1976) "The Death of the Oceans." *Vital Speeches,* 36(13), 411-414.

10. Fisher, J. (1985) "He's Pushing for New Laws to Keep the Peace in Space." *Philadelphia Inquirer,* February 10, 14A.

11. Fox, D.R. (1985) "Psychology, Ideology, Utopia, and the Commons." *American Psychologist,* 40(1), 48-58.

12. Hardin, G.J. (1968) "The Tragedy of the Commons." *Science,* 162, 1243-1248.

13. Hellick, A.L. (1984) "Managing the Oceans." *Wilson Quarterly,* 8(3), 70-86.

14. Holt, S.J. (1969) "The Food Resources of the Ocean." *Scientific American,* 221(3), 178-194.

15. Hough, E. (1958) "The Round-Up." In C. Neider (ed.), *The Great West.* New York: Bonanza Books, pp. 441-457.

16. Kraenzel, C.F. (1955) *The Great Plains in Transition.* Norman, OK: University of Oklahoma Press.

17. Lathem, E.C., ed. (1969) *The Poetry of Robert Frost.* New York: Holt, Rinehart and Winston.

18. Lam, S.H. and H.J. Taubenfeld (1970) *The Law Relating to Activities of Man in Space.* Chicago: University of Chicago Press.

19. Luard, E. (1984) "Who Owns the Antarctic?" *Foreign Affairs,* 62(5), 1175-1193.

20. MacLeish, A. (1935) "The Grasslands." *Fortune,* 12, 59.

21. Mereson, A. (1984) "The Longest Arm of the Law." *Science Digest,* 92(9), 30.

22. National Academy of Sciences (1975) *Population and Food.* NAS, Washington, DC.

23. Osgood, E.S. (1929) *The Day of the Cattleman.* Chicago: University of Chicago Press.

24. Pabst, R.A. (1976) "Fisheries." In D.L. Larson (ed.), *Major Issues of the Law of the Sea,* pp. 84-106. Durham, NH: The University of New Hampshire.

25. Repace, J.L., and A.H. Lowrey (1980) "Indoor Air Pollution, Tobacco Smoke, and Public Health." *Science,* 208(4443), 464-472.

26. Riegel, R.E. and R.G. Athearn (1971) *America Moves West.* Hinsdale, IL: The Dryden Press.

27. Sherif, M. (1958) "Superordinate Goals in the Reduction of Intergroup Conflict." *American Journal of Sociology,* 63, 349-356.

28. Sherif, M. (1964) "Creative Alternatives to a Deadly Showdown." In M. Sherif (1967) *Social Interaction,* Chicago: Aldine, pp. 455-463.

29. Sherif, M. and C.W. Sherif (1969) *Social Psychology.* New York: Harper and Row.

30. "Showdown on Smoking." (1983) *Newsweek,* June 6, 60-63, 67.

31. Wenger, D.M. and R.R. Vallacher (1977) *Implicit Psychology,* New York: Oxford University Press.

32. Weisskopf, W.A. (1983) "Moral Responsibility for the Preservation of Mankind." *Social Research,* 50(1), 98-125.

33. White, E.W. (1970) *Decision-Making for Space: Law and Politics in Air, Sea, and Outer Space.* West Lafayette, IN: Purdue University Studies.

34. Worster, D. (1979) *Dustbowl: The Southern Plains in the 1930s.* New York: Oxford University Press.

Epilogue:
a Vision for Tomorrow

TOWARD THE GREAT MILLENNIUM

by

Don Toppin

The Third Millennium A.D. can become The Great Millennium: one thousand years of peace and well-being for all the inhabitants of the global village. Never before has a guiding image of this magnitude been viable. Now the vision is clear, realizable and urgent. The darkness has become so deep that we are beginning to see the stars.

The challenge is colossal. The dream is the first step to reality. Billions of people are waiting to respond to wise farsighted leadership and a vision of hope and understanding. Hope, like fear, is contagious! The Great Millennium is an idea whose time has come.

We now live in one interdependent world with global communication, transportation, travel and trade. The next step is the globalization of understanding which transcends tribalism while reducing breakdowns and accelerating breakthroughs. The dream becomes the energizer.

The human race has become connected by the machine. The medium has become the message. Myriad impulses originating in every corner of the world crisscross and interlink the human system ever more tightly. The entire world has become a single community.

Modern wars are neither affordable nor winnable. Nuclear weapons have no military value, if used, except in the hands of terrorists. Starvation and sickness, as products of shortsightedness and ignorance, are no longer necessary. Many things are possible, including peace and well-being, as soon as enough human beings realize that the future of the human race is at stake.

It is now reasonable to prophesy that we are approaching the dawn of the greatest cultural epoch since the beginning of human life on earth provided that a fresh transcendent campaign for a positive future, already launched in the consciousness of billions, is as successful as it must be. The alternatives are too horrible to mention!

The options are clear. Time and again, supposedly inexorable forces have been reversed by human acts proceeding out of positive

Don Toppin is chairman of Toronto/2000 which launched the Great Millennium Campaign at Centrestage on February 12, 1986.

human decisions. Moreover, there seems to be a growing world-wide consensus in favor of peaceful progress toward a sane, sustainable global society.

Indeed, as violence and terrorism threaten, it is increasingly difficult, whether in the East or the West or the North or the South, to find anyone who is enthusiastic about continuing to live in the shadow of either socio-economic disaster or thermo nuclear holocaust. More and more, it is realized that the money spent on the global arms race could eliminate all global socio-economic problems and, at the same time, accelerate the trend toward global cooperation in human matters. The opportunities are already contained in the problems if so perceived.

This is an age of re-awakening, re-searching, re-thinking, and re-inventing. It is also an age of convergences and trade offs. In this fragile period of transition, small incremental changes in individual thought and action can tilt the balance toward appropriate social policies, locally and globally. The visions are clear for those who choose to see and consciousness is rapidly increasing at many significant levels.

The late great world visionary Buckminster Fuller speaks of "Six Billion Billionaires" meaning a world population by the year 2000 with each inhabitant enjoying a minimal standard of civilized life with facilities and choices much greater than the real billionaires of only a few years ago. Shortly before his departure, Bucky explained:

> For the first time in history, humanity has the capability to offer every individual a higher standard of living than any single individual has ever known. This can be accomplished through a design-science revolution. Design science is the effective application of the principles of science to the conscious design of our total environment.
>
> Neither the great political and financial power structures of the world nor the population in general realizes that an invisible revolution—metallurgical, chemical, electronic—now makes it possible to do so much with so little (in terms of material, energy and time for a given task) that there are enough resources for everyone. Selfishness is unnecessary! Everyone can win!
>
> With the finest aeronautical and engineering facilities of the world redirected from weaponry to livingry production, all humanity now has the option of becoming enduringly successful. All previous revolutions have attempted revengefully to pull the top down. If realized, this historically great revolution, the design-science revolution, will joyously elevate all humanity to unprecedented heights.

The Soviet futurist Igor Bestuzhev-Lada, past president of the International Association of Sociologists, believes "the world of tomorrow will be a world without arms, soldiers and wars. The billions that are dumped each year into the arms race will be more than enough for accomplishing the most daring projects. The transfer of the world economy to a peaceful state is perfectly feasible but, without halting the arms race, it is hard to count on the successful settlement of the many global problems including population, energy, minerals, resources, environment and food." As the mutual arms reduction programs become successful, the economic hardships of all hemispheres will begin to disappear.

As Chairman of the International Association for Arts in the Future, Takdir Alsijahbana, Rector of the National University of Indonesia, says: "There is no need for people to destroy each other." We are witnessing the greatest cultural explosion since 500 B.C. when transportation, communication, and trade humbly began as man climbed upon the horse and rode toward the moon. The taming and utilization of the horse, a generally-unrecognized milestone as important as the discovery of the wheel, portable type or electricity, seems to have contributed to a new world view as enunciated by Confucius, Buddha, Plato, Aristotle, Alexander and others and expressed in the Judeo-Christian and Moslem religions. According to this great oriental scholar, computers and satellites are now hastening another great leap forward in planetary consciousness which transcends all former boundaries. In the words of Peter Russell in his book *Global Brain,* we might well be headed toward a threshold point beyond which the momentum of rising consciousness will outweigh the inertia of the old ego-based model. If so, crossing this threshold would represent a major transition for humanity. When the "social atmosphere" rises sufficiently, enlightenment (understanding) will become the norm.

The book *Seven Tomorrows* by three SRI International futurists explodes the myth of a world conspiracy and shows clear alternatives that "can free people from the rigid lock of predeterminism." They emphasize that no one is in control of the current course of history, certainly neither Washington nor Moscow, contrary to widely-believed myths. Instead, humanity stands at a unique point: simultaneously, our problems are so acute and our communications network so widespread that, for the first time in world history, genuinely collective and democratic decisions are both demanded and possible.

The hour seems ripe for leaders of vision and good will from all cultures to join forces in addressing the critical concerns of our age. Indeed, the world is being tied together by modern communication, transportation, travel and trade. But as Orville Freeman, former President of Business International Corporation on Wall Street warns, "At this time of strain and major adjustment, the danger is that the world will fracture apart in an orgy or nationalist retaliation, protectionism, subsidization and a host of other devices that countries use to look after themselves and beggar their neighbors. A new group partnership of coordination and give-and-take is needed to replace the old hegemonic world structure. The necessary international institutions for survival in an interdependent world can be built or rebuilt and the world can be spared a nuclear war."

"The situation demands leaders who will shift the world's attention and its resources from maintaining East/West hostility to restoring the natural systems that ultimately sustain all societies," concludes Lester Brown in *State of the World*. "Acting in their own interests, these two countries could set the stage for demilitarizing the world economy. Once it starts, demilitarization, like militarization, could feed on itself."

To those who are able to see and understand, the critical path to The Great Millennium becomes clearly visible. Increasing public awareness, as generated by scientists, physicians, educators, clergymen, executives, scholars, artists, financiers and others (media specialists, etc.) and fostered by the communication explosion and the culture builders (us) will rapidly spread throughout the world until it becomes politically necessary to divert the annual trillion dollar weaponry loss to an annual trillion dollar "livingry" gain. Transnational institutions to facilitate the transition will come together. The psychological origins of the macrocrises will become widely recognized and confronted. Social and economic pressures will lift. Simultaneously, a scientific environmental design for symbiotic cooperation will converge from the collective intelligence and creative will of a global population who, at long last, has regained hope.

It does not diminish the significance of the convergences to suggest less the arrival of an era of goodwill than the sentiment that drew the Butcher and the Beaver together in Lewis Carroll's "Hunting of the Snark":

> The valley grew narrower and narrower still
> And the evening grew darker and colder
> 'Till (merely from nervousness, not from goodwill)
> They marched along shoulder to shoulder.

As the Butchers and the Beavers (East/West, labor/management, rightists/leftists, doves/hawks, etc.) learn that it is mutually advantageous to march shoulder to shoulder in the direction of a peaceful sustainable global society, they will also learn to understand each other better—without nervousness—and with growing good will, trust and hope.

To help facilitate the transition, we have the underrated, underused United Nations and its far-reaching agencies plus hundreds of forward-looking non-governmental groups and transnational organizations, who, even now, are trying to create a positive future by addressing a wide range of inter-related problems. Many of these organizations are capable of transformation to the new relevancies.

We can support these groups as well as making our personal contribution in our own unique ways. Indeed, each of us can share this *gift to posterity*.

Individually and collectively, because we are in harmony with a vast invisible network of other positive forces, we become co-creators of the miracle of The Great Millennium—a miracle which can be visualized and shaped—beginning right now.

Take an Active Part in Building Tomorrow . . . Today

Join the World Future Society

Join the 25,000 people from all over the world who want to make sense out of today's rapidly changing world. The World Future Society is unique. Since its founding in 1966, the Society has served as a neutral clearinghouse for people at the forefront of social and technological change. Through local chapters, seminars and conferences, and its many publications, the Society reaches out to those who want to explore the alternatives for tomorrow.
As a member of the World Future Society, you will receive:

THE FUTURIST
—The Society's bimonthly magazine of forecasts, trends, and ideas about the future. The latest in technological developments, trend tidbits, interviews, and in-depth articles give members a comprehensive look into tomorrow.

NEWSLINE
—An occasional newsletter exclusively for members of the World Future Society, NEWSLINE keeps members up-to-date on Society activities and reports on other items of interest, such as regional conferences.

RESOURCE CATALOG
—A twice-yearly guide to the hundreds of books, cassette tapes, and other materials carried by the Society bookstore. Members also receive discounts on these products.

CONFERENCES
—Special rates at all assemblies and conferences. The Society sponsors and organizes meetings to bring together futurists from around the world. Some 3,000 people attended the Fifth General Assembly in Washington, D.C., in June 1984.

LOCAL CHAPTERS
—Access to your local chapter. Over 100 cities in the United States and abroad have chapters for grass-roots support for future studies.

Take a part in building tomorrow. Send your check or money order for $25 for the first year's dues. You'll receive a one-year (six bimonthly issues) subscription to THE FUTURIST, the twice-yearly RESOURCE CATALOG and discounts from the Society bookstore, the occasional NEWSLINE, and special invitations and rates for meetings sponsored by the World Future Society. You may also join the local chapter in your area.

Send your order to:

World Future Society
4916 St. Elmo Avenue
Bethesda, Maryland 20814

TALKIN' BACK

TALKIN' BACK

Raising and Educating Resilient Black Girls

Dierdre Glenn Paul

Westport, Connecticut
London

Library of Congress Cataloging-in-Publication Data

Paul, Dierdre Glenn, 1964–
    Talkin' back : raising and educating resilient Black girls / Dierdre Glenn Paul.
        p. cm.
    Includes bibliographical references and index.
    ISBN 0–275–96195–8 (alk. paper)
    1. African American girls—Social conditions. 2. African American girls—Education. 3.
African Americans—Social conditions—1975– 4. Racism—United States. 5. Discrimination in
education—United States. 6. United States—Race relations. 7. United States—Social
conditions—1980– I. Title: Talking back. II. Title.
E185.86.P36 2003
305.23—dc21   2003053611

British Library Cataloguing in Publication Data is available.

Library of Congress Catalog Card Number: 2003053611
ISBN: 0–275–96195–8

First published in 2003

Praeger Publishers, 88 Post Road West, Westport, CT 06881
An imprint of Greenwood Publishing Group, Inc.
www.praeger.com

Printed in the United States of America

The paper used in this book complies with the
Permanent Paper Standard issued by the National
Information Standards Organization (Z39.48-1984).

10 9 8 7 6 5 4 3 2 1

Copyright Acknowledgments

The author and publisher gratefully acknowledge permission to reprint the following:

"Still I Rise," copyright © 1978 by Maya Angelou, from AND STILL I RISE by Maya
Angelou. Used by permission of Random House, Inc.

Excerpts from "Still I Rise" by Maya Angelou. UK copyright © held by Virago Press, a
subsidiary of Time Warner Books, UK. Used by permission of the publisher.

To my primary tributes to political activism, social change and Christianity: my children. I love you with my whole heart.

Dilemmas

Dilemmas are messy, complicated, and conflict-filled situations that require undesirable choices between competing, highly-prized values that cannot be simultaneously or fully satisfied.
—*Larry Cuban, professor, former social studies teacher, and superintendent* (How Can I Fix It?: Finding Solutions and Managing Dilemmas)

Searching for Solutions and Proposals for Action
Solving these problems[and dilemmas], the first thing is to see them.
—*Randall Robinson, author, founder, and president of TransAfrica* (The Debt: What America Owes to Blacks)

CONTENTS

ACKNOWLEDGMENTS

Very little is accomplished in life without the assistance of others. Although the writing of this book was dependent upon my labor and thought, the project could not have been brought to fruition without the invaluable support of others. As a result, I would like to thank those who have contributed to my success:

- God, from whom all blessings flow.
- My mother, Carolyn Pinkard Norris, and my grandmother, Helen Mary Pinkard, for serving as cheerleaders, mentors, and childcare providers. But for you, I wouldn't be at this point.
- My uncle, Edward Wendell Pinkard, for his sage wisdom and expert career guidance.
- Provost Richard Lynde and Associate Vice President Joan Ficke of Montclair State University for support and encouragement of my growth as a scholar and a leader.
- Montclair State University's Faculty Scholarship Incentive Program for the release time to complete this project.
- Tina Jacobowitz and the Agenda for Teacher Education in a Democracy for providing additional grant funding to complete the project.
- Graduate assistants Azure Diggs and Debra Tracht for their belief in this project and willingness to help.
- James Comer, president Freeman Hrabowski, and Janie Ward for their belief in this project.

- Editor Jane Garry, for contracting this book.
- Editor Marie Ellen Larcada for pushing me to always do a little better.
- Marcia Goldstein, Stephanie Mouton, Greenwood, and Thistle Hill for guidance and attention to detail.

Chapter 1

INTRODUCTION

The path of the scholar is at best a lonely one. In [her] search
for truth [she] must be the judge of [her] findings and [she]
must live with [her] conclusions. The world of the Negro
scholar is indescribably lonely; and [she] must, somehow, pursue truth down that lonely path while, at the same time, making
certain that [her] conclusions are sanctioned by universal standards developed and maintained by those who frequently do
not even recognize [her].

—John Hope Franklin, historian
(Race and History: Selected Essays 1938–1988)

The charge has been leveled that researchers of color who are culturally in
synch with their research participants cannot be objective "in their analyses of those problems which are so close to their life experiences" (Reyes
& Halcon, 1996, p. 97). This claim presupposes that objectivity truly
exists and it is more than an artificial contrivance.

The same criticism seems infrequently directed toward white
researchers who conduct research with and about white participants
(Smitherman, 1988). In fact, it appears that white researchers commonly
have the fewest restrictions placed on them. Yet I resist the essentialist trap
of stating that racial affiliation solely leads to understanding. Barriers like
internalized racism, gender, class distinction, and involuntary immigration
status versus immigrant minority status can prevent researchers who share
the same racial affiliation with those they research from understanding the
experiences presented or developing an empathic relationship. Anthropologist John Ogbu (1994) defines "immigrant minorities" as "people who
came to the United States more or less voluntarily because they believed
that this would lead to increased economic well-being, better overall
opportunities, or greater political freedom" (p. 63).

MY ROLE AS A BLACK WOMAN INTELLECTUAL

Comprehending that such a schizophrenic mindset regarding research on and by people of color exists, I state unequivocally that I am intimately connected to the topic of black girls. "It is personal because the women whose blood [courses] through my veins breathe amidst the statistics" (Giddings, 1984, p. 5). This topic is also intensely personal because I am the mother of a young daughter who must be taught to love and value herself, as well as navigate a society that routinely conveys the message that her blackness makes her unlovely. I am the mother of a son whom I must teach to see beauty and value in black women, working in partnership with us rather than working toward maintaining systems of subjugation and oppression that serve neither party. I do not wish for either child to equate beauty, intellect, status, and success with whiteness only. In fact, I must teach both children to resist such messages, and I must concomitantly counter those abrogating messages about blackness with positive ones. All of these tasks must be accomplished within the context of a society that remains racially unjust and in which the "Black Self is assigned the lowest status on America's racialized hierarchy" (Fordham, 1996, p. 343), even after September 11.

The act of teaching resistance is, itself, a political one, as is the act of parenting black children (Ward, 1996). Scholar Audre Lorde (1984) has eloquently depicted it in the following fashion:

> Raising Black children—male and female—in the mouth of a racist, sexist, suicidal dragon is perilous and chancy. If they cannot love and resist at the same time, they will probably not survive. And in order to survive, they must let go. This is what mothers teach—love, survival—that is, self-definition and letting go. (p. 74)

For the reasons delineated, I am unable to assume the role of a dispassionate researcher. I privilege a "passionate scholarship, science-making rooted in, animated by and expressive of our values" (Du Bois [1903] as quoted in Belenky, Clinchy, Goldberger, and Tarule 1986, p. 141).

Akbar (1985) has defined the general role of the black social scientist as altering the frameworks of dominant culture reality, so they might accommodate new frames of reality, marginalized viewpoints, and expanded paradigms. Black female intellectuals who conduct research function in this general capacity, but they often assume an added responsibility. In many instances, we are called on to further complicate the discourse by drawing attention to the dynamic of gender, as well as analyzing the synergistic intersections of race, class, gender, and the power relationships inherent in them. Black female intellectuals are often called on "to produce facts and theories about the Black female experience that will clarify a Black woman's standpoint for Black women" (Collins, 1991, p. 37). In the tradition of the black woman intellectual, I write to shape my own reality, privileging the black female experience and theorizing on black female epistemology.

I ascribe to a "Womanist," a term first introduced by Alice Walker (1983, p. xi), brand of research undergirded by one central premise. Inquiry should and does serve the purpose of advancing sociopolitical change and emancipation. "Social change is the starting point of science, and in order to understand the content, form, and consequences of patriarchy, the researcher must be actively involved in the fight against it; one has to change something before it can be understood" (Mies as quoted in Fonow & Cook, 1991, p. 6).

THE ANTITHESIS OF A MONOLITH

I am an U.S. citizen; therefore I also position this book within that context. Although blacks throughout the African diaspora share similar experiences of oppression and domination and have developed shared coping mechanisms, representative of strength, resilience, and growth, my own experiences have occurred within the borders of the United States, and that context shapes my thought (Paul, 2001). Although it is well known that all blacks did not arrive on American shores as slaves, the legacy of chattel slavery has wreaked a particular and distinct havoc on those brought here to plausibly endure the most brutal form of enslavement known thus far. The reference to "plausible endurance" reminds us that many did not even survive the Middle Passage.

In referring to "the black community," I am using the term (in a discerning fashion) to reflect those who share a common culture, common concerns, and common modes of survival, without contending that U.S. blacks should be viewed as a monolith. Anthropologist Brian Bullivant (Banks, 1993) defines culture as "the knowledge, ideas, and skills that enable a group to survive." Cultures can be formed on the basis of gender, socioeconomic status, religion, disability, and sexual orientation, as well as race and ethnicity. Dizard (1970) establishes two significant contributors to a collective or group identity. They are "a common thread of historical experience and a sense that each member of the collectivity, regardless of how distinct he [or she] may be, somehow shares in this historical experience, and [by] a sense of potency or strength inhering in the group" (p. 196). Yet varying cultural memberships can also create conflict.

THE TENETS OF CULTURAL PLURALISM

By focusing on the ways in which complex dilemmas impact the black community, I am not underestimating the ways in which these issues correspondingly impact other traditionally marginalized groups. Although I am committed to improving the plight of us all from historically disenfranchised groups, it would be an injustice and presumptuous to attempt to fully represent all of our interests (Paul, 2001). I can only write knowledgeably about what I have experienced, what I have lived (Paul, 2001). As such, I write from the theoretical construct of cultural pluralism, advanced by W. E. B. Du Bois. There are four tenets of cultural pluralism:

> (1) Each race has its own distinct and particular culture. (2) Different races can accept a common conception of justice and live together at peace in one nation-state. (3) Individuals must develop more and closer ties to the other members of their own race in order to preserve and enhance those cultural traits which mark it off from others. (4) ... the cultural pluralist hastens to add that [s]he does not say that any particular culture is superior or inferior to any other, only that they are different, and that members of each race must make a concerted effort to develop their own culture ... because each race must present its culture as a gift to the other races. (Boxill, 1995, p. 236)

"Although I have tried to compensate for the limits of my particular social ... history, I principally depend upon others to translate [and make applicable] across cultures" (Ruddick, 1980, p. 347).

THE NEED FOR THIS BOOK

For me, growing up as a young black girl was incredibly difficult and fraught with peril, although the experience also helped me to develop a strength, resilience, and adaptability that have made my life a fruitful one. My family, nuclear and extended, provided me with the support I needed to mitigate outside forces and influences that might have been deleterious. There were also teachers, health professionals, and "other mothers" who helped provide stability and reassurance, all proving invaluable in respect to my development. "Other mothers" have been defined as "women who assist bloodmothers by sharing mothering responsibilities" (Collins, 1991, p. 119).

Too often, the lives of black girls have been used to bolster positions focused on alleged deviance and pathology. For example, traditional science has supported the hypothesis that black girls experience precocious puberty (as evidenced by breast development and pubic hair); precocious puberty has been negatively associated with depression, social withdrawal, aggressive behavior, moodiness, and compromised adult height (Kaplowitz & Oberfield, 1999). Contemporary studies, however, suggest that the onset of puberty is occurring earlier in *both* white and black girls in the United States, and previous studies on the topic were flawed in respect to sampling and assessment standards (Kaplowitz & Oberfield, 1999).

The links established in the earlier studies among black women's sexuality, abnormality, and aberration appear as the norm in much of the traditional scientific literature. The connections also raise questions about a pervasive racism, which has historically used so-called science to support flawed truisms that black women are aberrantly sexual and fertile and thus a drain on the economy and an entity in need of reproductive control (even if that control is governmentally imposed). In a similar and more sinister vein, black women have been used as racial guinea pigs in perfecting complex gynecological surgeries (Breggin & Breggin, 1998; Scully, 1980), and poor black women have been exploited for the purpose of testing experimental and damaging birth control devices (Corea, 1977).

Within the pages of this book, it is my intention to avoid contributing to such characterizations of black girls and, by extension, black women. Blame would be more properly assigned to the obscure and complex systems that have, historically, failed black girls and continue to do so. For instance, as this book clearly outlines, black girls are not presently receiving equitable learning opportunities in schools. Many are achieving academic success in spite of their schooling. Plausibly, this factor might add to the widening educational gap between students of color and white students in U.S. schools. Some of the information presented here will assist classroom teachers, administrators, school counselors, and other school personnel in more successfully nurturing black girls and enhancing their chances for both personal and academic success.

Although I attempt to maintain candor and refuse to disguise problems that hinder the development of black girls (specifically) and the black community (generally), I opt to focus on triumph in this book. In *Talkin' Back: Raising and Educating Resilient Black Girls,* I seek to emphasize the strengths that black girls possess within the context of adaptive families, communities, and school systems. A history of success surrounds tripartite efforts involving families, communities, and schools. For example, birthrates for black teenagers have declined sharply over the past decade. Additionally, black middle-class teenage girls have been identified as the most effective contraceptive users in the contemporary United States (Maples, 2002).

Although this decline is obviously a success, it should also be viewed within the realm of a drop in birthrates for black women generally (U.S. Department of Health and Human Services, 1998). In examining the factors that appeared to impact girls to avoid teenage pregnancy, the following conditions were deemed essential:

- Parents and other adult mentors play key roles in encouraging young adults to avoid early pregnancy and to stay in school (U.S. Department of Health and Human Services, 1998).
- Public and private sector partners throughout communities—including parents, schools, businesses, media, health and human service providers, and religious organizations—must work together to develop comprehensive strategies (U.S. Department of Health and Human Services, 1998).

Each element of the tripartite enterprise contributed to the ultimate success. Thus I offer specific strategies designed to foster the efforts of parents and communities, as they work in partnership with schools, toward raising black girls who are well prepared to confront societal and educational challenges and still succeed.

METHODOLOGICAL CONCERNS

I want to add to the body of scholarship on black girls, but I also hope to serve as a catalyst and initiate a process of unlearning and relearning information on the black female experience. I would like to free readers and myself from the biases and misconceptions perpetuated by our academic training. In *Talkin' Back: Raising and Educating Resilient Black Girls,* I analyze the extant literature as it pertains to black pre- and early adolescent girls. Specifically, I focus on black girls in the middle grades (grades 5–8). I have selected this distinctive focus for myriad reasons. But the most prominent centers on the lack of attention it consistently receives. Presently, there is a dearth of research and information about black girls. And that which has been completed tends to focus on early childhood/elementary grades or late adolescence. Late adolescent black and Latino girls, in particular, appear as a precious target group for conservative think tanks and policymakers. In spite of research that eschews a link between increased welfare benefits and increased birthrates for teen mothers of color, late adolescent black and Latino girls have often been used to bolster racist, misogynist stereotypes perpetuated to maintain the status quo and blame the victim for her circumstances. Such attempts to shift blame have been used, quite effectively, to deflect attention from bureaucratic systems and political decision making that actually deplete our economy rather than the images of poor black and Latino welfare queens that are set forth to mask this fact.

For many youth, the changeover from elementary to middle school is a traumatic one, at best. The transition is not only plagued with academic uncertainty and a decline in self-esteem, but rapid physical, intellectual, and social change (Jackson & Davis, 2000). Research suggests that these problems are compounded for youngsters who are poor, from traditionally marginalized populations, and/or recent immigrants. These students are most prone to attend schools whose only distinctions center on being the most inefficacious, overcrowded, most segregated, and/or offering the fewest high-level courses (Jackson & Davis, 2000).

In this study, I utilize an interdisciplinary approach, synthesizing research from disciplines like history, psychology, and sociology, making it accessible and reader-friendly for educators, parents, community activists, and members of the church community. My hope and intention is to revisit the topic of black girls in subsequent scholarly works.

This book is in two parts. Part I, "Dilemmas," focuses on determining the quandaries surrounding the study of black girls and those issues impacting their lives, as well as rendering the parallel historical links precise. In Part I, I have purposely defined the neglected status of black girls in the United States as a dilemma as opposed to a problem. The distinction between a dilemma and a problem, as defined by scholar Larry Cuban, appears as follows. Dilemmas are "messy, complicated, and conflict-filled situations that require undesirable choices between competing, highly prized values that cannot be simultaneously or fully satisfied. Dilemmas then end up with good-enough compromises, not neat solutions" (2001, pp. 10–12). Problems, however, serve as the gap "between what is and what ought to be" (Cuban, 2001, p. 4).

In order to work toward a compromise on a complex dilemma, we must first understand its dynamics and the multifaceted complexity of those variables. Analyzing the dilemma's plausible genesis and historical links, potential correlations, and underlying assumptions are all components in arriving at some type of resolution.

There are three chapters in Part I. Chapter 2, "The Status of Black Women in the Contemporary United States," documents the accomplishments of black women in contemporary society and also illustrates the difficulties we continue to encounter on a routine basis. The chapter provides an accurate and intricate snapshot of life for the present-day black woman in the United States and the plausible implications of our struggle for the young black girls who will ultimately follow us.

Chapter 3, "All the Girls Are White, All the Boys Are Black, But Some of Us Are Brave," reinforces the need for this work on further defining and expanding the study on black girls. Although the ways in which black girls have been mistreated by the mainstream have consistently been documented and identified by a number of black women intellectuals, the ways in which our girls are treated within the community is also dangerous and potentially explosive. In this chapter, I explore the pervasive neglect of black girls in research literature and education.

Chapter 4, "Coping with the Legacy of Slavery and Its Links to Childhood and Life for Contemporary Black Girls," examines historical bonds to the contemporary dilemma impacting black girls. One of the chapter's major premises presents the conceptualization of black childhood as a new phenomenon in the United States. Additionally, the chapter emphasizes the point that life for slave children was difficult and life for young slave girls was even more difficult because it was exacerbated by the likelihood of sexual exploitation at the hands of adult men, white and black.

Part II, "Searching for Solutions and Proposals for Action" (chapters 5–8), demonstrates clearly that this book focuses more on the search for answers and developing action plans than defining and redefining problems. In my mind, an omnipresent narration sickness permeates American society. Too often, we remain so invested in defining and redefining problems and dilemmas that we lose sight of the plausible solutions available. In the process of becoming overwhelmed by the vastness and perplexity of societal problems, we become distracted from the pursuit of finding answers and realistic proposals for action. In many respects, the answers themselves are not always as insightful or productive as the process of arriving at those answers. Additionally, Part II is conceptually based on the theory of praxis as outlined by the late Brazilian educator Paulo Freire. The theory simply states that thought generates action and that action generates further thought. Within those parameters, I want to lead parents, communities, and schools to search actively for ways in which to strengthen their partnership and enhance the quality of care and nurturing they are able to give to black girls, both respectively and collectively.

Chapter 5, "The Role of Parents and Caregivers in Empowering Black Girls," analyzes the ways in which black parents can develop and encourage agency in their daughters and sons. The chapter focuses on how parents and family members can assist black girls in making a smoother transition toward womanhood. In an effort to make thoughtful, reflective decisions about parenting, parents must first be knowledgeable. Parents, especially of preadolescent and adolescent girls, must start with a basic understanding of racial identity development theory and adolescence and the ways in which those enigmatic processes will undoubtedly impact their daughters. Additionally, the chapter encourages parents to foster in their girls the ability to define black womanhood as per an internal standard rather than uncritically accepting an external ideal set forth by society.

Chapter 6, "What Is the Role of the Community?," outlines the roles and responsibilities of communities, community agencies, and mentors in raising resilient, empowered black girls. Chapter 7, "What Is the Role of Schools?," focuses on how schools can be enhanced to provide more nurturing environments for black girls' academic and social development. The chapter also suggests ways in which schools can forge more positive educational alliances with families and communities. Black girls specifically need to attend schools that focus on their empowerment, teaching them to voice and give legitimacy to their thoughts, speak for themselves, and recognize the multitude of options possible in their lives (Office of Juvenile Justice and Delinquency Prevention, 1998).

Finally, chapter 8, "Epilogue," discusses how the information presented in this book on black girls might impact educational policy, inform decision making, and lead to social change.

The appendices serve as resource guides for parents, caregivers, teachers, and other school personnel, as well as community activists. Appendix A is an annotated bibliography listing selected children's/adolescent literature titles that feature strong black female protagonists. Appendix B contains an annotated bibliography of reference and professional books that will help caregivers and concerned individuals create more nurturing spaces for black girls. Appendix C is a filmography that caregivers might use as critical discussion pieces with black girls.

In previous writings, I have explained my preference for the terms "black" and "white" as racial descriptors rather than "African American" and "Euro-American" by citing my desire to be inclusive and acknowledge the deep connection among all of the African diaspora. I have been recently led to rethink my position, especially after reading Patterson's discussion of such terms in his book *Rituals of Blood: Consequences of Slavery in Two American Centuries* (1998). Specifically, Patterson cites the negative connotations associated with the dictionary definition of "black" and the positive attributes attached to the definition of "white." He concludes,

> It is preposterous to assume that when Americans call each other "white" and "black" they are somehow able to mentally bracket the historically and culturally ingrained and dictionary sanctioned meanings of these terms. The decision of Afro-American leaders and their Euro-American allies ... to insist on a return to these terms during the sixties was linguistically naïve, culturally obtuse, socially inept, and politically stupid. (p. xxi)

After giving this position careful and deliberate reflection, I have decided that the terms "black" and "white" continue to be the most powerful in contemporary society. "Black is not just skin color [and] ... Whiteness, as a monopoly, is a subconscious construct that promotes aversion to any form of Blackness, especially within the political-legal system" (Anderson, 2001, pp. 24–26). In spite of vehement and politically correct protestations that "race," a word that first appeared with the evolution of the slave practice in the 16th century (Anderson, 2001), is no longer an issue, it remains so. The link between black and inferior is still made on a routine basis and globally; white skin still bestows privilege. "The sheer existence and size of a growing Black underclass is prima facie evidence of institutionalized racism that manipulates symbols, resources and power to advantage Whites over Blacks" (Anderson, 2001, p. 3). Thus, to posit the descriptors as the problem rather than the dilemma itself, seems like placing a bandage on a gaping wound.

Part I

DILEMMAS

Chapter 2

THE STATUS OF BLACK WOMEN IN THE CONTEMPORARY UNITED STATES

From the intricate web of mythology which surrounds the black woman, a fundamental image emerges. It is of a woman of inordinate strength, with an ability for tolerating an unusual amount of misery and heavy, distasteful work. This woman does not have the same fears, weaknesses, and insecurities as other women, but believes herself to be and is, in fact, stronger, emotionally than most men. Less of a woman in that she is less "feminine" and helpless, she is really more of a woman in that she is the embodiment of Mother Earth, the quintessential mother with infinite sexual, life-giving, and nurturing reserves. In other words, she is a superwoman.

—Michelle Wallace, scholar
(Black Macho and the Myth of the Superwoman)

The double burden syndrome of black womanhood, in which the synergistic disenfranchisement prompted by both race and gender is named, might be traced back to Harriet Jacobs. In her book, *Incidents in the Life of a Slave Girl* (1973), Jacobs wrote, "Slavery is terrible for men: but it is far more terrible for women. Superadded to the burden common to all [blacks], they [black women] have wrongs, and sufferings, and mortifications, peculiarly their own" (p. 77). Although she might have been one of the firsts to document the experience (in written form), her forebears undoubtedly felt this same tension. In many instances, those slave women who went before Jacobs presumably felt an identical encumbrance; they were denied the opportunity to fully use literacy. Therefore, they were denied the opportunity to have their thoughts privileged in this society that has, historically, used literacy and education as a means of silencing and further oppressing blacks. Traditionally, assigning the language of a subordinate group with attributes of inferiority, while concomitantly denying literacy development, have served as potent tools in the domination and subjugation of those groups who have been and remain historically disenfranchised.

But there are those who contend that this position regarding the black female's burden in society "lead[s] to images of Black women as conflicted and divided people rather than resourceful [and] strong" (Lightfoot, 1976, p. 241). Others have described it as exclusionary and challenge the very assertion that such an experience is specific to black women. To be precise, Patterson (1998) contends, "[The] only problem with the view is the assumption that it applies exclusively to Afro-American women. It was always the case in America that 'superadded' to the burden of being a male slave or male laborer was the burden of the assault of Afro-American men's integrity and identity as men" (Patterson, 1998, p. 8).

For this author, however, the validity of black women's double burden cannot be minimized. Another referent to this phenomenon of being disempowered by race and gender is *double jeopardy,* a term coined (in 1972) by Frances Beale, founding member of the Women's Liberation Committee of the Student Nonviolent Coordinating Committee (King, 1990). Without a doubt, we black females *do* experience conflicts associated with the dualism of our identities as women and blacks. The complex and powerful impact of our conflicts is even further compounded when the other oppressions we must endure (e.g., class based, sexual orientation, and disability—to name a few) are additionally considered.

Yes, it is true that black females are not the only ones who experience societal conflicts. Yes, it is also true that black female agency has played and continues to play a vital part in helping us cope with and survive multiple oppressions. Yet there are aspects of inter- and intragroup discrimination that cannot be explained without contemplating the convoluted, perplexing identifications with which black females are forced to live (Paul, 1999). Further, the burdens experienced do not negate black females' resilience or resistance to the status quo (Paul, 1999). Emphatically, it should be stated that these factors make the struggle of black women distinctive.

In this chapter, I document the accomplishments of black women in contemporary society, as well as analyze and explain those aspects of our lives that continue to adversely affect us. The anticipated outcome is to provide an accurate and intricate snapshot of life for the present-day black woman in the United States. In the process, a few legitimate questions might also be raised. For instance, why is it that the plight of U.S. black women and Latinas makes its way into the public consciousness with far less frequency and interest than global narratives on the status of women in countries deemed hostile to U.S. policy? Why is it that those crises that disproportionately impact black women are so routinely relegated to the periphery? Why is it that black women must fiercely struggle just to have our issues recognized, and what messages does this struggle send to the young black girls who will ultimately follow us?

USING OUR SUCCESSES AGAINST US

A contemporary phenomenon has sought to underscore the successes of black women, placing our accomplishments in direct contrast to the alleged failures of our black male counterparts. It appears that such high-lighting further disadvantages us and justifies the persistent lack of care and attention devoted to our issues, needs, and lives in both the contexts of the black community and the general population. On a routine basis, sta-tistics are used to substantiate the claim that our problems are not as criti-cal as they have been in the past nor do they reach the magnitude ascribed to those issues impacting black males, in particular. Such a divide-and-conquer strategy is merely a modern-day variation of the matriarch myth that seemed to proliferate with the 1965 *Moynihan Report*. The release contended that black women's dominance in the domestic sphere usurped black men's power, destroyed the black family, and led to the decline of the black community's status. Specifically, the report expressed this idea:

> At the heart of the deterioration of the fabric of the Negro society is the deterioration of the Negro family. It is the fundamental cause of weakness in the Negro community.... A fundamental fact of Negro American family life is the often reversed roles of husband and wife. (Rainwater & Yancey, 1967, pp. 5, 17)

Simply stated, we are to blame for the descent of black civilization rather than the horrific acts of institutionalized racism directed toward us in the past or those that continue to disenfranchise us in the present day. Please note the deliberate choice of the words "dominance," "power," and "status" because it remains debatable that we have ever had or fully utilized any of these, consistently, while existing within the borders of the United States.

Also, observe the fact that with this matriarch myth, as well as others, we become our own oppressors and attention is shifted from institutions, like slavery, for which we were not primarily responsible. So we are told once again, and under different circumstances, that we are to blame for our own lack of progress. The production of such images about us, but created by others, serves a number of purposes. Primarily, "race, class, and gender oppression could not continue without powerful ideological justifications for their existence" (Collins, 1991, p. 67).

"Typically, the privileged have utilized images as ways in which to sub-stantiate the contention that certain groups in society have limited resources and power because of flaws inherent in themselves or in the cul-tures to which they ascribe" (Paul, 2001, p. 71). Another prominent pur-pose for the maintenance of these flat and unidimensional images focuses on the issue of control and our own self-definition as a people. "As sub-jects, people have the right to define their own reality, establish their own identities, name their history. As objects, one's reality is defined by others, one's identity created by others, one's history named only in ways that define one's relationship to those who are subject" (hooks, 1989, pp. 42–43).

There can be little debate surrounding the contention that black women have made progress as a group and we will continue to make gains. Fur-ther, "if [we] are not able to articulate forceful new stories of progress ... based on new ideas, metaphors, and visions of what could be, then other, less democratic and more oppressive stories of progress will win the day" (Carlson & Apple, 1998, p. 4). But in these discussions of our overwhelming success, especially in comparison to black men, a great deal of information is decontextualized.

With the current extenuation of the matriarchy thesis, blame continues to be assigned to black women for failing to meet the implausible chal-lenge brought into existence with a constructed, Euro-centered femininity. We continue to assume blame for abandoning and emasculating black men, as well as compelling them to abandon us. The bottom line, as per the codified discourse set forth, is that both genders have inadvertently and intentionally colluded in black men's mythologized "failure."

For example, more black women than black men are enrolled in college at the present time (35% and 25% respectively) and have earned associ-ate's, bachelor's, master's, doctoral, and professional degrees. Since 1976, there has been a 219% rise in the first professional degrees awarded to black women, and a 53% jump in undergraduate degrees (Cohen & Nee, 2000). In 1992 black women received 63% of all bachelor's degrees awarded to blacks, 67% of master's degrees, 60% of doctoral degrees, and 55% of professional degrees received by black Americans (Cohen & Nee

2000; *Digest of Education Statistics,* 1996). Today, 35% of young black women go to college, and only 13.5% of young black females are high school dropouts (Cose 2003).

If taken at face value solely, these statistics could lead some to the assumption that the black community would be better served by focusing on how black males might be assisted in reaching the same levels of success as black women. Yet let's move beyond the most superficial reading of the statistics provided, instead opting to examine trends and tangential facts that should also be factored into the equation.

One of the most significant points is that black women's heightened presence in higher education and increased attainment of educational degrees should be considered within the parameters of the discussion that women, generally, have outperformed men in both respects. "It is important to note that the increase in female representation in institutions of higher learning observed between 1976 and 1995 is in no way specific to African American communities: Comparable trends are evident in other racial and ethnic groups" (Cohen & Nee, 2000, p. 6). Between 1977 and 1995, the number of black women to whom bachelor's degrees were conferred went from 12,300 to 23,600 (National Center for Education Statistics, 1997; Patterson, 1998). "In the aftermath of the women's liberation movement, females of all colors moved into the academy and the professions. In 1970 America's college population was predominantly male. Today it is 56% female" (Cose 2003, p. 49). Additionally, if in the last decade and a half, a disproportionate number of black men have suffered the near-genocidal effects of the criminal justice system, is it any wonder they are not enrolling in colleges and universities?

Another systemic issue impacting the rate of enrollment and degree attainment for black college-aged men relates to the ever-decreasing financial aid packages offered. Financial aid is shrinking for all enrolled in institutions of higher education; but it appears that black men are not being awarded financial aid at the same rate as black women (Cohen & Nee, 2000). One plausible explanation for this phenomenon is that black women seeking financial aid are usually heads of households with dependent children, and such households constitute the largest sector of Americans living in poverty. Black female householders (without a spouse present) make up 39.3% of those living below the poverty line (U.S. Census, 2001). In stark contrast, only 14.7% of black male householders (without a spouse present) live in poverty (U.S. Census, 2001).

As a result of the growth in incarceration rates for both black men and women, affirmative action attacks on higher education, shrinking financial aid, national economic decline, and resurgent poverty rates, the country is likely to experience decreasing rates of college enrollment and degree attainment for blacks, male and female.

Another misleading point regarding black women's status in postsecondary institutions centers on the benefits of a degree, once it is conferred.

> In 1997, the mean income for a Black woman with some college or with an associate degree was $19,643, whereas the mean income for a Black man with only a high school degree was $22,400.... A similar pattern is to be found among Black women with bachelor's degrees. Again, in 1997, the mean income of a Black woman with a bachelor's degree was $29,091.... Nonetheless, this $29,091 was nearly $6,000 less than the average $35,792 earned by a Black man with a bachelor's degree. (Cohen & Nee, 2000, p. 17)

Further, although black women currently perform at higher rates than black men in physics, mathematics, and computer science and receive more professional degrees than their male counterparts, they major in higher education courses of study (disciplines and professional tracks) that garner less prestige and earning potential (Cohen & Nee 2000; Patterson, 1998).

With this discussion of gains for black women, we lose credibility if we fail to acknowledge that life is better for many black women. Yet we cannot rest on the assumption that we have overcome racial and gender barriers. In many ways, the successes that black women have attained are received in spite of a generally antipathetic mainstream and only in pockets of our community. There remain large sectors of the black female population who are not doing well or progressing at the same rate. Poor black women in the United States are not witnessing or living the economic triumphalism that others are attributing to us. Black women are more frequently subject to poverty, with Hispanic female-headed households running an almost indistinguishable second (U.S. Census, 2000).

We cannot forget about these groups or cease to struggle to make life better for us all. For black women, there is a dialectic of struggle, a legacy of it (Collins, 1991, p. 22)

> Throughout the history of the United States, the interrelationship of white supremacy and male superiority has characterized the Black woman's reality as a situation of struggle—a struggle to survive in two contradictory worlds simultaneously, one white, privileged and oppressive, the other black, exploited and oppressed. (Cannon, 1985, p. 30)

THE OTHER SIDE OF BLACK WOMEN'S SUCCESS

Another questionable outcome associated with mythologizing (rather than critically examining) black women's successes in professional and academic spheres is the potential reinforcement of a compartmentalized view of black women's lives. As we can trace historically, there is an ongoing focus on function rather than personal well-being and life satisfaction. Such a stark and unbalanced characterization of our lives deflects attention from the weighty difficulties that continue to plague our health, social well-being, and relationships. The precarious nature of other aspects of our lives, like our social, emotional, and physical health, stands in grim contrast to the gains we have made in the academic and professional realms.

BLACK WOMEN'S HEALTH CRISES

Within the borders of the United States, the fact remains that black women (between the ages of 25 and 44) are the largest single group in the United States impacted by the HIV/AIDS epidemic at the present time. HIV has ranked first among causes of death in this group since 1993. Although black and Latino women comprise 21% of all U.S. women, 77% of AIDS cases reported among women in 1994 occurred among blacks and Latinas. The rate of transmission has been 16 times greater for black women than it has been for white women in the United States (Centers for Disease Control, 1995).

The statistics cited in relation to HIV/AIDS gain even more significance as we consider them in the context of black women's health crises generally. It appears as if black women are losing ground rapidly in reference to other health disorders as well. For example, for the first time in more than 70 years, fewer people in the United States are being diagnosed with cancer. But new cases of breast cancer in black women are on the rise (Griffin, 1998). More black women will also die from breast cancer, according to the National Cancer Institute (Griffin, 1998).

Although more mainstream media reports highlight eating disorders that disproportionately impact white women and adolescent girls, like anorexia nervosa and bulimia, many black women and girls have fallen prey to the eating disorder of obesity. "Sixty-six percent of African American women are overweight and 37% are technically obese, meaning they are 30% above ideal body weight. The figures for Mexican American women are similar: 66% overweight and 33% obese. For Caucasian women, the figures are slightly lower with 49% overweight and 24% obese" (Ferguson

2003). Further, black women, seemingly, have the most difficulty maintaining weight loss, according to the National Center for Health Statistics
(Hughes, 2000). The average clothing size for today's black woman is size
20; in 1998, it was 18.

Many black women have accepted the rhetoric that necessary concern
about and emphasis on maintaining our weight results from brainwashing
and indiscriminate acceptance of a Euro-centered beauty standard that
emphasizes thinness. Yet the facts are indisputable. Obesity is linked to
increased susceptibility to specific cancers, hypertension, diabetes, and
heart disease (Hughes, 2000). Further, black women suffering from obesity are more likely to suffer premature deaths (Hughes, 2000).

A number of black women's health concerns can be traced to the disproportionate rates at which we are affected by poverty, inadequate health
care, racial bias in diagnoses and treatment, as well as mistrust and fear of
health professionals among blacks. Quite specifically, poverty can result in
the lack of treatment or the early interruption of treatment, especially in
cases in which social service benefits are deficient or nonexistent (Seligsohn, 1994). Poverty has another adverse impact on black women's health
as well. Many of the health crises that black women experience can be
traced back to their diets. Poor blacks are more susceptible to malnutrition,
defined as not having enough to eat or subsisting on a diet that is unbalanced, high in fat and sugar. Whereas in some cases, malnutrition prompts
disease like cancer, diabetes, and heart disease, in other instances, malnutrition weakens the immune system, making people more susceptible to
infectious disease like hepatitis, HIV/AIDS, and tuberculosis.

SOCIAL AND EMOTIONAL WELL-BEING

Another quality of life issue impacting black women is the improbabil-
ity that we will marry. The fact remains that the majority of black women
in the United States will spend the majority of their adult lives in an
unmarried state, and most black men (regardless of socioeconomic status)
are opting against marriage. Aside from the apparent quality of life issues
(like the stress associated with raising children alone or the potential benefit attached to sharing life in a *committed* relationship that one's children
would potentially emulate), there are also economic implications. For
example, a legal marriage can ensure legal entitlement to child support and
financial responsibility for the children. Further, in a patriarchal society
such as ours, marriage is privileged and legally upheld. Thus those who
are married receive greater legal protections and benefits.

Other relationship difficulties are associated with black heterosexual relationships as well. For instance, research supports the assertion that black women have consistently had the highest rates of overall male partner-to-female partner violence and severe violence (McLoyd, Cauce, Takeuchi, & Wilson, 2000). According to the 1985 National Family Violence Survey, blacks were 58% more likely to report that arguments during the past year had escalated into physical violence (McLoyd et al., 2000). More than 15 years later, it appears that the trend of domestic violence in the black community continues to escalate. Black women also find themselves in a more precarious position when it comes to reporting domestic violence. This dilemma has been most eloquently characterized by scholar/activist Angela Davis in her caution: "We must learn how to oppose the racist fixation on people of color as the primary perpetuators of violence, including domestic and sexual violence, and at the same time to fiercely challenge the real violence that men of color inflict on women" (Davis, 2000). For numerous black women, the potential for harm that comes with delivering their men into the hands of police outweighs their desire to stop the domestic violence inflicted on them at the hands of black men.

Black women are also more prone to experience depression and other mental health disorders than white women are. "Black women are particularly vulnerable to mental health problems because of the added stressors in their lives. Such stressors include an increased number of personal negative events, exposure to the stressful life events of significant others, and chronic stressors such as exposure to painful incidents of discrimination" (Napholz, 1994).

Among ourselves, the black community, generally, and black women, specifically, are serious and complex questions about our ethics and values that we must explore. Questions include, What legacy are we leaving for those who follow us? How can we improve on our successes and fortify our collective areas of weakness? We must be vigilant about and committed to the issue of improving life for black girls, constantly analyzing and questioning the ways in which our successes and failures might both benefit as well as adversely impact their lives.

In order to enhance the quality of life for adult black women, we need to devise a strategy that consists of four major components:

- Starting early (with our children)
- Understanding the multidimensional complexity of the issues
- Working preventively and realistically

- Being political and confronting the white supremacy, sexism, and classism that looms under the surface

Starting early means raising both black girls and black boys for partnership. Many have heard the denigrating adage that black mothers love their
sons and raise their daughters, while others privilege the equally damaging
characterization that black parents raise black girls defensively.

> Even in homes where a man is present, the pervading belief in the black
> community that girls need to learn to take care of themselves, and that boys
> need to be protected from the ever-present racist evils "out there," cause
> some parents to push their sons and daughters in different directions. These
> differing expectations for boys and girls give rise to adult men and women
> who are at one another's throats, unable to fulfill one another's romantic
> expectations. (Chapman, 1995, p. 26)

We must start early teaching both genders the skills that will help them
transform black female-male relationships rather than abandon them. Both
genders need to be taught to work toward extending the capacity to love
and expressing love in healthy rather than oppressive ways. Specific to this
book, we must raise black girls who remain independent and assertive, but
girls who are also adaptable and cooperative in decision making (Chapman, 1995). Concomitantly, we must raise black boys who are not intent
on replicating oppression and suppressing black women's strength.
Instead they should be nurtured to be interdependent and empathic (Chapman, 1995).

Some might question my choice to focus on black heterosexual relationships in this chapter. This choice is a weighted one and based on the fact that
the majority of black women seem to choose heterosexual relationships. In
research conducted (in 1994) by professor of psychiatry and biobehavioral
science Gail E. Wyatt, only 7% of the women surveyed self-identified as
having female sexual partners in adulthood (Wyatt, 1997). Further, as it
stands, black male-female relationships are currently in the greatest jeopardy, and predictions indicate that their plight will worsen before it
improves. As opposed to abandoning them because they are challenging and
problematic, both genders need to accept the challenge and work toward
transforming the situation. In many ways, our group survival and culture
depends on our ability to metamorphose our present circumstance.

To paraphrase, Mencken has said that for every complex problem, there
is a simple solution that does not work. No simple solutions exist for the

precarious state of black women's lives. Yet there are many instances in which we, as a society, become so enmeshed in a problem's complications that we become paralyzed and unable to move toward resolution. But certain steps are quite easily implemented that would move us closer to the goal of making life better for black females. This book explores the ways in which the black community can enhance the quality of life for black girls and women by starting early, analyzing the dilemmas we (as a community) face, and offering realistic recommendations for change that will possibly impact local, state, and national public policy initiatives.

Chapter 3

ALL THE GIRLS ARE WHITE, ALL THE BOYS ARE BLACK, BUT SOME OF US ARE BRAVE

I am my mother's daughter and the drums of Africa still beat in
my heart. They will not let me rest while there is a single Negro
boy or girl without a chance to prove his[/her] worth.
—Mary McLeod Bethune, activist and educator
(quoted in Tamara Nikuradse's *My Mother Had a Dream:
African American Women Share Their Mothers'
Words of Wisdom*)

During a January 19, 1998, telecast of *The Charlie Rose Show,* the question, Why do you write?, was posed to Nobel Prize winner Toni Morrison. In her eloquent, melodic, and reflective fashion, Morrison responded, "I wanted to read that book that I wrote, and I couldn't find it anywhere. But certainly there was a sense that there was a void" (p. 5). Her words have since resonated within me and echoed my own sentiments.

I will not go as far as to say there are no extant books and/or journal articles on the education and socialization of young black girls, nor am I inadvertently commenting on the quality of other such works in this forum. Yet it is accurate to state that only a small body of such work exists. A small cadre of black women researchers like Janie Ward (1995), Signithia Fordham (1993), Jacqueline Jordan Irvine (1991), Joyce Ladner (1971), and Sarah Lawrence Lightfoot (1976) have devoted time and thoughtfulness to the study of black girls.

For example, in her seminal *Tomorrow's Tomorrow: The Black Woman* (1971), sociologist Ladner sets the stage for inquiry with her four-year ethnographic study on black adolescent girls in an urban center. Ladner characterizes the writing of the book as her "attempt to reconceptualize the 'deviance/pathology' model of black family life and black women [instead casting us] as resourceful, normal women ... simply trying to cope with some of the harsher realities of life" (p. xii).

More recently, researchers Erkut, Fields, Sing, and Marx (1996) renew Ladner's call with the following admonition:

> The major point we raise is that the questions that have guided most research on adolescent girls have not been informed by the wisdom of women and girls who are different from the white, middle class mainstream. Nor have there been sufficient investigations of the diverse experiences of all girls. (p. 62)

Thus, in many respects, I am merely responding to the calls set forth and attending to a story that remains virtually invisible and neglected.

BLACK GIRLS: UNDERREPRESENTED AND IGNORED

In 1976 Sarah Lawrence Lightfoot declared that black girls were an underrepresented population in the extant educational research. Quite specifically, she wrote,

> One of the great struggles that arise when documenting the early experience of black girls in schools is that they have not been the focus on the agenda of social science research. As one reads through the literature in search of some mention of the special identity and experience of black girls in school, one is struck by the blank slate.... Their shadowy status in the literature is a reflection of the more general cultural orientation towards young black girls. (1976, p. 239)

Twenty-two years later, scholar Annette Henry repeated Lightfoot's protestation. In an article entitled "Invisible and Womanish: Black Girls Negotiating Their Lives in an African-Centered School in the USA" (1998), Henry stated, "Black girls are invisible in social science theory and practice in qualitative ways. Interpretive studies on Black girls and schooling are meager (p. 154) ... research on race, class, gender, and schooling rarely focus on the complexities that face young girls of African heritage but rather tend to perpetuate the popularized discourse of the 'endangered Black male'" (p. 153).

Although some progress has been made and guarded optimism seems appropriate, these scholars' conclusions remain solidly applicable today.

Black girls have been included (to a certain extent) in recent feminist research and writing on education and schooling. Books directed toward the academic community, for example, the American Association of University Women Educational Foundation's *How Schools Shortchange Girls: The AAUW Report* (1992) and Peggy Orenstein's *Schoolgirls: Young Women, Self-Esteem, and the Confidence Gap* (1994), have taken a more balanced approach to the subject. They have addressed, in substantive ways, the lives of girls of color within the broader context of girls, which usually translates to white girls. Yet black girls continue to be studied less frequently than white boys, black boys, and white girls. The underrepresentation of black girls in the existing gender research literature is momentous. With a glaring and consistent lack of attention to those issues directly impacting black girls, questions about the generalizability and/or applicability of both data and conclusions put forth in such gender research should be posed and prompted (Erkut et al., 1996).

Black girls' neglect in social science appears as a continuing pattern seen in relation to black women generally. Frequently, the experiences and concerns of black women are subsumed under the category of black or female. On her own merits, the black female tends to receive little attention. "The experience of black women is apparently assumed, though never explicitly stated, to be synonymous with that of either black men or white females; and since the experiences of both are equivalent, the discussion of black women in particular is superfluous (King, 1988, p. 268).

Although books targeted toward the academic community have attempted to be more inclusive, recent books directed to the general public (e.g., Pipher's *Reviving Ophelia: Saving the Selves of Adolescent Girls,* 1994; Pollack's *Real Boys: Rescuing Our Sons from the Myths of Boyhood,* 1998; and Wolf's strangely uneven blend of memoir and pseudoscience in *Promiscuities: The Secret Struggle for Womanhood,* 1997) appear as an uninterrupted continuation of a traditional social science that has either directly ignored the concerns of people of color and/or universalized and privileged the experience of whites.

These books (all touted as *New York Times* bestsellers) convey the popular notion that the white adolescent experience is ubiquitous. Pipher and Pollack do make rather transparent efforts to include a few children of color with whom they have worked, although the majority of the cultural markers and examples used are Euro-centered. But Wolf makes no such veiled attempts and boldly tells the reader what is already apparent. Her book, *Promiscuities,* is neither about nor for women and girls of color. She states,

> The lives that follow are not representative. All the women whose stories I
> recount are white and more or less middle class, and the sexual codes they
> were learning were mostly white, middle class codes. White middle class
> American girls are members of a tribe, just like any other subculture, with
> certain clothing, language patterns, and belief systems. The book is about
> one subset of that tribe. (p. xxvii)

Although Wolf's approach to issues of equity and diversity is stark in its
blatant disregard, another strategy used by contemporary feminists also
disadvantages black girls. This trend (that seemingly results from a desire
to be inclusive) describes and examines the experience of U.S. black girls
under the rubric of "girls of color," "immigrant girls of color," or "urban
girls" as per books like *Beyond Appearance: A New Look at Adolescent
Girls* (Johnson, Roberts, & Worrell, 1999). The rationale for such classification has been that it serves as a way to underscore that race (in the
United States) is no longer relegated to black and white solely (Daniel,
1999). Other racial/ethnic groups should be acknowledged and considered as well. Whereas I do not have difficulty accepting and/or acknowledging other people from traditionally marginalized groups and I have
recognized our common bonds and struggles, I view this strategy in
another fashion. It seems to serve as yet another way in which to discredit
the history and experience of blacks within the United States and gloss
over the history of slavery on these shores as well as its long-lasting
impact on the social, economic, and political infrastructures within the
African American community.

With the seemingly benign mode of categorizing black girls with
recent immigrants, no distinction need be made between those who
arrived in the United States involuntarily and those who came willingly.
Immigrant minorities come to this country with the understanding that
problems in the new land will be and/or can be overcome with a strong
work ethic and educational opportunity (Ogbu, 1994). The viewpoints of
involuntary immigrants, however, are vastly different. "Not only do
involuntary immigrants not have a 'homeland' situation with which to
compare their present selves and future possibilities, but they use white
Americans as a basis for comparison and usually end up with negative
conclusions and resentment" (Ogbu, 1994, p. 65). If black Americans are
lumped together with immigrant minorities, in the guise of being inclusive, our collective "failure" in contrast to other "successful" or more
easily assimilable groups of color can be reinforced and white guilt can
be assuaged.

BLACK GIRLS AS A FOOTNOTE IN THE DISCOURSE ON THE ENDANGERED BLACK MALE

Another noteworthy point centers on the fact that many national discussions about *our* children, in communities throughout the United States (both white and of color), appear focused on boys and young men. A plausible reason for such emphasis is that boys' pain is more apt to manifest in the form of violence, whether self-inflicted or directed toward others, than that of girls. Anecdotal accounts and statistics suggest that growing up male in the United States is becoming increasingly difficult, and without a doubt, the dilemma is compounded for males of color. The anxieties expressed by the black community regarding the status of black men and boys are consequential, meritorious, and fact based.

Current statistics indicate that black men die at greater rates than white men, white women, and black women. Further, they are the only racial group whose rate of suicide is rising. One of the fastest growing suicide rates is among young black men between the ages of 20 and 24 (Pryor, 2001).

The schooling of black boys appears equivalently dismal. During the Reagan-Bush era, a number of research studies concluded that black males, particularly those from families of low socioeconomic status, were disproportionately represented in public school grade retention, school suspensions, and disciplinary actions (Bennett & Harris, 1981; Campbell, 1982; Lee & Slaughter-Defoe, 1995).

Also, during the early 1980s, the Office of Civil Rights pointedly questioned the National Academy of Sciences Panel on Placing Children in Special Education regarding the placement of excessive numbers of black boys, incommensurate to their numbers in the general population, in classes for the educable mentally retarded (Heller, Holtzman, & Messick, 1982; Hilliard, 1994).

More than 15 years later, they remain notably underrepresented in classes for the intellectually gifted and talented, and black boys remain disproportionately placed in special education. "While only16% of the total school enrollment (in the 1970s), black children represented 38% of the students in classes for the educationally mentally retarded. After more than 20 years, black children constitute 17% of the total school enrollment and 33% of those labeled mentally retarded—only a marginal improvement" (Losen & Orfield, 2002, p. xvi). "Most disturbing was that in wealthier districts, contrary to the expected trend, black children, especially males, were more likely to be labeled mentally retarded" (Losen & Orfield, 2002, p. xxiv).

Further, it has been confirmed that difficulties in the referral process, assessment bias, and a lack of cultural synchronization all contribute to the rise in special education placements among black and Latino children and youth (Paul, In press). Presently, people of color comprise only 13% of the extant teaching corps and even a smaller percentage of school psychologists and administrators (NCES, 1993). Thus an educated conjecture would suggest that the majority of such placements are based on observations and evaluations made by white teachers, school psychologists, and other school professionals who may be culturally out of synch with our boys. Cultural synchronization is a harmony established between the cultural systems of schools, diverse groups of learners, and the communities from which those learners come (Gay, 1993; Irvine, 1991). School professionals who "are often cultural outsiders in the communities where they work may misunderstand or misinterpret the cultural nuances present.... This lack of cultural continuity can result in cultural misunderstanding, student resistance, low expectation for student success, and self-fulfilling prophecies of student failure" (Paul, 2000b, p. 247).

Black boys are more prone to be diagnosed as having attention deficit-hyperactivity disorder (ADHD), a disorder whose very existence might and should be challenged. With that diagnosis, the drugging of our boys (especially with Ritalin) immediately follows. Estimates suggest that 10% to 12% of all boys between the ages of 6 and 14 in the United States have been diagnosed as having attention deficit disorder and are being treated with Ritalin. It has even become more commonplace than might be expected for school systems to request court intervention, sometimes compelling parents to place their children on Ritalin.

America now uses 90% of the world's Ritalin—more than five times the rest of the world combined. In 1990, 900,000 American children were prescribed Ritalin. In 1997, 2.5 million were—and 80% of those are boys (Breggin, 1998). I frequently ponder the correlation between the increased diagnoses of ADHD in children and the sixfold increase in Ritalin production between 1990 and 1995, as documented by the U.S. Drug Enforcement Administration (Breggin, 1998).

It is also interesting to note that "drug companies, as well as government agencies and researchers, view the African American poor as an 'underdeveloped market.' Drug advocates lament that the 'African American community believes that children are being overmedicated" (Breggin, 1998, p. 283).

For this author, the facts and figures presented, in no way, describe a deficit in black boys, their families, or communities. Instead, they depict a bureaucratic web, capitalistic opportunism, and institutional racism that continue to disenfranchise our boys and maintain a permanent underclass. In large part, the widespread victimization of black boys through schools is ongoing, with devastating implications. One such implication might be the ways in which poorly educated, urban center black and Latino males feed the "prison industrial complex," a term popularized by Angela Davis. The term questions the very essence of a system in which the containment of black and brown bodies has become an industry, an industry that bolsters capitalism with its modern-day form of chattel slavery (Paul, 2000a). With 14 million entangled in the penal system, America's rate of imprisonment is the highest on the planet, surpassing even that of Russia (Cose, 2000). "As late as the 1990s, nearly 60% of Whites, Hispanics, and Asian-Americans continued to perceive black people as inferior, undeserving of justice, and innately criminal. Justice for blacks in a system that reflects such bias and indifference is virtually impossible" (Anderson, 2001, p. 23).

Between 1985 and 1996, total expenditures on state-prison activities increased twofold, going from a little less than $13 billion to more than $27 billion (Cose, 2000). Another provocative thought lies in the premise that while it can cost approximately $71,000 to house an inmate in New York's Rikers Island (a prison), it can cost under $10,000 to educate a child in the New York City public school system (Cose, 2000; Kozol, 1991). For me, at least, the added expense of imprisonment has to prove beneficial in some real and tangible ways because the cost ineffectiveness of this proposition is stark.

A LONG-STANDING AND MUFFLED DEMAND FOR INCLUSION

Yet, with a clear acknowledgment of the claims and concerns that directly center on black boys and men, these discussions inadvertently have another set of implications that are not as easily discernible. In this discussion of the endangered black male, some are unable or unwilling (except in the most cursory of fashions) to acknowledge that concerns about black girls and young women are consequential as well.

For instance, we are frequently reminded of the overwhelming black and Latino male presence in prisons and jails. Is it not equivalently consequential that there has been a 126% increase in the number of black women arrested? In 1991 the largest racial group of women in state prison was black (46%). That figure has increased significantly over the past 11 years. More than half of those women are serving time for nonviolent offenses, particularly those related to the use and distribution of drugs (U.S. Department of Justice, 1994). The emerging profile for adult female inmates appears as follows. More than 4 in 10 women offenders report a history of physical or sexual abuse. Nearly 6 in 10 grew up in a household with at least one parent absent. Women prisoners are likely to be poor, undereducated, and single parents. Approximately 20% of women offenders also served a sentence as a juvenile (Office of Juvenile Justice and Delinquency Prevention, 1998). Is it less important that 78% of all women in prison are mothers? In fact, more than 69% of black female inmates in state prisons have children under age 18 (U.S. Department of Justice, 1994). Approximately 46% of women with children under 18 self-disclosed that they speak with their children via telephone at least once a week. Forty-five percent exchanged letters and cards with their children, and 9% were visited by their children (U.S. Department of Justice, 1994).

With the facts and figures just presented, one point is made transparent and a myth is dispelled. These mothers are not "absent." They are still involved in the parenting of their children, although physically separated from them. Yet significant questions are also raised about the impact of incarceration on mothering. For example, "since mothers are often described as their children's first teachers, what might these women's children learn from them? Is it possible that, among other lessons, some will learn the same disempowerment and disenfranchisement that led their mothers to prison? Others might learn that survival comes at a tremendously high cost. Exponentially, the dilemma involving imprisoned women is momentous" (Paul, 2001).

On the academic front, black girls have substantially lower dropout rates and higher college enrollment rates than black boys. But it seems their success is attained in spite of the school systems they attend (AAUW Educational Foundation, 1992). For example, in the study *Gender Gaps: Where Schools Still Fail Our Children* (American Institutes for Research, 1998, p. 33), it was discovered that "black girls demonstrate academic strengths at every assessment point. In the fourth grade, they outpace black male classmates in science, reading, geography, and history. In eighth grade, they retain an advantage over black male classmates in science, reading, and history. In the twelfth grade, they score equally with black boys in mathematics, and retain an advantage in reading." But, in spite of these gains, they still do not feel good about the schools they attend.

"It is nothing short of amazing that females succeed in school at all. After reading the research and studying the reports from female students

themselves, one is struck by the resiliency and tenacity that it takes to per-
severe in an environment so demeaning and adverse (Masland as quoted in
Gay, 2000, p. 66). For many black girls in particular, school is perceived
as more of a hindrance than a help. This group of girls is "often stigma-
tized by teachers and undermined by low expectations ... the survival
skills they've mastered are considered a liability" (Orenstein, 1994, p.
160). Another interesting note centers on the fact that while black youth,
generally, have positive self-esteem as related to attractiveness and social
worth (Gibbs, 1985; Ward, 1990), black girls (as a group) seem to more
frequently suffer the effects of low academic self-esteem. "One of the prevailing views is that self-esteem (how good one feels about oneself) and
positive self perceptions of ability (self-perceived competence) are more
important in determining an individual's level of achievement than actual
ability" (Erkut & Marx, 1995, p. 2).

Traditionally, black children have been categorized as having low self-esteem. Much of the support for this hypothesis was based on the work of the
Clarks' (1939) doll test or a replication of that test (e.g., GoPaul-McNicol,
1992). More recent works suggest, however, that self-esteem is not as unidimensional as it appears in those tests:

> To accurately measure either self-concept or self-esteem, at least three pri-
> mary and one or more secondary factors must be distinguished. The primary
> factors refer to academic self-esteem, peer acceptance or social self-esteem,
> and personal self-esteem. The fourth factor is associated by some authors
> with physical appearance and physical competence, while others see it as a
> by-product of the family context. (Madhere, 1991, p. 48)

Research focused on black females in the early elementary grades
yielded findings that suggest this group of black girls is more prone to suffer from low academic self-esteem (Damico & Scott, 1987). A correlational relationship can be established between the decreased academic
self-esteem experienced and the treatment received from teachers. For
example, black girls in the early elementary school classroom interact less
frequently with their white female teachers than do their white counterparts, and they are more apt to be ignored, even though they initiate interactions more often than other race/gender groups. Additionally, they
receive less reinforcement than other children from their teachers
(AAUW, 1992; Damico & Scott, 1987). Usually, the positive feedback
young black girls receive is focused on social rather than academic skills
and assisting teachers with nonacademic tasks.

A further nuanced view, as presented in research by Irvine (1991), suggests that the "inconspicuousness of Black females in the classroom begins in the upper elementary grades, not in the lower grades, as is true for their White female counterparts" (p. 71). Upper elementary grade black girls tended to isolate themselves with other black females, received fewer positive feedback statements, received fewer response opportunities in class, and were subject to attempts of both black and white males to force them into periphery service roles (Irvine, 1991). It seems the trend of mistreatment of black girls in school continues into their junior high school years and beyond. According to Irvine (1991, p. 75), black girls in junior high:

- continue to receive less academically oriented reinforcement from teachers;
- become invisible, rarely interacting with teachers or peers;
- are more likely to work alone;
- receive more negative and procedural status;
- are left out of friendship networks.

It is also well documented that girls' "self-esteem and confidence in their competence, particularly with regard to math and science, drop precipitously during their middle school years, narrowing their later choices of course work and career path" (Research for Action, 1996).

"Further, for black females and Hispanic students with respect to MR [mental retardation], communities that spend more for education show greater disproportionality" (Oswald, Coutinho, & Best, 2002, p. 10). Girls of color and those who are poor are also more apt to be tracked into remedial classes (American Institutes for Research, 1998). Because of the fact that race, gender, and socioeconomic status often mediate determinations of academic skill and proficiency, there is an increase of more subjective disabilities like reading/learning disabilities and behavioral disorders (American Institutes for Research, 1998). "Nonwhite and nonaffluent students—girls and boys—are especially likely to have their abilities overlooked" (American Institutes for Research, 1998, p. 21).

Another disturbing trend involves the issue of increased violence and aggression displayed by young women, although it is not surprising in a society that privileges violence and war:

Many teachers, and girls themselves, are saying they're seeing an increase in relational aggression, or girls being particularly [m]ean to one another. It see[m]s that girls are engaging in more backbiting, gossip, and trying to control other girls' behavior; often it becomes violent.... Many girls these days confuse jealousy and possessiveness with love. They're getting the message that other women are not to be trusted and are seeing other girls as a threat. (Ward cited in Villarosa, 2002)

"Girls learn competition from their mothers. Male unavailability is a huge issue for Black women, so women end up competing with other women for a partner" (Wyatt cited in Villarosa, 2002).

Other disquieting statistics related to black girls and violence include the following:

- Black teen girls are almost twice as likely as white girls and in 1999 were 22% more likely than black boys to be victims of crime.
- 7.1% of black girls say they feel unsafe going to high school, compared with 4.3% of white girls and 4.9% of black boys; 4.8% of black girls carry weapons to high school, compared with 1.6% of white girls.
- Delinquency cases involving all girls rose 83% from 1988 to 1997, with a 106% hike among black girls, compared with a 74% rise among white girls. (Villarosa, 2002, p. 8)

For all students, the rising epidemic of school violence (in its varying forms) is costly because fear can be explicitly linked with lower academic performance, posttraumatic stress disorder, illness, as well as absence without illness.

Also related to the issue of female aggression and violence is the issue of juvenile delinquency as it pertains to females. Arrests of juvenile females have steadily increased, and although their crimes used to be classified more frequently as nonviolent (e.g., curfew violations, running away, or unruly behavior), they are now more likely to be arrested for robbery, assault, drug trafficking, and gang activity (Office of Juvenile Justice and Delinquency Prevention, 1998). Nationally, girls are becoming involved in the criminal justice system at younger ages. Approximately 70% have a history of sexual abuse. They are more apt to be classified as learning/reading disabled or emotionally handicapped (Office of Juvenile Justice and Delinquency Prevention, 1998). Black girls are disproportionately represented in the female offender population, comprising more than 50% of those in secure detention (Office of Juvenile Justice and Delinquency Prevention, 1998). Additionally, black female offenders are more likely to receive a more severe disposition at their arrest, intake hearings, and in court (Office of Juvenile Justice and Delinquency Prevention, 1998). White girls are more

likely to be referred to mental health facilities than juvenile justice facilities
(Office of Juvenile Justice and Delinquency Prevention, 1998).

It would be difficult to deny we live in a violent culture, privileging war
and the abuse of power, that perpetuates brutality in our young people.
Unfortunately, however, far too many of our young learn such lessons in
their own homes. When parents and caregivers lash out in violence at their
children because spankings and beatings made them "better people," they
concomitantly teach their children that might rather than reason rules the
day. When parents/caregivers are verbally and emotionally abusive, they
teach their children that the way to resolve conflict is through words that
kill. All parents/caregivers must come to understand that the primary purpose for discipline is to teach rather than punish. What lessons are taught
when we use excessively harsh forms of punishment in the name of
preparing our children for the future?

Yet we must also examine the ways in which schools perpetuate violence against children of color. The use of institutional violence teaches
our children significant lessons as well. After all, what do children learn
when they are suspended from school or expelled? What do they learn
when school personnel express their low expectations for them? What is
learned when ill-trained teachers (who in too many instances are cultural
outsiders) use school administrators to "control" the behavior of children
and youth whom they are afraid of and who belong to cultures with which
the teachers have had very little interaction?

Traditionally, requests that black girls and women also be considered (in
discussions on the plight of black America, included in the dialogue, and
made privy to the proposals presented and solutions posited) seem to go
unrecognized. Many of us tacitly accept the flawed truism that to privilege
and validate the lives of black boys and men, we must underestimate and
denigrate the experiences of black girls and women. In the process, we
reinforce a pervasive and invariable sexism in the black community that is
infrequently admitted and/or debated. The reinforcement of this catego-
rization as an either/or proposition deepens psychic wounds for both genders and jeopardizes our advancement collectively.

The most salient point is that black children are suffering in the contemporary United States. In a most compelling fashion, Marian Wright Edelman (2001, p. 122) has described the plight of black children in the United
States as follows:

> Every five seconds during the schoolday, a Black public school student is
> suspended, and every forty-six seconds during the schoolday, a Black high

school student drops out. Every minute, a Black child is arrested and a Black baby is born into poverty. Every hour, a Black baby dies. Every four hours, a Black child or youth under twenty dies from an accident, and every five hours, one is a homicide victim. And every day, a Black young person under twenty-five dies from HIV infection.

Rates of child poverty are highest for black and Latino populations in the United States at 30% and 28%, respectively. Black and Native American/Alaskan Native children have the highest infant mortality rates in the nation (Weinick, Zuvekas, & Cohen, 2000). Black children (under the age of 13) comprise two thirds of the new pediatric AIDS cases reported. In a similar respect, there was a 300% rise (between 1987 and 1992) in the likelihood that a New York child under age 15 would contract tuberculosis, and more than half of those living with tuberculosis are black (Seligsohn, 1994). Black children are also among those who most frequently live in poverty. Therefore, they are more prone to contracting communicable diseases, less likely to receive prescription drugs, and less likely than white children to have access to appropriate health care and treatment (Weinick et al., 2000).

Child victimization rates, within the general public, are appalling. Approximately 1.5 million children have experienced physical abuse, more than 1 million are neglected, and approximately 500,000 have experienced sexual victimization (Thompson & Kaslow, 2001). Yet black and Native American children are abused at a little less than twice the rate of their proportion in the national child population, according to the U.S. Department of Health and Human Services (Patterson, 1998).

In relation to their rates of victimization, black children are more frequently placed in foster care (Tremmel, 2002). Forty-two percent of the nation's black children are ensnared in foster care's bureaucratic web; their status as black children virtually ensures that they will remain in the system longer than other children, be moved more frequently, and be less likely to return home or adopted than white children (Tremmel, 2002).

Traditionally, black teenagers committed suicide at significantly lower rates than white teenagers did. The suicide rate for white children was 157% greater than that for black children of the same age bracket in 1980. Yet the gap decreased to 42% by 1995 (Pryor, 2001). The largest increase was a 214% rise for black teenagers in the South (Pryor, 2001).

For this author, at least, the lives of *both* black girls and boys could be assigned more value and investment in our present-day society. But in order to understand present-day circumstances, we must examine links to the past and the way in which black childhood has emerged.

Chapter 4

COPING WITH THE LEGACY OF SLAVERY AND ITS LINKS TO CHILDHOOD AND LIFE FOR CONTEMPORARY BLACK GIRLS

> She always talked about roots, about values that were anchored in loving yourself, but also in loving your people. Your roots. "Little people make big people," she would say, "and big people become small people when they forget where they came from."
>
> —Gloria Wade-Gayles, author and scholar
> (as quoted in Tamara Nikuradse's *My Mother Had a Dream: African American Women Share Their Mothers' Words of Wisdom*)

A recent addition to American popular culture film imagery has been the love narrative, in which the slaveholder and the enslaved fall in love. The challenge becomes even more intriguing as the plot of love against insurmountable odds (e.g., time, society, and racism) plays itself out before viewers. The most notable of these late films focus on the relationship between American president Thomas Jefferson and Sally Hemings. Two specific films I reference in this discussion are *Jefferson in Paris* (dir. James Ivory, 1995) and *Sally Hemings: An American Scandal* (dir. Charles Haid, 2000). Both films are worth mentioning for myriad reasons, among them that both films coincided with a national discourse challenging the very existence of a sexual relationship between the two, Jefferson and Hemings.

Die-hard historians on one side of the issue contend that Jefferson's principles and sense of morality would have averted his sexual dalliance with a slave. Others claim that Jefferson's vitriolic racism would have prevented him from even contemplating a sexual liaison with a black. After all, Jefferson's writings attest, unequivocally, to his unapologetic racism and his feelings that blacks are physically unattractive, malodorous, and intellectually inferior. In his own *Notes on the State of Virginia,* Jefferson wrote,

> They [Blacks] secrete less by the kidneys, and more by the glands of the skin, which gives them a very strong and disagreeable odour.... They are at least as brave, and more adventuresome. But this may perhaps proceed from a want of forethought, which prevents their seeing danger till it be present.... Their griefs are transient.

By most accounts, Sally Hemings (half sister of Jefferson's wife) would not have fit Jefferson's characterization of a black. Born to a white father and biracial mother, Sally (also referred to as Dashing Sally) has been described as "being nearly white in appearance with 'straight hair down her back' (Gordon-Reed, 1997). Further, the personal accounts of many slaveholders inform us that avowed racism does not negate attraction to blacks or sexual dalliances with one's slaves.

On the other side of the debate stand historians and scholars like Fawn Brodie and Annette Gordon-Reed, who refer to the dates and circumstances of Hemings's conceptions and births, most of which supported the assertion that Jefferson had, undoubtedly, fathered Hemings's children.

Yet, as far as I am concerned, the scandal regarding the sexual relationship extends further. In *Jefferson in Paris,* Hemings is portrayed as a brown-skinned, coquettish enchantress who actively pursued a relationship with Jefferson. For example, in one scene, a bright-eyed, nubile Sally jumps about Jefferson's bedroom, weaving tales of haunts and spirits as Jefferson sits bemused on his bed. A similar scene occurs *in Sally Hemings: An American Scandal.* In that scene, a seductive Sally eyes Jefferson coyly at a ball.

Although I am certain that attractions did surface, how could there be a "basis for 'delight, affection, and love' as long as white men, by virtue of their economic position, had unlimited access to Black women's bodies?" (Davis, 1981, pp. 25–26). "It was as oppressors—or, in the case of non-slaveowners, as agents of domination—that white men approached Black women's bodies" (p. 26). Further, it remains debatable that Jefferson's relationship with Sally Hemings could be termed as loving because he owned her for 38 years. Ultimately, she was freed two years after his death.

Why is it that Hollywood has chosen to privilege this so-called love story featuring two characters' capacity to love in spite of the power differential that existed between them? In some respects, it seemed as if these film narratives' primary purpose was to construct an icon of Jefferson, known for possessing an "almost Hitlerian phobia of blacks and race-mixing" (Gordon-Reed, 1997, p. 136) as the quintessential American man in the fullness of his humanity, in spite of his obvious propensity toward slaveholding and human bondage. Potentially, audiences were supposed to overlook this flaw, seeing instead this tragic hero's capacity to love and appreciate beauty regardless of where it might lie.

In both film narratives, however, it appears as if Hollywood simply "forgot" the details of this tale. For examples, Sally was plausibly 14 or 15 years old at the start of her relationship with a 43-year-old Jefferson (Gordon-Reed, 1997). A 14-year-old Sally accompanied Jefferson's 9-year-old daughter Mary to Paris in 1787, where Jefferson had served as a minister to France since 1784. Sally stayed with the Jefferson family (in Paris) for 26 months, and evidence suggests she returned to the United States pregnant with Thomas Jefferson's child. Why is this detail (regarding Sally's age) insignificant in these celluloid portrayals? Further, why didn't this portrait evoke the same degree of outrage that came with Showtime's film adaptation of Nabokov's *Lolita* (dir. Adrian Lyne, 2000) featuring a "love" affair between a pubescent white girl and her middle-aged white male lover?

It seems that, as with the entire issue of American chattel slavery, the American public also wishes to minimize the child victimization and sexual abuse that came with the institution. Thus, for many slave children, childhood itself was lost or stolen.

CHILDHOOD: A RELATIVELY NEW PHENOMENON

The concept of childhood, itself, is relatively new. If considered in its most comprehensive definition, the concept of childhood in the United States is little more than 150 years old (Postman, 1982):

> The period between 1850 and 1950 represents the high watermark of childhood. In America, to which we must give our exclusive attention, successful attempts were made during these years to get all children into school and out of factories, into their own clothing, their own furniture, their own literature, their own games, their own social world. In a hundred laws, children were classified as qualitatively different from adults; in a hundred customs, assigned a preferred status and offered protection from the vagaries of adult life. (p. 67)

In his celebrated *The Disappearance of Childhood* (1982), Postman presents an insightful argument that the printing press and the European reinvention of education precipitated the emergence of childhood (which he categorizes as a social artifact). "Where literacy was valued highly and persistently, there were schools, and where there were schools, the concept of childhood developed rapidly" (p. 39). Thus the point of initiation into childhood began with the process of learning to read.

Postman traces children's clothing and distinctive jargon to 16th- and 17th-century Europe in an interesting and insightful fashion. But it is equally interesting that, throughout the book, Postman remains unrepentant about his blatant Eurocentricism and obvious belief that civilization began in Europe. By basing the book's major premises on these belief systems, contributions from Africa (in particular) appear irrelevant and wholly without merit.

I highlight these features of Postman's work, not as a way to identify racism as specific to him, but instead to present such approaches to content as standard fare in conceptualizations of childhood. For this author, the formation of childhood includes more origination points than Europe. What did the vast cultures of the world outside of Europe contribute to the concept? Another major point of contention centers on the fact that if childhood is a relatively new phenomenon in the United States, it is an even newer one as it pertains to black children in the United States.

According to Postman, the primary distinctions between childhood and adulthood center on the heightened governmental protection of children's status and the sheltering of children from adult secrets, particularly those of a sexual nature. Therefore, I make the claim that enslaved children were not offered governmentally protected status or shielded from adult secrets. For instance, "even the most cursory look at historical data shows that [enslaved] children made large contributions to the nation's economic growth" (King, 1985, p. 41).

CHILDHOOD IN THE CONTEXT OF SLAVERY

Much of what we know about childhood within the context of slavery suggests it was virtually nonexistent. The exploration of childhood, within the context of North American slavery, is exceedingly significant when we consider that the majority of those in bondage in the United States (prior to the Civil War) were born in North America rather than in Africa (King, 1995). From slave narratives and traditional research alike, it becomes immediately apparent that the quality of life for enslaved children could best be characterized as extraordinarily meager. The defenselessness of slave children adds another dimension to the difficulty of their lives.

By most accounts, life for enslaved children was not without toil or burden. "Slaves were forced to confront adult situations of work, terror, injustice, and arbitrary power at early ages" (King, 1995, p. xviii). For example, both boys and girls worked, even during early childhood. Most of the work done by children (prior to their teenaged years) consisted of babysitting, completing kitchen and household chores, as well as toting water to thirsty field hands, fetching mail, and tending to the needs of livestock (White, 1985). Yet, under most circumstances, the ages at which slaves engaged in regular routines varied according to slaveowners and the size of their holdings (King, 1985).

Additionally, it appears as if there was no specific socialization for children as it pertained to sex roles during the years prior to adolescence. Aside from completing similar work tasks, boys and girls also played the same games and wore similar clothing (White, 1985). For the most part, enslaved parents were more concerned their children learn the implicit racial codes that came with slavery. "Parents were more concerned that children, regardless of sex, learn to walk the tightrope between the demands of whites and the expectations of blacks without falling too far in either direction" (White, 1985, p. 93).

Enslaved parents taught their children other lessons in race solidarity as well. For example, they taught their children to value collectivity rather than individualism (King, 1985). For slaves, it was much more important to work toward the common good because they were able to ward off punishments and unpleasant work assignments in this fashion.

> Many enslaved parents demonstrated an unfailing love for their offspring and socialized them to endure slavery by paying deference to whites while maintaining self-respect. This embodied a major act of resistance and equipped children to defend themselves on the psychological battlefield. Parents, whether together or alone, taught their youngsters how to tolerate inhumane acts and degradation while maintaining their humanity and keeping their spirit intact. (King, 1985, pp. 67–68)

It appears that sex-role socialization came for young black female slaves with adolescence, as well as with menarche (the point at which girls were also considered to have approached adulthood). During adolescence, young female slaves were placed in the female world of work called the "trash gang," composed (for the most part) of pregnant women, women with nursing infants, and elderly females (White, 1985). The tasks of the trash gang included raking stubble, pulling weeds, and doing light hoeing.

It was during this time as well that most slave girls caught the attention of men, black and white, on the plantations, and slave mothers' most prominent role became teaching their daughters to ward off sexual advances. Much of the sexual exploitation that black females experienced at the hands of white men was based on the sexual mythology that black women were sexually wanton and animalistic in respect to their genitalia and sexual proclivities (King, 1985). Another factor that impacted the likelihood with which black females encountered sexual victimization centered on the fact that they had no legal or social recourse, unlike white women.

"In the long run, however, a mother could do little more than hope that her daughter made it through adolescence and young womanhood unscathed by sexual abuse" (White, 1985, p. 96). Enslaved parents knew, all too well, that they had no real protection from sale, and any intervention used to shield their daughters from the advances of white men could result in potential sale and the dissolution of the family unit. Data suggests that enslaved females usually had their first child during their 19th year (approximately two years earlier than their white female counterparts) (White, 1985). This figure, however, is misleading as it might suggest to some that enslaved females started having sexual intercourse in their late teens. In this fashion, some might accept the premise that the young women participated in sexual decision making more fully than they actually did, and the sexual abuse they experienced as children is minimized.

It seems that the possibility of sexual abuse for enslaved female children loomed large and was widespread. "The lack of empirical evidence [regarding sexual exploitation of enslaved girls] does not mean it did not occur. It is more likely that the immorality and inhumanity associated with the practice forced those responsible to hide evidence of their involvement" (King, 1985, p. 110). Additionally, the likelihood that young enslaved boys were sexually abused and coerced into homosexual and heterosexual acts by adults should not be overlooked either, nor should the fact that enslaved female children were exposed to same-sex sexual contact with adult women. Yet the focus of this chapter is centered on drawing attention to the most prevalent form of sexual abuse and degradation ... that inflicted upon young black girls, at the hands of adult men, black and white.

THE LEGACY OF SLAVERY ON CONTEMPORARY BLACK CHILDHOOD

Indisputably, the institution of chattel slavery held devastating consequences for black people, the black family, and black children. Further, the impact of slavery on these groups and structures remains manifest today. "It [has been] extremely difficult for Black people to progress when the same hands that held the whip still hold almost all of the wealth and power" (Anderson, 2001, p. 2).

For example, research suggests that having children out of wedlock as a culturally accepted practice among U.S. blacks might have emerged during slavery; thus it can be defined as new and potentially specific to the United States. In many African societies, having children outside of marriage is frowned on, although premarital sex is not (Giddings, 1984). In many societies, a marriage was not considered consummated until after the birth of a child (White, 1985).

Although many view slavery as being primarily a means of obtaining free labor, it was more specifically about the reproduction and breeding of slaves (Davis, 1981; Giddings, 1984; King, 1995; White, 1985). Thus motherhood enhanced the status of the slave woman in ways that marriage could not (White, 1985). "For a master could save the cost of buying new slaves by impregnating his own slave, or for that matter having anyone impregnate her" (Giddings, 1984, p. 37). So the potential correlational link between slave women having children outside of marriage and its sanction under the institution of slavery is easily established.

As discussed in previous chapters, black women and children remain one of the largest sectors of those classified as living below the poverty line, and this dilemma can be directly linked to the legally sanctioned fragmentation and unprotected status of black families during slavery. In more instances than not, the institution of slavery itself ran counter to black families remaining intact. For slaveholders, most of the benefits of black families remaining together (while in bondage) could be categorized as emotional and social. "Many slaveowners acknowledged conjugal relationships, recorded slave births by family units, and insisted upon monogamy. They reasoned that marriage and children fostered 'happiness' and usurped restiveness" (King, 1995, p. 2). Yet the proprietary nature of slavery contradicted the very notion of mental health and social well-being. As such, marriage did not yield conventional advantages for the enslaved.

> Slave women could not depend on their husbands for protection against whippings or sexual exploitation. Slave couples had no property to share, and essential needs like food, clothing, and shelter were not provided by slave husbands. Thus slave men could not use the provision of subsistence goods as leverage in the exercise of authority over women. In almost all

> societies where men consistently dominate women, their control is based on
> male ownership and distribution of property and/or control of certain cul-
> turally valued subsistence goods. The absence of such mechanisms in slave
> society probably contributed to female slave independence from slave men.
> (White, 1985, p. 153)

The legacy left with this institutionalization of slavery is vast and far
reaching. It pointedly validates the belief that in American society,
founded on the principle of capitalism, economic solvency is paramount.
It continually outweighs social welfare concerns or concerns about
humanity. Two of slavery's most problematic legacies center on poverty
and the devaluation of the marital bond. As per the cautions of sociologists, the situation is bound to worsen before it improves.

Generally speaking, the number of families headed by single mothers
(in the United States) has increased 25% since 1990, totaling more than
7.5 million (Kantrowitz & Wingert, 2001). Demographics suggest that
more than half of the children born in the 1990s will spend at least a portion of their childhoods in a single-parent home. In 1998 only 36% of
black children lived in two-parent families, in contrast to 74% of whites
and 64% of Latinos (Kantrowitz & Wingert, 2001).

Most contemporary women, who are poor, would be considered working poor, especially because welfare reform initiatives have made it
exceedingly difficult for women and their families to receive federal aid.
Most black women who escape poverty do so by taking advantage of educational and training opportunities. White women, conversely, more frequently escape poverty by "marrying up," defined as marrying someone
more financially stable. Although rates of marriage are low and divorce
high for the general population in the United States, the rates of marriageability are extremely low in the black community. As a result, many black
women will probably remain unmarried and poor. Exponentially, the children of these women will also remain poor, and those born to them subsequently will also likely be enculturated into poverty. Children living in
single-parent homes are "seven times more likely to experience poverty
and 17 times more likely to end up on welfare and to have a propensity for
emotional problems, discipline problems, early pregnancy and abuse"
(Kantrowitz & Wingert, 2001, p. 51). Unfortunately, this is the present
legacy we bequeath to far too many of our children.

Part II

SEARCHING FOR SOLUTIONS
AND PROPOSALS FOR ACTION

Chapter 5

THE ROLE OF PARENTS AND CAREGIVERS IN EMPOWERING BLACK GIRLS

Each generation of African Americans, usually but not exclusively parenting figures or family members, prepares the next generation for the challenge of being African American in a society that devalues them.

—Beverly Greene, psychologist
(as quoted in S. Hansen, J. Walker,
and B. Flom's *Growing Smart:
What's Working for Girls in School*)

As indicated in chapter 4, the primary responsibility of enslaved parents was to teach their children to resist and survive slavery. In many ways, that responsibility remains parallel for black parents in contemporary society; we continue to teach our young to maneuver racism and white supremacy, surviving them emotionally intact. Today we must serve as our "children's first tutors in learning self-respect; forming a positive, race-conscious identity; understanding their histories; and navigating in an environment that is infrequently kind" (Paul, 2000a, p. 23). Another vital lesson for black children centers on becoming discerning enough to know when to attribute lack of success to individual effort and when to attribute it to societal forces.

Most of these lessons occur within the homespace, for obvious reasons. *Homespace* serves as an important socializing setting in which black children first develop attitudes specific to their own cultural affiliations and learn coping strategies for living in a society that privileges both white skin and masculinity. "Homespace is a primary site of resistance" (Ward, 1996, p. 87).

For the benefit of both their daughters and sons, black parents can develop and encourage agency in their children and concurrently teach them the skills of empowerment. "Agency" is defined as being self-possessed, confident, willing to take risks, as well as demonstrating leadership capabilities (Bern, 1981). Empowerment is much broader in scope and characterized as

> the process by which people, organizations, or groups who are powerless or marginalized a) become aware of the power dynamics at work in their life context, b) develop the skills and capacity for gaining some control over their lives, c) which they exercise, d) without infringing on the rights of others, and e) which coincides with actively supporting the empowerment of others in their community. (McWhirter, 1994, p. 12)

Within the framework of this chapter, I seek to provide black parents with suggestions for raising daughters who are self-confident, assured, and prepared to deal with the academic and social barriers they will inevitably face. In an effort to make thoughtful, reflective decisions about parenting, parents must first be knowledgeable. Parents, especially of preadolescent and adolescent girls, must start with a basic understanding of racial identity development theory and adolescence and the ways in which those enigmatic processes will undoubtedly impact their daughters. Although this book is geared toward the healthy development of black girls, the recommendations here might assist the parents of black boys as well.

UNDERSTANDING RACIAL IDENTITY DEVELOPMENT

This book originates from the premise that most parents/caregivers of black children want to instill a sense of race consciousness in their children and deem it an important ingredient for success. The formation of racial identity begins very early in life. Racial identity, not to be confused with racial category, is defined as "a sense of group or collective identity based upon one's perception that he or she shares a common racial heritage with a particular racial group (Helms, 1993, p. 7). Infants (as young as 6 months) notice skin color differentiations (Katz, 1993). By the time children reach preschool, they readily question color difference and learn to attach value to such difference (Clark & Clark, 1947; Derman-Sparks, Tanaka Higa, & Sparks, 1980; GoPaul-McNicol, 1992; Powell-Hopson, 1985; Trager & Yarrow, 1952).

The emergence of racial identity is the "move from least healthy, White-identified stages of identity to most healthy, self-defined racial transcendence" (Helms, 1993, p. 17). Thus racial identity theory could also be considered developmental and process oriented. Although a number of psychologists have sought to explain the process of black racial identity development (among them Naim Akbar, James Banks, William Cross, and Charles Thomas), we use Cross's model of Nigrescence (or becoming black) because it is one of the most well known. The traditional Cross model (1971, 1978) has stages that include Preencounter, Encounter, Immersion/Emersion, and Internalization. Because only two of the stages, Preencounter and Encounter, occur during childhood, they are the ones we explore in relative depth.

During the Preencounter stage, black children begin to see themselves in contrast to the mainstream culture, yet they tend to take on the views of the dominant culture. In this initial stage, the black child "absorbs many of the beliefs of the dominant White culture, including the idea that it is better to be White. The stereotypes, omissions, and distortions that reinforce notions of White superiority are breathed in by Black children as well as White" (Tatum, 1997, p. 55).

A counterexplanation is presented by clinical psychologist Marguerite A. Wright, who proposes that "by eight, children understand that their skin color is a permanent part of their bodies (Wright, 1998, p. 181). Thus, by extension, they start to become more aware of the implications attached to skin color during the middle childhood years, extending from age 8 to 12. It is at this developmental point that children's growing sense of skin-color difference becomes transformed into an understanding of race (Wright, 1998). "At this age, black children, and to a lesser extent children of other oppressed racial minorities, are also becoming aware of their low social status relative to other racial groups" (Wright, 1998, p. 178). Yet "children's self-image in middle childhood is still influenced mostly by the treatment they receive in their families, schools, and communities" (p. 178).

It is also important to highlight the way in which notions of white superiority play themselves out within group as well as across groups. Black children must deal with color difference in the context of the broader society, and they must also deal with color distinctions and the intragroup attachment to color value referred to as *colorism.* "Given that color-consciousness is rooted in the social, political, and economic conditions that existed during slavery, colorism is often manifested as a preference for lighter skin tones over darker ones; however, discrimination against persons with lighter skin tones occurs as well" (Robinson & Ward, 1995, p. 258). Research findings suggest that, even in contemporary society, skin color still matters (Robinson & Ward, 1995).

The Encounter stage of Cross's development ladder is usually sparked by an incident or series of incidents. "Transition to the Encounter stage is typically precipitated by an event or series of events that force the young person to acknowledge the personal impact of racism. As a result of a new and heightened awareness of the significance of race, the individual begins to grapple with what it means to be a member of a group targeted by racism" (Tatum, 1997, p. 55). Parents/caregivers can help alleviate the pain attached to these epiphanal experiences by sharing their own personal narratives that involve coping with race. "In sharing their own personal, often painful experiences, African American parents transmit to their children the knowledge that they have been there too and they can see what their children see, feel their pain, and share their frustration" (Ward, 1996, p. 91).

Cross has identified this stage as evolving during late adolescence and early adulthood, but substantial data suggests that this process of experiencing the Encounter stage may occur as early as junior high school (Phinney & Tarver, 1988). Research also suggests an increased intensity inherent in this stage for black girls in integrated settings (Tatum, 1997).

Black girls, in particular in this instance, must learn to thrive in a society that routinely conveys its disrespect and contempt for blackness even post–September 11. Since September 11, we have been led to believe that racism is no longer an issue in the United States, especially in the face of an "exotic" brown collective enemy. If focused on this enemy, we might ignore the enemy at home. We might disregard the increased poverty and corporate corruption the nation is experiencing, accept the fact that a significant number of citizens here (many of whom are black and female) are worse off since the George W. Bush administration took office, and/or tolerate the fact that racism and classism can still run rampant and virtually unchecked on the homefront (Paul, 2002).

UNDERSTANDING ADOLESCENCE

Adolescent girls are always in the process of negotiating their lives, intuiting circumstances, weighing alternatives, as well as making and revising choices (Research for Action, 1996). Unfortunately, the experience of adolescence becomes even more complicated for girls than boys (in some respects) as young women "still move toward adulthood in a society that

THE ROLE OF PARENTS AND CAREGIVERS 53

continues to denigrate women, especially women of color" (Research for Action, 1996, p. 1). Psychologist Erik Erikson (1977) describes the process of adolescence as a period during which young people grapple with the question of who they will become as well as who they are. Specifically, Erikson (1977) states, "identity formation depends upon the interplay of what young persons at the end of childhood have come to mean to themselves and what they now appear to mean to those who become significant to them" (p. 106). Adolescence is characterized as the period of experimentation, strong identification with certain people and groups, active fantasy lives, and probing into various philosophies, vocations, and the self (Liebert & Wicks-Nelson, 1981).

Yet we must highlight that adolescence takes on a decidedly different cast for black girls. "Girls of color face a different set of experiences and issues because of different socialization patterns and their need to deal with the multiple burdens of racism, cultural discrimination, and gender bias in society" (Hansen, Walker, & Flom, 1995a, p. 10). In addition to establishing her identity as a woman, a black girl becomes even more aware of her status as a black (Goodman, 1972).

In a small-scale study of girls of color at the exclusive Emma Willard School in Troy, New York, researcher Janie Ward (1990) determined that the black girls she interviewed were intensely aware of their double-jeopardy status. She also discovered that double-jeopardy standing could prove potentially affirming and empowering while concomitantly burdensome.

> The process of being and becoming black provides young women with three essential opportunities for growth. First, there is an opportunity for role negation—the repudiation of both race- and gender-based stereotypes. Second, there is an opportunity to create a new and personally defined identity on one's own terms. And third, when opportunities for leadership are provided, there's a chance to effect change in one's social environment by developing and pursuing one's personal commitments. (Ward, 1990, p. 228)

The most important of the three, however, as per psychologist Janet Helms, is the ability to move from a perception of one's self that is externally derived to one that evolves inwardly. "Women's healthy gender identity development involves movement from an externally and societally based definition of womanhood to an internal definition in which the woman's own values, beliefs, and abilities determine the quality of her womanhood" (Ossana, Helms, & Leonard, 1992, p. 403).

Helms sums up this progression toward healthy self-esteem for black women in a developmental model of Womanist identity that appears solidly based on Cross's model of racial transcendence. The Helms model has four stages that are very closely aligned with the stages Cross outlined. They include Preencounter, Encounter, Immersion/Emersion, and Internalization. As with the Cross model, the Preencounter and Encounter phases are the only phases of Helms's model that may occur during childhood.

In stage 1 of the Helms's Womanist Identity Model, Preencounter, the girl conforms to societal views about gender, holds a constricted view of women's roles, and unconsciously thinks and behaves in ways that devalue women and esteem men as reference groups. In the second stage, Encounter, she begins to question the accepted values and beliefs of the Preencounter stage as a result of contact with new information and/or experiences that heighten the personal relevance of womanhood and suggest alternate ways of being.

For parents, it becomes incredibly tempting to dismiss the behavior of preadolescent and adolescent girls by saying they are temperamental, secretive, and more difficult to handle than boys are. Many parents/caregivers spend sleepless nights wondering how the sweet, even-tempered child they once knew has become so adversarial. In some ways, it seems that our girls are purposely pushing us away and keeping us "out of their business." Truthfully, they are! They are attempting to forge identities that are separate and distinct from those of their mothers in the only ways they know, and that venture involves creating social and emotional distance from adults.

DEVELOPING AGENCY IN BLACK GIRLS

As recently as a few months ago, a participant in a professional development session I conducted (based on this book) questioned me about the ways in which black mothers relate to their daughters. She observed that a number of the black mothers with whom she came in contact (as a school nurse) seemed disconnected and almost hostile to their daughters. Then she contrasted this behavior with her perceptions of the ways these same women treat their sons. Some of the information she received from direct interaction, and some was obtained anecdotally from the girls she counseled.

Contrary to her beliefs, however, data suggests that, as with white girls, black girls confide more in their mothers, and their mothers give them more advice on personal matters. "In addition, adolescent girls choose their mothers as their confidantes on a number of personal topics such as family problems and feelings, school, career, and the future" (Cauce, et al., 1996, p. 106). In another small-scale study (of 93 middle school respondents and 22 black girls) conducted by Erkut and Marx (1995), 96% of the African American respondents indicated there was an adult woman in their lives with whom they could talk about things, and mothers (32%) were most frequently mentioned. With this study and the one conducted by Ward (to which I also allude in this chapter), however, particular attention must be paid to the studies' small scale and limited geographic scope as they remind us that the findings are not necessarily generalizable. Another surprising point emphasizes that most adolescent-parent arguments are related to topics like the completion of chores and homework more frequently than sex and drug use (Cauce et al., 1996). Tangentially, it should be noted that many adolescent-parent arguments centered on relationships usually involve the selection of same-gender friends. In the Erkut and Marx (1995) study referenced previously, the majority of black respondents indicated that they felt their parents did not like their friends. During preadolescence, girls' friendships become more significant to them, and the family begins to lose its position of primary importance (Ladner, 1971). Yet it is very important to highlight that much of the more recent research cited in Part II indicates that, although it might slip from its primary position, the relationships shared by black girls and their families (mothers in this instance) are in no way diminished in value.

Returning to the discussion with the session participant, I accepted the fact that the inquiry of the session participant (to whom I alluded) was genuine. As a white woman, she sincerely questioned a phenomenon she did not understand; concurrently, however, she helped give credence to the age-old adage that black mothers raise their daughters and love their sons. Although I believe her perception is based on a misinterpretation of black mothers' intentions, her beliefs also have some degree of credibility, and they were supported by some of the black session participants as well.

The contention that black mothers love their sons more than their daughters is problematic in a number of ways. One such difficulty was identified earlier and centers on the traditional assignment of blame to mothers (across lines of race and ethnicity) for the problems their children experience, even after those children have reached adulthood and the age of personal accountability. Yet the role that black mothers (in this instance) play is even more complex and multilayered.

In modern-day society, the incredible enigma of balancing power and powerlessness remains potent for black mothers. Although immense power is inherent in the capabilities of giving and sustaining life and remaining strong in the face of incredible adversity, we are still forced to contemplate the powerless ways in which we may appear to our children. We may do little wrong in the eyes of our offspring, but those children also see our powerlessness to control the inequities that impact our lives as we work for wages that are still not reflective of our worth and battle some fathers to play more significant roles in their children's lives and make routine child support payments (Paul, 2001). This last point leads to another problem attached to the notion that black mothers demonstrate blatant favoritism toward their sons. If we accept this premise, then black fathers are almost totally absolved from the responsibility of fully participating in the day-to-day grind, as well as joys, of parenting.

In my estimation, a more salient question to focus on during the professional development session was this: "What can we as parents, caregivers, community members, and school personnel do (specifically) to be more supportive of our black girls?" It is this question that drives this chapter and the ones that follow.

FOSTERING DIALOGUE

Studies indicate that, in some instances, black children's television viewing rates exceed their parents' 40-hour work week (Bush, Smith, & Martin, 1999). Data also suggests that black teens are more prone to use television as a source of guidance and to learn dating behavior (Bush et al., 1999). Yet the point of this discussion is not to identify the evils of television, because I believe that point is debatable. This discussion seeks to emphasize that with so much television viewing, as well as engagement with cell phones, laptops, and X-Boxes, not a lot of time remains for family dialogue. The majority of American families no longer sit down to dinner together. On average, many parents spend mere minutes talking with their children each day. One of the most common complaints parents make about their school-aged children is "my kids won't talk to me." The situation becomes exacerbated as those children reach preadolescence and adolescence.

The reasons that our children do not converse with us are manifold and varied, but more importantly, we must not accept the situation as normal. As parents/caregivers, we must make the time to engage in dialogue with our children each day, especially as adolescence prompts them to keep more and more information to themselves or share it with their friends. The first step of "doing parenting" might involve talking with our daughter(s) and fostering open lines of communication.

Most conversations occur spontaneously and without much delibera-tion, so that might be the best form for conversations with your child to take. Engage them in *parallel conversations,* defined by psychotherapist Ron Taffel (1991) as conversations in which the two participants are not necessarily focused on one another. Such conversations come out of the moment, and they are unplanned and unexpected. These conversations can occur during travel time or while you and your child are engaged in some collaborative task like completing household chores or watching televi-sion. Conversations can also result from common interests, so learn some-thing about your child's interests and talk about those things.

In my mind, these aspects of communication are relatively easy. A harder task is developing the art of listening. Many children do not talk with their parents because their parents do not listen. Parent/caregivers frequently spend all too much time talking *at* their children, and that talk includes lecturing, giving unsolicited advice, and scolding. We must develop the skill of listening if we genuinely want children to talk. By tak-ing the time to listen to and talk with your child, you are sending the truly important message that the child's thoughts are valuable. That leads us to the next point, developing self-worth and autonomy in girls.

DEVELOPING AUTONOMY IN GIRLS

Many of my women friends (across lines of race and socioeconomic sta-tus) were brought to womanhood under the principle that a woman should get an education, just in case. After all, she might need it, in the event that her marriage ends and she is forced to be self-sufficient.

Today, black parents are faced with a distinctive paradox. They must continue to raise girls who are able to fend for themselves because the rate of marriageability remains much lower than average in the black commu-nity. Concurrently, they must help their daughters learn a sense of balance between family and work and ways in which to operate interdependently with black men, in particular, and men, generally. This balance (in spite of the family's configuration) proves essential as many career women have discovered that institutions do not love you back. They frequently take extensively and give far too little in return. It is possible for a woman to give her life to an institution (whether it be a job, profession, or church), only to discover she has forever lost the opportunity to raise children, fos-ter a loving relationship with another adult, and truly self-actualize.

Parents must start early, instilling a sense of self-worth in their girls, and cultivating the belief that women have something of value to offer, and it is not specific to the pleasure our bodies can potentially offer. Girls should regularly be complimented on their intellect, confidence, and capabilities. This process begins with the way we speak to our children and the messages we send forth about those children.

Some parents/caregivers are all too comfortable speaking to their children in ways in which they would be ashamed to speak to co-workers and friends. Some parents/caregivers unwittingly erode their children's self-esteem with the things they say and the underlying message transmitted that the child does not meet parental expectations in some way. Children who grow up in this fashion carry these feelings of inadequacy into adulthood, and these feelings will probably manifest in some form.

Parents can jump-start this process of instilling self-confidence with small acts of kindness, as well as those that are more substantive in nature. Girls need to be afforded opportunities to explore options that are not defined by constricting gender roles, in addition to determining their own interests, strengths, and ambitions.

For example, "in no academic area does the nexus between race and gender claim more casualties than in the areas of mathematics and science—and no group has been more excluded than African-American girls" (Adenika-Morrow, 1996). Parents can work toward narrowing this gap by presenting young girls with toys that would be traditionally targeted for boys, games that emphasize critical thinking and problem solving, in addition to trips that expose them to typically described male interests like technical museums, science fairs, and agricultural festivals. In the home, we can engage our daughters in problem solving by asking their opinions on appropriate household matters, supplying them opportunities to conduct hands-on experiments, encouraging them to read expository nonfiction books, as well as develop a level of comfort interacting with computer technology.

Presenting college as an option and an expectation early on is an experience that all children should have. On a routine basis, I hear some parents express the belief that college is not for everyone; they propose that one can still do well in life without advanced education of some sort. In my mind, such thoughts are dated in most instances. In his book *How to Succeed in Business Without Being White* (1997), Earl Graves, publisher and chief executive officer of *Black Enterprise* magazine, projects job growth in the millennium in three broad areas:

- outsourcing (independent companies that offer services conventionally rendered in-house by corporations and public entities);

- computer technology, telecommunications, multimedia software, and on-line entertainment;
- health care and other services for aging baby boomers.

The greatest opportunities will presumably be contained within the second category, indicates Graves. Labor Bureau forecasters suggest that technicians will comprise one fifth of the work force by 2005. The number of jobs in computer-related fields will increase by 90%.

With the present economic decline, corporate graft surfacing, rates of unemployment rising, and the demands of the workplace increasing, more is required to get and maintain jobs. The nation has rapidly transitioned from an industrial-based society to one that is technologically advanced and undergirded by an information substructure. As a result, workers must be able to analyze, interpret, and process complex data, as well as understand sophisticated computer programs with minimal assistance.

Thus parents/caregivers should talk with their youngsters about the importance of education and the need for advanced training (in whatever capacity that might be). Parents should also take children on college visits (starting in middle school) and discuss the relevance of historically black colleges and universities. These institutions are such an important aspect of black history and may face extinction if our young people fail to value them or consider them as viable options for higher education.

BUILDING EDUCATIONAL PARTNERSHIPS

As a parent/caregiver concerned about your child's educational development, start early in initiating a relationship with your child's teacher. Focus on developing a relationship built on mutual trust and respect, rather than one that is adversarial. Express your willingness to work in partnership with the teacher and school, yet emphasize that your primary concern is your child and her or his healthy development and academic competence. Emphasize your role as an advocate for your child.

Along with meetings with your child's teacher, send notes and call periodically to check on your child's progress. During parent-teacher conferences, share information about your views on education and the ways in which you foster your child's intellectual growth at home. If you routinely read stories, share titles and suggest the teacher read them in class. If your child demonstrates talent in areas your child's teacher might be unaware of, share that information. Also share information about your culture and your family. You may also elect to use conference times and parent-teacher communications to clarify classroom practices and homework procedures as well. Homework serves as a reinforcement of work done in class. Therefore, ask the teacher to provide tips and pointers on the ways in which you might assist in facilitating learning. In addition, ask that the teacher send periodic updates regarding the academic content and concepts that will be addressed.

Yet, in addition to developing children's intellectual needs, we must also nurture their social and emotional lives. One way to foster this growth is to encourage healthy, productive friendships.

ENCOURAGING GIRLS TO TAKE PERSONAL RESPONSIBILITY FOR THEIR BODIES

Parents/caregivers need to promote friendships between girls and boys, in addition to those that spawn from the intragender group. Our daughters and sons need to spend time nurturing friendships with each other, forming bonds of comfort and building trust. In this fashion, young people cultivate an understanding that the genders are similar in some ways, yet they are vastly different in others.

As parents, we must teach our girls that the way to ensure a relationship is not based on sex (whether it is oral, genital, or anal). I need to distinguish in this way as some young people are being misled to believe oral and anal sex are acceptable because they do not lead to a loss of the hymen and thus virginity remains intact. Sex (in any form) before one is ready is harmful. The most effective way to develop a lasting relationship is to postpone intercourse, taking time to become well acquainted with and develop respect for each other.

Yet what about young girls who are already sexually active? Well, just because you have had sex does not mean you must or should continue. For this group, the motivations and decision making surrounding sexual activity need to be analyzed. This set of young people should be encouraged to ask questions like these: Why am I having sex? Is this truly my choice, or is it my partner's choice? Am I taking precautions to prevent sexually transmitted diseases (STDs) and pregnancy? In the event that precautions fail, am I prepared to cope with the consequences of my behavior? How do I negotiate condom use with my partner? Will my partner support me and trust my decision making if I decide against having or continuing a sexual relationship? How might my decision to be sexually active impact my future and my family?

As parents, we will not always be able to intervene or prevent our children from making decisions that are not, necessarily, in their best interest.

What we can do, however, is provide them with the tools and information needed to make the best decisions possible. Further, parents/caregivers need to accept the fact that while girls can more easily manifest the consequences of sexual activity, no girl can become pregnant without a boy. Therefore, our message to boys must be consistent with those we transmit to girls. Here, as well, we need to discuss the postponement of sex until a strong friendship is formed. Also, rather than just viewing sex for boys as conquest or proof of manhood, we need to start talking to young men about the consequences of their sexual decision making, as well as our expectations of them in the event that they impregnate someone else's daughter.

Parents (and fathers, in particular) can treat their daughters in the same fashion they would expect their daughter's future life partner to treat her. Parents/caregivers can present their girls with gifts like flowers, dinner, tickets to a play or concert, and trips that indicate I value you, so girls expect a certain standard of behavior from their dates. The message has already been conveyed: "I am worth something. I am special whether I am in a relationship or not." Our daughters should view relationships as means of securing companionship and opportunities to grow rather than viewing them as entitlements that present them with the opportunity to be taken care of.

Thus we need to encourage our daughters regarding self-care and self-love. What are the things that girls need to do for themselves to make them feel appreciated? We should encourage our girls to take pleasure in the small things like eating healthy foods, taking a bubble bath, exercising, reading a book, writing a letter, and/or staying at home and eating chocolates (once in a while) for that matter. Girls need to look within for validation and establish strong networks so they do not grow up believing validation from males is the only kind of validation that matters. Another thing that parents can do to assist their daughters is to empower them economically.

GIRLS AND ECONOMIC EMPOWERMENT

I, personally, would like to see my daughter and my son (respectively) married to mates who love God and respect, love, and remain committed to my child. As a single parent, life is very challenging for me. It is difficult handling a responsibility that should be shared between two parents (no matter how much I love my children). It is difficult raising children with one set of emotional, financial, and intellectual resources when two sets would prove optimal. Although I desire a married life for my daughter and son, I must help both children develop a contingency plan so they can be economically self-sufficient.

Blacks spend more than $270 billion a year on consumer goods, and since the 1990s, consumer spending by blacks has increased to approximately 54% (Bush et al., 1999). Blacks also tend to spend more in such product categories as personal care items, women's accessories, jewelry, and infant and toddler clothing (Bush et al., 1999). Unfortunately, however, most of our money is spent outside of our communities, and it does very little to enhance the quality of our lives. On a consistent basis, we make other communities rich and have very little to show for it.

Girls are taught, in many instances, to be especially incompetent in respect to managing finances. The first lesson regarding money management that daughters need to understand is money's value and the importance of spending and saving wisely. It is very difficult to teach financial literacy in adulthood, and the consequences of financial illiteracy are staggering; "widespread 'financial illiteracy' is evident on two levels—rising personal bankruptcy and a nearly incomprehensible national debt" (Godfrey & Edwards, 1994, p. 14).

Although it is truly important to save money, it is also vital to spend money in a fiscally responsible way and demonstrate effective financial decision making. For these reasons, we should introduce children to the concepts of budgeting and banking as soon as they are able to comprehend them. Teaching our daughters (and sons) about the benefits of budgeting can only be accomplished in an experiential fashion. Allowance is a great place to start, and, without a doubt, allowance should be tied to work. In this manner, we develop a strong work ethic in the young while concomitantly teaching moral and ethical values like commitment and citizenship. Chores are part of each person's responsibility to the family and its effective management.

Many other fiscal lessons remain to be taught, but this is a good place to begin. Ultimately, parents might be able to introduce more complicated concepts like buying stocks and understanding wills and trusts. The only way we can overcome the financial difficulties that will inevitably come in this life is to prepare for them.

Chapter 6

WHAT IS THE ROLE OF
THE COMMUNITY?

When messages of white society say, "you can't," the well-functioning black family and community stand ready to counter such messages with those that say, "You can, we have, you will."

—Janie Ward, scholar and professor of education
("Racial Identity Formation and Transformation,"
in *Making Connections: The Relational Worlds of
Adolescent Girls at Emma Willard School*)

I do not routinely engage in nostalgia or reminisce over the good old days. Instead, I prefer to look at the progress we (as a people) have made, and I stay fixed on what remains to be realized in the future. But I do mourn the loss of "community" within many contemporary black residential areas. The "community" to which I refer is defined as a "collective thinking, seeing and behaving as a 'we,' not as a 'me'" (Anderson, 2001, p. 66). Community might also be distinguished as a sign of "commitment and the potential for power," rather than a mere locality in which people live near one another (p. 65).

I do not think this loss of community has solely evolved because we, as a people, want it that way. Instead, a combination of factors has created this untenable situation we are presently faced with, a situation that has us in fear of our children and ourselves, distances us from our neighbors, and creates adversarial relationships where cordial ones once existed.

THE URBAN CENTER: PARADISE LOST

At the turn of the twentieth century, urban centers in the North were described as lands of milk and honey (Banks, 1991); they were thought to hold chances for actualizing great promise and fulfilling dreams. With northern manufacturers needing laborers, a significant number of blacks fled the South and its denial of their legal rights, natural disasters (like floods and the boll weevil), and the inequities of the sharecropping system. "The Great Migration radically redefined the nation's African American population, nearly reversing the ratio of urban and rural residents and removing some 40 percent of black residents from the Old South. Between 1910 and 1930, an estimated 1.2 million African American migrants moved to the North, increasing the black populations in northern urban centers by 300 percent" (Massood, 2003, p. 12).

The trend of black migration from the South continued post–World War II. Between the 1960s and 1970s, approximately 1.5 million more migrated from the South to the North and the West (Massood, 2003). The black population increase in northern cities also intensified with the influx of third-wave immigrants (a number of whom originated from the Caribbean and Africa) during the late 20th century. When the Immigration Reform Act of 1965 became effective in 1968, the United States experienced its largest wave of immigrants since the turn of the century. Approximately 78.6% more immigrants entered the United States in the decade between 1971 and 1980 than entered during the period 1951 to 1960. Immigration to the United States continued at a rapid rate between 1981 and 1988, and almost 5 million immigrants settled in the United States at that time (Banks, 1994).

Unfortunately, the trek to the North (expected to offer flourishing opportunities and unforeseen treasures for black newcomers) actually presented many more perils. Extreme violence, race riots, and gross discrimination in employment and housing awaited the new black immigrants from the South instead (Banks, 1991). In many respects, the situation has worsened over the past 25 years, with the disappearance of businesses and a shift to a customer-service, high-tech-oriented form of industry. The new economy requires complex critical thinking skills that underfinanced and poorly staffed schools servicing major U.S. cities fail to foster consistently in their young charges. Added to these difficulties is the loss of housing and resurfacing of gentrification in urban centers. These changes have "stimulated [an] influx of criminal activities [that] undermines the strong sense of solidarity that once permeated the community" (Wacquant & Wilson, 1989, p. 14).

There has been another outcome as well. The increase in criminal activity and heightened concerns for personal and family safety have led to a mass exodus from cities to the surrounding suburbs by a rising black middle class. This process, however, has not been seamless. "Anytime blacks were able to breach the wall of restrictive covenants, brokers' steering and mortgage redlining to begin to integrate a neighborhood, white flight and resegregation quickly followed" (Kunen, 1996, p. 33).

Thus, for many U.S. metropolises, the forecast remains bleak as their economic bases continue to destabilize, loss of services heightens, and a widespread neglect of cities and their residents pervades. For New York City and Washington, D.C., in particular, but not to the exclusion of other parts of the United States, the events of September 11, 2001, only served to further devastate already precarious infrastructures. Despite this chapter's focus on municipalities, we must recognize that rural areas as well continue to languish as a result of the extreme poverty and substandard living conditions faced by their residents.

Albeit many difficulties have come with urbanization, the most significant has been the emotional and social distance created between us, especially in areas of extreme poverty that are far too frequently located in urban centers. For example, whereas approximately two thirds of middle-class blacks belong to at least one formal organization, such as a block club, a community organization, a political party, a school-related association, or a sports, fraternal, or other social group, it is more common for extremely poor area residents to belong to no organization (Wacquant & Wilson, 1989). Additionally, black women who reside in areas of extreme poverty are least likely to know most of their neighbors (Wacquant & Wilson, 1989). The "great barrier to black social and economic mobility is isolation from the opportunities and networks of the middle class" (Crain as quoted in Kunen, 1996, p. 36). Whereas this loss is significant for us all, it is greatest for our children.

THE DANGERS OF URBAN CENTERS FOR BLACK GIRLS

Many of our children, especially our girls, will grow up in neighborhoods representative of danger and fear. "One of the consequences of these pervasive community influences upon the child is that they superimpose [an] emotional precocity on the girl that often exceeds her chronological years" (Ladner, 1971, p. 52). In spite of the fact that the danger is real and ubiquitous, it does not typically make its way to the various media outlets as frequently as the violence perpetrated against white children. For this reason, many black girls (from an early age) must learn to live defensively. Routinely, they are faced with potential pitfalls and adult decisions they should not be forced to make (Cauce et al., 1996).

In times past, the immediate and extended families served as the primary socializing agents in the black community (Ladner, 1971).

> Frequently, girls spent their growing up years in the care of extended kin. Grandmothers acted as permanent babysitters while the actual parents were away working.... The influence of the extended family upon the socialization of young Black girls [was] often very strong. Many children grew up in three-generation households and they absorbed the influences of grandmother and grandfather as well as mother and father. (Ladner, 1971, p. 50)

Currently, grandparents and other extended family members do not always live in such close proximity or maintain contact with the family's children. The ways in which divorce and separation reinforce distance among children, parents, and extended family members (on both sides) must also be considered. As a result, many present-day family members do not share the same level of sustained contact with young people that extended families of the past have.

The lack of physical proximity and the impact of divorce and separation are further compounded by the implications of poverty with which many urban center residents must learn to cope. "Of all other factors that can influence childhood sexual activity, poverty has been most strongly linked with abusive early-childhood experiences" (Wyatt, 1997, p. 62). When the quality of family life diminishes, the likelihood that the child will be protected from harmful experiences concomitantly decreases (Wyatt, 1997). "More than 60 percent of Black teen mothers are concentrated in poor, racially segregated neighborhoods that have poor housing, high crime rates, and inadequate schools. Many teen mothers have [also] been victims of childhood sexual abuse" (Office of Juvenile Justice and Delinquency Prevention, 1998).

In the Erkut and Marx (1995) study of middle school girls cited in chapter 5, black and Puerto Rican female respondents indicated a "keen awareness of the physical dangers which surrounded their urban existence" (p. 42). In the same study, black girls' advice to their parents included a respect for "space," and they distinguished this need from that sought more regularly by white respondents for "independence." "The space they seemed to be seeking was relief from the protectiveness and controls parents place on girls because of the physical dangers in their outside environment" (p. 42).

Unfortunately, neither parents/caregivers nor community leaders in many such neighborhoods have been successful in ridding them of antisocial adult behavior because for many such areas, the community power base remains outside its borders as well as its grasp (Ladner, 1971). For numerous children, the village is no longer present to raise them.

THE NEED FOR EFFECTIVE COMMUNITY PROGRAMMING

One of the contemporary realities with which we are faced is that too many American young people spend the hours from 3 P.M. to 6 P.M. (in the afternoons) unsupervised. Data suggests that out-of-school hours, for young people who are supervised by caring adults, can be filled with occasions to spend time with friends, engage in sports-based activities, and pursue hobbies and pastimes. For the many home alone, in contrast, out-of-school hours pose grave dangers for substance abuse, crime, violence, and high-risk sexual activity leading toward unwanted pregnancy and STDs.

A correlation has also been established between early sex play among children and being raised in large cities (Wyatt, 1997). Research suggests that the following characteristics (specific in many ways to the urban reality) might lend themselves to the increased likelihood of early sex play:

- having both parents or a single parent, head of household, at work;
- children having more unsupervised time;
- children receiving greater exposure to sex-related information. (Wyatt, 1997)

Yet an important distinction must be made between youngsters being alone and their actions during the time they are unsupervised. Mere time spent alone is not a critical contributor to jeopardy for young people. "Rather it is what young people do during that time, where they do it, and with whom that leads to [both] positive and negative consequences" (Carnegie Council on Adolescent Development, 1994).

For these reasons, community programs can serve as invaluable resources to working parents and their children. Community programming also has the potential to supplement limited school resources and extend the services that schools offer. Yet, at present, they remain a vastly untapped resource. More than 17,000 national and local youth organizations currently exist in the United States, including those launched by religious youth groups, sports organizations, museums, public libraries, and recreation departments. But many of these programs uniformly fail to attract young people past the ages of 11 or 12 (Carnegie Council on Adolescent Development, 1994).

THE POTENTIAL BENEFITS OFFERED BY
EFFECTIVE COMMUNITY PROGRAMMING

For a number of plausible reasons, community programs have traditionally fallen short in their efforts to service youngsters, their families, and communities. They are recurrently plagued with problems, many of which are inextricably linked with their inconstant financial status. For example, significant numbers of community programs have high turnover rates among staff members and lack the financial resources required to advance their missions. These programs are "chronically under-financed and suffer from the low morale of dedicated staff [members] forced to limit vital services. Recruiting and preparing committed adult leaders—both paid and pro bono—is a constant challenge" (Carnegie Council on Adolescent Development, 1994).

Adequate financing for a respective community program must be sustained long enough for it to yield results (Office of Juvenile Justice and Delinquency Prevention, 1998). Community programs are more vulnerable to cuts in federal funding than schools and major social service agencies. They are more apt to rely almost totally on grant funding, contributions, and/or other forms of so-called soft money, that is, money on which an organization cannot depend from year to year. For example, there is never a guarantee that grant funding will be renewed or that programs developed with such funds will continue. In most instances, program continuation and funding are contingent on program evaluation; the program must prove it is viable, effectual, and that the funding awarded is well spent. Therefore, "program developers should construct valid and reliable ways to determine whether activities or interventions produce desired goals" (Carnegie Council on Adolescent Development, 1994). Program developers must also ensure that their programs are well governed, efficiently managed, and fiscally responsible.

Yet, above all, if community programs are to flourish, program developers must have a commitment to quality education for young people, a clear vision for success, and creative ingenuity. All of these qualities would apply to the following exemplars of community programming: the Brooklyn (New York) Children's Museum and the Congress of National Black Churches' (CNBC) Project SPIRIT (which serves as an acronym for strength, perseverance, imagination, responsibility, integrity, and talent).

The Brooklyn Children's Museum, founded in 1899 and one of the first to admit unaccompanied children, takes a multitiered approach to programming for children and youth. Young people (ages 7 to 15) can enroll (on their own) in the Kids Crew, which operates afternoons, weekends, holidays, and during school vacations. More than 1,500 youngsters are members, including the 100 who visit one to four times a week. The next tier is that of Junior Curator for youngsters ages 10 to 17. Junior Curators are trained to assist staff members in all areas of the museum. The final tier helps young people (ages 14 to 18) secure meaningful employment as they work part time in the exhibition, education, collection, or administration programs. Families of the young people in the various programs are also involved in museum programming (Carnegie Council on Adolescent Development, 1994).

The CNBC's Project SPIRIT aims to instill the qualities of strength, perseverance, imagination, responsibility, integrity, and talent in the youth it serves, many of whom would be classified as academic underachievers with leadership potential. The youth component is centered on the after-school program and its activities, which include the following:

- snacks, prayer, and times for meditation;
- tutoring, reading, writing, and mathematics;
- activities aimed at developing black cultural and ethnic pride;
- a weekly rites-of-passage curriculum that culminates in an end-of-the-year ceremony.

Parents of youngsters in the program participate in weekly education sessions focused on child development and effective parenting strategies. Clergy and laity of participating churches (classified as service providers) are enrolled in a 15-session workshop series designed to assist them in more effectively mentoring youth and sensitize them to the needs and concerns of young people (Carnegie Council on Adolescent Development, 1994).

Although we need all community-based organizations, we (as a people) especially benefit from those that serve out of a sense of commitment to the survival and edification of the black community. In a similar vein, we all benefit when programs are developed with the needs of girls and young women (another traditionally marginalized group) in mind. As much as possible, girls should have a say in program design, implementation, and evaluation. Research indicates that more successful programs regularly incorporate the suggestions of their young participants.

COMMUNITY PROGRAMMING FOR GIRLS AND YOUNG WOMEN

Community-based programs established for girls and young women, in particular, have the capacity to supply female participants with access to female mentors, in addition to facilitating their transition to womanhood and reinforcing cultural values (Hansen, Walker, & Flom, 1995a). Personally, I prefer the term "mentor" to "role model" because the latter seems to connote a passive image to be emulated. "A mentor is more aggressively involved with a protégé. The word 'mentor' has an intellectual [undertone].... Because mentors provide some intellectual guidance, they also must be respected intellectually" (T. L. Banks, 1995, p. 329). In reviews of promising youth programming, the single most favorable aspect was invariably described as a charismatic program staff; staff who had "been there" themselves and understood those issues that are so important to adolescent girls (Office of Juvenile Justice and Delinquency Prevention, 1998).

Via innovative community programming models, girls can receive opportunities to develop an internally derived sense of success, envision a wide repertoire of possibilities, and acquire necessary skills as critical readers of the cultures they inhabit (Research for Action, 1996). They must also be able to honor themselves as complex individuals with emerging visions, sophisticated critical thinking abilities, and a wide array of options about who they are, as well as who they wish to become (Research for Action, 1996). Within this process of realizing their potential and achieving self-actualization, girls should make regular connections with engaged and caring adult mentors.

Prototypical community programs for girls should include the following dimensions: same-sex mentors and same-sex bonding, celebrations emphasizing rites of passage to adulthood, reinforcement of culture and academics, parental and community involvement, and a safe haven (Hansen et al., 1995a). Exemplary programs must also demonstrate sensitivity to the real-life impediments girls encounter, some of which plausibly interfere with their full participation in after-school and weekend programs. In addition, this programming must actively assist them in overcoming such barriers. For example, girls of all ages often have weighty child care obligations and must often provide care for younger siblings and/or their own children. In order for after-school and weekend programs to reach this group of potential participants, girls must be encouraged to bring younger children with them, and on-site child care should be furnished (Hansen et al., 1995a). For this reason, programs need to highlight comprehensive care and serve as wide a cross section of children and young people as possible.

Community organizations can provide black girls, in this instance, and all children, generally, safe, supervised recreation facilities, opportunities to gather, and time during which to explore their burgeoning identities and enhance self-esteem. This exploration might take place on the sports field as well as through tutorials and internships. As one facet of the programs they offer, community groups can promote girls' development by encouraging their participation in youth sports leagues and athletics. Such occasions accentuate the skills of team building and collaboration, in addition to preparing young women for possible leadership and coaching roles.

Yet some believe that after-school and weekend programs for girls should be primarily sports based, citing the growth of girls' participation in school and community-based athletic programs with the passage of Title IX of the Education Amendments of 1972, as well as the positive characteristics (acknowledged earlier) that girls develop as a result of participation in sports (Weiler, 1998).

For black girls, however, athletic participation has not correlated to higher grades or a decline in their dropout rate as it has for white females (Weiler, 1998). So although black girls should receive opportunities to participate in sports, especially those that exclude low-income girls, like swimming, tennis, ice skating, and gymnastics, they should also be exposed to the arts and academic enrichment in these programs. Black girls, like other girls, have broad interests and should be presented with the opportunity to develop those interests.

Another benefit rendered by community programs is that they afford girls chances to potentially resolve their issues in the context of single-sex gatherings. Data suggests that this strategy of single-sex grouping has even proven successful with adults who are coping with serious issues like drug addiction and domestic violence. Single-sex gatherings afford participants with the freedom to drop artifice and engage in the hard work of identity exploration and character building. Typically, participants in coed groups focus more on making a good impression on the opposite sex than they do on honestly working through their issues. Additionally, whereas schools have experienced a number of legal challenges surrounding the constitutionality of single-sex groupings, community groups are not necessarily faced with the same encumbrance. The public seems more accepting of such configurations in settings outside of school.

THE POWER OF MENTORING YOUNG GIRLS

Community organizations do make tremendous improvements in the quality of life for numerous young people, but the role that dedicated individuals can play must not be minimized. Young people, girls in this instance, need involved adults who will advocate for them, and sometimes those adults are not family members. A young person might not feel comfortable revealing certain experiences and feelings to her parents/caregivers or extended family members. Mentors, most definitely, fill that void.

The role of mentor is primarily an educational one for the mentee and the mentor alike. Mentors should be trained, so they share a common set of understandings about girls and the various cultures to which they belong. Yet the mentor also serves to teach her mentee many life skills and strategies that will boost her self-esteem and help her become successful. Through the mentoring relationship, mentees can learn problem-solving strategies, anger management, conflict resolution, and the art of negotiation (Kanfer, Englund, Lennhoff, & Rhodes, 1995). Mentors are also able to share personal experiences that resonate with the realities of girls' lives and present models of survival and growth (Office of Juvenile Justice and Delinquency Prevention, 1998).

There are many ways to initiate the process of serving as a mentor. For first timers, participating in a firmly established program (e.g., Jack and Jill, Big Sisters, or the Girl Scouts) might prove beneficial. Through these stable vehicles, mentor training modules are usually introduced; these modules assist mentors in forming the strategies and dispositions (e.g., patience, trust, and understanding the dynamics of adolescence) requisite to competent mentoring of preadolescent and adolescent girls. Participating in an established program also proves the least time-consuming approach for busy people. Yet the options of starting a mentoring group on one's own or informally mentoring young people in one's community also exist.

In any event, the role of mentor is an essential one in the healthy development of young girls. The effective mentor can play an affirming role in the life of her mentee. Without a nurturing and supportive adult, and without confidence in her own judgment or abilities, the girl is far more likely to turn to peers for validation and establish an identity that conforms to external standards of beauty, womanhood, and success (Office of Juvenile Justice and Delinquency Prevention, 1998).

Chapter 7

WHAT IS THE ROLE OF SCHOOLS?

I am more convinced than ever of the importance of reinventing community, both within our schools and within our neighborhoods. This sense of place, of belonging, is a crucial building block for the healthy development of children and adolescents. And it is especially crucial for young people who are growing up in disadvantaged circumstances—the young people who face the most serious obstacles on the pathway to adulthood.

—James P. Comer, psychiatrist and co-chair, Task Force on
Youth Development and Community Programs
(as quoted in the Carnegie Council on Adolescent
Development's *A Matter of Time,* 1994)

On May 17, 1954, a unanimous Supreme Court handed down the landmark *Brown v. Board of Education of Topeka* ruling. The *Brown* case served as the culminating suit in a series of school desegregation cases. The decision, clearly a victory in almost every conceivable way, decreed that "separate educational facilities are inherently unequal" and the concept itself violates the Constitution's equal protection clause. On a global front, the credibility of the United States had been damaged by the widely broadcast inequitable social conditions that existed for blacks in the 1950s. Both the government and the NAACP lawyers argued that the *Brown* decision would assist in legitimizing U.S. political and economic policies (Ladson-Billings, 1999). On a national level, the decision offered reassurance to blacks that the freedom and equality attained for others (during World War II) could be realized at home as well.

Symbolically, the immediate impact of *Brown* was meaningful and decisive because a spate of school desegregation activity was generated in the late 1950s and early 1960s. Quite specifically, the desegregation efforts of Central High School in Little Rock, Arkansas, the New Orleans public schools, the University of Mississippi, the University of Alabama, and the University of Georgia were all underway. By the 1970s, school desegregation/civil rights battles were also being fought in northern cities, one of the most memorable in the Boston public school system (Ladson-Billings, 1999).

In many ways, *Brown v. Board of Education of Topeka* also paved the way for the Civil Rights Amendment and Title IX of the Elementary and Secondary Education Act of 1965 (ESEA). As a result of the success of *Brown* and the gains made during the civil rights movement of the 1960s and 1970s, blacks "demanded more control over the institutions in their communities and also demanded that all institutions, including the schools, more accurately reflect their ethnic cultures" (Banks, 1994, p. 27). They called for more black teachers and school administrators, textbooks that accurately mirrored African American history and culture, and schools that resonated a heightened sensitivity to African American needs and concerns (Banks, 1994, p. 27). Recognizing the impact of black collectivity, other historically disenfranchised ethnic groups (e.g., Mexican Americans, Asian Americans, and Puerto Ricans) made similar demands for political, economic, and educational change (Banks, 1994). In a similar fashion, Title IX and the Women's Educational Equity Act came to fruition because women demanded equality in all arenas, including the schools (Sleeter & Grant, 1994).

At the present time, however, it appears as if many of these educational victories to which I allude have been slowly and steadily eroding.

THE REVERSAL OF EDUCATIONAL FORTUNE

Although desegregation remains the order of the day (in a de jure fashion), its potential has never been fully realized. Skeptics might even contend that *Brown* was never designed to impact real and substantive change; instead it was always destined to serve as a mere symbolic representation. In any event, after approximately 40 years of desegregation, the separation of black children in America's schools remains firmly entrenched and unwavering. Nationally, more than one third of black public school students attend schools that are racially and economically segregated. In most instances, these schools' student enrollments hover around 90% to 100%

from traditionally marginalized ethnic groups (e.g., black, Latino, and Asian/Pacific Islander). In the Northeast, the country's most segregated region, half of all black students attend such schools (Kunen, 1996).

In myriad ways, the synergy of legal revisionism and residential segregation has effectively ended America's visionary efforts to integrate its public schools (Kunen, 1996). Routinely, legal rulings made (post-*Brown*) seem to send this message: "we still agree with the goal of school desegregation, but it's too hard, and we're tired of it, and we give up" (Hansen as quoted in Kunen, 1996, p. 32). Another factor that has made desegregation nearly impossible to accomplish has been white flight from major U.S. cities to the surrounding suburbs. For example, in 1972—the year blacks sued to desegregate Boston's schools—some 90,000 students were enrolled in the public school system, 54,000 of them white. As of September 1995, some 63,000 students remained, barely 18% white (Lukas, 1996, p. 34). Surprisingly, however, blame for the dismantling of desegregation cannot be solely relegated to whites because black leaders also initiated protests to end such efforts. Because black children frequently bore the brunt of desegregation plans, forced in too many instances to travel long distances to schools where they were not welcome, many black leaders felt it was incumbent on them to protect the interests of their communities and constituencies (Kunen, 1996).

Disillusionment and discontent over the missed potential of desegregation has intensified with time, and critics have even come to question the very foundation on which the case was initially based. "The whole discussion of desegregation is corrupted by the fact that we mix up race and class. You don't gain anything from sitting next to somebody with a different skin color. But you gain a lot from moving from an isolated poverty setting into a middle class setting" (Orfield as quoted in Kunen, 1996, p. 36).

Racial and economic segregation in public schools also surfaces in the teaching corps. People of color continue to comprise less than 20% of the teaching force, even at the writing of this book. "A minority teaching force of this size would mean that the average student, who has about 40 teachers during her/his precollegiate years (grades K–12), can expect at best to encounter only two teachers who are members of a minority group during her/his entire school career" (Irvine, 1991, p. 40).

As a result, many of those who will teach students of color are white, female, middle class, and have had very little direct and prolonged contact with people of color. Approximately 35% of students enrolled in the nation's public schools in 1995 were students of color (Banks, 2000). Women constitute more than 70% of the teaching corps. Further, "whereas a growing percentage of students are poor and live in large urban areas, increasing numbers of teachers are middle class and reside in small- to medium-size suburban communities" (Gay, 1993, p. 35).

In a Spring 2000 study I conducted at Montclair State University (MSU) (Paul, 2001), it was confirmed that a number of our teacher education students hold negative images of urban students and have limited exposure to such students or settings. Their negative perceptions also influence, in part, their self-described decisions not to teach in urban centers. I do not cite these study findings to suggest these students' struggles are specific to them or MSU. Instead, I present them as representative.

Most of the preservice teachers we educate need opportunities to challenge critically the misconceptions and preconceived notions they have regarding people of color and, by extension, students of color. "Attitudes and values do not develop instantaneously. It is necessary that teacher education programs provide for early, guided, cross-cultural contact beginning in the first years of college and extending throughout the program" (Hilliard, 1974, p. 50). Lack of relevant, accurate information and opportunities for critical inquiry lead to critical misunderstanding that can, in fact, manifest itself in a lack of cultural synchronization in the K–12 classroom. Culture, itself, is "emergent, contested, and consequently always in the process of being constructed, reconstructed as an historical production" (Carlson & Apple, 1998, p. 1). Thus culture plays an essential role in classrooms and schools, as it does in society at large. Cultural synchronization is a harmony established between the cultural systems of schools, diverse groups of learners, and the communities from which those learners come (Gay, 1993; Irvine, 1991). Thus teachers who are cultural outsiders to the communities in which they work many times misunderstand and misinterpret the cultural nuances present.

Another factor lending itself to the racial and economic imbalance present in today's public schools has been the home schooling movement. Some parents view home schooling as an opportunity to provide their children with one-on-one engagement and more vigorous curricula, but a number of parents use home schooling as a way to keep their children from interacting with children of other races, ethnicities, and religions, thus limiting exposure to thought and perspectives considered progressive and/or liberal. Further, no compelling data indicates that home schooling is actually more effective than attendance in the nation's better public schools or its private schools. For too many home-schooled children, there is too much variability in their curricula, no way of truly ascertaining the content they are learning, and (far too frequently) they are being taught by parents who have not been trained to deliver educational services. Unfortunately, the recently passed No Child Left Behind Act (NCLB) provides home schools with greater freedom from federal educational regulations and exempts them from all testing requirements.

After decades of revolution in America's public schools to make them more democratic and reflective of the pluralistic society in which we live, it is safe to say that "American education remains deeply undemocratic—it is segregated by race/class/gender and it serves to perpetuate inequality. It is also not geared to make the majority of students critical intellectuals" (Fraser, 1997, p. 142). Added to the difficulties that U.S. public schools have faced and are continuing to experience are the attempts of the George W. Bush administration to decimate public education through the gradual wearing away of federal funding via NCLB. Too frequently, this funding (Title I, in this instance) has traditionally benefited schools serving the neediest student populations most.

MANY CHILDREN OF COLOR LEFT BEHIND AND PUSHED OUT

H.R. 1, The No Child Left Behind Act, passed on May 23, 2001, supposedly serves as a reauthorization of the ESEA. The cornerstones of NCLB include the following:

- increased accountability for states, school districts, and schools;
- greater choice for parents and students, particularly those attending low-performing schools;
- more flexibility for states and local educational agencies (LEAs) in the use of federal education dollars;
- a stronger emphasis on reading, especially for the country's youngest children. (U.S. Department of Education, 2002)

President Bush and his secretary of education, Rod Paige, have exaggerated the results of this approach in Houston during Bush's tenure as Texas governor. The pair fails to divulge that although the number of Houston students who passed statewide achievement tests went from 44% to 64%, the gains were boosted by an "abysmal dropout rate" (Winters, 2001). Underperforming students, under constant pressure, simply surrendered and left school prematurely. A report published in 2001, by Johns Hopkins University, ranked Houston 28th in school completion out of the nation's 35 largest school districts. Less than half of ninth graders in most of Houston's schools systems failed to reach graduation (Winters, 2001).

Relatively few people would quarrel with the point that the American public education system, especially in its service to poor children and students of color, needs an overhaul. Yet they should challenge whether H.R. 1 (NCLB) is the solution. Without a doubt, the challenges faced by most public school districts (especially those servicing urban and rural areas) are numerous and vast. Among the most prominent of the problems are historic underfunding, mismanagement, and pervasive neglect; and yes, there is enough blame to go around here because the neglect emanates from both the mainstream and the various communities of color. But, while President Bush boasts that the law (NCLB) emanates from his "deep belief in our public schools" (Bush as quoted in U.S. Department of Education, 2002), the most pernicious aspects of NCLB center on the use of Title I funds to subsidize private schools and the creation of educational policy that seems to serve corporate interests rather than those of children, a silent constituency.

In the interest of fairness, however, the current law appears to modify the initial hard line taken by the White House on school vouchers. The mitigation was necessary, rather than a demonstration of goodwill, because most Democrats would not have been able to support the law in its prior state. Formerly, the White House proposed that parents who were seeking a way out of the public schools could use Title I funding to execute their plans. During that time, the media trotted out many black parents who passionately expressed their support of school vouchers. Such government subsidies would alleviate the financial burden attached to sending their children to private schools. Yet these parents often seemed unclear on the point that public schools are, by design, supportive of public interests and should not be used to subsidize private education. Additionally, such proposals could violate the constitutional clause separating church and state because four fifths of private schools have religious affiliations (Hadderman, 2000).

Most importantly, however, these parents failed to understand that private schools are frequently more successful in their efforts to educate because they have the ability to select in and select out. They do not admit "problems" (however they might be defined) or keep them, once discovered. Many private schools also require parental involvement, in the forms of both financial commitment and support of school activities. Public schools, many times, have no such mandates. Public schools must work with that which they have. They do not have the ability to deny certain children access to schooling or coerce parents to support their children's educations (in a legally protected manner, at least). For that reason, public schools in some of the most poverty-stricken areas will continue to educate America's children poorly, and in some instances, they may even do a worse job because they will not have the funds they once had to improve.

In the form of H.R. 1, parents now have the choice of removing their children from low-performing public schools (after those schools have received sufficient time to improve) and placing them in better *public* schools. Additionally, they can only use funds from Title I for the purpose of providing their children with *supplementary* educational services. These services include tutoring, after-school services, and summer school programs offered by private schools and faith-based contractors (Boehmer, 2001). At the time of this writing, NCLB fails to outline guidelines for educating special needs populations. Additionally, the sole solution the law presents for dealing with the intransigent problem of pervasive and deep-seated racism (that manifests in the form of inequitable rates of per-pupil expenditure and widespread neglect of urban schools) is to increase accountability through mandatory testing.

In the end, I predict that H.R. 1 will actually do little to improve public education aside from opening it up as a new frontier for corporate interests to control. After all, although education is a "feel good" issue that politicians routinely use to garner public support, "the real prize is the more than $100 billion dollars … spent annually in urban school districts for building construction, school supplies, textbooks, food services, testing programs, and Internet infrastructure and services" (Anderson, 2001, p. 100).

You might wonder about the connection between this discussion and the topic of black girls. For me, the relationship is quite explicit. Black children, generally, have suffered and continue to suffer in 20th- and 21st-century schools. The burden is made heavier for black girls because they are impacted by multiple oppressions in many instances. To change their educational plight, we must change the plight for *all* black children and that specific to black girls concomitantly. Further, if there is to be any recognizable change, any time soon, parents and communities must take their legitimate roles as educational partners much more seriously and return to the times past when they actually made demands of the federal government on behalf of, rather than in opposition to, the public school system.

A CRY FOR PARENTAL INVOLVEMENT

Many teachers, school administrators, and other school personnel have accepted more than their fair share of criticism regarding the failure of public schools, but many of us believe (and appropriately so) that the public, including parents, should be held accountable as well. A number of school systems seem almost synchronous in their criticism that a majority of parents/caregivers are minimally involved in their children's schooling. As a result, some public schools have opted to mandate parental involvement. Teachers, principals, and other school personnel know that children whose parents/caregivers are involved in their educations are more apt to achieve academically and feel more successful about their school performances. In an evaluation of 66 studies, researchers associated parental support with higher grades and test scores, better attendance, more homework done, fewer placements in special education, more positive attitudes and behavior, higher graduation rates, and greater enrollment in postsecondary education (Jackson & Davis, 2000, p. 196).

Yet, although the necessity of parental involvement has never been questioned, the process of defining expectations for it has traditionally proven problematic. In more than a few instances, requests made by schools for parental participation have quickly degenerated. The end result is that parents merely serve time in school rather than engaging in meaningful activities that really assist children and schools. By and large, schools would be better served if they examined their own policies, both those that are overt and hidden, in an effort to enhance parental involvement.

For example, school personnel may elect to examine the language they use when conversing with parents. For some parents, returning to school systems (via their children) that previously disenfranchised them evokes feelings of trepidation and rage. As educators, we need to think about the language we use with this group of parents, in particular, as well as the tacit messages we transmit to all parents. Is the language of school personnel jargon free? Are complex concepts explained in ways that are easy for parents/caregivers to understand? Are homework concepts introduced to parents (via workshops and instruction sheets) prior to when their children turn to them for homework help? Are parents encouraged to sit in on classes and become involved in the school community, including school decision making? Are school meetings and workshops scheduled at times when working parents can attend? Is it possible that multiple sessions of a specific meeting might be scheduled, in an effort to reach as many parents as possible? Could on-site babysitting services be provided for parents whose meeting attendance is negatively impacted because they cannot find additional child care services and/or afford them?

We must also examine the most basic social justice points surrounding this issue. For example, do parental involvement mandates preclude the participation of poor parents? Far too frequently, those who are able to spend time in school are those whose professions and lifestyles afford them the time and money to take more active roles in their children's educations. Do educators, inadvertently, send the message to poor parents that the only roles they might play in their children's academic lives are those of enforcer and/or reinforcer of school behavioral codes and expectations?

In considering how parental support might be enhanced, we must also examine whether teachers and other school personnel have received adequate training in working effectively with parents and demonstrating appropriate respect for children, their families, and communities. If there is a difficulty in this respect, it might appear more pronounced in cross-cultural exchanges. As indicated earlier, many teachers have had very little (if any) sustained contact with people from traditionally marginalized ethnic groups.

USING THE VEHICLE OF TEACHER EDUCATION TO IMPROVE THE QUALITY OF LIFE IN SCHOOLS FOR BLACK CHILDREN

"The single most important factor for achieving excellence in education is the quality of the teacher" (Michelli, 2001, p. 2). In addition to facilitating the processes of learning and teaching and demonstrating a suitable grasp of content, teachers are frequently called on to serve as culture brokers and advocates for their students of color as well. Culture brokers are defined as those "who thoroughly understand different cultural systems, [are] able to interpret cultural symbols ... mediate cultural incompatibilities, and ... establish linkages across cultures that facilitate the instructional process" (Gay, 1993, p. 37). The ability of many teachers to serve in the capacities of culture brokers and advocates is often impeded by their lack of familiarity with the cultures to which their students and their families ascribe.

> While teachers and administrators of the school may not share the same cultural perspectives as the families of minority children, the school has a clear role to play in the developmental process. Teachers and administrators seeking to be supportive of this venture toward identity development and self-understanding can help students make sense of what they see in the world; specifically the major social inequities in the United States and the evidence of racism and sexism. These are two important educational lessons for children of all colors, but even more critical for black women. (Ward, 1990, p. 229)

All of our children need a teaching corps dedicated to such struggle, one that recognizes the potentially disenfranchising nature of educational practices and policies like ability grouping, classes for the gifted and talented, national standards and curricula, special education, standardized testing, and tracking. We need teachers who are knowledgeable enough about the global community, American democracy, and their roles in relationship to and partnership with others so they refuse to perpetuate unjust and undemocratic educational practices reflective of political policies that are equivalently unjust and undemocratic. We need teachers who understand the unwieldy process of change and take their roles as change agents seriously, whether they choose to navigate it through small, yet noteworthy, modifications and/or radical reconstruction.

Well-educated persons need multiple forms of knowledge and ways in which to access that knowledge. Thus we need teachers whose educations afford them the ability to convey the concept of *access to knowledge* to their students. This ability does not translate to students' access to a minimum wage job in a neighboring suburb and/or the maintenance of the status quo. Further, it does not seek to reinforce the widening gulf between those who have and those who have not. Instead we are talking about access to full democratic participation, the ability to use one's life to change one's reality and improve the quality of life in one's community.

Far too frequently, teacher education students are herded into multicultural education courses that could, at best, be subtitled "Fat Kids That Dance," in reference to "the preponderance of ethnic cooking and dancing in this [additive curricular] approach to multicultural education" (King & Ladson-Billings, 1990, p. 23). Yet prior to respecting and appreciating the cultural affiliations others bring, one must start with the self. Teacher education students need opportunities to unpack their own distinctive cultural identities. These explorations need to occur in "safe" classroom spaces in which "meaningful, productive dialogue [can] raise consciousness and lead to effective action and social change" (Tatum, 1997, p. 193). These classroom spaces should be designed to provide students with a comfort zone in which to ask naïve questions, examine myths, and explore issues of race, without the hindrances of embarrassment or value judgments.

I would like students to have such meaningful opportunities (early in their college careers) and then be presented with occasions to serve in community agencies, schools, and social service agencies, paired with seminar classes during which they work toward understanding and processing those experiences with a pedagogically skilled mentor. In this way, they might potentially be able to realize the humanity, strength, and resilience present in the communities, families, and children they will ultimately go on to serve. The pairing of the immersion experience with debriefing sessions is of paramount importance because the experience alone could produce the reverse response, reinforcing the prejudice or stereotype rather than plausibly eliminating it (Ladson-Billings, 1995).

And now let's move forward and discuss the creation of safe school spaces for black girls. In this instance, safe space "speaks to legitimacy, and, in this sense, describes an ideological space where a student can belong, feel at home, and be free from bias, stereotypes, and harassment. Schools and classrooms that accept and understand an individual's ways of knowing, thinking and being can be such places. A hospitable place for learning is a place where a girl can be herself and pursue her work in comfort" (Hansen et al., 1995a, p. 18).

SAFE SCHOOL SPACES THAT ENHANCE THE DEVELOPMENT OF BLACK GIRLS

The difficulties that black girls encounter in schools have been well documented in this book and other scholarly venues. Next we focus on what schools can do to improve academic life for black children, generally, and black girls specifically.

Most are in full agreement concerning the definite need for school improvement. But authentic school change is not initiated with toothless education reform policies disseminated from the White House. Real school change involves the efforts of many, at many different levels. It involves grassroots efforts, as well as those that are organized and systematic. It also results from a heartfelt need and the belief that all of our children rather than a select few deserve quality educations.

Black girls specifically need to attend schools that focus on their empowerment, teaching them to voice and give legitimacy to their thoughts, speak for themselves, and recognize the multitude of options possible in their lives (Office of Juvenile Justice and Delinquency Prevention, 1998). Additionally, black girls need to attend schools that emphasize a future orientation. "An orientation toward the future serves as a protective factor by allowing girls to see beyond immediate life circumstances" (Office of Juvenile Justice and Delinquency Prevention, 1998). Girls who value and strive toward educational achievement tend to possess a compelling sense of the future (Benard, 1993).

For black girls to reach optimal levels of academic success (that cannot be ascertained through mere test scores alone), innovative learning strategies must be implemented and schools must assist students to envision the setting as an academic community. Black girls must also be prepared to

assume their rightful roles as authentic members of that academic community. In that sense, curriculum needs to reflect and mirror adequately
the values, experiences, and contributions of women and traditionally disenfranchised ethnic groups (Office of Juvenile Justice and Delinquency
Prevention, 1998).

In classrooms, cooperative learning should be encouraged and focus on
the collective good emphasized. K–12 students should receive opportunities to work collaboratively as often as possible. For decades, educators
have been told we must prepare people who are able to compete in the
workforce, and we have accepted the unjust criticism from industry that
we ill-prepare workers. In my estimation, the criticism is unfair because it
is frequently made without a clear understanding that the workplace has
changed. For most corporate entities, the values encouraged center on
teamwork and cooperation. If we are called to truly prepare people for success in their work lives, we must continue to teach them strategies for
working effectively as a unit.

A tangential point centers on the size of most urban center schools and
classes. Too frequently, black girls attend schools and classes that are
overcrowded and foster an atmosphere of namelessness and anonymity.
Too many times, girls who resist school rules and act out are more apt to
be recognized than those girls who follow the rules and might be described
as model students, when both sets of girls are in need of nurturing and
development.

"The key principle is to create groupings of students and educators
small enough to stimulate the development of close, supportive relationships" (Jackson & Davis, 2000, p. 123) A growing body of research documents the advantages of small schools for all students.

> Small schools tend to be safer, to have higher attendance rates, and to have
> better participation rates in a wide range of activities; at a high school level,
> they have significantly lower dropout rates. [Small schools] are repeatedly
> found to benefit students' achievement, attitude toward school social behav-
> ior, interpersonal relationships, self-esteem, and feelings of 'belonging-
> ness.' In addition, teachers' attitudes and collaboration are more positive in
> small schools than in large ones. Students from low-income families have
> been found to benefit the most from being educated in small schools. (Jack-
> son & Davis, 2000, p. 124)

We must also present black girls with opportunities to work with challenging subject matter, and teachers must have the expectation that they
will achieve with the proper educational guidance. Counselors as well

need to suggest high-level classes and express high expectations for girls. Traditionally, schools have emphasized success in literacy development and the humanities for girls, at the expense of their proficiency in mathematics and science. Although current data suggests that the gap between female and male students (in respect to achievement in science and mathematics) is closing for the mainstream population, it remains firmly in place for black girls. In order to tackle this problem, we (in the academic arena must devise creative ways to address the exclusion of black girls who choose to pursue study in mathematics, science, and engineering. For example, some school programs have worked "in partnerships with mathematics, science, and engineering clubs for minority students at colleges and universities" (Adenika-Morrow, 1996). "Undergraduate participants of these clubs provide high school girls with experiences with college students who look like them and have had similar experiences" (Adenika-Morrow, 1996). Study findings suggest that this approach is successful.

Black girls need opportunities to become computer literate in a sophisticated fashion. "A competitive nation cannot allow girls to write off technology as exclusively male domain. Teachers will need to be prepared to deal with this issue" (Ford, 1998, p. viii). Once again, although research suggests the gender gap is closing between white girls and white boys, the gap remains clearly intact for black students.

Within any respective school setting, all members of the school community (e.g., principals, teachers, counselors, school nurses, psychologists, social workers, secretaries, custodians, and others) need to communicate an ethic of care and nurturance to girls (Hansen et al., 1995b, p. 3). Schools need to emphasize the total health and well-being of their students.

In the American Association of University Women's commissioned study *Girls in the Middle: Working to Succeed in School* (1996), the researchers suggest that middle school girls use three consistent strategies for navigating the school terrain. Those strategies include the following:

- Speaking out: tending to assert themselves, speaking out and insisting on being heard in both friendly and unfriendly circumstances.
- Doing school: Some girls behave in ways that have been traditionally expected of them in school, doing what is asked and speaking in turn.
- Crossing borders: Girls crossing borders between different cultures or sets of norms and expectations may achieve success in school and with peers as well as in their communities, becoming proficient in two or more codes of speech and behavior and gaining stature as "schoolgirls/cool girls." (Research for Action, 1996, pp. 14–15)

"School adults need to notice the different ways that girls negotiate school. This requires observing girls in hallways and classrooms, asking girls questions, attending to girls' voices. It is also important that adults understand girls' needs to try out strategies in the process of forming identities and recognize that girls' strategies may shift" (Research for Action, 1996, pp. 14–15). In addition to strategies for achieving academic success, girls need intervention and leadership strategies (e.g., problem solving, assertive communication, efficacious decision making, conflict resolution skills, and peer mediation strategies) for navigating this society. For black girls, in particular, they must learn to cope with multiple oppressions and concomitantly still succeed. School adults also need to model critical thought, reflection, and critical consciousness. They must model effective problem solving and encourage inquiry.

Chapter 8

EPILOGUE

Bringing the gifts that my ancestors gave, I am the dream and hope of the slave. I rise
I rise
I rise.

—Maya Angelou, poet and scholar
(as quoted in Tamara Nikuradse's *My Mother Had a Dream:
African American Women Share Their Mothers'
Words of Wisdom* and excerpted from the presidential
inaugural poem "Still I Rise")

Fully engaged in the last stages of completing this book, I have tried to anticipate criticisms and determine whether I have missed any essential points. Although most of these potential criticisms are easily dismissed (in my mind at least), one remains omnipresent. Will some contend that this book is anachronistic? Will there be bafflement about the virtual need to teach black girls to resist racism in a society that some believe has effectively conquered its racist past? To a certain extent, my concern is irrational. After all, this book is not written for people who hold such views, and, based on the title alone, they would not have cause to read my thoughts.

Yet clearly there will be those who choose to read this work solely to dissect it and attempt to prove its premises flawed. There will be those who actually believe that discussions of racism, such as those contained within this book, are shortsighted and naïve. This group will point to the increases in interracial marriages and the children produced from such unions, as if to suggest that the issues of race and racism have totally dissipated. They will cite the black middle class that rose during the 1990s, but it is falling just as quickly during the new millennium. In most instances, this group will inadvertently overlook black unemployment rates that are presently skyrocketing and other such indicators that suggest the black middle class just might be losing ground.

Some of this book's critics might even express the belief that discussions of racism are downright retrograde and unpatriotic, especially as we, the United States, have entered a manufactured war with a brown, collective enemy. If we, as a nation, are focused on an "exotic" and murderous brown enemy, we might ignore the increasing poverty the nation is experiencing or accept the fact that many citizens here are worse off since the Bush administration was selected into office.

At the basest level of acknowledgment, one must admit that racism is not as blatant a practice as it once was. Some limited progress has been made in respect to race relations in the United States. Yet make no mistake: Racism is just as insidious a practice as it ever was, although, at present, it takes a more subtly nuanced and high-tech form. In contemporary society, race (when used by the mainstream) "has become metaphorical—a way of referring to and disguising forces, events, classes, and expressions of social decay and economic division far more threatening to the body politic than biological 'race' ever was" (Morrison, 1992, p. 63). There are now code words that signify blackness, even though blackness itself remains unmentioned (Paul, 2001). For example, "welfare," "affirmative action," "quotas rather than excellence," "angry," "criminal," and "homeless" all seem to equate with blackness in the contemporary American psyche. These images of blackness remain fixed in the minds of politicians and their constituents as they institute insouciant policy initiatives (Paul, 2001).

Text and talk constitute the social and political dimensions of structural racism in present-day society (Smitherman & van Dijk, 1988). In this sense, "talk and text not only may hurt you, they also may hurt you more effectively, more systematically, and more permanently (Smitherman & van Dijk, 1988, p. 11). Talk, text, and the presentation of racialized images impact public policy.

The new form of racism makes this book relevant and practical. Black girls must be taught to create new visions of progress and success for themselves. They must learn that the neglect from which they suffer is not because they are deficient in some way. Instead they must learn it is society that is deficient. They must learn to navigate this society while remaining emotionally intact and spiritually healthy. This book, *Talkin' Back: Raising and Educating Resilient Black Girls,* is my contribution toward such an effort. Using the book as a vehicle, I have tried to emphasize the ways in which families, community agencies, and schools can work to ensure that subsequent generations of black girls achieve greater degrees of success than their forebears did. All of us must work together to make certain that black girls receive the same opportunities and attention that their contemporaries do.

APPENDIX A:
A RESOURCE GUIDE

SUGGESTED CHILDREN'S BOOKS FEATURING BLACK FEMALE PROTAGONISTS

A number of the book selections listed here are taken from my previous book, *Raising Black Children Who Love Reading and Writing: A Guide from Birth Through Grade Six* (2000a). The compilation of the original list represented a collective effort. In our opinion, the books on that list were the very best children's literature had to offer.

In this book, I have significantly modified and shaped that initial list so it more accurately reflects the distinctive focus on black girls in the middle school grades (5–8). In consideration of literary merit, cultural authenticity, and personal predilection, I have added new selections. Some of the students in my class "READ 400—Initial Inquiry into Literacy Development" (Fall 2002 semester) shared selections that they read and wrote summaries for me. I especially wish to thank Francesca Amato, Stephanie Burke, and Diana DeCarlo.

However, as the author, I am solely responsible for this book's content. Any omissions or questionable choices were based on a great deal of thought and sound rationales.

This annotated list emphasizes the connection among all of the African diaspora and therefore includes the stories of children and their families throughout Africa, the Caribbean, and South America.

Poetry

Brown Honey in Broomwheat Tea
Author: Joyce Carol Thomas
Illustrator: Floyd Cooper
Publication Date: 1993

This book features a beautiful collection of poems about family, individuality, and pride of heritage. Told from a young girl's perspective, the narrator admonishes us to love ourselves and be proud of who we are. She is young, spirited, and happy! The poems discuss her mother, father, and sister, as well as the vicissitudes of life and the careful choice of the place one occupies in the world. Floyd Cooper's paintings will capture the hearts of readers.

Picture Storybooks

Aida
Author: Leontyne Price
Illustrators: Leo and Diane Dillon
Publication Date: 1990

Opera singer Leontyne Price lends a skillful hand to this retelling of Verdi's opera of the same name. Ethiopian princess Aida falls in love with Radames, an Egyptian general. Yet the love shared between the two ultimately ends in tragedy. The colorful, glossy pages of this picture storybook superbly depict the honor, beauty, courage, and emotion of its central characters.

Amazing Grace
Author: Mary Hoffman
Illustrator: Caroline Binch
Publication Date: 1991

Grace, a young girl who loves stories and imaginative play, wants to play the lead in the school play, *Peter Pan*. Yet Grace's schoolmates tell her she can't because she is black and a girl. Ultimately, Grace comes to realize that she can do anything she sets her mind to. Hoffman has created a strong and confident character in Grace, who does not allow society to define her identity or her dreams. She believes in herself, and a supportive family encourages her.

Aunt Flossie's Hats (and Crab Cakes Later)
Author: Elizabeth Fitzgerald Howard
Illustrator: James Ransome
Publication Date: 1991

Sarah and Susan love to visit Great-Great-Aunt Flossie on Sunday afternoons. Each unique hat of Aunt Flossie's that the girls try on reminds her of a time past. The elder and younger generations enjoy time together through the sharing of tea, cookies, crab cakes, and stories. The illustrations in this book, oil paintings, are outstanding.

Chicken Sunday
Author/Illustrator: Patricia Polacco
Publication Date: 1992

Following church each Sunday morning, Miss Eula Mae, her grandsons Stewart and Winston, and their special neighbor and adopted sister always enjoy a delicious chicken dinner together. In appreciation of those special times provided by Miss Eula, the children decide to sell decorated eggs so they can buy her a hat she has longed for. In the process, the children are accused of a wrongful act in their neighborhood and must prove their innocence. The concepts of familial love, devotion, acceptance, and the worth of one's reputation are particularly noteworthy in this story.

Cornrows
Author: Camille Yarbrough
Illustrator: Carole Byard
Publication Date: 1979

Great Grammaw shares history with her family as they inquire about the artistry involved in her hair cornrowing. She lovingly recounts her own memories, as well as those of her ancestors, and simultaneously elucidates the history of braids. This story reflects the pride and beauty of black people. The illustrations, completed in black and white, present soft, fluid, and loving representations of blackness.

The Day Gogo Went to Vote: South Africa, 1994
Author: Elinor Batezat Sisula
Illustrator: Sharon Wilson
Publication Date: 1996

This wonderful story is told from the perspective of a young girl living in Soweto at the time of its first democratic election. Thembi becomes an active participant in her great-grandmother's first voting experience. This is a story of frustrations, struggle, joy, and ultimately respect. Through this picture storybook, the reader simultaneously shares in South Africa's contemporary history and experiences the warm, intergenerational ties shared between child and great-grandparent.

Flossie and the Fox
Author: Patricia C. McKissack
Illustrator: Rachel Isadora
Publication Date: 1986

In this story, which is quite reminiscent of the traditional "Little Red Riding Hood," the wolf meets up with and is outsmarted by the intelligent and sassy Flossie. Set in the American South and told in black English vernacular, this amusing tale is a joy to read.

Goin' Someplace Special
Author: Patricia C. McKissack
Publication Date: 2001

Tricia Ann, a young black girl growing up in segregated Nashville, Tennessee, loves to go to her "special place." On her way to her special place, Tricia faces the prejudice, ridicule, and embarrassment associated with the Jim Crow laws that ruled the day. It is hard to cope with being relegated to the back of the bus and not sitting on certain benches because she is black. Yet, in spite of the fact that these laws hurt her, they cannot suppress her spirit or stop her from going to her special place. Holding her head high and staring in the face of adversity, she makes her way.

Grandpa's Face
Author: Eloise Greenfield
Illustrator: Floyd Cooper
Publication Date: 1988

Tamika and her grandfather share a special relationship. One day during Grandpa's play rehearsal, she sees a side of him she has never seen before. As a result, Tamika becomes afraid she will lose her grandfather's love one day. Perhaps one of this book's most distinguishing features is the wonderful illustrations. They are so vivid and realistic, they seem to leap off the page.

Happy to Be Nappy
Author: bell hooks
Illustrator: Chris Raschka
Publication Date: 1999

Black hair has been and remains a controversial topic in the black community. But hooks does a masterful job of treating it with dignity and respect in this book for young primary readers. Her beautiful, melodic descriptions prompted this author's daughter to announce, "Mom, I like this book because our hair is good in this book!"

I Like Me!
Author: Deborah Connor Coker
Illustrator: Keaf Holliday
Publication Date: 1995

Nia has a bright smile and an enthusiasm for everything she does. From ballet to running races, Nia enjoys herself and likes her life. She is versatile and cheerful. Children will like her instantly and identify with her genuine qualities.

I Love My Hair!
Author: Natasha Anastasia Tarpley
Illustrator: E. B. Lewis
Publication Date: 1998

Young Keyana loves the distinctiveness of her hair. She is able to wear it in braids, ponytails, or an afro. Her hair is a great source of pride for her and a rich reminder of her heritage.

Jamaica's Find
Author: Juanita Havill
Illustrator: Anne Sibley O'Brien
Publication Date: 1986

Jamaica finds a worn and seemingly much-loved stuffed animal in the park. She decides to keep him. With the help of her family, however, Jamaica learns lessons about loss and empathy. Ultimately, she must decide whether or not the toy should be returned.

Just Us Women
Author: Jeanette Caines
Illustrator: Pat Cummings
Publication Date: 1982

In this simple and straightforward tale, the young narrator and her Aunt Martha take a road trip to North Carolina in Aunt Martha's brand-new car. Along the way, they encounter new and exciting adventures. The illustrations are absolutely stunning in their detail.

Ma Dear's Aprons
Author: Patricia C. McKissack
Illustrator: Floyd Cooper
Publication Date: 1997

A testament to the life of Leanna Crossley Bowens (McKissack's great-grandmother) is lovingly presented in this fictional tribute. Her young son David Earl tells the story of Jonelle, a domestic worker at the turn of the 20th century, as he remembers the daily tasks associated with each distinctive apron she wore. In her customary way, McKissack also presents information on racism and responses to it in a dignified and subtle manner. The beautifully nuanced and textured artistry of Floyd Cooper complements the text.

Me and Neesie
Author: Eloise Greenfield
Publication Date: 1975

Through her invisible friend Neesie, young Janell lives out her fears, joys, and life changes. Because most children have imaginary friends (at one point or the other), many readers will compare and relate Janell and Neesie's adventures to their own.

Mirandy and Brother Wind
Author: Patricia C. McKissack
Illustrator: Jerry Pinkney
Publication Date: 1988

Mirandy is looking for a dance partner for the upcoming cakewalk and sets her sights on Brother Wind. She establishes an elaborate plan to ensure that she secures her partner and wins the cakewalk. But just how does one cajole the wind?

Mufaro's Beautiful Daughters
Author/Illustrator: John Steptoe
Publication Date: 1987

Through the genre of fable, the story is told of Mufaro's two beautiful daughters, Manyara, who is ill tempered, and Nyasha, who is sweet and kind. The two venture before the king, who is attempting to choose a wife. Steptoe magnificently captures the essence of African culture and people. Based on the landscape of Zimbabwe and the faces of family members, Steptoe's illustrations are brought to life. The golden landscapes, fuchsia skies, and emerald green forests create a vision of Africa in the reader's mind.

My Painted House, My Friendly Chicken and Me
Author: Maya Angelou
Photographer: Margaret Courtney-Clarke
Publication Date: 1994

This wonderful book explores the rich culture and tradition of the small South African village of Ndeble through the eyes of 8-year-old Thandi. Thandi lives with her mother, her aunts, her brother, and her best friend, a chicken. Angelou's prose and Courtney-Clarke's photos truly capture the wonderful aesthetic beauty of the small village. The combination of the two elements enables readers to experience the art, culture, and social dimensions of Ndebele from an insightful, fresh perspective.

No Mirrors in My Nana's House
Author: Ysaye M. Barnwell
Illustrator: Synthia Saint James
Publication Date: 1998

This book is a visual feast to behold! Synthia Saint James's use of brilliant and vivid color brings life to Barnwell's text, which focuses on the loving intergenerational relationship shared between a young girl and her nana. In her nana's eyes, she sees her reflection, a reflection filled with beauty, hope, and possibility.

The Patchwork Quilt
Author: Valerie Flournoy
Illustrator: Jerry Pinkney
Publication Date: 1985

By helping her grandmother make a family quilt, young Tanya comes to realize the quilt is more than a simple blanket. It represents her family history. The wonderful watercolors used in this book's illustrations aptly depict the characters' individuality and sense of self through the use of diverse hairstyles, hair colors, and skin hues. A strong family bond is further expressed and the family unit esteemed in this loving portrait.

The Story of Ruby Bridges
Author: Robert Coles
Illustrator: George Ford
Publication Date: 1995

Based on a true story, this picture storybook shares the story of a little first-grade girl placed in the position of integrating an all-white school in New Orleans during the tumultuous 1960s. The inner strength this youngster possesses is both haunting and uncanny. She appears nearly unaffected by the negativity that surrounds her. She is able to move forward, in spite of threats, jeers, and harassment.

Sukey and the Mermaid
Author: Robert San Souci
Illustrator: Brian Pinkney
Publication Date: 1992

One warm afternoon, Sukey escapes from her abusive stepfather, Mister Jones, to the water's edge where she sings a song she has heard. In response to the song, Mama Jo (a mermaid) appears. The friendship between Mama Jo and Sukey alters both lives permanently. This story is based on an early African American folktale about mermaids. The illustrations vividly capture its magical setting. Readers of all ages will enjoy this tale.

Sweet Clara and the Freedom Quilt
Author: Deborah Hopkinson
Illustrator: James Ransome
Publication Date: 1993

Sukey has separated Clara from her mother, but she is determined to reunite with her one day and escape North to freedom. As a seamstress, Clara is recruited to sew a "freedom quilt," which ultimately serves as a map and guides Clara and other slaves to freedom. Clara's resourcefulness and courage make this story an inspirational and educational chapter in African American history.

Tar Beach
Author/Illustrator: Faith Ringgold
Publication Date: 1996

Young Cassie's vivid imagination enables her to fly. Her flight allows her to own pieces of New York City, which she generously shares with her family. Her fantastic travels and magic powers allow her to fondly recount times spent with family and friends on "tar beach," in addition to potentially righting the wrongs of discrimination and racism.

Tell Me a Story, Mama
Author: Angela Johnson
Illustrator: David Soman
Publication Date: 1989

A young girl loves to hear stories of Mama growing up, whether she was getting into mischief or finding a puppy. She likes these tales so much that she finishes them for Mama. Fortunately, Mama does not mind. This engaging story emphasizes the bond between parent and child, as well as the importance of passing the oral tradition from one generation to the next.

Two Mrs. Gibsons
Author: Toyomi Igus
Illustrator: Daryl Wells
Publication Date: 1996

This story is about the two Mrs. Gibsons a young girl loves. Throughout the book, she describes both of the women and their close relationship. The older Mrs. Gibson has "chocolate" skin, sings with the girl at church, and gives big hugs. The other Mrs. Gibson has "vanilla" skin, writes in Japanese, and cooks food from Japan. The young narrator explains that she loves both of these women, even though they seem very different. The book is exciting because of the quasi-mystery element of figuring out the women's relationship to the girl. It keeps readers engaged and very interested in the outcome.

What I Want to Be
Author: P. Mignon Hinds
Illustrator: Cornelius Van Wright
Publication Date: 1995

Maya loves to visit her grandmother. She has fun rummaging through an old trunk. Everything she finds reminds her of something she might want to be when she grows up. From archaeologist to underwater scientist to firefighter to dress designer, Maya imagines herself busy at work. Her grandmother reminds her that she can be whatever she chooses, but she should always do her personal best.

What Mary Jo Shared
Author: Janice May Udry
Illustrator: Elizabeth Sayles
Publication Date: 1966, 1991

Shy Mary Jo tried diligently to work up the nerve to share something different from the other children in her class for show-and-tell. Each time she decides on something, another student seems to get the same idea. Finally, Mary Jo decides to share one of her most prized and valued possessions.

INTERMEDIATE CHAPTER BOOKS

Book of Black Heroes, Vol. 2: Great Women in the Struggle
Authors: Toyomi Igus, Veronica Freeman Ellis, Diane Patrick, and Valerie Wilson
        Wesley
Publication Date: 1991

Great Women in the Struggle is a resource guide that outlines the accomplishments of black women. The book includes brief biographical sketches of well-known figures like Rosa Parks, Harriet Tubman, and Madame C. J. Walker, and it also includes lesser known women (for many young readers at least) like civil rights activist Fannie Lou Hamer, African queen-warrior Nzingha, and the first black woman lawyer, Charlotte E. Ray. It is a fine contribution to black history for the young.

The Gift Giver
Author: Joyce Hansen
Publication Date: 1980

After reading this book, readers will understand how the qualities of friendship, patience, and tolerance can enhance their lives. The plot revolves around Doris, a fifth grader, who lives in the Bronx and befriends a boy, Amir, living in a neighborhood foster home. These two special children learn from, as well as give to, each other. The story is realistically told and destined to evoke emotion.

Ida B. Wells-Barnett: A Voice Against Violence
Author: Patricia and Frederick McKissack
Publication Date: 1991

Crusader for justice and believer in the might of the pen, Ida Wells-Barnett's life story is introduced to young readers. The authors McKissack aptly present Wells-Barnett as a courageous and intelligent woman, deeply committed to liberation for blacks that extended beyond mere physical fetters. In this easy-to-read book, Wells-Barnett is also presented as a model for young readers to emulate and one who prompted social and political change through the use of literacy.

I Thought My Soul Would Rise and Fly: The Diary of Patsy, a Freed Girl
Author: Joyce Hansen
Publication Date: 1997

In this amazing narrative, Hansen presents us with a rare find in the preadolescent Patsy, an orphaned protagonist who stutters and was born with a limp. The ratification of the Thirteenth Amendment and the abolishment of slavery in the United States were difficult for adult slaves to process because the concept of freedom and its implications were new to them. It was even more difficult for young Patsy. She must struggle with her desires to belong to a family, protect her newfound literacy abilities, and challenge the popular notions regarding disability, in addition to making sense of freedom's distinctive dimensions and the ways in which they will change her life. Through Patsy, Hansen skillfully leads readers to examine their views on self-definition, intellect, and family (all within the context of a little-studied period in children's literature).

Last Summer with Maizon
Author: Jacqueline Woodson
Publication Date: 1990

Eleven-year-old Margaret Tory grapples with life's harsh truths as she struggles to accept her father's death and her best friend's departure to boarding school. Both life-altering experiences occur during the same summer. These experiences also help Margaret discover her own strengths and develop a sense of self-reliance.

Phoebe the Spy
Author: Judith Berry Griffin
Publication Date: 1977

During the American Revolution, a young Phoebe is sent to General George Washington's home to discover the identity of the man planning to kill him. Phoebe, frightened and unsure, watches and listens, ultimately saving General Washington's life. Phoebe's courage and initiative should prove inspirational for all children.

A Picture of Freedom: The Diary of Clotee, A Slave Girl
Author: Patricia C. McKissack
Publication Date: 1997

Part of the *Dear America* series, *A Picture of Freedom* presents a complex and sophisticated view of slavery and places a human face on its ravages. McKissack consistently demonstrates a gift for presenting the harsh historical truth of slavery in a manner that is palatable for young readers. Through the young eyes of the intelligent and strong Clotee, the reader learns about the power of literacy and the significant resistance movement that helped the enslaved escape slavery.

Thank You, Dr. Martin Luther King Jr.!
Author: Eleanora Tate
Publication Date: 1990

Mary Elouise envies her classmate, Brandy. A chocolate-brown Mary Elouise wishes that she had Brandy's blond hair and blue eyes. Very early in life, Mary Elouise has realized that Brandy is considered beautiful and she is not (according to society's standards). Through performance in the school play and the nurturing guidance of Miz Imani, Mary Elouise must take a more loving look at herself and question the societal concept of beauty and femininity.

Whose Side Are You On?

Author: Emily Moore

Publication Date: 1988

Barbra is failing in math until her nemesis, T.J., assists by tutoring her. Through this act of kindness, Barbra begins to see T.J. in a different light, and first love begins to bloom as well.

YOUNG ADULT BOOKS

Black Ice

Author: Lorene Cary

Publication Date: 1991

In the form of autobiographical narrative, Cary describes her transition (in 1971) from the Philadelphia school system to the exclusive and prestigious St. Paul's boarding school in New Hampshire. Along with the usual angst that comes with adolescence, Cary must adapt to her new environment and make sense of her learnings on the interworkings of race, class, gender, and power.

Blue Tights

Author: Rita Williams-Garcia

Publication Date: 1988

Fifteen-year-old Joyce Collins has her heart set on being a dancer, but she faces constant criticisms and self-recriminations regarding the African-ness of her body and dance style. Through participation in an African dance troupe, Joyce faces some important self-truths that affect the way she sees dance and herself.

The Dear One

Author: Jacqueline Woodson

Publication Date: 1991

Twelve-year-old Afeni, a Swahili name that means "dear one," is coping with her parents' divorce and her grandmother's death when her mother informs her that a college friend's 15-year-old daughter will be living with them until the girl delivers her baby. Afeni is angry that she will have to share both her mother and her bedroom with Rebecca. *The Dear One* is a textured novel that illuminates the differences between Afeni's suburban life and Rebecca's urban one, as well as broaches the topic of teen pregnancy both thoughtfully and realistically.

Freedom Songs

Author: Yvette Moore

Publication Date: 1991

During the spring and summer of 1963, 14-year-old Northerner Sheryl Williams's life is forever altered, with her mother's dream and a trip South. With that trip and exposure to her Uncle Pete, Sheryl starts to understand the harsh injustices associated with Jim Crow segregation and racism. She also starts to understand the role she can potentially play in the political change process. At the same time, she learns a great deal about herself—both her strengths and weaknesses.

The Friends

Author: Rosa Guy

Publication Date: 1973

Phyllisia, newly immigrated from the Caribbean, cultivates an understanding of herself in the midst of dealing with the harsh realities of unsympathetic classmates, a mother battling breast cancer, and an insensitive father. She must also come to terms with her own newly forged identity as a Caribbean American.

I Hadn't Meant to Tell You This

Author: Jacqueline Woodson

Publication Date: 1994

In an interesting reversal for children's and adolescent fiction, Marie (a popular middle-class black girl) forms an unlikely friendship with a poor and troubled white girl named Lena. The loss of their mothers draws the girls to each other and helps them support one another through trying times. One of those trying times, however, threatens to destroy the relationship they share. A good book leaves its reader wanting more. In this case, Woodson's book does just that.

Journey to Jo'burg

Author: Beverly Naidoo

Publication Date: 1986

Determined to find their mother and inform her of their baby sister's grave illness, Naledi and her younger brother, Tiro, journey from their small South African village to the metropolis of Johannesburg. The excursion results in a number of revelations about apartheid and the realities associated with life as black South Africans during a time of siege.

Like Sisters on the Homefront

Author: Rita Williams-Garcia

Publication Date: 1995

Fourteen-year-old mother Gayle gets a wake-up call when her mother gets fed up and sends her (with a one-way ticket) South to live with her religious aunt and her family in a small rural town. On this personal journey, Gayle learns a great deal about life, compassion, and the depth of love.

Plain City

Author: Virginia Hamilton

Publication Date: 1993

Twelve-year-old Buhlaire Marie Sims is having difficulty fitting in. She feels that people are judging her because of where she lives, how she looks, and her mom's risqué profession. Most importantly, however, she feels there is something missing in her life—knowledge about her father, who she believes is missing in action in Vietnam. In trying to find out more about her father, Buhlaire learns a great deal about herself.

Rainbow Jordan
Author: Alice Childress
Publication Date: 1981

All at once, 14-year-old Rainbow must cope with an unreliable mother, the demands of growing up female, and her own burgeoning sexuality. Yet, in the process, she also learns to accept love and cultivate an understanding of interdependence. Rainbow and her foster mother, Miss Josie, must discover ways in which to rely on one another, if they are to make it safely through the tough times in life.

Roll of Thunder, Hear My Cry
Author: Mildred Taylor
Publication Date: 1976

Nine-year-old Cassie Logan narrates the story of her family during one year in Depression-era Mississippi. The events encompass school, a wayward friend, and the start of a cooperative. At the heart of these events is the racism that confronts the Logans on a daily basis, each family member's individual and varied response, and the family's resolve to remain strong and viable. Taylor's understated writing belies the power of Cassie's story and will leave readers pensive regarding the issues addressed and the ways in which they would respond or have responded in similar situations.

Ruby
Author: Rosa Guy
Publication Date: 1976

This book is profound and ahead of its time in the world of young adult fiction. Eighteen-year-old Ruby Cathy meets the girl of her dreams in Daphne Duprey, who is young, sophisticated, and selfish. Ruby experiences all of the passion of first love, but she must also cope with the dilemma of coming out and revealing her forbidden affair.

The Shimmershine Queens
Author: Camille Yarbrough
Publication Date: 1989

Ten-year-old Angie has to cope with classmates who pick on her, a mother who is depressed, and the other pressures associated with simply being a child. It seems like things will never get any better until Cousin Seatta arrives and shares some words of wisdom. Those simple words about self-love and pride in one's heritage change Angie's entire outlook on life. It might prove beneficial for parents to peruse this book first because some might object to the language used.

Sojourner Truth: Ain't I a Woman?
Authors: Patricia C. McKissack and Frederick McKissack

Publication Date: 1992

The respect is evident in the McKissacks' biographies both for the young readers in their audience and the subject (in this instance Sojourner Truth). Much of what most readers know about Truth centers on her involvement in the first wave of the women's rights movement and her speeches against slavery. Yet there was so much more. In this work, readers develop an admiration for Truth as a woman, a mother, and a person of great intellect and courage. In this well-written chronicle, the authors present their readers with a wealth of information on Truth, Truth's contemporaries, and the time period.

Stitching Stars

Author: Mary E. Lyons

Publication Date: 1993

As a biography of African American quilter Harriet Power, the history of quilting and its significance is explored. Through this book, we learn as much about the art of quilting as we do about the life history of Harriet Powers. For women like Powers, each quilt served as a story being retold. The craftsmanship and beauty captured the folktales and religious stories told through the quilts.

Toning the Sweep

Author: Angela Johnson

Publication Date: 1993

Three generations of black women come together, and each holds on to a separate truth about life, death, and themselves. Emmie and her mother, Diane, travel to the desert to bring her grandmother back home with them. Ola, however, is suffering from terminal cancer. During the trip, Emmie comes to the end of her childhood, the beginning of womanhood, the connection that exists in families, and the power of friendship.

Young, Black, and Determined: A Biography of Lorraine Hansberry

Authors: Patricia and Frederick McKissack

Publication Date: 1998

In this skillfully done biography, the McKissacks present a loving and dignified portrait of Lorraine Hansberry, black intellectual and advocate for social justice. Intensive research obviously shaped this book, and the high regard with which the McKissacks apparently hold their young readers is very evident.

APPENDIX B:
RESOURCES FOR CAREGIVERS
AND TEACHERS

Culturally Responsive Teaching: Theory, Research & Practice
Author: Geneva Gay
Publication Date: 2000

Gay provides educators with theory, research, and pragmatic practices for educators interested in improving the school performance of underachieving students in U.S. public schools. With its personal stories and interesting examples, this book proves a wonderful resource and a practical guide.

Different and Wonderful: Raising Black Children in a Race-Conscious Society
Authors: Darlene Powell Hopson and Derek S. Hopson
Publication Date: 1990

In this sensitively written book, the Hopsons (practicing psychologists and parents) share their insights on raising black children who are able to appreciate the multiple ways in which their blackness might prove affirming. The Hopsons provide parents/caregivers with quizzes, practical tools, and parenting anecdotes that make the job of parenting black children easier.

*I'm Chocolate, You're Vanilla: Raising Healthy Black and Biracial Children in a
   Race-Conscious World*
Author: Marguerite A. Wright
Publication Date: 1998

For some readers, the views expressed in *I'm Chocolate, You're Vanilla* may be far too conservative. In some instances, it appears as if the significance of race is being downplayed. Yet Wright's experience as a clinical psychologist (working frequently with children and their families) and the practical advice she offers makes the book a worthwhile read.

Kids Who Succeed: The No-Nonsense Guide to Raising a Child Who'll Be a Winner in Tomorrow's World
Author: Beverly Neuer Feldman
Publication Date: 1987

In *Kids Who Succeed*, Dr. Feldman does a skillful job of providing caregivers with uncomplicated techniques for raising children with the skills and dispositions vital for success in contemporary society. Through the use of practical tips, games, and tasks, as well as commonsense measures, Feldman's book serves as a wonderful aid to parents and caregivers.

A Mentor Manual for Adults Who Work with Pregnant and Parenting Teens
Authors: Frederick H. Kanfer, Susan Englund, Claudia Lennhoff, and Jean
        Rhodes
Publication Date: 1995

The complex responsibility of mentoring is laid out in simple and easy steps in this informative guide. Kanfer et al. take their readers through all the necessary dimensions of relationship building from the development of trust to jump-starting a stalled relationship with one's mentee.

*Money Doesn't Grow on Trees: A Parent's Guide to Raising Financially Respon-
        sible Children*
Author: Neale S. Godfrey with Carolina Edwards
Publication Date: 1994

In this invaluable guide on teaching children and teens money management strategies, Godfrey does an incredible job of introducing the most basic concepts (e.g., determining allowance) as well as more sophisticated skills like acquiring stocks and bonds. Founder of the First Children's Bank and an expert on family finances, Godfrey presents a wealth of information in this must-have book.

*Overcoming the Odds: Raising Academically Successful African American Young
        Women*
Authors: Freeman A. Hrabowski, Kenneth I. Maton, Monica L. Greene, and
        Geoffrey L. Greif
Publication Date: 2002

A companion volume to *Beating the Odds: Raising Academically Successful African American Males,* this book delineates study findings on a group of fresh-men entering the University of Maryland in Baltimore County. The university's president is the first author. Based on interviews with the young women and their parents/caregivers, the researchers share inspiring stories and effective strategies for raising black girls who are geared toward success.

Parenting by Heart
Author: Dr. Ron Taffel with Linda Blau
Publication Date: 1991

This book is probably one of the best I have read on the subject of parenting. Because children do not come with instructions attached to their backsides and they can often push parents to the very limits of their patience, this guide provides parents with the strategies needed to remain in control of their emotions and model effective problem solving and conflict resolution. Taffel also takes a very compassionate and pragmatic approach to parenting that is very refreshing.

*Raising Black Children: Two Leading Psychiatrists Confront the Educational,
        Social and Emotional Problems Facing Black Children*
Authors: James P. Comer, M.D., and Alvin F. Poussaint, M.D.

Publication Date: 1975, 1992

Using a question-and-answer format, Drs. Comer and Poussaint provide sound and thorough advice on approximately a thousand special concerns expressed by black parents. The book spans the behavior and issues facing black children from infancy through adolescence. The book is reader-friendly and serves as an excellent reference tool.

Raising Black Children Who Love Reading and Writing: A Guide from Birth Through Grade Six

Author: Dierdre Glenn Paul

Publication Date: 2000

Building on the premise that the foundations of educational success and literacy begin in the home, this book stresses the need for early involvement in the learning process. It challenges the traditional notion that issues surrounding child development and parent education are apolitical and neutral. This guide also includes an annotated bibliography featuring exemplary adolescent and children's literature.

The Skin We're In: Teaching Our Teens to Be Emotionally Strong, Socially Smart, and Spiritually Connected

Author: Janie Victoria Ward

Publication Date: 2000

With a progressive and proactive stance on blackness and raising black teens, psychologist Ward explores issues like developing a race-conscious identity, teaching healthy resistance (to racism) strategies, spirituality, and interracial dating in this helpful book. *The Skin We're In* is based on a study Ward conducted on parenting.

"Why Are All the Black Kids Sitting Together in the Cafeteria?": And Other Conversations About Race

Author: Beverly Daniel Tatum

Publication Date: 1997

With skilled precision and practical terms, Dr. Tatum presents the complex issue of race and racial development in an easily comprehensible manner. She helps parents, caregivers, teachers, school personnel, and laypeople understand the ways in which black, white, and multiracial identities develop. Concomitantly, Psychologist Tatum provides real-life examples and current research, and she focuses on communication across racial boundary lines.

APPENDIX C:
ANNOTATED FILMOGRAPHY

Within the context of modern-day society, we must accept the truism that the media is a potent and ubiquitous influence. In spite of the fact that some would claim its purposes are centered on entertainment and education, the media (in all of its varied forms) is designed to generate profit. As per the dictates of this particular discussion's focus on film, I would like to share the following quotation:

> Film is no longer the product of a self-contained industry but one of a range of cultural commodities produced by multinationals or conglomerates whose main interest is more likely to be electronics or petroleum than the construction of magical images for the screen. (Graeme Turner as quoted in Miklitsch, 1997, p. 261)

Humanitarian concerns have been and remain of secondary importance for movie executives.

With this information in hand, parents and caregivers must be uncommonly vigilant in protecting their children from the negative portrayals that are sometimes advanced by the media. In times past, forbidding one's child to see certain films and denying permission to attend movies with questionable content might have proven sufficient. In a number of instances, such prohibitions effectively deterred a child from viewing controversial movies. But the mixed blessing of videotape has increased the likelihood that children will be exposed to these movies in spite of our best efforts. Additionally, as many parents/caregivers have discovered, forbidding a child to do something is usually much more effective when they are younger. Yet, with older children, it is rarely as effectual. So what is a capable parent/caregiver to do?

In my estimation, parents/caregivers are still responsible for establishing guidelines for film viewing with their children. They should be aware of the film rating a particular film received as well as the reviews it received. Most importantly, however, your child should not be permitted to view any film you have not seen. In far too many instances, parents/caregivers lose credibility with their children because they berate a film they have not even seen. One should always speak from a knowledgeable position. If after viewing a particular film, you determine it is unsuitable for your child, you can justifiably provide the child with reasons supporting your decision.

Additionally, if your child goes to a friend's home to watch a movie or receives an invitation to go to the movies with a friend's family, you are both obligated and entitled to receive information on the film to be viewed. You are also within your rights to decline or postpone the offer, if the responses you receive are less than satisfactory or you have not had an opportunity to view the film in question.

I would caution, however, that all films with difficult subject matter should not be avoided. Some such films will provide you with the opportunity to use the film experience as a springboard for discussion with your child. Ask your child questions about the ways in which characters are portrayed. Ask about the film's themes or editorial choices that helped construct particular realities as they appeared in the film.

In this technologically driven world in which we live, it is of crucial importance that we teach our children to be critical consumers of the media. We need to provide our youngsters with the analytical tools needed to talk about films and the media; as well as to understand that film images are to be explored and questioned rather than passively accepted. Young people must be educated to detect the ways in which " print and nonprint texts that are part of [their] everyday live[s] help to construct their knowledge of the world and the various social, economic and political positions they occupy within it (Alvermann, Moon, & Hagood, 1999, pp. 1–2).

In this annotated filmography, I provide a list of suggested films that focus on black womanhood. For the most part, the films featured on this list were first released for general distribution in the United States. They are also available through most video rental stores and telecasts. I realize there may be obvious omissions. Yet I have chosen to include films about which I am passionate or I ardently believe they tackle tough topics in distinctive ways. Finally, I would like to provide one caveat for parents/caregivers who opt to use this list. Please preview these films, prior to watching any of them with your child.

The Color Purple
Director: Steven Spielberg
Release Date: 1985

For most of Celie's life, she has been abused and mistreated. Her life is transformed, with the help of an unlikely influence, and she embarks on a journey of self-discovery and self-love.

Crooklyn

Director: Spike Lee

Release Date: 1994

Young Troy, the only girl in a family of boys, can rely on the love of her parents and her close network of family and friends. Then her life is turned upside down with the death of her mother.

Down in the Delta

Director: Maya Angelou

Release Date: 1998

Loretta is a troubled single mother of two who needs to turn her life around. With the aid of her mother and a summer in rural Mississippi, she learns lessons about life, love, and family.

Eve's Bayou

Director: Kasi Lemons

Release Date: 1997

Growing up in the prominent Batiste family looks charmed from the outside. But appearances are deceiving and being a member of it (with all of its secrets and lies) proves exceedingly difficult for Eve, the middle child.

Girls Town

Director: Jim McKay

Release Date: 1995

Three high school seniors must deal with life, love, and survival after a fourth friend commits suicide following a rape.

Holiday Heart

Director: Robert Townsend

Release Date: 2000

The Warrior Women, a drug-addicted mother and her preadolescent daughter, find refuge and comfort in an unlikely source.

Just Another Girl on the I.R.T.

Director: Leslie Harris

Release Date: 1993

A smart and spirited Brooklyn girl, with lots of attitude, begins to examine her values when she becomes pregnant.

Love and Basketball

Director: Gina Prince-Bythewood

Release Date: 2000

Monica must make a choice between pursuing her dreams as a basketball player or maintaining her relationship with her boyfriend Quincy, putting her dreams on hold while helping him pursue his. Can she have both?

Mama Flora's Family
Director: Peter Wemer
Release Date: 1998
    Based on a novel by Alex Haley, the film chronicles the life of Mama Flora, her children, and grandchildren.
Queen
Director: John Eman
Release Date: 1993
    This miniseries chronicles the life of Alex Haley's paternal great-grandmother, Queen, born to a slave mother and her white slaveowner.
Ruby Bridges: A Real American Hero
Director: Euzhan Palcy
Release Date: 1999
    A wise 6-year-old courageously serves as the first black to integrate the New Orleans public school system.
Sarafina
Director: Darrell James Roodt
Release Date: 1992
    Set in South Africa during the Soweto student uprisings, a teacher shares lessons with her students that extend beyond the 3 Rs—reading, writing, and arithmetic.

BIBLIOGRAPHY

Adenika-Morrow, T.J. (1996). A lifeline to science careers for African American females. *Educational Leadership, 53*(8), 80.

Akbar, N. (1985). Our destiny: Authors of a scientific revolution. In H. P. McAdoo and J. H. McAdoo, (Eds.) *Black Children: Social, educational, and parental environments* (17–31). Newbury Park, CA: Sage Publications.

Alvermann, D., Moon, J.S., & Hagood, M.C. (1999). *Popular culture in the classroom: Teaching and researching critical media literacy.* Newark, DE: International Reading Association.

American Association of University Women (AAUW) Educational Foundation. (1992). *How schools shortchange girls: The AAUW report.* New York: Marlowe & Company.

American Association of University Women (AAUW) Educational Foundation. (1996). *Girls in the middle: Working to succeed in school.* Washington, DC: American Association of University Women Educational Foundation.

American Institutes for Research. (1998). *Gender gaps: Where schools still fail our children.* Washington, DC: American Association of University Women Educational Foundation.

Anderson, C. (2001). *PowerNomics: The national plan to empower Black America.* Bethesda, MD: PowerNomics Corporation of America.

Banks, J.A. (1991). *Teaching strategies for ethnic studies* (5th ed.). Needham Heights, MA: Allyn & Bacon.

Banks, J.A. (1994). *Multiethnic education: Theory and practice* (3rd ed.). Needham Heights, MA: Allyn & Bacon.

Banks, J. A. (2000). Series foreword. In G. Gay. *Culturally responsive teaching: Theory, research, and practice.* New York: Teachers College Press.

Banks, T. L. (1995). Two life stories: Reflections of one black woman law professor. In K. Crenshaw, N. Gotanda, G. Peller, and K. Thomas, (Eds.) *Critical race theory: Key writings that formed the movement* (329–336). New York: New Press.

Belenky, M. F., Clinchy, B. M., Goldberger, N. R., and Tarule, J. M. (1986). *Women's ways of knowing: The Development of self, voice, and mind.* New York: Basic Books.

Benard, B. (1993). *Turning the corner: From risk to resiliency.* Portland, OR: Northwest Regional Educational Laboratory.

Bender, M. (2000, July). Suicide and older African-American women.*Mortality, 5*(2), 158.

Bennett, C. & Harris, J. J. (1981). *A Study of the causes of disproportionality in suspensions and expulsions of male and black students*: Part I: Characteristics of disruptive and non-disruptive students. Washington, DC: U.S. Department of Education.

Bern, S. (1981). *Bern sex role inventory: Professional manual.* Palo Alto, CA: Mindgarden.

Boxill, B. R. (1995). Segregation or assimilation? In J. Arthur & A. Shapiro, (Eds.), *Campus Wars: Multiculturalism and the politics of difference* (235–248). Boulder, CO: Westview Press.

Breggin, P.R. (1998). *Talking back to Ritalin: What doctors aren't telling you about stimulants for children.* Monroe, ME: Common Courage Press.

Breggin, P.R., & Breggin, G.R. (1998). *The war against children of color: Psychiatry targets inner city youth.* Monroe, ME: Common Courage Press.

Brent, L. (Harriet Jacobs) (1973). *Incidents in the life of a slave girl.* New York: Harcourt Brace Jovanovich.

Bullivant, B. M. (1993). Culture: Its nature and meaning for educators. In J. A. Banks and C. A. M. Banks, (Eds.), *Multicultural education: Issues and Perspectives* (29–47). Needham Heights, MA: Allyn & Bacon.

Bush, A.J., Smith, R., & Martin, C. (1999). The influence of consumer socialization variables on attitude toward advertising: A comparison of African-Americans and Caucasians. *Journal of Advertising, 28*(3), 13.

Cannon, K. (1985). The Emergence of a Black feminist consciousness. In L. M. Russell, (Ed.) *Feminist interpretations of the Bible* (30–40). Philadelphia: Westminster Press.

Carlson, D., & Apple, M.W. (1998). Introduction: Critical educational theory in unsettling times. In D. Carlson & M.W. Apple (Eds.), *Power/knowledge/ pedagogy: The meaning of democratic education in unsettling times* (1–38). Boulder, CO: Westview Press.

Campbell, E. L. (1982). *School discipline: Policy: Procedures, and potential discrimination—A study of disproportionate representation of minority pupils in school suspensions.* New Orleans, LA: Mid-South Educational Research Association.

Carnegie Council on Adolecent Development. (1994). *A Matter of time: Risk and opportunity in the out-of-school hours*. New York: Carnegie Corporation of New York.

Cauce, A. M., Hiraga, Y., Graves, D., Gonzales, N., Ryan-Finn, K., and Grove, K. (1996). African American mothers and their adolescent daughters: Closeness, conflict, and control. In B.J.R. Leadbetter & N. Way (Eds.), *Urban girls: Resisting stereotypes, creating identities* (pp. 85–99). New York: New York University Press.

Centers for Disease Control. (1995). *What is safer sex? Factsheet.* ss.admin@safersex.org.

Chapman, A. B. (1995). *Getting good loving: How black men and women can make love work*. New York: One World/Ballantine Books.

Civil Rights Project. (2001a). *Community and school predictors of overrepresentation of minority children in special education*. Cambridge, MA: Harvard University.

Civil Rights Project. (2001b). *Exploring relationships between inappropriate and ineffective special education services for African American children and youth and their overrepresentation in the juvenile justice system*. Cambridge, MA: Harvard University.

Clark, K. B., & Clark, M. P. (1939). The development of consciousness of self in the emergence of racial identification in Negro preschool children. *Journal of Social Psychology, 10,* 591–597.

Clark, K. B., & Clark, M. P. (1947). Racial identification and preferences in Negro children. In T. M. Newcomb & E. L. Hartley (Eds.), *Readings in social psychology* (pp. 169–178). New York: Henry Holt.

Cohen, C. J., & Nee, C. E. (2000). Educational attainment and sex differentials in African American communities.*American Behavioral Scientist* 11(7), 1–38.

Collins, P. H. (1991). *Black feminist thought: Knowledge, consciousness, and the politics of empowerment*. New York: Routledge.

Comer, J. P., & Poussaint, A. F. (1992). *Raising black children: Two leading psychiatrists confront the educational, social and emotional problems facing black children*. New York: Plume.

Committee on Education and the Workforce. (2001, May 23). *House passes President Bush's No Child Left Behind education bill (H.R.1)*. http://edworkforce. house.gov/press107.

Cooley, C. H. (1902). *Human nature and the social order*. New York: Charles Schribner's Sons.

Corea, G. (1977). *The hidden malpractice: How American medicine mistreats women*. New York: Jove/HBJ Books.

Cose, E. (2000, November 13). America's prison generation. *Newsweek*, pp. 42–49.

Cose, E. (2003, March 3). The Black gender gap. *Newsweek*, 46–51.

Crenshaw, K., Gotanda, N., Peller, G., & Thomas, K. (1995). *Critical race theory: The key writings that formed the movement.* New York: New Press.

Cross, W. E., Jr. (1971, July). The Negro-to-Black conversion experience: Toward a psychology of black liberation. *Black World, 20*(9), 13–27.

Cross, W. E., Jr. (1978). Models of psychological nigrescence: A literature review. *Journal of Black Psychology, 5*, 13–31.

Cuban, L. (2001). *How can I fix it?: Finding solutions and managing dilemmas.* New York: Teachers College Press.

Damico, S., & Scott, E. (1987). Behavior differences between black and white females in desegregated schools. *Equity and Excellence in Education, 23*, 63–66.

Daniel, J. H. (1999). Introduction. In N. G. Johnson, M. C. Roberts, and J. Worrell, (Eds.) *Beyond appearance: A New look at adolescent girls* (111–113). Washington, DC: American Psychological Association.

Davis, A. Y. (1981). *Women, race & class.* New York: Vintage Books.

Davis, A. Y. (2000, Fall). The color of violence against women. *Color Lines, 3*(3). http://www.arc.org/C_Lines/CLArchive/story3_3_02.html.

Derman-Sparks, L., Tanaka Higa, C., & Sparks, B. (1980). Children, race and racism: How race awareness develops. *Bulletin, 11*(3 & 4), 3–9.

Dizard, J. E. (1970). Black identity, social class, and black power. *Journal of Social Issues, 26*(1), 195–207.

Du Bois, W. E. B. (1903). *The souls of black folk.* New York: Fawcett.

Edelman, M. W. (2001). What we can do ... In T. Smiley (Ed.), *How to make black America better* (pp. 121–124). New York: Doubleday.

Erikson, E. (1977). *Toys and reason: Stages in the ritualization of experience.* New York: Norton.

Erkut, S., & Marx, F. (1995). *Raising competent girls: An exploratory study of diversity in girls' views of liking one's self.* Wellesley, MA: Center on Research for Women, Wellesley College.

Erkut, S., Fields, J. P., Sing, R., and Marx, F. (1996). Diversity in girls' experiences: Feeling good about who you are. In B. J. R. Leadbetter and N. Way, (Eds.) *Urban Girls: Resisting stereotypes, creating identities.* New York: New York University Press.

Feldman, B. N. (1987). *Kids who succeed: The no-nonsense guide to raising a child who'll be a winner in tomorrow's world.* New York: Fawcett Crest.

Ferguson, M. (2003). A Growing problem: Race, class, and obesity among American women. *Diversity or Division?: Race, class and America at the Millennium.* http://journalism.nyu.edu/pubzone/race-class/othergirlsstuff.html.

Fonow, M. M., & Cook, J. A. (1991). Back to the future: A look at the second wave of feminist epistemology and methodology. In M. M. Fonow & J. A. Cook (Eds.), *Beyond methodology: Feminist scholarship as lived research* (pp. 1–15). Bloomington and Indianapolis: Indiana University Press.

Ford, M. (1998). Foreword. In American Institutes for Research, *Gender gaps: Where schools still fail our children*. Washington, DC: American Association of University Women Educational Foundation.

Fordham, S. (1996). *Blacked out: Dilemmas of race, identity, and success at Capital High*. Chicago, IL: The University of Chicago Press.

Franklin, J. H. (1989). *Race and history: Selected essays 1938–1988*. Baton Rouge: Louisiana State University Press.

Fraser, J. W. (1997). Reading, writing and justice: School reform as if democracy matters. Albany, NY: State University of New York.

Frederick D. Patterson Research Institute of the College Fund/UNCF. (1997). A preview. In *African American Education Data Book* (vol. 1). http://www.patterson-uncf.org/.

Gay, G. (1993). Building cultural bridges: A bold proposal for teacher education. In F. Schulz (Ed.), *Annual editions: Multicultural education 95/96* (pp. 34–40). Guilford, CT: Dushkin/Brown & Benchmark.

Gay, G. (2000). *Culturally responsive teaching: Theory, research, and practice*. New York: Teachers College Press.

Gibbs, J. T. (1985). City girls: Psychosocial adjustment of urban black adolescent females. *Sage: A Scholarly Journal on Black Women, 2*, 28–36.

Giddings, P. (1984). *Where and when I enter: The Impact of Black women on race and sex in America*. New York: Bantam Books.

Gilman, S. L. (1985, Autumn). Black bodies, white bodies: Toward an iconography of female sexuality in late nineteenth-century art, medicine, and literature. *Critical Inquiry, 12*, 204–242.

Godfrey, N. S., & Edwards, C. (1994). *Money doesn't grow on trees: A parent's guide to raising financially responsible children*. New York: Simon & Schuster.

Goldstein, A. (2001, December 14). *The Bush education plan: A test of will*. http://www.time.com.

Goodman, J. A. (1972). Institutional racism: The crucible of black identity. In J. A. Banks & J. D. Grambs (Eds.), *Black self concept: Implications for education and social science*. New York: McGraw-Hill.

GoPaul-McNicol. S. (1992). Racial identification and racial preference of black pre-school children in New York and Trinidad. In K. H. Burlew, W. C. Banks, H. P. McAdoo, & D. A. Azibo (Eds.), *African American psychology*. Newbury Park, CA: Sage.

Gordon-Reed, A. (1997). *Thomas Jefferson and Sally Hemings: An American controversy*. Charlottesville: University Press of Virginia.

Graves, E. (1997). *How to succeed in business without being white: Straight talk on making it in America*. New York: HarperBusiness.

Griffin, R. (1998, October 24). Black women and breast cancer. *America, 179*(12), 20.

Hadderman, M. (2000). Educational vouchers. *Eric Digest, No. 137*. Eugene, OR: ERIC Clearinghouse on Educational Management.

Haid, C. (Director). (2000). *Sally Hemings: An American scandal.* [Motion picture]. United States: Columbia Broadcasting System.

Hansen, S., Walker, J., & Flom, B. (1995a). *Growing smart: What's working for girls in school.* Washington, DC: American Association of University Women Educational Foundation.

Hansen, S., Walker, J., & Flom, B. (1995b). *Growing smart: What's working for girls in school* (Executive Summary and Action Guide). Washington, DC: American Association of University Women Educational Foundation.

Heller, K. A., Holtzman, W. H., & Messick, S. (Eds.). (1982). *Placing children in special education: A strategy for equity.* Washington, DC: National Academy Press.

Helms, J. E. (1993). *Black and white racial identity: Theory, research, and practice.* Westport, CT: Praeger.

Henry, A. (1998). 'Invisible and womanish': Black girls negotiating their lives in an African-centered school in the USA. *Race, Ethnicity & Education* 1(2), 151–170.

Hilliard, A. G. (1994). Misunderstanding and testing intelligence. In J. I. Goodlad & P. Keating (Eds.), *Access to knowledge: The continuing agenda for our nation's schools* (rev. ed.) (pp. 145–157). New York: College Entrance Examination Board.

Hilliard, A. G. (1974). Restructuring teacher education for multicultural imperatives. In W. A. Hunter, (Ed.) *Multicultural education through competency based teacher education.* Washington, DC: American Association of Colleges of Teacher Education.

Holden, G. W. (1997). *Parents and the dynamics of child rearing.* Boulder, CO: Westview Press.

hooks, b. (1989). *Talking back: Thinking feminist, thinking black.* Boston: South End Press.

hooks, b. (1992). *Black looks: Race and representation.* Boston: South End Press.

Hull, G. T., Scott, P. B., and Smith, B. (1982). *All the women are white, all the blacks are men, but some of us are brave: Black women's studies.* New York: The Feminist Press.

Hughes, Z. (2000, March). Why so many black women are overweight—and what they can do about it. *Ebony, 55*(5), 92.

Irvine, J. J. (1991). *Black students and school failure: Policies, practices, and prescriptions.* New York: Praeger.

Ivory, J. (Director). (1995). *Jefferson in Paris* [Motion picture]. United States: Touchstone Pictures.

Jackson, A. W., & Davis, G. A. (2000). *Turning points2000: Educating adolescents in the 21st century.* New York and London: Teachers College Press.

Johnson, N. G., Roberts, M. C., and Worrell, J. (1999). Beyond appearance: A new look at adolescent girls. Washington, DC: American Psychological Association.

Kanfer, F. H., Englund, S., Lennhoff, C., & Rhodes, J. (1995). *A mentor manual: For adults working with pregnant and parenting teens.* Washington, DC: The Child Welfare League of America.

Kantrowitz, B., & Wingert, P. (2001, May 28). Unmarried, with children. *Newsweek,* pp. 46–55.

Kaplowitz, P. B., & Oberfield, S. E. (1999). Reexamination of the age limit for defining when puberty is precocious in girls in the United States. *Pediatrics, 104*(4), 936.

Katz, P. (1993, May). *Development of racial attitudes in children.* Presentation at the University of Delaware.

King, D. K. (1990). Multiple jeopardy, multiple consciousness: The context of a black feminist ideology. In M. R. Malson, E. Mudimbe, J. F. Barr, & M. Wyer (Eds), *Black women in America: Social science perspectives* (pp. 265–295). Chicago and London: University of Chicago Press.

King, J. E. and Ladson-Billings, G. (1995). Multicultural teacher education: Research, practice, and policy. In J. A. Banks and C. A. M. Banks, (Eds.) *Handbook of research on multicultural education* (747–759). New York: Macmillan.

King, W. (1985). *Stolen childhood: Slave youth in nineteenth century America.* Bloomington & Indianapolis: Indiana University Press.

Kozol, J. (1991). *Savage inequalities: Children in America's schools.* New York: HarperPerennial.

Kunen, J. S. (1996, April 29). The integration of integration. In F. Schulz (Ed.), *Annual editions: Multicultural education 97/98* (pp. 32–37). Guilford, CT: Dushkin/McGraw-Hill.

Ladner, J. A. (1971). *Tomorrow's tomorrow: The black woman.* Lincoln and London: University of Nebraska Press.

Ladson-Billings, G. (1999). Just what is critical race theory and what's it doing in a nice field like education? In L. Parker, D. Deyhle, & S. Villenas (Eds.), *Race is … race isn't: Critical race theory and qualitative studies in education* Boulder, CO: Westview Press (7–30).

Lee, C. D. & Slaughter-Defoe, D. T. (1995). Historical and sociocultural influences on African American education. In J. A. Banks and C. A. M. Banks, (Eds.) *Handbook of research on multicultural education* (348–371). New York: Macmillan Publishing.

Liebert, R. M., & Wicks-Nelson, R. (1981). *Developmental psychology* (3rd ed.). Englewood Cliffs, NJ: Prentice-Hall.

Lightfoot, S. L. (1976). Socialization and education of young black girls in school. *Teachers College Record, 78*(2), 239–262.

Lorde, A. (1984). *Sister outsider.* Freedom, CA: The Crossing Press.

Losen, D. J. & Orfield, G. (2002). Introduction: Racial Inequity in Special Education. In D. J. Losen & G. Orfield (Eds.). *Racial Inequity in Special Education* (pp. xiii–xxxvii). Cambridge, MA: Harvard Educational Press.

Lukas, J. A. (1996). The need for a tougher kind of heroism. In F. Schulz (Ed.), *Annual editions: Multicultural education 97/98* (p. 34). Guilford, CT: Dushkin/McGraw-Hill.

Madhere, S. (1991). Self-esteem of African American preadolescents: Theoretical and practical considerations. *Journal of Negro Education, 60*(1), 47–61.

Maples, J. (2002). *Black teens 'deliberate' in family planning.* http://www.uah.edu/HTML/Research/ResRev/LS/story2.html.

Mapp, K. (1997). Making the connection between families and schools. *The Harvard Education Letter, 8*(5), 1–3.

Massood, P. J. (2003). *Black City Cinema.* Philadelphia: Temple University Press.

McLoyd, V. C., Cauce, A. M., Takeuchi, D., & Wilson, L. (2000). Marital processes and parental socialization in families of color: A decade of research. *Journal of Marriage & the Family, 62*(4), 1070.

McWhirter, E. H. (1994). *Counseling for empowerment.* Alexandria, VA: American Counseling Association.

Michelli, N. (2001). *Teacher education in the new millennium: The View from New York City.* The College Board Review.

Mies, M. (1983). Towards a methodology for feminist research. In G. Bowles and R. Klein, (Eds.) *Theories of women studies.* Boston, MA: Routledge and Kegan Paul.

Miklitsch, R. (1997). Punk pedagogy or performing contradiction: The risks and rewards of anti-transference. In H. A. Giroux & P. Shannon (Eds.), *Education and cultural studies: Toward a performative practice.* New York: Routledge.

Morrison, T. (1992). *Playing in the dark: Whiteness and the literary imagination.* New York: Vintage Books.

Morton, P. (1991). *Disfigured images: The historical assault on Afro-American women.* Westport, CT: Praeger.

Napholz, L. (1994, November). Sex role orientation and psychological well-being among working black women. *Journal of Black Psychology, 20*(4), 469–482.

National Center for Children in Poverty. (2001). *Child poverty fact sheet (June 2001): Child poverty in the United States.* http://cpmcnet.columbia.edu/dept/nccp/ycpf.html.

National Center for Education Statistics. (1996). *Digest of Education Statistics.* Washington, DC: U.S. Department of Education, Office of Educational Research and Improvement.

National Center for Education Statistics. (1993). America's teachers: Profile of a profession. Washington, DC: U.S. Department of Education, Office of Educational Research and Improvement.

Office of Juvenile Justice and Delinquency Prevention (1998, Oct.). *Guiding principles for Promising Female Programming.* Washington, D.C.: Office of Juvenile Justice and Delinquency Prevention.

Ogbu, J. U. (1994). Overcoming racial barriers to equal access. In J. I. Goodlad & P. Keating (Eds.), *Access to knowledge: The continuing agenda for our nation's schools* (rev. ed.) (pp. 59–89). New York: College Entrance Examination Board.

Omolade, B. (1994). *The rising song of African American women.* New York: Routledge.

Orenstein, P. (1994). *Schoolgirls: Young women, self-esteem, and the confidence gap.* New York: Doubleday.

Ossana, S. M., Helms, J. E., & Leonard, M. M. (1992). Do "Womanist" identity attitudes influence college women's self-esteem and perceptions of environmental bias? *Journal of Counseling and Development, 70,* 402–408.

Oswald, D. P., Coutinho, M. J., & Best, A. M. (2002). Community and School Predictors of Overrepresentation of Minority Children in Special Education. In D. J. Losen & G. Orfield (Eds.). *Racial Inequity in Special Education* (pp. 1–13). Cambridge, MA: Harvard Educational Press.

Patterson, O. (1998). *Rituals of blood: Consequences of slavery in two American centuries.* Washington, DC: Civitas Counterpoint.

Paul, D. G. (1998). Bridging the cultural divide: Reflective dialogue about multicultural children's books. *The New Advocate, 11*(2), 241–251.

Paul, D. G. (1999). Images of Black females in children's/adolescent literature. *Multicultural Review* 8(2), 34–41, 59–65.

Paul, D. G. (2000a). *Raising black children who love reading and writing: A guide from birth through grade six.* Westport, CT: Bergin & Garvey.

Paul, D. G. (2000b). Rap and orality: Critical media literacy, pedagogy, and cultural synchronization. *Journal of Adolescent & Adult Literacy, 44*(3), 246–252.

Paul, D. G. (2001). *Life, culture, education on the academic plantation: Womanist thought and perspective.* New York: Peter Lang.

Paul, D. G. (2002, May). Coming apart at the seam. *Cultural Studies/Critical Methodologies* 2(2), 197–200.

Paul, D. G. (In press). The Train Has Left—No Child Left Behind leaves Black and Latino literacy learners waiting at the station. *Journal of Adolescent and Adult Literacy.*

Phinney, J. S., & Tarver, S. (1988). Ethnic identity search and commitment in black and white eighth graders. *Journal of Early Adolescence, 8*(3), 265–277.

Pogrebin, L. C. (1991). *Deborah, Golda, and me: Being female and Jewish in America.* New York: Anchor Books.

Population Reference Bureau. (2001). *Sexual violence against women.* Washington, DC: Population Reference Bureau.

Postman, N. (1982). *The disappearance of childhood.* New York: Vintage Books.

Powell-Hopson, D. & Hopson, D. S. (1988). Implications of doll color preferences among black preschool children and white preschool children. *Journal of Black Psychology* 14, 57–63.

Pryor, D. (2001). *Suicide: Life's curtain of darkness.* www.Blackwomenshealth. com.

Rainwater, L., & Yancey, W.L. (1967). *The Moynihan report and the politics of controversy.* Cambridge, MA: MIT Press.

Research for Action. (1996). *Girls in the middle: Working to succeed in school.* Washington, DC: American Association of University Women Educational Foundation.

Reyes, M. & Halcon, J. J. (1982). Racism in academia; The old wolf revisited. In T. Beauboeuf-Lafontant & D. S. Augustine, (Eds.) (1996). *Facing racism in education,* second edition. Cambridge, MA: Harvard Educational Review (Reprint series no. 28), 89–105.

Rivers, C., Barnett, R., & Baruch, G. (1979). *Beyond sugar and spice: How women grow, learn and thrive.* New York: Ballantine Books.

Robinson, R. (2000). *The Debt: What America owes to blacks.* New York: Dutton.

Robinson, T.L., & Ward, J.V. (1995). African American adolescents and skin color. *Journal of Black Psychology, 21*(3), 256–274.

Rose, C. (1998, Jan. 19). Toni Morrison suggests 'Paradise' defined by inclusion (interview transcript) (1–8). Denver, CO: All News.

Ruddick, S. (1980). Maternal Thinking. *Feminist Studies*, 6(2), 342–363. Scully, D. (1980). *Men who control women's health: The mis-education of obstetrician-gynecologists.* Boston: Houghton Mifflin.

Seligsohn, D. (1994, November/December). The new underclass and re-emerging diseases. *World Health, 47*(6), 25.

Sleeter, C.E., & Grant, C.A. (1994). *Making choices for multicultural education: Five approaches to race, class, and gender* (2nd ed.). Englewood Cliffs, NJ: Merrill.

Smitherman, G. (1988*).* Discriminatory discourse on Afro-American speech. In G. Smitherman & T. A. van Dijk, (Eds.) *Discourse and discrimination.* Detroit, MI: Wayne State University Press.

Taffel, R. (1991). *Parenting by heart.* Reading, MA: Addison-Wesley.

Tatum, B.D. (1997). *"Why are all the Black kids sitting together in the cafeteria?": And other conversations about race.* New York: Basic Books.

Thompson, M. P., Kaslow, N. J., Kingree, J. B., Rashid, A., and Puett, R. (2001). Violence and victims. *American Journal of Community and Psychology* 16(2), 115–126.

Trager, H.G., & Yarrow, M.R. (1952). *They learn what they live.* New York: Harper.

Tremmel, P.V. (2002, January 8). Child welfare discourse fails to factor in racial bias. *Northwestern News.* http://www.northwestern.edu/univ-relations/ media_relations/releases/01_2002/childwelfare.html.

U.S. Census. (2001). Table 17: Poverty status of families in 1999 by type, race, and Hispanic origin, March 2000. *Current Population Survey, March 2000: Racial Statistics, Population Division.* http://www.census.gov/population/ socdemo/race/black/pp1–142/tab17.txt.

U.S. Census. (2002). Table 2: Poverty among families according to the official poverty measure, 2000. *Poverty in the United States: 2000,* pp. 60–214, Table A. http://www.ssc.wisc.edu/irp/faqs/faq3dir/povtab00-two.htm.

U.S. Department of Education. (2002, March 18). *No Child Left Behind Act of 2001: Executive summary.* http://www.ed.gov/offices/OESE/esea/ exec-summ.html.

U.S. Department of Health and Human Services. (1998). *A national strategy to prevent teen pregnancy: Annual report 1997–1998.* Washington, DC: U.S. Department of Health and Human Services.

U.S. Department of Justice. (1994). *Bureau of Justice statistics bulletin: Women in prison* (NCJ-145321). Annapolis Junction, MD: U.S. Department of Justice Office of Justice Programs.

Villarosa, L. (2002). Our girls in crisis. *Essence, 33*(1), 1–8 . . ./fulltext.asp?result-SetId = R00000005&hitNum = 1&booleanTerm = ward%2c%20janie& fuzzyTern.

Wacquant, L. J. D., & Wilson, W. J. (1989, January). The cost of racial and class exclusion in the inner city. In *The Annals of the American Academy of Political and Social Science.* Newbury Park, CA: Sage.

Walker, A. (1983). *In search of our mothers' gardens: Womanist prose.* San Diego, CA: Harcourt Brace Jovanovich.

Wallace, M. (1979). *Black macho and the myth of the superwoman.* New York: Dial.

Ward, J. V. (1990). Racial identity formation and transformation. In C. Gilligan, N. P. Lyons, & T. J. Hanmer (Eds.), *Making connections: The relational world of adolescent girls at Emma Willard School.* Cambridge, MA: Harvard University Press.

Ward, J. V. (1996). Raising resisters: The role of truth telling in the psychological development of African American girls. In B. J. R. Leadbetter & N. Way (Eds.), *Urban girls: Resisting stereotypes, creating identities* (pp. 85–99). New York: New York University Press.

Weiler, J. (1998). The athletic experiences of ethnically diverse girls. *ERIC/CUE Digest,* p. 131.

Weinick, R. M., Zuvekas, S. H., & Cohen, J. W. (2000). Racial and ethnic differences in access to and use of health care services, 1977 to 1996. *Medical Care Research and Review, 2000 Supplement I, 57,* 36.

White, D. G. (1985). *Ar'n't I a woman?: Female slaves in the plantation South.* New York: Norton.

Winters, R. (2001, February 7). *Teacher in chief.* http://www.time.com.

Wolf, N. (1997). *Promiscuities: The Secret struggle for womanhood.* New York: Fawcett Columbine.

Woollett, A., & Phoenix, A. (1996). Motherhood as pedagogy: Developmental psychology and the accounts of mothers of young children. In C. Luke (Ed.), *Feminisms and pedagogies of everyday life* (pp. 80–102). Albany: State University of New York Press.

Wright, M.A. (1998). *I'm chocolate, you're vanilla: Raising healthy black and biracial children in a race-conscious world.* San Francisco: Jossey-Bass.

Wyatt, G.E. (1997). *Stolen women: Reclaiming our sexuality, taking back our lives.* New York: Wiley.

INDEX

About the Author

DIERDRE GLENN PAUL is a professor of Literacy Education, Montclair State University, New Jersey. She is also the author of *Raising Black Children Who Love Reading and Writing: A Guide from Birth Through Grade Six* (Bergin & Garvey) and *Life, Culture and Education on the Academic Plantation: Womanist Thoughts and Perspective.*